Using MS-DOS®

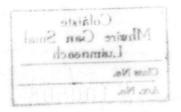
Using MS-DOS®

Kris Jamsa

Osborne **McGraw-Hill**

Berkeley, California

Osborne **McGraw-Hill**
2600 Tenth Street
Berkeley, California 94710
U.S.A.

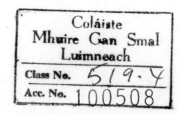

For information on translations and book distributors outside of the
U.S.A., please write to Osborne **McGraw-Hill** at the above address.

A complete list of trademarks appears on page 747.

Using MS-DOS®

234567890 DODO 898

ISBN 0-07-881442-1

Copy Editor: Barbara Conway
Word Processor: Bonnie Bozorg
Proofreaders: Kay Luthin, Juliette Anjos
Technical Illustration: Peter Hancik
Production Supervisor: Kevin Shafer

CONTENTS

Part Two:
Getting the Most From DOS

Preface

With the tremendous success DOS has experienced since its introduction in 1981, countless computer books have emerged that deal specifically with DOS, its commands, and its user interface. Admittedly, several very useful DOS books have emerged that have helped users get started with DOS. However, there is a large difference between getting started with DOS, and using DOS and your computer efficiently. This book not only gets you started with DOS, it also teaches you tricks and shortcuts that allow you to quickly get the most from your computer investment.

How Is This Book Different?

DOS is a very important topic. All of the other DOS books on the market place DOS foremost. However, without users there would be no need for DOS and DOS books. This book differs from all of the others because it puts the user first and foremost. This is the only book available that teaches you how to use DOS in a logical step-by-step manner. The book does so by using a series of 15-minute lessons that you can perform each day for a one-month period. Where other books discuss DOS, this book teaches it! You won't find a better method of learning DOS anywhere.

What's in This Book?

In most books, you'd probably find a chapter-by-chapter description at this point, one which uses terms that you've never heard to discuss topics that you don't yet understand. But this book is different. Instead, what you'll find in this book is a set of lessons that will teach all users (regardless of their current level of expertise), how to get the most from DOS and, hence, from their computers. Each lesson is short, straightforward, and, in most cases, even fun!

Disk Package

One of the most common frustrations of computer users is to forget the format of a specific command. If you have this book readily available on your bookshelf, Part Four (the Command Reference Section) lists the formats of each DOS command. In addition, the disk package, DOS HELP provides you with on-line help for each of the DOS commands. Since you are already working at your computer, why should you have to look anywhere else for information on DOS commands?

The disk package comes in a solid disk folder, which is ideal for carrying your floppy disks with you when you travel or when you go to work or school. The complete cost of the package is only $17.95 plus $2.00 shipping and handling ($5.00 for foreign orders).

Please send me the disk package that accompanies *Using MS-DOS*. My payment for $19.95 ($17.95 plus $2.00 for shipping and handling or $5.00 for foreign orders) is enclosed.

Name _____

Address _____

City _____ **State** _____ **Zip** _____

Kris Jamsa Software, Inc. Box 26031 Las Vegas, Nevada 89126

Getting Started

Part One

Welcome to DOS and your personal computer. DOS is simply a program that you must have in order to perform useful tasks with your computer. Rather than describing DOS in one or two sentences, this entire book describes the various aspects of DOS. If you have a computer background but are new to DOS or to the personal computer, you will find DOS to be powerful and easy to learn. If you have never used a computer, you should put aside all of your fears. More than 10 million users have learned to use DOS, and each of them was new to DOS at some point. They've mastered DOS, and so will you.

Getting the Most from DOS

"I don't want to be a DOS expert—I just want to know enough to get my job done."

"I don't have time to learn DOS."

"I use Lotus 1-2-3, not DOS."

Sound familiar? These quotes reflect the fact that most users do not want to become system experts—they just want to get the most from their computers in the shortest possible time. If you follow the DOS lessons presented in this text, you will soon find not only that the computer is your ally, but also that it is a critical partner in your success.

Simply stated, when you complete the last lesson in this book, you will be a sophisticated DOS user. Knowledge of DOS puts you in control of your computer. No matter what you use your computer for (be it word processing, spreadsheets, or programming), if you understand DOS, you will save time and effort.

Your Commitment

This book is based on the premise that no one has time to learn DOS. However, you do not have time to be ineffective with your computer. This book will teach you how to save time, effort, and money by using DOS (and hence your computer) more effectively. You must be willing to give 15 minutes a day—no more, no less. In 30 days, you will not only find yourself mastering DOS but also answering the questions of all those who are yet to learn the secrets.

Unlike other DOS books, this book does not confuse you with long chapters, endless examples, and difficult scenarios. Instead, it puts you in the driver's seat. Just as you did not learn to drive a car by standing on the sidewalk, you cannot learn to use DOS simply by reading a book.

This book is built on 15-minute sessions at your computer. Each chapter introduces you to a fundamental DOS concept. Several examples of the concept are also presented. Next, the concept is put to use. This is your hands-on time; you must be at the computer. Following each hands-on section is a summary of material presented in the chapter and a glossary that reviews important new terms.

Do not skip lessons—each lesson is built on its predecessor. Just as a pilot should have a working knowledge of landing before taking off, so, too, should you have a solid foundation of the DOS basics before you try something more complicated.

Put Your Fears Aside

Many people are intimidated by the very notion of using computers. In contrast, children have no preconceptions about computers, and they master them quickly. Set aside all of your fears, and you will find that your computer is a valuable tool. Many adults were afraid of their cars when they first learned to drive, and yet the car has made their lives much easier. So, too, will your computer. There is no reason to worry about catastrophic results—if you simply follow the lessons as they are presented in this text, you cannot damage your computer.

A critical factor in learning is that you must enjoy what you are learning. The lessons in this book are short, and you will gain considerable confidence with each one. Take time to review, experiment, and just play. You will find that using your computer can be fun. Your mastery of DOS will also lead you to many years of productivity. With that, it's time to get started.

1 *System Components*

This chapter examines the hardware components that make up your personal computer. For those of you who have worked with computers before, much of this information will be review; however, this chapter also introduces the standard terminology that is used throughout this text. For those of you who are just getting started, this chapter will put you at ease with each piece of equipment found in your computer system, as shown in Figure 1-1.

Following an examination of the various parts of your computer, this chapter walks you through start up of your computer and gives you a checklist that you can use to ensure that your system is working correctly.

Input, Processing, and Output

Most new users are intimidated the first time they sit at a computer simply because they have seen countless examples of the computer's tremendous capabilities. After all, computers affect just about every aspect of our lives. It seems that everywhere you go, computers are being used to simplify another difficult task. Such fears are quite understandable. To minimize unease at the computer, you must keep the computer's capabilities in perspective. Here's how.

No matter what task the computer is performing (be it word processing, billing, or hospital patient monitoring), it does so in three

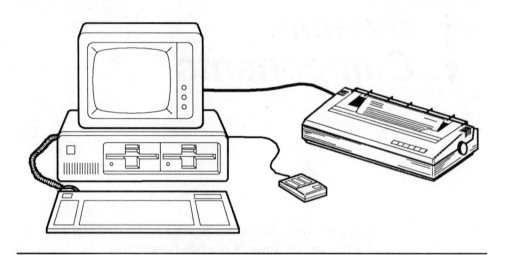

Figure 1-1. *Components of the computer system*

steps: input, processing, and output. Input is the act of getting information, or data, into the computer. For example, each month you may get consolidated bills that contain your credit card purchases for the previous month, as shown here:

Payment Coupon				

DUE DATE	TOTAL NEW BALANCE
07-20-88	1,595.79
	MIN. MONTHLY PMNT.
	10.00

POSTING MO.	DAY	ACTIVITY SINCE LAST STATEMENT		CHARGES		PAYMENTS AND CREDITS	
06	08	COMPUTER SHOP	S. FRANCISCO	1,500	00		
06	18	PAYMENT - THANK YOU				3,579	78
06	25	DISK STORE	BERKELEY	75	84		
06	30	BOOK STORE	CONCORD	19	95		
			TOTAL	1,595	79	3,579	78

B
e
f
o
r
e
a
c
o
m
p
u

Input

Input is the process of getting information (data) into the computer for processing.

---

ter can generate this list, each of these charges had to be input into the computer, as shown here:

Figure 1-2 illustrates several sources of input for your computer.

The second step performed by the computer is processing. This step can be as simple as adding two numbers or as complex as determining which of the many million credit card purchases that occur each

Figure 1-2. *Input devices*

Processing

Processing is the execution of a computer program (software) to convert input to a desired output.

month belong on your credit card bill. Processing is often associated with your computer's chassis, shown here:

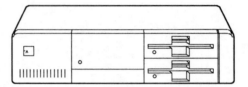

The chassis contains the central processing unit (CPU), the computer's memory, disk drives, and other boards (internal hardware components) that will be discussed throughout this text.

The final step is output—the printing or display of useful information to the end user. Figure 1-3 shows that your computer has many sources of output. Using the previous charge card example, your monthly bill is an example of output, as shown in Figure 1-4.

So regardless of the computer's application, the three steps of input, processing, and output are followed. Given this basic understanding of data processing, you should be able to classify your hardware components as either input or output devices.

Output

Output is the display or printing of meaningful information for the end user.

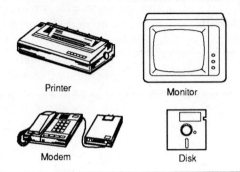

Figure 1-3.   *Output devices*

What's in a Name

Throughout this text the term *personal computer*, or *PC*, will be used to mean any personal computer capable of running DOS, such as an IBM PC or PC-compatible clone. Today countless vendors produce computers that are IBM PC compatible. Basically, two computers are

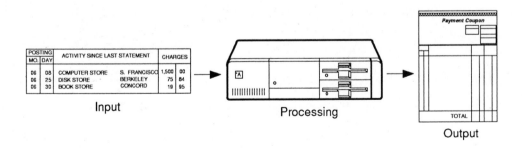

Figure 1-4.   *Credit card bill output*

compatible if they can run the same programs or exchange information stored on disk. In most cases you can even freely swap hardware components (such as the screen or the keyboard) between compatible computers without experiencing adverse effects.

Not all personal computers are compatible. You should find, however, that computers advertised as IBM PC compatible will prove to be 99 percent compatible with the IBM PC. The differences are usually subtle. All of these computers will execute MS-DOS.

8088, 80286, and 80386

As previously stated, a computer performs three basic tasks: input, processing, and output. Recall that within the computer's chassis resides the computer's memory and central processing unit (CPU). The CPU chip is the personal computer's workhorse—it is where program processing occurs.

The name of your CPU depends on your computer type (IBM PC, PC AT, or Compaq 386). For example, the IBM PC uses a CPU called the 8088, while the PC AT uses the 80286. The major difference between processors is speed. Table 1-1 compares the three commonly used CPU chips found in personal computers.

Although it is important to have a basic appreciation of these processors, you can essentially ignore the computer's processor type once you become an end user, because MS-DOS and PC-compatible software run on any of these processors.

Taking a Closer Look at Your Computer's Chassis

In addition to its memory and CPU, your computer's chassis houses your computer's disk drives, as shown here:

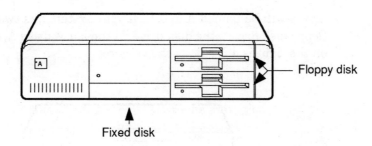

Floppy disk

Fixed disk

Disks store information and programs (such as your word processor). Later chapters will examine specifically how DOS stores information on a disk, but for now, just keep in mind that disks store programs and data.

Depending on your system configuration, your computer will have one or more floppy disk drives and possibly a fixed disk. Each disk drive has a single-letter name (A, B, C, and so on). Your floppy disk

Processor Chip	Speed	Computer	Usage	Unique Features
8088	Slowest	IBM PC	16-bit processor 8-bit bus	First PC with a megabyte address space
80286		IBM PC AT	16-bit processor 16-bit bus	Protected mode
80386	Fastest	IBM PS/2 Model 80 Deskpro 386	32-bit processor 32-bit bus	Protected mode; memory management by using hardware

Table 1-1. *Comparison of 8088, 80286, and 80386 Chips*

drives will be named A and B. If your system has two side-by-side floppy disk drives, the disk drive on the left is drive A, and the drive on the right is drive B, as shown here:

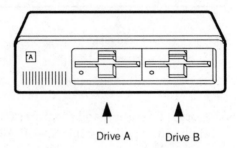

Drive A   Drive B

Likewise, if your system has two half-height floppy disk drives, the upper disk is drive A and the lower disk is drive B, as shown here:

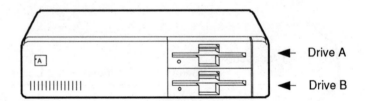

◄— Drive A

◄— Drive B

If your system has a fixed, or hard, disk, you will refer to it as drive C, as shown here:

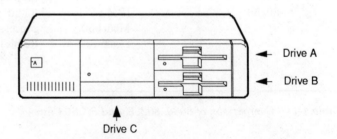

◄— Drive A

◄— Drive B

Drive C

Finally, if your computer has a single floppy disk drive, your floppy disk will be named drive A and your fixed disk, if present, will be named drive C.

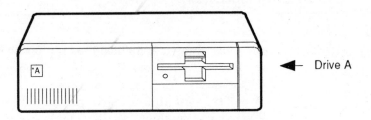

For those who are not familiar with fixed disks, here is a brief introduction. Fixed and floppy disks both exist for one purpose: to store data and programs. Fixed disks are faster, can store more information, and are more expensive than floppy disks. Also, fixed disks are not removable, unlike the floppy disks that you will work with in the next chapter. Table 1-2 compares floppy and fixed disks.

Disk Type	Speed	Storage	Cost	Removable	Damageable
Floppy	Much slower than fixed	380,000 to 1,200,000 characters	25 cents to several dollars	Yes	Yes
Fixed	Fast	10,000,000 to several hundred million characters	$300 to $1000+	No	Yes

Table 1-2. *Comparison of Floppy and Fixed Disks*

To the end user, fixed and floppy disks are treated in the same manner, and you will execute DOS commands in the same way.

Additional Hardware

Each of the systems examined thus far has been a standard personal computer configuration. Many users, however, add other devices to their computers. Three of the most common are shown in Figure 1-5.

A *mouse* is an input device that can simplify the way you use software packages. Many software packages require you to extensively use your keyboard arrow keys. A mouse offers a simpler and often faster alternative. Not all software, however, supports the mouse interface, so be sure that your software supports a mouse before you purchase this device.

Many computers must exchange data with or access a larger computer that is at a geographically different location. A *modem* is a device that allows your computer to transfer data to another computer over telephone lines. The two types of modems common to personal computers are internal and external modems. Internal modems

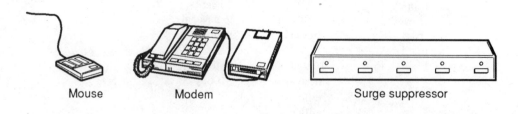

Mouse   Modem   Surge suppressor

Figure 1-5.   *Most common computer accessories*

are contained within your computer's chassis; external modems reside outside of your computer.

A convenient and strongly recommended accessory is a power surge suppressor and distributor. When this device is placed between your wall outlet and your computer, it protects your computer if, for some reason, a large power surge comes across your power lines. Many computers have been damaged or destroyed by a lightning strike that actually occurred several miles from the computer. A surge suppressor is therefore a smart precaution. Also, most suppressors allow you to turn on several different devices independently by using easy-to-access switches.

Getting Powered Up

Configuring most personal computers today is quite straightforward. Ignoring your printer for the moment, you should simply have to plug in your chassis and screen display, and then plug your keyboard and screen display into your computer chassis, as shown here:

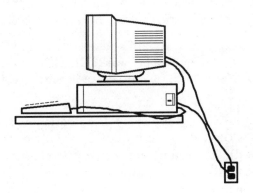

With no disks in your floppy disk drives, turn on your screen display and computer chassis. Your computer will begin its power-on sequence, during which it ensures that its internal components are working correctly and that each device is properly connected.

If your computer encounters an error during this period of time, it will display an error message on your screen. Write down this message so you can read it to your computer retailer. Turn off your system and wait a few seconds (about 10), and then repeat the power-on sequence. In some cases cycling your computer's power in this manner will clear the error.

If successful during the initial power-on sequence, most computers will display on the screen a count of your computer's memory that it finds operational. If displayed, record the last number shown so that you know how much memory is present within your computer.

Next, if your computer does not have a floppy disk in drive A or a fixed disk with DOS installed (by your retailer), it will invoke a version of the BASIC programming language that resides within your computer's hardware. If this occurs, your system is successfully installed and you are ready to use DOS. (Chapter 2 explains how to start DOS.) If you encounter errors, follow this checklist to help you isolate the error:

1. Can you hear your computer's fan running? If not, make sure that your computer is properly plugged in. If your computer is plugged in correctly, test the wall outlet with a working appliance. If your computer still does not work, you may be having a problem with its power supply.

2. Does your screen display work? Check that it is properly receiving power. Next, be sure your screen is connected to the computer's chassis.

3. Does your computer display its operational memory? If your system begins the display count but does not complete it, you have a problem with your computer's memory. Cycle the power on your system to see if this error goes away. If it does not, your retailer will have to repair your system.

4. Record other error messages so you can read them to your computer retailer.

Hands-On Practice

You have just seen several examples of possible personal computer configurations. In this section you will get comfortable with *your* computer system. Start with your disk drives. Using Figure 1-6 as a guide, locate disk drives A and B (if you have two floppy drives) and drive C (if you have a fixed disk drive) on your computer. You should know where your drives are before beginning with DOS.

Next, examine your computer's power cabling. If you have several plugs connected to a power outlet, strongly consider a power surge suppressor. Not only will you find the power distributor convenient, it can also protect your computer investment. If your chassis and screen display are plugged in, check your keyboard and video display to ensure that they are connected to your computer's chassis. If so, you are ready to turn on your system.

If you have a floppy disk in drive A, remove it. Next, turn on your screen display and computer chassis. You will hear your computer's fan start as your computer begins its power-on sequence.

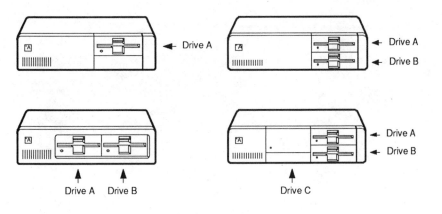

Figure 1-6.   *Disk drive locations*

Record any error messages for your retailer. If you computer displays a prompt similar to

```
A>
```

or

```
C>
```

you either have a DOS disk in drive A or you have DOS installed on a fixed disk. In either case, you are ready for the next chapter.

Summary

Regardless of the application, computers perform three steps: input, processing, and output.

The central processing unit (CPU) is your computer's workhorse. It is responsible for running the programs that your computer executes.

Depending on your computer's type (IBM PC, PC AT, or Compaq 386), your processor's name will differ (8088, 80286, or 80386). Essentially, the major differences between processors is speed and cost.

Each of the disk drives on your computer has a single-letter name starting with A. Your floppy disks will be named A and B, while your fixed disk will be drive C.

Each time you turn on your computer, it performs a power-on sequence in which it examines its internal hardware components and operational memory. If successful, the computer will either start DOS or invoke a version of BASIC stored in the computer's hardware.

Glossary

Input is the process of getting information into the computer so that the computer can process it.

Output is the process of printing or displaying meaningful information to the end user.

The *CPU* is the computer's central processing unit, which is responsible for executing the program that your computer is running.

Disks store programs and information. A disk can be either a fixed or a floppy disk. Although functionally equivalent, fixed disks are faster, can store more information, and are more expensive than floppy disks.

2 *Getting Started With DOS*

Chapter 1 examined many of the components, or hardware, that make up your computer. In general, hardware is the cables, cabinets, and boards that comprise your computer. However, hardware is only one part of the picture. Without software, your hardware is basically powerless. This chapter will examine your first PC software—MS-DOS. You will learn how to start DOS, set your computer's date and time, and reset your system without having to cycle your computer's power.

What Is Software?

Software is computer programs, such as a word processor, a spreadsheet, or even DOS. A computer program is simply a list of instructions that the computer is to perform. Software tells your computer hardware what to do so it can function.

Before your computer can execute a program, the program must reside in your computer's memory. For example, DOS will see that your programs are loaded from disk into your computer's memory, thus giving you the ability to run other programs.

Software is classified as either application software or system software. *Application software* includes such programs as a word processor, a spreadsheet program, or even computer games. *System software,* however, helps your computer function and allows you to

---

Your System

Hardware is the cables, cabinets, and boards that make up your computer.

Software is computer programs. Software tells hardware what to do. DOS is special software that allows you to run other programs on your computer.

---

run other programs. The most common example of system software is the operating system that oversees the computer and its resources.

What Is DOS?

As was just mentioned, DOS is software: however, DOS is a special program. DOS stands for "disk operating system." An operating system is your computer's resource manager that allows you to run programs, store information on disk, and use other devices (such as your system printer). Before you can run any of your other software packages, DOS must be present in your computer's memory. It is the operating system for the IBM PC and PC compatibles. As illustrated in Figure 2-1, DOS is your interface to your computer and application software.

PC DOS Versus MS-DOS

Many users are often confused by the terms "MS-DOS" and "PC DOS." Quite simply, both are operating systems for personal computers. The difference lies in the developer—MS-DOS was written by Microsoft (MS), and PC DOS was developed by IBM. If you have an IBM PC, you are probably using PC DOS; if you are using a PC compatible, you are probably using MS-DOS.

To the end user, these operating systems are functionally identical: each serves as your interface to your personal computer and

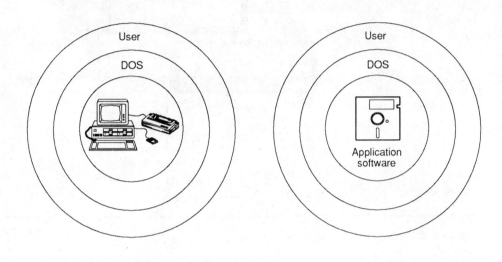

Figure 2-1. *DOS interfaces between the user and the computer or application software*

software, and the commands for each are identical in form and function. The commands found in this book will run under either PC DOS or MS-DOS.

What You Get

MS-DOS comes on two floppy disks, shown in Figure 2-2. The first disk, labeled "Program Disk," is the disk that you will use later in this chapter to start DOS. The second disk, labeled "Supplemental Programs Disk" contains utility programs that will be discussed in later chapters. This disk also contains GWBASIC, which is a version of the BASIC programming language for PC-compatible computers.

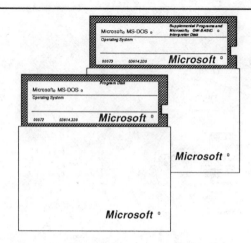

Figure 2-2.   *DOS comes on two floppy disks*

Floppy Disk Drives

The type of floppy disk drives your computer has depends on the type of personal computer you have. Three of the most common floppy disk drives are discussed here.

The first two types of disk drives are for standard 5 1/4-inch floppy disks and are shown in Figure 2-3. The difference between these two disk drives is the disk drive latch, which you open to insert a disk and close once your disk is in place.

Notice there is a disk activation light on both of these disk drives, which tells you when DOS is accessing the disk. Each time DOS reads information from or writes information to a floppy disk, it turns on the disk activation light. Never open the disk drive while the activa-

---

Warning: Never open your disk drive latch while the disk activation light is on. If you do, you will risk destroying your disk and the information it contains.

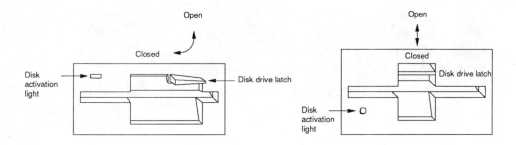

Figure 2-3.   *Two types of disk drives*

tion light is on; you could destroy your disk and lose the information
it contains.

When you insert a floppy disk into a disk drive, always do so with
the label facing up, so that the end of the disk containing the label is
the last end to enter the disk drive, as shown in Figure 2-4.

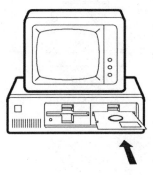

Figure 2-4.   *Inserting a disk*

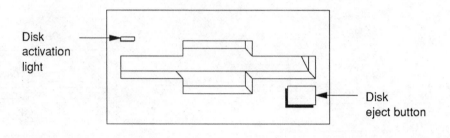

Figure 2-5.   *Front view of a microfloppy disk drive*

The third type of disk drive is a microfloppy disk drive, illustrated in Figure 2-5. This type of drive is specific to a 3 1/2-inch microfloppy disk, which is shown in Figure 2-6. With the success of laptop personal computers and the IBM PS/2 line of computers, 3 1/2-inch disks are becoming much more commonplace. Later chapters will discuss

Figure 2-6.   *A microfloppy disk*

how DOS treats these disks in a manner identical to standard 5 1/4-inch floppy disks.

If you are using microfloppy disks, again insert the disk so that the label is facing up and is inserted last. Regardless of your disk drive type, be careful when you insert your floppy disks into the disk drive. They are easily damaged.

Chapter 1 examined your personal computer's power-on sequence. As you will soon discover, DOS is started in a similar way. The only difference is that you will insert your DOS disk in drive A before you turn on your computer's power.

Hands-On Practice

This section assumes that you are using your original MS-DOS disks. Follow these procedures to start, or boot, DOS whether you are using a floppy disk or fixed disk system. Take your DOS disk labeled "Program Disk" and insert it into drive A. Be sure that your disk drive latch is closed once you insert the DOS disk into the drive, as shown in Figure 2-7.

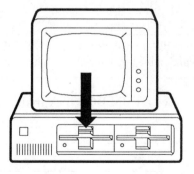

Figure 2-7. *Close the disk drive latch after inserting the disk*

Next, turn off your computer's power. Wait approximately 10 seconds, and then turn your computer's power back on. Your computer will once again perform its power-on sequence. Next, you will see the drive activation light for drive A come on. Your computer is reading DOS from the floppy disk into memory, as shown here:

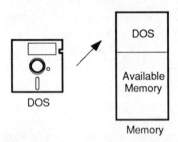

Remember, your computer cannot execute a program until that program resides in memory. DOS is no exception.

Once loaded into memory, DOS will prompt you to enter the current date:

```
Current date is Thu  3-31-1988
Enter new date (mm-dd-yy):
```

If your system is instead displaying BASIC, make sure that you have DOS in drive A and that the disk drive latch is closed. Likewise, if your screen displays the message

```
Non-system disk or disk error
Replace and strike any key when ready
```

you do not have a valid DOS disk in drive A. Finally, if your screen contains

```
A>
```

you are not using your *original* DOS disk. The characters "A>" are the DOS prompt, which will be discussed later in this chapter.

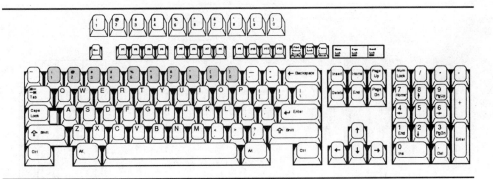

Figure 2-8. *Location of numeric keys on the keyboard*

If no error messages appear and your system is prompting you for the current date, use the numeric keys at the top of your keyboard (shown in Figure 2-8) to type in today's date in the form

mm/dd/yy

where *mm* is the current month (1 to 12, as shown in Table 2-1), *dd* is the current day (1 to 31), and *yy* is the current year (88). Your screen will now display

```
Current date is Thu  3-31-1988
Enter new date (mm-dd-yy): 12-25-88
```

Number	Month	Number	Month
1	January	7	July
2	February	8	August
3	March	9	September
4	April	10	October
5	May	11	November
6	June	12	December

Table 2-1. *Numbers Corresponding to Months of Year*

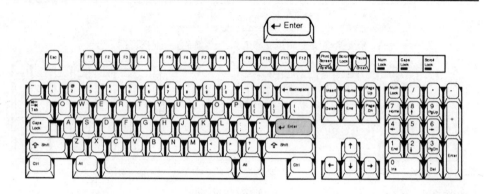

Figure 2-9.   *Location of ENTER key on the keyboard*

Next, press ENTER (Figure 2-9 shows where this key is on the keyboard). If the date that you just typed in is invalid or if you have entered an invalid character, DOS will display

```
Current date is Thu  3-31-1988
Enter new date (mm-dd-yy): 25-12-88

Invalid date
Enter new date (mm-dd-yy):
```

Remember that the month precedes the day. Simply re-enter the date properly.

Once you have successfully entered the current date, DOS prompts you for the current time:

```
Current date is Thu  3-31-1988
Enter new date (mm-dd-yy): 12-25-88
Current time is 17:27:53.10
Enter new time:
```

Again, using the numeric keys, enter the current time in the format

Military Time	Standard Time	Military Time	Standard Time
0	12:00 A.M.	13	1:00 P.M.
1	1:00 A.M.	14	2:00 P.M.
2	2:00 A.M.	15	3:00 P.M.
3	3:00 A.M.	16	4:00 P.M.
4	4:00 A.M.	17	5:00 P.M.
5	5:00 A.M.	18	6:00 P.M.
6	6:00 A.M.	19	7:00 P.M.
7	7:00 A.M.	20	8:00 P.M.
8	8:00 A.M.	21	9:00 P.M.
9	9:00 A.M.	22	10:00 P.M.
10	10:00 A.M.	23	11:00 P.M.
11	11:00 A.M.		
12	12 Noon		

Table 2-2.   *Military Time Compared to Standard Time*

hh:mm:ss

where *hh* is the current hour in military time (Table 2-2 compares military and standard times), *mm* is the current minutes (0 to 59), and *ss* is the current seconds (0 to 59):

```
Current date is Thu  3-31-1988
Enter new date (mm-dd-yy): 12-25-88

Current time is 17:27:53.10
Enter new time: 10:30:00
```

If you have entered a value in error, DOS will display

```
Current date is Thu  3-31-1988
Enter new date (mm-dd-yy): 12-25-88

Current time is 17:34:19.94
Enter new time: 32:12:00



Invalid time
Enter new time:
```

Simply re-enter the time and press ENTER. DOS will now display

```
Current date is Thu  3-31-1988
Enter new date (mm-dd-yy): 12-25-88

Current time is 17:27:53.10
Enter new time: 10:30:00
Microsoft (R)   MS-DOS(R)   Version 3.30
              (C)Copyright Microsoft Corp 1981-1987


A>
```

The characters "A>" are the DOS prompt—this is the way DOS asks
you what to do next.

Congratulations! You have just successfully started DOS. This is
as difficult as things will get. Simply press ENTER, and DOS will display a second prompt, "A>". In later chapters you will learn about the
DOS commands. These commands are entered (or typed in) at this
DOS prompt.

Now you can repeat the process, but this time you will do one thing
differently. Rather than cycling your computer's power to start DOS,
hold down the CTRL, ALT, and DEL keys (the location of these keys on
the keyboard is shown in Figure 2-10). You must hold all of these keys
down at the same time, so you will have to use both hands. This
keyboard combination directs DOS to restart itself. When you hold
down these keys at the same time, your screen display will clear and
the disk activation light on drive A will illuminate as your computer
loads DOS into memory.

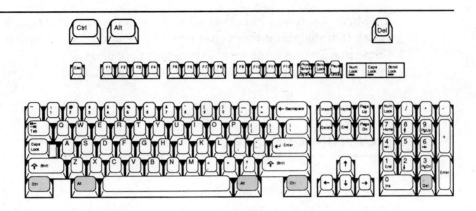

Figure 2-10. *Location of* CTRL, ALT, *and* DEL *keys*

DOS will prompt you to enter the current date, just as before. When you enter today's date, DOS will prompt you for the current time, just as it did when you first started up DOS. Enter the current time and DOS will again display the A> prompt, as shown here:

```
Current date is Thu  3-31-1988
Enter new date (mm-dd-yy): 12-25-88

Current time is 17:27:53.10
Enter new time: 10:30:00
Microsoft (R)   MS-DOS(R)   Version 3.30
              (C)Copyright Microsoft Corp 1981-1987


A>
```

Starting DOS

You can start DOS in two ways. First, with DOS in drive A, simply turn on your computer's power. Second, again with DOS in drive A, press the CTRL, ALT, and DEL keys all at the same time.

Many of you may have purchased a system with a battery-powered clock that maintains the correct system date and time. If the date and time that DOS is displaying is correct, simply press ENTER at the date and time prompts. DOS will leave the date and time unchanged.

Turning Off Your Computer

Later chapters will show how to execute programs from the DOS prompt. Always let these programs complete before shutting down your computer. In other words, only turn off your computer when DOS is displaying its prompt. If you turn off your computer while a program is running, you run the risk of destroying the information contained on your disks.

Summary

DOS is the disk operating system for the IBM PC and PC compatibles. An operating system oversees your computer and each of its resources. In general, an operating system serves as an interface between hardware and application software.

DOS allows you to run other programs, store data on disk, and use other devices, such as your system printer.

Two operating systems exist for the IBM PC and PC compatibles: PC DOS and MS-DOS. Both are functionally equivalent. The difference is that IBM developed PC DOS and Microsoft developed MS-DOS. To the end user, each will appear identical in function and format.

Every disk drive contains a small disk activation light that tells you when DOS is reading information from or writing information to the disk contained in the drive. Never open the disk drive latch when this light is on.

To start DOS you have two alternatives. First, with DOS in drive A, you can simply power on your computer. Second, if DOS is already active, you can press the CTRL, ALT, and DEL keys simultaneously to restart DOS.

Once loaded into memory, DOS will prompt you for the current date and time. Once you enter the date and time, DOS will display its prompt.

Glossary

Hardware is the cables, cabinets, and boards that comprise your computer.

Software is computer programs. A computer program is simply a list of instructions for the computer to perform.

An *operating system* is the software that oversees your computer, each of its resources, and the programs that you run. DOS is the operating system for the IBM PC and PC compatibles.

Booting DOS means starting DOS. Throughout this text, the terms will be used interchangeably.

The DOS *prompt*, which is often called the A prompt (A>), signals that DOS is ready for you to enter a command. Throughout this text you will be asked to type in specific commands at the DOS prompt. In later chapters you will see that the prompt is not always A>.

3 *Issuing DOS Commands*

Chapter 2 discussed how to start, or boot, DOS. At that time you learned that DOS is your interface to your computer's hardware and your application software. In this chapter you will begin using several of the basic capabilities of DOS. You will learn how to protect your floppy disks, issue several DOS commands, and how to make working copies of your original DOS disks so that you can place your originals safely back on the shelf. Before starting this chapter, you should have at least two unused floppy disks.

Write-Protect Notch

Examine your DOS Program disk. In the upper-right corner of your disk is an opening called the write-protect notch, shown in Figure 3-1. When this notch is completely visible, DOS is free to write information to the disk and erase information that the disk contains. In most cases you will want DOS to be able to write to your disk, so you will leave this notch fully exposed.

You do not want to risk erasing any of the information that is contained on your original DOS disks, however, so to protect your disk, you must must cover this notch with a write-protect tab, shown in Figure 3-2. When you purchase floppy disks, several write-protect

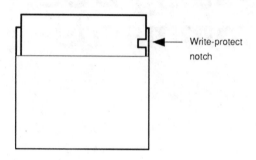

Write-protect
notch

Figure 3-1.   *A disk's write-protect notch*

tabs are included in the package. Simply peel off one of these tabs
and wrap it around your DOS disk, as shown here:

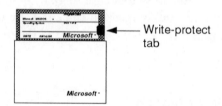

Write-protect
tab

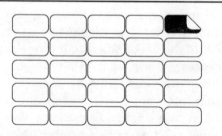

Figure 3-2.   *Write-protect tabs*

Write Protecting Your Disk

DOS allows you to write protect your disks, which prevents an errant command from modifying the contents of the disk. In most cases you will want DOS to be able to write to your disks. In such cases you should leave the disk's write-protect notch fully exposed. However, always write protect your DOS Program and Supplemental Programs disks by covering the write-protect notch with a write-protect tab.

If your DOS disk is currently in drive A, you can remove it as long as the disk activation light is not on. Repeat this process, write protecting your Supplemental Programs disk, as shown here:

Later in this text, you will see how DOS responds when you attempt to modify a disk that is write-protected. For now, however, simply remember that without write-protect tabs, the data on your disk can be erased by an errant DOS command.

If you are using 3 1/2-inch microfloppy disks, they too can be write-protected. In this case, rather than using a write-protect tab, you must turn the disk over and slide the write-protect switch down, exposing the opening, as shown in Figure 3-3.

DOS Commands

In addition to overseeing your computer's resources and allowing you to run other software programs, DOS also provides you with several

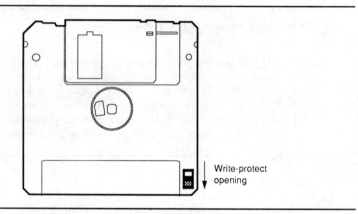

Write-protect
opening

Figure 3-3.   *Write-protect switch on microfloppy disk*

useful utilities, called commands, that you can access from the A>
DOS prompt. You will examine three simple, but useful, commands
here. To issue these commands, your computer must be at the A>
DOS prompt.

If your computer is not running, simply place DOS in drive A and
turn on your computer's power, as discussed in Chapter 2. Once the
DOS prompt is displayed on your screen, press ENTER several times.
This should place several characters on your screen display, as shown
here:

```
A>
A>
A>
A>
```

Next, at the last DOS prompt, simply type in **CLS**, as shown here:

```
A>
A>
A>
A>
A> CLS
```

Then press ENTER. DOS will respond to your command by clearing the screen display and placing the A> prompt in the upper-left corner of the screen.

CLS, your first DOS command, stands for "clear screen." Regardless of your screen contents, CLS will always clear the screen and place the DOS prompt back in the upper-left corner of the screen.

Believe it or not, you are already very familiar with the next two DOS commands that will be examined—DATE and TIME. These two commands allow you to set or display your system's current date and time. Again from the DOS prompt, type in **DATE**, so your screen displays this:

```
A> DATE
```

Press ENTER, and DOS invokes the DATE command, which prompts you for the current date:

```
A> DATE
Current date is Mon 12-26-1988
Enter new date (mm-dd-yy):
```

Does this look familiar? This is the same prompt to which you responded during DOS system start up. If you are satisfied with the current system date, press ENTER. This causes DOS to leave the current date unchanged, which is useful when you simply need to display the current date for a moment without changing it.

Throughout this text the format of each DOS command will be presented. The command's *format* tells you the information that you can type in at the DOS prompt. The format of the DATE command, for example, is

DATE [*mm-dd-yy*]

The word "DATE" is the DOS command. The characters [*mm-dd-yy*], however, deserve some additional discussion. Any characters that are contained within brackets are optional. For example, you can issue the DOS DATE command without specifying a date, like this:

```
A> DATE
```

However, the DATE command format indicates that you can also include a date in the command:

```
A> DATE 12-25-88
```

In this case, DOS will set the current system date to December 25,
1988. Since you have specified the date that you desire, DOS does not
have to prompt you for one. However, if you had specified an invalid
date, such as

```
A> DATE 25-12-88
```

the DATE command would respond by displaying

```
A> DATE 25-12-88

Invalid date
Enter new date (mm-dd-yy):
```

As you did in Chapter 2, type in the correct date and press ENTER.
    The DOS TIME command allows you to set your computer's sys-
tem time. The format for the TIME command is

```
TIME [hh:mm [:ss [.hh]]]
```

Don't panic! You will learn what each set of brackets means. First,
simply issue the TIME command without specifying a time:

```
A> TIME
```

DOS will prompt you for the current system time, as shown here:

```
A> TIME
Current time is 13:09:41.65
Enter new time:
```

In the same manner that you specified a time during DOS system start up, type in the desired time and press ENTER. If you are satisfied with the current time, simply press ENTER to leave it unchanged.

As previously stated, the multiple brackets in the TIME command format deserve additional explanation.

[*hh:mm* [*:ss* [*.hh*]]]

In this case, the multiple brackets tell you that several different parts of the time are optional. In fact, since there are three sets of brackets, you can specify the time in three separate ways. First, you can specify hours and minutes, ignoring [*:ss*[*.hh*]]:

```
A> TIME  12:30
```

Second, you can specify seconds, ignoring [*.hh*]:

```
A> TIME  12:30:00
```

Third, you can specify the time down to hundredths of a second:

```
A> TIME  12:30:00.99
```

When you specify a valid time, DOS will update the current system time and redisplay its prompt. If your time is invalid, however, DOS will display

```
A> TIME  12:61
Invalid time
Enter new time:
```

Simply type in the correct time and press ENTER.

Issuing an Invalid Command

Periodically you may misspell a DOS command when you type it at the DOS prompt. When this occurs, DOS will display

```
Bad command or file name
```

This message is telling you that DOS did not understand the command you typed in. If this occurs, examine the command that you typed in; you have probably just mistyped the command. Re-enter the correct command at the new DOS prompt. If you are certain that you have typed in the command correctly, make sure that you have your DOS Program disk in drive A, not the Supplemental Programs disk.

Making a Working Copy

One of the most important precautions that you can take with all of your software programs is to make working copies of the disks that you will use on a daily basis. This allows you to put your original disks back on the shelf in a safe location. Before you make a duplicate copy of a disk, make sure that your original disk is write-protected.

The final DOS command that will be examined in this chapter is DISKCOPY, which allows you to make a copy of a disk, as shown in Figure 3-4. To issue the DISKCOPY command, you must have your DOS disk in drive A. If you have a system with two floppy disk drives, you will copy the contents of the disk in drive A to the disk in drive B, as shown in Figure 3-5. However, if you only have one floppy disk drive, you will perform a single-drive disk copy in which you repeatedly exchange the disk you are copying with the target disk in the disk drive. This process is illustrated in Figure 3-6.

A simplified format of the DISKCOPY command is

DISKCOPY [*source_disk.*] [*target_disk.*]

where *source_disk* is the single-letter name (A or B) of the disk drive containing the disk to copy. Likewise, *target_disk* is the letter for the disk drive containing the disk to which you are copying. For example, the command

```
A> DISKCOPY  A:  B:
```

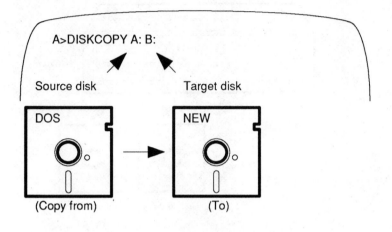

Figure 3-4. *DISKCOPY target and source disks*

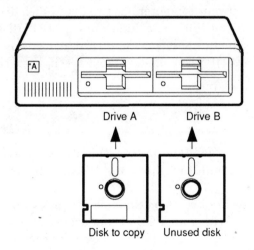

Figure 3-5. *Copying disks on a two-floppy disk drive system*

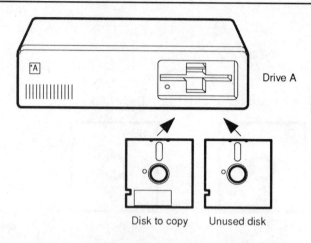

Drive A

Disk to copy   Unused disk

Figure 3-6.   *Copying a disk on a single-floppy disk drive system*

directs DOS to copy the contents of the disk in drive A to the disk in drive B. This format is the most common for the DISKCOPY command. In fact, if your computer has two floppy disk drives, this is the command that you will use to duplicate your DOS disks.

If your system has only one floppy disk drive, you will simply invoke the DISKCOPY command without specifying a source or target disk drive:

```
A> DISKCOPY
```

Remember, items that appear within the brackets of a command format are optional. In either case, DOS duplicates your disks as desired.

Consider the most common example of a disk copy, using two floppy disk drives. With your DOS disk in drive A, the following DISKCOPY command directs DOS to duplicate the contents of the disk in drive A to the disk contained in drive B:

```
A> DISKCOPY  A:  B:
```

Before proceeding with the disk copy, DOS will prompt you to place
the source disk (disk to copy) into drive A, as shown in the following
example::

```
A> DISKCOPY  A:  B:

Insert SOURCE diskette in drive A:

Insert TARGET diskette in drive B:

Press any key when ready . . .
```

DOS prompts you to place the target disk into drive B. Press ENTER,
and DOS will begin copying the contents of the source disk to the target disk. The following will be displayed:

```
A> DISKCOPY  A:  B:

Insert SOURCE diskette in drive A:

Insert TARGET diskette in drive B:
Press any key when ready . . .

Copying 40 tracks
9 Sectors/Track, 2 Side(s)


Formatting while copying
```

During the copying process, you will first see drive A's disk activation light turn on for a period of time. This is because DOS is reading
the information to copy from this drive. Then you will see drive B's
activation light turn on as drive A's turns off. DOS is now writing the
information to the disk in drive B. This process will repeat until DOS
has copied the entire disk. Once the copying operation is complete,
DOS will display

```
Copy another diskette (Y/N)?
```

To copy an additional disk, type **Y**. If you do not want to copy other disks, type **N**.

If DOS displayed the message

Bad command or file name

instead of invoking DISKCOPY, and you are sure that you have correctly entered the command, double check what disk you have in drive A. You must have your DOS Program disk in the drive, not the Supplemental Programs disk.

Labeling Your Disks

To organize your disks you should place labels on them that describe their contents, as shown here:

You should get extra disk labels with your box of disks each time you purchase a box of floppy disks.

Always write your disk description on your label before you put the label on your disk. It is best never to write on a label that is already on a disk, as shown in Figure 3-7; this could damage your disk, and you can lose the information that it contains. If you must do this, use a felt-tip pen.

Make your labels as meaningful as possible. You will have to use these labels to determine your disk contents for many years to come.

Hands-On Practice: CLS, DATE, and TIME

The three commands you will use in this section are very straightforward. From the DOS prompt, type **CLS**, like this:

```
A> CLS
```

DOS will acknowledge your command by clearing your screen display and placing the DOS prompt in the upper-left corner of the screen.

Next, invoke the DOS DATE command by typing **DATE** at the DOS prompt:

```
A> DATE
```

DOS will in turn prompt you to enter a new system date. In this case, simply press ENTER to leave the system date unchanged. The following will be displayed.

Figure 3-7.   *Writing on a label already on a disk can damage the disk*

```
A> DATE

Current date is Mon 12-26-1988
Enter new date (mm-dd-yy):
```

Next, use DATE to set your system date to January 1, 1989, like this:

```
A> DATE 01-01-89
```

When successful, use DATE to reset the system date to today's date.
Use the DOS TIME command to display the current system time:

```
A> TIME
Current time is 13:29:11.66
Enter new time:
```

Again press ENTER to leave the system time unchanged. Next, use the
DOS TIME command to set the current system time to 10:30 A.M.:

```
A> TIME 10:30
```

Use TIME to reset your computer to the correct system time.

Next, you will make a working copy of your DOS disks. These copies
are so named because they are the disks that you will work with on
a daily basis. Which one of the following DISKCOPY operations you
will perform depends on your system configuration. Even if you have
two floppy disk drives, you should practice the single-drive disk copy.

Two-Floppy Disk Drive System

Place your DOS Program disk in drive A and issue the following command to begin the copying process.

```
A> DISKCOPY A: B:
```

DOS will respond by displaying the following information and instructions on what to do next.

```
A> DISKCOPY  A:  B:

Insert SOURCE diskette in drive A:

Insert TARGET diskette in drive B:

Press any key when ready . . .
```

Leave your original DOS Program disk in drive A (it is the disk that you want to copy). Next, place an unused disk in drive B and press ENTER. DISKCOPY will copy the contents of the disk in drive A to the disk in drive B, displaying

```
A> DISKCOPY  A:  B:

Insert SOURCE diskette in drive A:

Insert TARGET diskette in drive B:

Press any key when ready . . .

Copying 40 tracks
9 Sectors/Track, 2 Side(s)


Formatting while copying

Copy another diskette (Y/N)?
```

You need to copy the contents of your Supplemental Pro-grams disk, so type **Y** to perform a second copy. DISKCOPY responds with

```
Insert SOURCE diskette in drive A:

Insert TARGET diskette in drive B:

Press any key when ready . . .
```

Place your DOS Supplemental Programs disk in drive A and an un-used disk in drive B. Press ENTER to begin the copy. While this copying process is proceeding, label your working DOS Program disk. Remember to write on the label before placing it on the disk.

Once DISKCOPY finishes the second copy, simply type **N** in response to the prompt

```
Copy another diskette (Y/N)?
```

DISKCOPY terminates and returns to the DOS prompt. Label a working Supplemental Programs disk, and place the originals safely on your shelf.

Single-Floppy Disk Drive System

Place your DOS Program disk in drive A and issue the command

```
A> DISKCOPY
```

DOS will respond with the display

```
A> DISKCOPY

Insert SOURCE diskette in drive A:

Press any key when ready . . .
```

Leave your original DOS Program disk in drive A (it is the disk that you want to copy) and press ENTER. DISKCOPY will begin reading the contents of the disk in drive A, and the following will be displayed:

```
A> DISKCOPY

Insert SOURCE diskette in drive A:

Press any key when ready . . .

Copying 40 tracks
9 Sectors/Track, 2 Side(s)
```

Next, DISKCOPY will ask you to place your target disk in drive A:

```
A> DISKCOPY

Insert SOURCE diskette in drive A:

Press any key when ready . . .

Copying 40 tracks
9 Sectors/Track, 2 Side(s)

Insert TARGET diskette in drive A:

Press any key when ready . . .
```

At this time, remove the source disk, place an unused disk in drive A, and then press ENTER. DISKCOPY will now write information to the new disk. You may need to repeat this process of exchanging source and target disks one more time.

Since you need to copy the contents of your Supplemental Programs disk, type **Y** to perform a second copy. DISKCOPY will respond with

```
Insert SOURCE diskette in drive A:

Press any key when ready . . .
```

Place your DOS Supplemental Programs disk in drive A and press ENTER to begin the copying process. While this copy is proceeding, label your working DOS Program disk. Remember to write on the label before placing it on the disk. Once DISKCOPY is done with the second copy, type **N** in response to the prompt

```
Copy another diskette (Y/N)?
```

DISKCOPY will terminate and return you to the DOS prompt. Label your working Supplemental Programs disk, and place your originals safely on your shelf.

Summary

In addition to overseeing your computer and its resources, DOS provides you with many very useful utilities, called commands, that you can execute from the DOS prompt.

The CLS command directs DOS to clear the contents of your screen display and place the DOS prompt in the upper-left corner of your screen.

The DATE and TIME commands allow you to modify or display the current date and time.

Many DOS commands used throughout this book will have optional information that you can specify (such as a date or time). When you examine the format of these commands, the optional information will appear between brackets, like this: [*optional*].

There are two important safeguards for your original software: write protection and working copies. To write protect a disk, cover the write-protect notch that appears in the upper-left corner of the disk. Once a disk is write-protected, DOS cannot inadvertantly erase its contents. Making working copies of your disks, which you will use on a daily basis, frees you to place your original disks safely on your shelf.

The DOS DISKCOPY command allows you to make working copies of your disks. DISKCOPY fully supports systems with one or two floppy disk drives.

Glossary

A *write-protected* disk is a disk whose write-protect notch has been covered. Once a disk is write-protected, DOS cannot modify its contents.

A DOS *command* is a utility program provided with DOS that you can execute from the DOS prompt. CLS, DATE, TIME, and DISKCOPY are examples of DOS commands.

The *source disk* is the disk that contains information that you want to transfer to another location. The *target disk* is the disk to which the information is being copied.

4 Getting Started With DOS Files

Previously in this text you learned that disks exist for only one reason—to store programs and information. DOS keeps track of all of the information on your disk by placing the programs and data into a storage facility called a file. Think of a DOS file as a file in your filing cabinet; both are designed to store information. In later sessions you will use DOS to create disk files, modify the information they contain, examine their contents, and eventually get rid of them when they are no longer needed.

DOS File Names

Each of your DOS files has a unique name. DOS file names have two parts: an eight-character file name and an optional three-character extension. DOS uses a period to separate the file name from the extension, as shown here:

```
filename.ext
```

In your DOS disks, for example, you will find the following file names:

4201.CPI	ANSI.SYS	APPEND.EXE
ASSIGN.COM	ATTRIB.EXE	CHKDSK.COM
COMMAND.COM	DISKCOMP.COM	DISKCOPY.COM
DISPLAY.SYS	DRIVER.SYS	SYS.COM

Later in this text you will create your own files. When you do so, you must follow the rules for naming files. The following file names are valid under DOS:

BOOK.RPT	SCIENCE.NTS	DEBBIE.LTR
A.A	A	A.DAT
SEPT.PAY	BILLS.OCT	XMAS.LST

These file names, however, are invalid:

File Name	Reason for Invalidity
.COM	No file name given
BOOK..RPT	Period is not a valid file name character
SPACE AGE	Blank is not a valid file name character
NAMETOOLARGE	Only eight-character names are valid
NEW.FILE	Extension can only be three characters in length

DOS allows you to use all of the characters of the alphabet (uppercase and lowercase) in your file names, as well as these characters:

DOS File Names

All of the DOS files on your disk have unique names. A DOS file name has two parts. The first is an eight-character file name. The second part is an optional three-character extension. DOS separates the file name and extension with a period.

filename.ext

DOS allows you to use any of the characters in the alphabet, along with the following characters within your file names:

~ ! @ # $ % ^ & ( ) - _ { } '

~ ! @ # $ % ^ & ( ) - _ { } '

Using this set of characters, you can create very meaningful file names.

SALES.88!	SALES(A).88	MY-PAY.SEP
EXPENSES.$$$	PHONE.#S	RAISES.^^^
TAXES.%%%	J&B.CST	MY_SALES.INF

What's in a Name?

The three-letter extension in a DOS file name can tell you a great deal about the file. For the sake of standardization, DOS predefines the following file extensions:

Extension	Function
COM	DOS command file
EXE	DOS command file
SYS	DOS operating system file
BAT	DOS batch file
CPI	DOS code page information file

The function of each of these files will be examined later in this book. For now, keep in mind that DOS predefines these extensions. Likewise, the following extensions have become accepted standards for personal computer users:

Extension	Function
TXT	Text or word processing file
DAT	Data file
BAK	Backup file
LTR	File containing a letter
RPT	File containing a report
BAS	File containing a BASIC program

Given the following list of DOS files, you can determine the contents of each file by examining their extensions:

File Name	Extension	Function
DISKCOPY	COM	DOS command
GRANDMA	LTR	File containing a letter
ANSI	SYS	DOS operating system file
CONFIG	BAK	Backup file
AUTOEXEC	BAT	DOS batch file
CHAPTER4	TXT	Text file

What Is a Directory?

DOS stores your programs and information on disk in separate files. To organize this collection of files on your disk, DOS stores your files in a facility called a directory. You will hear, therefore, the term "directory listing" used to describe a list of the files on your disk. In fact, DOS provides a directory command, DIR, that allows you to list the files contained in your directory.

Listing the Files on Your Disk

Place your DOS Program disk in drive A and issue the command

```
A> DIR
```

DOS will display a list of all of the files on your disk, as shown in Figure 4-1. Many of these files are DOS commands.

DIR is a DOS command; therefore, it has a complete command format:

DIR [*file_specification*] [/P][/W]

```
Volume in drive A is MS330PP01
Directory of  A:\

4201        CPI    17089    7-24-87    12:00a
5202        CPI    459      7-24-87    12:00a
ANSI        SYS    1647     7-24-87    12:00a
APPEND      EXE    5794     7-24-87    12:00a
ASSIGN      COM    1530     7-24-87    12:00a
ATTRIB      EXE    10656    7-24-87    12:00a
CHKDSK      COM    9819     7-24-87    12:00a
COMMAND     COM    25276    7-24-87    12:00a
COMP        COM    4183     7-24-87    12:00a
COUNTRY     SYS    11254    7-24-87    12:00a
DISKCOMP    COM    5848     7-24-87    12:00a
DISKCOPY    COM    6264     7-24-87    12:00a
DISPLAY     SYS    11259    7-24-87    12:00a
DRIVER      SYS    1165     7-24-87    12:00a
EDLIN       COM    7495     7-24-87    12:00a
EXE2BIN     EXE    3050     7-24-87    12:00a
FASTOPEN    EXE    3888     7-24-87    12:00a
FDISK       COM    48919    7-24-87    12:00a
FIND        EXE    6403     7-24-87    12:00a
FORMAT      COM    11671    7-24-87    12:00a
GRAFTABL    COM    6136     7-24-87    12:00a
GRAPHICS    COM    13943    7-24-87    12:00a
JOIN        EXE    9612     7-24-87    12:00a
KEYB        COM    9041     7-24-87    12:00a
LABEL       COM    2346     7-24-87    12:00a
MODE        COM    15440    7-24-87    12:00a
MORE        COM    282      7-24-87    12:00a
NLSFUNC     EXE    3029     7-24-87    12:00a
PRINT       COM    8995     7-24-87    12:00a
RECOVER     COM    4268     7-24-87    12:00a
SELECT      COM    4132     7-24-87    12:00a
SORT        EXE    1946     7-24-87    12:00a
SUBST       EXE    10552    7-24-87    12:00a
SYS         COM    4725     7-24-87    12:00a
        34 File(s)    5120 bytes free
```

Figure 4-1.   *List of files in DOS Program disk*

The use of the qualifiers (that is, the items within brackets) will be
explained later in this chapter. For now, remember that items appearing within brackets are optional. For this reason you can simply
type in **DIR** at the DOS prompt to display all files in your directory.

Here is an example of the information that DIR actually displays

```
Volume in drive A is MS330PP01
Directory of  A:\

4201        CPI    17089    7-24-87    12:00a
5202        CPI    459      7-24-87    12:00a
ANSI        SYS    1647     7-24-87    12:00a
APPEND      EXE    5794     7-24-87    12:00a
ASSIGN      COM    1530     7-24-87    12:00a
ATTRIB      EXE    10656    7-24-87    12:00a
CHKDSK      COM    9819     7-24-87    12:00a
COMMAND     COM    25276    7-24-87    12:00a
COMP        COM    4183     7-24-87    12:00a
COUNTRY     SYS    11254    7-24-87    12:00a
DISKCOMP    COM    5848     7-24-87    12:00a
DISKCOPY    COM    6264     7-24-87    12:00a
SELECT      COM    4132     7-24-87    12:00a




SORT        EXE    1946     7-24-87    12:00a
SUBST       EXE    10552    7-24-87    12:00a
SYS         COM    4725     7-24-87    12:00a
            34 File(s)    5120 bytes free
```

There are several components to this list that should be explained.
First, DOS tells you the disk drive where the directory you are listing is located. In this case, DOS is in drive A.

Disk
drive

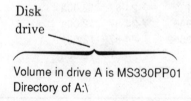

```
Volume in drive A is MS330PP01
Directory of A:\
```

Next, DOS displays a listing of the files on disk. Note how DOS separates the eight-character file name from the three-character extension.

DISKCOPY⏝COM 6264   7-24-87 12:00a

             File name
             extension

DOS displays three additional fields. The first is the size of the file in bytes.

DISKCOPY   COM ⏝6264⏝   7-24-87 12:00a

              File size
              in bytes

One byte represents one character of the alphabet; for example, if your file size is 4096 bytes, the file contains 4096 characters. Many of the concepts that will be discussed in this book refer to size in terms of bytes. It is simplest to associate a byte with a character of the alphabet.

The next field in the directory listing tells you the date when the file was created or last modified.

What Is a Byte?

For discussions in this book, a byte is simply a character of the alphabet. DOS uses bytes to specify many sizes. If, for example, your file size is 512 bytes, visualize the file as containing 512 characters.

```
DISKCOPY    COM   6264      7-24-87  12:00a
```

Creation
date

Each time you modify a file's contents, DOS updates this field.

```
DISKCOPY    COM   6264      7-24-87  12:00a
```

Creation
time

DOS also displays the file's creation or modification time.

The last field in the directory tells you how much disk space you still have available for creating files.

```
34 File(s)    5120 bytes free
```

Note that DOS specifies the amount of available disk space in bytes.

One of the first things you will probably notice when you issue the DIR command is that your files scroll rapidly past on the screen. To alleviate this problem, you can use one of the optional DIR command qualifiers, /P, as shown here:

```
A> DIR /P
```

The /P qualifier directs DIR to pause with each screenful of file names, and the following message is displayed:

```
Strike a key when ready . . .
```

Using the command

```
A> DIR /P
```

on your DOS Program disk will result in the output that is shown in Figure 4-2.

```
Volume in drive A is MS330PP01
Directory of  A:\

4201        CPI    17089    7-24-87    12:00a
5202        CPI    459      7-24-87    12:00a
ANSI        SYS    1647     7-24-87    12:00a
APPEND      EXE    5794     7-24-87    12:00a
ASSIGN      COM    1530     7-24-87    12:00a
ATTRIB      EXE    10656    7-24-87    12:00a
CHKDSK      COM    9819     7-24-87    12:00a
COMMAND     COM    25276    7-24-87    12:00a
COMP        COM    4183     7-24-87    12:00a
COUNTRY     SYS    11254    7-24-87    12:00a
DISKCOMP    COM    5848     7-24-87    12:00a
DISKCOPY    COM    6264     7-24-87    12:00a
DISPLAY     SYS    11259    7-24-87    12:00a
DRIVER      SYS    1165     7-24-87    12:00a
EDLIN       COM    7495     7-24-87    12:00a
EXE2BIN     EXE    3050     7-24-87    12:00a
FASTOPEN    EXE    3888     7-24-87    12:00a
FDISK       COM    48919    7-24-87    12:00a
FIND        EXE    6403     7-24-87    12:00a
FORMAT      COM    11671    7-24-87    12:00a
GRAFTABL    COM    6136     7-24-87    12:00a
GRAPHICS    COM    13943    7-24-87    12:00a
Strike a key when ready . . .                          ←——— Pause
JOIN        EXE    9612     7-24-87    12:00a
KEYB        COM    9041     7-24-87    12:00a
LABEL       COM    2346     7-24-87    12:00a
MODE        COM    15440    7-24-87    12:00a
MORE        COM    282      7-24-87    12:00a
NLSFUNC     EXE    3029     7-24-87    12:00a
PRINT       COM    8995     7-24-87    12:00a
RECOVER     COM    4268     7-24-87    12:00a
SELECT      COM    4132     7-24-87    12:00a
SORT        EXE    1946     7-24-87    12:00a
SUBST       EXE    10552    7-24-87    12:00a
SYS         COM    4725     7-24-87    12:00a
            34 File(s)    5120 bytes free
```

Figure 4-2.   *Output from the DIR command with the /P qualifier*

You have probably noticed that DIR supports a second command qualifier, /W. The /W qualifier directs DIR to only display the file name and extension, so there is room to display the names of five files across your screen. If, for example, you issue the command

```
A> DIR  /W
```

with your DOS disk in drive A, the output will be like that shown in Figure 4-3.

There is one more qualifier in the DIR command that needs explanation: the optional file specification. You can consider a DOS file specification as equivalent to a file name. To list the directory information (size, date, and time) for a specific file, you can use the DIR command, as shown here:

```
A> DIR  FILENAME.EXT
```

For example, when you enter the command

```
A> DIR  DISKCOPY.COM
```

```
Volume in drive A is MS330PP01
Directory of  A:\

4201      CPI   5202       CPI   ANSI      SYS   APPEND  EXE ASSIGN   COM
ATTRIB    EXE   CHKDSK     COM   COMMAND   COM   COMP    COM COUNTRY  SYS
DISKCOMP  COM   DISKCOPY   COM   DISPLAY   SYS   DRIVER  SYS EDLIN    COM
EXE2BIN   EXE   FASTOPEN   EXE   FDISK     COM   FIND    EXE FORMAT   COM
GRAFTABL  COM   GRAPHICS   COM   JOIN      EXE   KEYB    COM LABEL    COM
MODE      COM   MORE       COM   NLSFUNC   EXE   PRINT   COM RECOVER  COM
SELECT    COM   SORT       EXE   SUBST     EXE   SYS     COM
    34 File(s)    5120 bytes free
```

Figure 4-3.   *Output from the DIR command with the /W qualifier*

DIR will display

```
Volume in drive A is MS330PP01
Directory of  A:\

DISKCOPY      COM    6264   7-24-87   12:00a
              1 File(s)    5120 bytes free
```

The command

```
A> DIR  FORMAT.COM
```

displays directory information about the file FORMAT.COM. If you specify a file name that does not exist, such as

```
A> DIR  XXX.XXX
```

DIR will display

```
Volume in drive A is MS330PP01
Directory of  A:\

File not found
```

This error message tells you that the file XXX.XXX does not reside on disk.

Matching a Group of Files

A file specification can actually be more complex than a simple DOS file name. DOS provides you with two special characters, called wildcard characters, that you can use within your file specifications. These characters are the asterisk (*) and the question mark (?).

As you know, DOS file names have an eight-character file name followed by an optional three-character extension. If you place a ques-

---

? Wildcard Character

The DOS ? wildcard character directs DOS to match any character to the question mark in a file specification.

Example: DIR DISK????.COM

---

tion mark within any of these 11-character locations, DOS will match any character at that location. For example, the DOS Program disk includes two files with similar names: DISKCOPY.COM and DISK-COMP.COM. Because only the last two characters of these names differ, you can use the question mark in these locations to find both files in the directory. Therefore, the command

```
A> DIR  DISKCO??.COM
```

will display

```
Volume in drive A is MS330PP01
Directory of  A:\

DISKCOMP      COM     5848   7-24-87   12:00a
DISKCOPY      COM     6264   7-24-87   12:00a
              2 File(s)     5120 bytes free
```

As long as the first six characters of the file name match DISKCO, the question marks direct DOS to ignore the last two characters.

The second and more powerful DOS wildcard character is the asterisk. When you use the asterisk, you are telling DOS that not only do you not care about the character at the position containing the asterisk, but you also do not care about any of the characters that follow it. For example, at the command

```
A> DIR  DISK*.COM
```

DOS will display

```
Volume in drive A is MS330PP01
Directory of  A:\
DISKCOMP        COM     5848   7-24-87   12:00a
DISKCOPY        COM     6264   7-24-87   12:00a
                2 File(s)     5120 bytes free
```

Likewise, given the command

```
A> DIR  D*.COM
```

DOS will again display

```
Volume in drive A is MS330PP01
Directory of  A:\

DISKCOMP        COM     5848   7-24-87   12:00a
DISKCOPY        COM     6264   7-24-87   12:00a
                2 File(s)     5120 bytes free
```

Note that DOS matches characters in the file name up to the position of the asterisk.

DOS also allows you to use the asterisk and question mark in the three-character file extension. This command, for example,

```
A> DIR  A*.*
```

will display

```
Volume in drive A is MS330PP01
Directory of  A:\

ANSI            SYS    1647   7-24-87   12:00a
APPEND          EXE    5794   7-24-87   12:00a
ASSIGN          COM    1530   7-24-87   12:00a
ATTRIB          EXE    10656 7-24-87   12:00a
                4 File(s)     5120 bytes free
```

---

* Wildcard Character

The DOS * wildcard character directs DOS to ignore not only the character in the position containing the asterisk, but also all of the characters that follow the asterisk.

Example: DIR DI*.*

As previously stated, if you do not include a file specification with your DIR command, DOS will display all of the files in your directory. Given what you know now about the asterisk wildcard, you can see that the commands

```
A> DIR
```

and

```
A> DIR *.*
```

are functionally equivalent.

Earlier you found that DOS defines several file extensions for specific types of files. Knowing this, you can use the DOS wildcard characters to display the different file types. First, DOS defines its commands as either EXE or COM files. Figure 4-4 lists the directory entries for each extension.

We also know that DOS defines files with the extension SYS as system files. Here is a list of SYS files:

```
Volume in drive A is MS330PP01
Directory of  A:\

ANSI         SYS    1647   7-24-87   12:00a
COUNTRY      SYS    11254  7-24-87   12:00a
DISPLAY      SYS    11259  7-24-87   12:00a
DRIVER       SYS    1165   7-24-87   12:00a
             4 File(s)    4096 bytes free
```

```
A> DIR *.EXE

Volume in drive A is MS330PP01
Directory of  A:\
APPEND        EXE    5794     7-24-87    12:00a
ATTRIB        EXE    10656    7-24-87    12:00a
EXE2BIN       EXE    3050     7-24-87    12:00a
FASTOPEN      EXE    3888     7-24-87    12:00a
FIND          EXE    6403     7-24-87    12:00a
JOIN          EXE    9612     7-24-87    12:00a
NLSFUNC       EXE    3029     7-24-87    12:00a
SORT          EXE    1946     7-24-87    12:00a
SUBST         EXE    10552    7-24-87    12:00a
9 File(s)    5120 bytes free


A> DIR *.COM

Volume in drive A is MS330PP01
Directory of  A:\
ASSIGN        COM    1530     7-24-87    12:00a
CHKDSK        COM    9819     7-24-87    12:00a
COMMAND       COM    25276    7-24-87    12:00a
COMP          COM    4183     7-24-87    12:00a
DISKCOMP      COM    5848     7-24-87    12:00a
DISKCOPY      COM    6264     7-24-87    12:00a
EDLIN         COM    7495     7-24-87    12:00a
FDISK         COM    48919    7-24-87    12:00a
FORMAT        COM    11671    7-24-87    12:00a
GRAFTABL      COM    6136     7-24-87    12:00a
GRAPHICS      COM    13943    7-24-87    12:00a
KEYB          COM    9041     7-24-87    12:00a
LABEL         COM    2346     7-24-87    12:00a
MODE          COM    15440    7-24-87    12:00a
MORE          COM    282      7-24-87    12:00a
PRINT         COM    8995     7-24-87    12:00a
RECOVER       COM    4268     7-24-87    12:00a
SELECT        COM    4132     7-24-87    12:00a
SYS           COM    4725     7-24-87    12:00a
             19 File(s)    5120 bytes free
```

Figure 4-4.   *Directories of EXE and COM files*

Remember that DOS allows you to use the qualifiers /P and /W in conjunction with your wildcard characters, as in these commands:

```
A> DIR *.EXE /W

A> DIR *.* /P
```

Hands-On Practice

Put your DOS disk in drive A and check that your disk drive latch is closed. At the DOS prompt, type **DIR** and press ENTER.

```
A> DIR
```

DOS will display a directory listing of all of the files in your directory. If your files scrolled by too quickly, use the command

```
A> DIR /P
```

and DOS will display your files one screenful at a time. Press ENTER at the prompt to continue with each screenful of file names. Note the various file sizes and the amount of available disk space that your disk contains.

Suppress the display of the size, date, and time fields by using the /W qualifier.

```
A> DIR /W
```

Now try using the DOS wildcard characters * and ?. First, list all of the files on your disk by using

```
A> DIR *.*
```

Then use question marks to obtain the same result.

```
A> DIR  ????????.???
```

Use the command

```
A> DIR  *.COM
```

to display files containing many of the DOS commands.
Next, use the DOS question mark qualifier in this command:

```
A> DIR  DISKCO??
```

DOS will display

```
Volume in drive A is MS330PP01
Directory of  A:\

DISKCOMP      COM     5848   7-24-87   12:00a
DISKCOPY      COM     6264   7-24-87   12:00a
2 File(s)    4096 bytes free
```

If you do not specify a file extension, DOS will display all the files
that match the file name given. If you specify a file name that does
not reside on your disk, such as

```
A> DIR  X
```

DOS will display

```
File not found
```

Note that this error message differs from

```
Bad command or file name
```

which DOS displays when you specify an invalid command.
To see the difference between the use of * and ?, issue the command

```
A> DIR  DISKCO?Y
```

DOS will display

```
Volume in drive A is MS330PP01
Directory of  A:\

DISKCOPY       COM      6264   7-24-87   12:00a
               1 File(s)     5120 bytes free
```

Now issue the command

```
A> DIR  DISKCO*Y
```

In this case DOS will display

```
Volume in drive A is MS330PP01
Directory of  A:\

DISKCOMP       COM      5848   7-24-87   12:00a
DISKCOPY       COM      6264   7-24-87   12:00a
               2 File(s)     5120 bytes free
```

Remember, the asterisk tells DOS to ignore not only the character at the location containing the asterisk, but also all of those characters that follow.

For practice, take out your DOS Program disk and insert the Supplemental Programs disk. Issue several DIR commands to examine the files on this disk.

Summary

DOS stores your programs and information on disk in files.

Under DOS, files have a two-part name: the first eight characters are the file name, and the last three characters comprise the file extension. DOS separates the file name and the extension with a period, as in

filename.ext

The DOS DIR command allows you to list all of the files contained in your directory. By default, DIR will display each file's name, extension, size, and creation/modification date and time.

DOS allows you to use two wildcard characters, the asterisk (*) and the question mark (?), to specify a group of files. The question mark directs DOS to match any character to the question mark. The asterisk, on the other hand, directs DOS to ignore not only the character in the location of the asterisk, but also all of those that follow.

Glossary

A *file* is a disk storage facility that contains your programs and information.

A *directory* is a list of file names. The DOS DIR command allows you to display all of the files in your directory.

DOS supports two *wildcard characters,* the question mark (?) and asterisk (*), which help you group files. The question mark directs DOS to match any character to the question mark. The asterisk, on the other hand, directs DOS to ignore not only the character in the location of the asterisk, but also all characters that follow.

5 *Getting the Most From Your Keyboard*

New DOS users are often impressed when they watch seasoned veterans entering DOS commands and displaying a mastery of the keyboard. Unfortunately, for many users it takes months (or sometimes longer) to understand the secrets of getting the most from their keyboards. As you will see in this chapter, however, this does not have to be the case. This chapter teaches you all of the DOS keyboard secrets. By using the keyboard combinations that you will examine here, you will find that you can enter commands much faster and much easier.

Standard Keyboards

Figures 5-1 and 5-2 illustrate the keyboards commonly found on the IBM PC and PC AT. Although the keyboards differ slightly in appearance, they are identical in terms of function.

Even if you do not like to type, the lessons you will learn in this chapter will put you at ease with your PC keyboard.

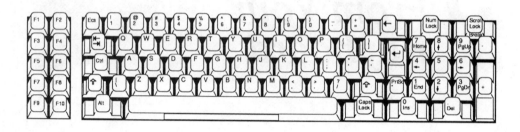

Figure 5-1.   *The IBM PC keyboard*

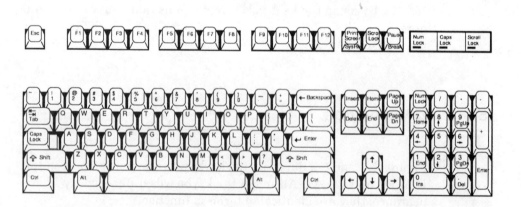

Figure 5-2.   *The PC AT keyboard*

BACKSPACE Key

Eventually, every DOS user will make a typographical error when entering DOS commands. For example, if you enter

```
A> DARE
```

you have misspelled the DATE command as DARE. With the cursor positioned immediately following the letter "E," press BACKSPACE twice to delete the last two letters typed. Figure 5-3 shows the location of the BACKSPACE key on the keyboard. Your screen now displays

```
A> DA
```

You can now correct your error and issue the command

```
A> DATE
```

The BACKSPACE key simply erases the character that immediately precedes the cursor.

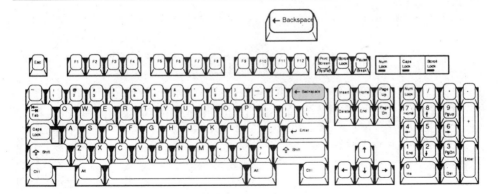

Figure 5-3. *Location of* BACKSPACE *key*

CTRL-ALT-DEL **Key Combination**

You may recall the CTRL-ALT-DEL key combination that was used earlier in this text to restart DOS. In any key combination of this kind, you must hold down all of the keys specified in the sequence given. In this case, you first hold down CTRL, then ALT, and then DEL, and you must keep them depressed simultaneously in order for DOS to restart. The location of these three keys on the keyboard is shown in Figure 5-4.

> **WARNING**: Be careful when you use this keyboard combination. Many of your software programs will open DOS files in order to store information. If you reboot DOS while one of these programs is running, you will run the risk of destroying the data file and losing the information that it contains.

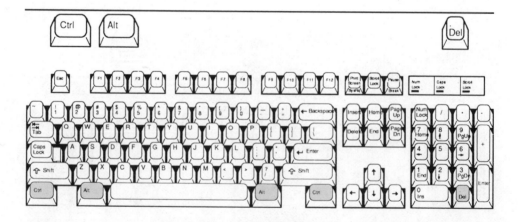

Figure 5-4.   *Location of* CTRL, ALT, *and* DEL *keys*

CTRL-BREAK *Key Combination*

Periodically you may invoke a DOS command in error, or you may decide that you want to terminate a command before it completes. DOS allows you to stop many applications simply by pressing the CTRL-BREAK key combination. Figure 5-5 shows the location of these two keys on the keyboard.

For example, if you issue the DOS DISKCOPY command

```
A> DISKCOPY  A:  B:

Insert the SOURCE diskette in drive A:

Press Enter to continue.
```

and then decide to terminate it before it continues, you can press the CTRL-BREAK combination. DOS will terminate the application, display

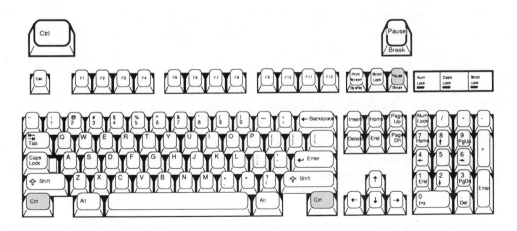

Figure 5-5.   *Location of the CTRL and BREAK keys*

the characters "^C," and redisplay its prompt for your next command.

```
A> DISKCOPY  A:  B:

Insert the source diskette in drive A:

Press Enter to continue.^C

A>
```

DOS also allows you to press the CTRL-C key combination for this same purpose. This is why DOS displays ^C above. The ^ character is often called the control character. ^C, therefore, stands for control C. If, for example, you want to terminate the DOS DATE command

```
A> DATE
Current date is Tue  4-05-1988
Enter new date (mm-dd-yy):
```

simply press CTRL-C, and DOS will display

```
A> DATE
Current date is Tue  4-05-1988
Enter new date (mm-dd-yy): ^C

A>
```

The function of CTRL-BREAK and CTRL-C is identical: both direct DOS to terminate the current program.

CTRL-S Key Combination

In Chapter 4, you first issued the DOS DIR command, and you found that the directory output scrolled past you very quickly. One solution was to include the /P directive in the DIR command:

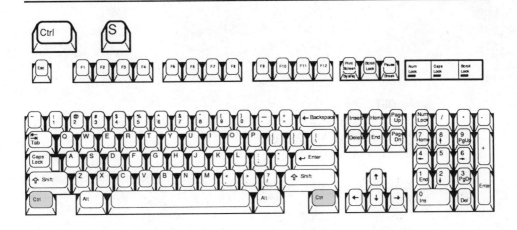

Figure 5-6. *Location of* CTRL *and* S *keys*

```
A> DIR  /P
```

Not all DOS commands, however, have a qualifier such as /P. DOS provides you with an alternative: the CTRL-S key combination. The location of these keys is shown in Figure 5-6. CTRL-S directs DOS to suspend temporarily the output of the current program. For example, if you issue the DOS DIR command and then press CTRL-S, DOS will suspend the output of your command, as you can see in Figure 5-7. If you then press any key, DOS will resume the program's output, as shown in Figure 5-8.

DOS Function Keys

Your PC keyboard has several keys labeled F1 through F10 (some keyboards have additional keys). These keys are your keyboard func-

```
A> DIR

Volume in drive A is MS330PP01
Directory of  A:\

4201        CPI    17089    7-24-87    12:00a
5202        CPI    459      7-24-87    12:00a
ANSI        SYS    1647     7-24-87    12:00a
APPEND      EXE    5794     7-24-87    12:00a
ASSIGN      COM    1530     7-24-87    12:00a
ATTRIB      EXE    10656    7-24-87    12:00a
CHKDSK      COM    9819     7-24-87    12:00a
COMMAND     COM    25276    7-24-87    12:00a
COMP        COM    4183     7-24-87    12:00a
COUNTRY     SYS    11254    7-24-87    12:00a
DISKCOMP    COM    5848     7-24-87    12:00a
DISKCOPY    COM    6264     7-24-87    12:00a
DISPLAY     SYS    11259    7-24-87    12:00a
DRIVER      SYS    1165     7-24-87    12:00a
EDLIN       COM    7495     7-24-87   12:00a
EXE2BIN     EXE    3050     7-24-87   12:00a
FASTOPEN    EXE    3888     7-24-87   12:00a
FDISK       COM    48919    7-24-87   12:00a
FIND        EXE    6403     7-24-87   12:00a
FORMAT      COM    11671    7-24-87   12:00a
GRAFTABL    COM    6136     7-24-87   12:00a
```

(CTRL-S pressed here by the user)

Figure 5-7.   *Suspension of output by using* CTRL-S

```
Volume in drive A is MS330PP01
Directory of  A:\

4201            CPI     17089    7-24-87    12:00a
5202            CPI     459      7-24-87    12:00a
ANSI            SYS     1647     7-24-87    12:00a
APPEND          EXE     5794     7-24-87    12:00a
ASSIGN          COM     1530     7-24-87    12:00a
ATTRIB          EXE     10656    7-24-87    12:00a
CHKDSK          COM     9819     7-24-87    12:00a
COMMAND         COM     25276    7-24-87    12:00a
COMP            COM     4183     7-24-87    12:00a
COUNTRY         SYS     11254    7-24-87    12:00a
DISKCOMP        COM     5848     7-24-87    12:00a
DISKCOPY        COM     6264     7-24-87    12:00a
DISPLAY         SYS     11259    7-24-87    12:00a
DRIVER          SYS     1165     7-24-87    12:00a
EDLIN           COM     7495     7-24-87    12:00a
EXE2BIN         EXE     3050     7-24-87    12:00a
FASTOPEN        EXE     3888     7-24-87    12:00a
FDISK           COM     48919    7-24-87    12:00a
FIND            EXE     6403     7-24-87    12:00a
FORMAT          COM     11671    7-24-87    12:00a
GRAFTABL        COM     6136     7-24-87    12:00a
GRAPHICS        COM     13943    7-24-87    12:00a
JOIN            EXE     9612     7-24-87    12:00a
KEYB            COM     9041     7-24-87    12:00a
LABEL           COM     2346     7-24-87    12:00a
MODE            COM     15440    7-24-87    12:00a
MORE            COM     282      7-24-87    12:00a
NLSFUNC         EXE     3029     7-24-87    12:00a
PRINT           COM     8995     7-24-87    12:00a
RECOVER         COM     4268     7-24-87    12:00a
SELECT          COM     4132     7-24-87    12:00a
SORT            EXE     1946     7-24-87    12:00a
SUBST           EXE     10552    7-24-87    12:00a
SYS             COM     4725     7-24-87    12:00a
          34 File(s)     5120 bytes free
```

Figure 5-8.   *Resumption of output by pressing any key*

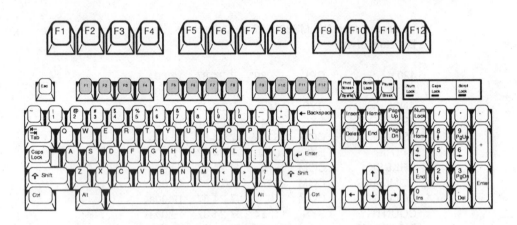

Figure 5-9.   *Location of function keys*

tion keys, shown in Figure 5-9. Several of these keys are helpful in simplifying your keyboard entry. If you issue the DOS DIR command

```
A> DIR
```

DOS will display all of the files in your directory, as was discussed in Chapter 4. To repeat this command, you have several choices. First, you can simply type **DIR**. Second, you can press the F1 function key three times. Third, you can press the F3 function key once. Regardless of which method you select, DOS will display

```
A> DIR
```

DOS has this capability because the previous DOS command is saved in an area called the command buffer. The PC function keys manipulate the text stored in this buffer, which in turn greatly simplifies your keyboard entry.

The F1 function key copies a single character from the command buffer. For example, assume that your previous command was

```
A> DIR
```

Pressing F1 upon completion of the command will result in

```
A> D
```

If you press F1 again, the display will be

```
A> DI
```

Pressing F1 a third time directs DOS to display

```
A> DIR
```

Pressing F1 a fourth time has no effect. You have used up all the characters from the previous command buffer. Press ENTER and allow the DIR command to complete. Now press the F3 function key. DOS will immediately display

```
A> DIR
```

Just as the F1 function key directs DOS to copy a single character from the keyboard buffer, F3 directs DOS to copy the entire command buffer.

You can use these commands in conjunction to simplify your efforts. For example, if you enter the command

```
A> DISSCOPY  A:  B:
```

the following message will be displayed:

```
Bad command or file name

A>
```

Your goal is to change the second "S" in DISSCOPY to a "K," yielding DISKCOPY. To do so, press the F1 key three times. DOS will display

```
A> DIS
```

Next, type **K** so the display is

```
A> DISK
```

To copy the remainder of the previous command buffer, press F3, and the command is correct.

```
A> DISKCOPY
```

F1 and F3 are the function keys that you will use most often. DOS also defines the function keys F2, F4, and F5 for command editing.

The F2 function key directs DOS to copy all of the characters immediately preceding the character that you type after pressing F2. For example, given the command

```
A> DIR  FORMAT.COM

Volume in drive A is MS330PP01
Directory of  A:\

FORMAT          COM   11671    7-24-87    12:00a
                1 File(s)  5120 bytes free
```

if you press F2 and then type **F**, DOS will copy all of the letters up to the letter "F" from the command buffer, yielding

```
A> DIR
```

The F4 function key will copy all of the letters in the command buffer including, and immediately following, the letter that you type after pressing F4. If you make a mistake while you are typing in your command, but you have not yet pressed ENTER, the F5 function key allows you to edit the current command. For example, assume that you have mistyped the DISKCOPY command, as shown here:

```
A> DIKKCOPY  A:  B:
```

Before you press ENTER, press F5. DOS will display

> A> DIKKCOPY A: B:@

You can now press the F1 function key twice, type **S**, and then press the F3 function key. The screen will display this:

> A> DIKKCOPY A: B:@
> DISKCOPY A: B:

Your command is now correct. You can press ENTER to invoke it.

ESC Key

If you have partially entered your command and you decide that you want to cancel it, press the ESC key. Figure 5-10 shows the location of the ESC key.

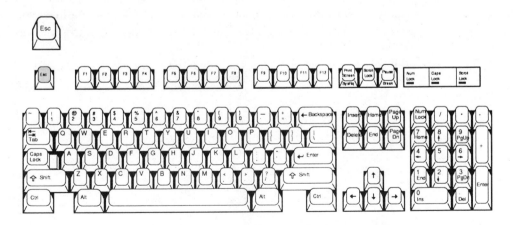

Figure 5-10. *Location of ESC key*

For example, assume that you have typed in

```
A> DISKCOPY A: B:
```

If you then decide you do not want to perform the DISKCOPY operation, you can press either the CTRL-BREAK key combination or the ESC key, which will give the following display:

```
A> DISKCOPY A: B: \
```

After you press ESC, press ENTER, and DOS will ignore the command and repeat the prompt:

```
A> DISKCOPY  A: B: \

A>
```

INS Key

There may be times, as you enter your DOS commands, when you need to insert characters into the command buffer. DOS allows you to do this with the INS key. Its location on the keyboard is shown in Figure 5-11.

For example, assume that you have just entered the command

```
A> DISCOPY
```

which results in the following error message:

```
Bad command or file name

A>
```

You can easily correct this error by first pressing F1 three times so that the command now appears as:

```
A> DIS
```

Next, press the INS key and type **K**.

```
A> DISK
```

Finally, press F3 to copy the text remaining in the command buffer. Your command is now correct.

```
A> DISKCOPY
```

INS directs DOS to insert the new text before the letters that remain in the command buffer. Had you not pressed INS, the result of your efforts would have been

```
A> DISKOPY
```

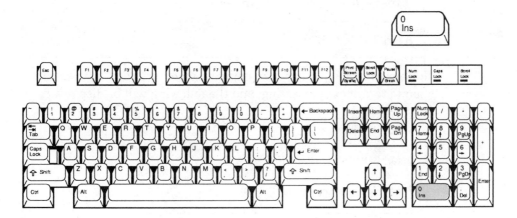

Figure 5-11.   *Location of* INS *key*

Notice that the "K" was typed over the "C" in your original command instead of being inserted in front of it.

Hands-On Practice

At the DOS prompt, issue the DOS DATE command

```
A> DATE
```

Terminate this command by pressing the CTRL-BREAK key combination, and the display will be

```
A> DATE

Current date is Tue  4-05-1988
Enter new date (mm-dd-yy): ^C

A>
```

Invoke DISKCOPY as shown here:

```
A> DISKCOPY  A:  B:
```

Rather than completing this command, use the CTRL-C key combination to terminate processing, and the following will be displayed:

```
A> DISKCOPY  A:  B:

Insert SOURCE diskette in drive A:

Press any key when ready . . .^C
```

As you can see, DOS allows you to terminate your programs with either the CTRL-C or CTRL-BREAK key combination.

```
A> DIR

Volume in drive A is MS330PP01
Directory of  A:\

4201        CPI   17089   7-24-87   12:00a
5202        CPI   459     7-24-87   12:00a
ANSI        SYS   1647    7-24-87   12:00a
APPEND      EXE   5794    7-24-87   12:00a
ASSIGN      COM   1530    7-24-87   12:00a
ATTRIB      EXE   10656   7-24-87   12:00a
CHKDSK      COM   9819    7-24-87   12:00a
COMMAND     COM   25276   7-24-87   12:00a
COMP        COM   4183    7-24-87   12:00a
COUNTRY     SYS   11254   7-24-87   12:00a
DISKCOMP    COM   5848    7-24-87   12:00a
DISKCOPY    COM   6264    7-24-87   12:00a
DISPLAY     SYS   11259   7-24-87   12:00a
DRIVER      SYS   1165    7-24-87   12:00a
EDLIN       COM   7495    7-24-87  12:00a
EXE2BIN     EXE   3050    7-24-87  12:00a
FASTOPEN    EXE   3888    7-24-87  12:00a
FDISK       COM   48919   7-24-87  12:00a
FIND        EXE   6403    7-24-87  12:00a
FORMAT      COM   11671   7-24-87  12:00a
GRAFTABL    COM   6136    7-24-87  12:00a
```

(CTRL-S pressed here by the user)

Figure 5-12.   *Suspension of output by using CTRL-S*

```
Volume in drive A is MS330PP01
Directory of  A:\

4201        CPI    17089    7-24-87    12:00a
5202        CPI    459      7-24-87    12:00a
ANSI        SYS    1647     7-24-87    12:00a
APPEND      EXE    5794     7-24-87    12:00a
ASSIGN      COM    1530     7-24-87    12:00a
ATTRIB      EXE    10656    7-24-87    12:00a
CHKDSK      COM    9819     7-24-87    12:00a
COMMAND     COM    25276    7-24-87    12:00a
COMP        COM    4183     7-24-87    12:00a
COUNTRY     SYS    11254    7-24-87    12:00a
DISKCOMP    COM    5848     7-24-87    12:00a
DISKCOPY    COM    6264     7-24-87    12:00a
DISPLAY     SYS    11259    7-24-87    12:00a
DRIVER      SYS    1165     7-24-87    12:00a
EDLIN       COM    7495     7-24-87    12:00a
EXE2BIN     EXE    3050     7-24-87    12:00a
FASTOPEN    EXE    3888     7-24-87    12:00a
FDISK       COM    48919    7-24-87    12:00a
FIND        EXE    6403     7-24-87    12:00a
FORMAT      COM    11671    7-24-87    12:00a
GRAFTABL    COM    6136     7-24-87    12:00a
GRAPHICS    COM    13943    7-24-87    12:00a
JOIN        EXE    9612     7-24-87    12:00a
KEYB        COM    9041     7-24-87    12:00a
LABEL       COM    2346     7-24-87    12:00a
MODE        COM    15440    7-24-87    12:00a
MORE        COM    282      7-24-87    12:00a
NLSFUNC     EXE    3029     7-24-87    12:00a
PRINT       COM    8995     7-24-87    12:00a
RECOVER     COM    4268     7-24-87    12:00a
SELECT      COM    4132     7-24-87    12:00a
SORT        EXE    1946     7-24-87    12:00a
SUBST       EXE    10552    7-24-87    12:00a
SYS         COM    4725     7-24-87    12:00a
          34 File(s)    5120 bytes free
```

Figure 5-13.   *Resumption of output by pressing any key*

Issue the DOS DIR command. Before you press ENTER to actually invoke the command, be ready to suspend output by pressing the CTRL-S key combination. The output will appear as in Figure 5-12. To resume output, press any key and output will appear, as you can see in Figure 5-13.

Once the DIR command is completed, press F1 three times and the DIR command will be entered again.

```
A> DIR
```

Press ENTER to invoke the DIR command. When this command is completed, press F3. DOS will immediately display

```
A> DIR
```

As you can see, the function keys F1 and F3 can greatly simplify your command entry. The impact of these keys will become much more important in later chapters when you examine complex commands such as this:

```
A> XCOPY C:\*.*  /S
```

Continually rekeying such complex commands can become tedious.

Enter the following command with an error, which results in an error message:

```
A> DISCOPY
Bad command or file name

A>
```

Press F2 and then immediately type **C**. DOS will display

```
A> DIS
```

Next, press INS and type **K**. Your screen should now contain the following display.

A> DISK

Finally, press F3, yielding the corrected command:

A> DISKCOPY

Because you do not want to execute this command, press ESC and then ENTER. DOS will display

A> DISKCOPY \

A>

Next, type **DARTE**, but do not press ENTER.

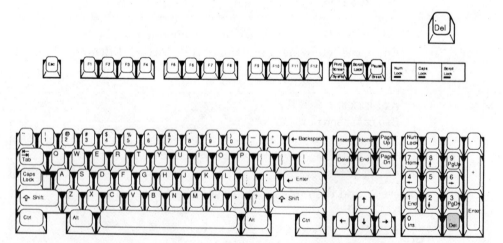

Figure 5-14.   *Location of the* DEL *key*

Key	Function
F1	Copies one character from the previous command buffer to the current command buffer
F2	Copies all of the characters that precede the next character that you type from the previous command buffer to the current command buffer
F3	Copies all of the characters from the previous command buffer to the current command buffer
F4	Copies all of the characters (including and following the next character that you type) from the previous command buffer to the current command buffer
F5	Allows you to edit the current command buffer
INS	Allows you to insert characters in the current command line
DEL	Allows you to delete the character that precedes the cursor from the current command line
ESC	Cancels the current command line without executing it
CTRL-ALT-DEL	Restarts DOS
CTRL-BREAK or CTRL-C	Terminates the current program
CTRL-S	Temporarily suspends program output

Table 5-1. *DOS Editing Keys*

```
A> DARTE
```

Press F5, which allows you to edit your current command, and the screen will display

```
A> DARTE@
```

Now press F1 twice to display

```
A> DARTE@
DA
```

Use DEL to delete the letter "R." The location of DEL is shown in Figure 5-14. Now press F3 to display

```
A> DARTE@
DATE
```

Your command is now ready for you to press ENTER.

As you can see, knowledge of your keyboard can save you time and effort. DOS provides you with tremendous command editing capabilities. Table 5-1 outlines the function of each key discussed in this chapter. Experiment with each one. You will use each of them throughout this book. This was your first step in becoming a sophisticated DOS user.

Summary

DOS stores each command that you enter in an area called the command buffer.

Using the PC keyboard knowledgeably allows you to edit the previous command in order to simplify your command entry.

Glossary

DOS stores your previous command in an area called the *command buffer*.

Your keyboard has several keys labeled F1 through F10. These keys comprise your keyboard's *function keys*, which can be used to edit the previous command and thus simplify your command entry. Many third-party software packages rely on the function keys for user input.

6 *Preparing Your New Disks for Use by DOS*

Thus far, the only disks that you have used have been your original DOS disks and the working copies of DOS that you made in Chapter 3. These disks have been more than sufficient so far, but eventually you will need to use additional disks to store your files and programs. Before you can use a disk, you must prepare the disk specifically for use by DOS.

Each time you purchase floppy disks, the original disk manufacturer has no way of knowing if you are buying the disks for use on an IBM PC under DOS, for an Apple, or even for a Commodore computer. Since each of these systems store data differently on disk, the disk manufacturer does not prepare the disks for use on a specific system. Instead, you must do this yourself by using the DOS FORMAT command.

A First Look at FORMAT

Place your write-protected DOS Program disk in drive A. At the DOS prompt, enter the following command:

```
A> FORMAT  A:
```

DOS will respond with

```
A> FORMAT  A:
Insert new diskette for drive A:
and strike ENTER when ready
```

Remove your floppy disk and place a brand new floppy disk in drive A. Press ENTER to continue. DOS will display the following as it begins preparing your disk for use:

```
A> FORMAT  A:
Insert new diskette for drive A:
and strike ENTER when ready

Head:  0 Cylinder:   0
```

In later chapters you will learn how DOS actually stores information on your disk. At that time, many of the messages displayed by FORMAT will make more sense. For now, however, it is enough to understand that DOS is preparing both sides of your disk (sides 0 and 1) for use by DOS. The cylinders that FORMAT is referring to are similar to the grooves in a record album, as you can see in Figure 6-1. DOS uses these cylinders to record information on disk.

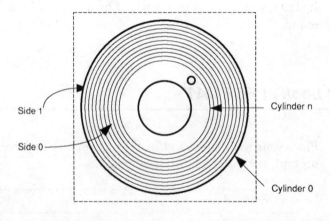

Figure 6-1.   *Tracks that make up a disk*

Depending on what version of DOS you have, FORMAT may at this stage display this prompt:

> Enter desired volume label (11 characters, RETURN for none)?

FORMAT is asking you to enter a name for your disk. DOS disk names, or volume labels, can contain up to 11 characters and should clearly define what is contained in the disk. You can use the characters that are valid for DOS file names within your disk name. Here are some examples of disk names you might use

PAYROLL	TAXES	ORDERS	CHAPTER_1
MISC	OLD-FILES	PHONE_#S	DOS3.3

If you do not want to assign a name to your disk (although naming your disks is a good practice), press ENTER.

When you have entered your volume label or have simply pressed ENTER, FORMAT continues by displaying

```
A> FORMAT A:
Insert new diskette for drive A:
and strike ENTER when ready

Head:  0 Cylinder:   0

Format complete

            362496 bytes total disk space
            362496 bytes available on disk

Format another (Y/N)?
```

If you want to prepare several disks, type **Y**. If you only want to format one disk, type **N**, and FORMAT will terminate.

Your new disk is now ready for use under DOS. If your system displays the following message instead of the DOS prompt,

```
Insert disk with \COMMAND.COM in drive A
and strike any key when ready
```

place your DOS Program disk in drive A and press ENTER. DOS will then display its command prompt.

What If FORMAT Encounters Errors?

Although floppy disk technology has improved tremendously over the past few years, periodically a floppy disk may contain damaged locations in the recording media that are unsuited for storing information. One of FORMAT's primary tasks in preparing your disk for use by DOS is to locate these areas and mark them as unusable. When FORMAT discovers bad locations on a disk, it will display something like the following:

```
362496 bytes total disk space
5120 bytes in bad sectors
357376 bytes available on disk
```

In this case, the disk contains damaged space that consumed 5120 bytes. Most disks today do not experience errors when they are formatted. If several of your disks have errors, strongly consider a different disk brand.

Two-Floppy Drive System

If your computer has two floppy disk drives, A and B, place your DOS Program disk in drive A and a new, unused disk in drive B. Issue the command

```
A> FORMAT B:
```

DOS will respond with

```
A> FORMAT B:
Insert new diskette for drive B:
and strike ENTER when ready
```

Press ENTER to begin preparing the new floppy disk for use by DOS, and the following display will appear

```
A> FORMAT B:
Insert new diskette for drive B:
and strike ENTER when ready

Head:  0 Cylinder:   0
```

FORMAT may prompt you to enter a disk name. If so, type in a valid name, and FORMAT will continue by displaying

```
A> FORMAT B:
Insert new diskette for drive B:
and strike ENTER when ready

Head:  0 Cylinder:   0

Format complete

          362496 bytes total disk space
          362496 bytes available on disk

Format another (Y/N)?
```

In this case, type **N** to terminate the program.

What's on the New Disk?

Now that you have successfully formatted a new disk, let's find out what DOS has put on it. Place your newly formatted disk in drive A. Issue the DOS DIR command, and you will see the following:

```
A> DIR

Volume in drive A has no label
Directory of  A:\

File not found
```

As you can see, FORMAT does not place any files on your disk. It prepares the disk for use under DOS, and DOS is then free to store files on the disk.

Building a Bootable Disk

Leave your newly formatted disk in drive A. Use the CTRL-ALT-DEL key combination to restart DOS. Your screen display should clear, and the disk drive activation light for drive A should illuminate. Rather than booting DOS, however, your system will display

```
Non-System disk or disk error
Replace and strike any key when ready
```

This message tells you that the disk in drive A does not contain the files that DOS requires to start. This makes sense because no files are on the disk. To start DOS, replace your DOS Program disk in drive A and press any key to continue.

There may be times, however, when you want to create a disk that is bootable under DOS. FORMAT allows you to do this by placing the /S qualifier in your FORMAT command, as shown here:

```
A> FORMAT  A:  /S
```

or

```
A> FORMAT  B:  /S
```

Both of these commands direct FORMAT not only to prepare a disk for use by DOS, but also to place onto the disk the files that DOS requires to start.

After copying the system files to the target disk, the format process would continue as it did when the files were not copied. The entire process would be displayed as follows:

```
A> FORMAT  B:
Insert new diskette for drive B:
and strike ENTER when ready

Head:  0 Cylinder:   0

System transferred

Format complete

                362496 bytes total disk space
                78848 bytes used by system
                283648 bytes available on disk

Format another (Y/N)?
```

Note the amount of disk space that is consumed by the DOS files in order to make the disk bootable. This explains why you probably do not want to make all of your disks bootable. In so doing, you consume

Bootable DOS Disk

In order for your disk to be bootable by DOS, you must use the /S qualifier or the DOS FORMAT command:

A> FORMAT A: /S

FORMAT will in turn place all of the files on the target disk that DOS requires to boot.

almost 1/6 of the disk's storage capabilities.

If you were to place this disk in drive A and issue the DOS DIR command, DOS would display

```
A> DIR

Volume in drive A has no label
Directory of  A:\

COMMAND      COM     25276    7-24-87  12:00a
             1 File(s)  283648 bytes free
```

As you can see, FORMAT places the COMMAND.COM file on the disk.

What Is COMMAND.COM?

The COMMAND.COM file contains many of your DOS commands (such as CLS, DATE, and TIME). Each time your system boots, DOS loads these commands into memory. Because these commands are always stored inside your computer's memory, they are called internal commands. No matter what disks you are using, you can always execute these internal commands from the DOS prompt. The commands DISKCOPY and FORMAT, however, are too large for DOS to always keep in memory. DOS stores these external commands on disk and only places them into memory when the command is invoked, as shown in Figure 6-2.

To better illustrate this concept, make sure that a newly formatted disk (one not formatted with system files) is in drive A, and issue the DOS DIR command:

```
A> DIR

Volume in drive A has no label
Directory of  A:\

File not found
```

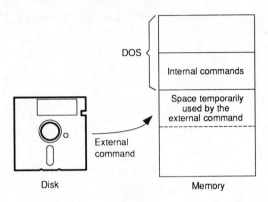

Figure 6-2.   *The running of programs within DOS*

DIR is an internal DOS command present in memory. This explains why you do not see a file called DIR.COM.

Next, issue the DOS DISKCOPY command.

```
A> DISKCOPY
Bad command or file name

A>
```

DOS Commands

DOS has two types of commands: internal and external. DOS internal commands, such as DATE, TIME, DIR, and CLS, always reside in your system's memory and you can execute them regardless of the disks that you have in your drives. External commands, such as FORMAT and DISKCOPY, reside on disk. When you invoke an external command, DOS must be able to locate the file on disk.

The DISKCOPY.COM file, which contains the disk copy program, is not on this disk. Therefore, DOS cannot find it to execute the command.

1.2MB Drives

If your computer is an IBM PC AT or AT compatible, you probably have a disk drive called a 1.2MB drive. This drive uses a different floppy disk (called a quad-density disk) that is capable of storing almost four times as much information as a standard 5 1/4-inch floppy disk. If you are using quad-density disks, the output of the FORMAT command will be

```
A> FORMAT  A:
Insert new diskette for drive A:
and strike ENTER when ready

Head:   0 Cylinder:   0

                1213952 bytes total disk space
                1213952 bytes available on disk

Format another (Y/N)?
```

There may be times when you want to exchange files with a user who only has a 360K standard floppy disk. If the 1.2MB disk drive is your only drive, you need a method of formatting standard 360K floppy disks in this drive. FORMAT provides a method: using the /4 qualifier, as shown here:

```
A> FORMAT  A:  /4
```

The only time you will issue FORMAT in this way is when you are using a 360K (double-sided, double-density) disk in a quad-density (1.2MB) disk drive.

Those who have 360K floppy disk drives will never need to use this qualifier.

Warning!

Be careful when you invoke the DOS FORMAT command. FORMAT will overwrite the contents of any disk, whether it is a new or a used disk. If you format a disk that you are using to store programs or information, that data is lost. You cannot recover the information stored on a floppy disk once you have formatted it. Therefore, treat the FORMAT command with care.

What About DISKCOPY?

You may be wondering why, if you must format all new disks, you did not have to when you used DISKCOPY. As it turns out, DISKCOPY examines your target disk. If that disk is brand new, DISKCOPY automatically formats the disk prior to the copy. That is why, when you use a new disk as your target disk, DISKCOPY displays this:

```
Formatting while copying
```

In all cases new disks must be formatted before they can be used by DOS.

Hands-On Practice

Place your DOS Program disk in drive A. If your system has only one floppy disk drive, issue the command

```
A> FORMAT A:
```

If your computer has two floppy disk drives, issue the command

```
A> FORMAT B:
```

In either case DOS will prompt you to place a new disk into either drive A or B and to then press ENTER. FORMAT will prepare your floppy disk for use by DOS. Next, FORMAT may prompt you to enter a disk name:

```
Enter desired volume label (11 characters, RETURN for none)?
```

Type in **MISC**, for miscellaneous, and press ENTER, and the following will be displayed:

```
Enter desired volume label (11 characters, RETURN for none)? MISC
```

FORMAT will then display the following.

```
                362496 bytes total disk space
                362496 bytes available on disk

Format another (Y/N)?
```

Type **N** to terminate the program.

Place your newly formatted disk in drive A. Issue the DOS DIR command:

```
A> DIR

Volume in drive A has no label
Directory of  A:\

File not found
```

Remember that, by default, FORMAT does not place any files on your disk. DOS can execute the DIR command because DIR is an internal DOS command that resides in memory.

Leave your new disk in drive A and issue the FORMAT command:

```
A> FORMAT  A:
Bad command or file name

A>
```

This command fails because FORMAT is an external command that resides on disk. Because this disk contains no files, DOS cannot find the FORMAT.COM file required to execute the command.

Use the CTRL-ALT-DEL key combination to restart DOS. Since your newly formatted disk is not bootable (you did not use /S), your system will display

```
Non-System disk or disk error
Replace and strike any key when ready
```

Place your DOS Program disk in drive A and press ENTER. DOS will boot and display its prompt. Issue the following command and note the display:

```
A> DIR  FORMAT.COM

Volume in drive A is MS330PP01
Directory of  A:\

FORMAT          COM     11671  7-24-87   12:00a
                1 File(s)  4096 bytes free
```

As you can see, this disk contains the external FORMAT command.

Next, use the /S qualifier to build a bootable disk. Issue one of the following commands. Which one you use depends on your system configuration.

```
A> FORMAT /S
A> FORMAT B: /S
```

When the FORMAT command is completed, place the newly formatted disk into drive A and issue the DOS DIR command.

```
A> DIR

Volume in drive A has no label
Directory of  A:\

COMMAND       COM     25276 7-24-87    12:00a
              1 File(s)  283648 bytes free
```

Remember, the COMMAND.COM file contains your internal DOS commands. As you can see, this disk contains only enough information to get DOS started. You may be asking, "Where did all of the disk space go?" In addition to the COMMAND.COM file, FORMAT places two hidden files on your disk that actually perform the DOS start-up procedure. Although they do not appear in your directory listing, they are hidden on disk to prevent you from accidentally deleting them. You will examine these files in later chapters.

Use the CTRL-ALT-DEL key combination to restart DOS. Once your system boots, replace your newly formatted disk in drive A with your DOS Program disk.

Summary

You must prepare all of your new disks for use under DOS by using the DOS FORMAT command.

Each of your disks can have a unique 11-character volume label, or name. During the disk format process, FORMAT will prompt you to enter a disk name. A good practice is to assign unique names to your disks.

One of FORMAT's primary purposes is to locate damaged locations on your disks and to mark them as unusable by DOS. Each time FORMAT completes, it will display a summary of the amount of unusable space on your disk.

FORMAT prepares a disk for use by DOS; it does not place any files on the disk.

If you need to create a disk that is bootable under DOS, you must use the FORMAT /S qualifier. By so doing, you direct FORMAT to place files on the disk that DOS requires to start.

The COMMAND.COM file contains your DOS internal commands, such as CLS, DIR, DATE, and TIME. Each time DOS starts, it reads these commands from disk into memory. Therefore, you can always execute these commands, regardless of the disks in your drives, because these commands are already present in memory.

An external DOS command, on the other hand, resides on disk instead of in memory. Commands such as DISKCOPY and FORMAT are too large to reside in memory all of the time. DOS loads these external commands into memory from disk when you invoke them from the DOS prompt.

FORMAT will overwrite the contents of your target disk, whether that disk is new or used; therefore, take care when you issue the FORMAT command.

Glossary

A *cylinder* on your disk is conceptually similar to the grooves in a record album. DOS uses cylinders to record the information on your disks. In later chapters you will see that the number of cylinders is dependent upon your disk type.

A *volume label* is a name for a DOS disk. DOS allows you to assign a unique 11-character name to your disks. The characters valid for DOS file names are also valid for volume labels.

A *quad-density* disk is a 1.2MB disk capable of storing four times as much information as a standard 5 1/4-inch disk. If you are using an IBM PC AT or AT compatible, you probably have a 1.2MB disk drive on your system.

DOS has two command types. DOS *internal commands*, such as DATE, DIR, and CLS, are always stored in memory. You can always execute internal commands regardless of the disks that you have in your drives. *External commands,* however, such as FORMAT and DISKCOPY, reside on disk. When you invoke them, DOS must be able to locate the file containing the command on disk.

7 *Manipulating DOS Files*

In Chapter 4 you found that DOS stores your programs and information on disk in a storage facility called a file. You also learned that all of the files in your DOS directory have a unique two-part name: an eight-character file name and an optional three-character extension. DOS separates the file name from the extension with a period, as shown here:

filename.ext

You also examined the DOS wildcard characters * and ? and found that they allow you to perform commands that affect a group of files.

In this chapter you will use your knowledge of DOS file names and wildcard characters to copy, rename, and delete DOS files. The commands that you will learn in this chapter are ones you will use on a daily basis.

Making Copies of Your DOS Files

Put the copy of the bootable disk that you made in Chapter 6 in drive A and issue the DOS DIR command.

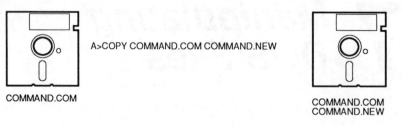

A>COPY COMMAND.COM COMMAND.NEW

COMMAND.COM

COMMAND.COM
COMMAND.NEW

Figure 7-1.   *Copying COMMAND.COM to COMMAND.NEW*

```
A> DIR

Volume in drive A has no label
Directory of  A:\

COMMAND        COM     25276     7-24-87   12:00a
               1 File(s)  283648 bytes free
```

At this point the COMMAND.COM file is the only file on this disk. Use the DOS COPY command to duplicate its contents, as shown here:

```
A> COPY  COMMAND.COM  COMMAND.NEW
              1 File(s) copied

A>
```

This command directs DOS to copy the contents of the COM-MAND.COM file, placing its contents into the COMMAND.NEW file. Figure 7-1 illustrates this process.

Now you issue the DOS DIR command.

```
A> DIR
```

DOS will display

```
A> DIR

Volume in drive A has no label
Directory of  A:\

COMMAND      COM     25276     7-24-87    12:00a
COMMAND      NEW     25276     7-24-87    12:00a
             2 File(s)  258048 bytes free

A>
```

You can see that the size of both files is the same. The COPY command directs DOS to make an identical copy of each file. You can now use the COMMAND.NEW file to create a third file, as shown here:

```
A> COPY  COMMAND.NEW  TESTFILE.COM
```

A directory command of your files now displays

```
A> DIR

Volume in drive A has no label
Directory of  A:\

COMMAND      COM     25276     7-24-87    12:00a
COMMAND      NEW     25276     7-24-87    12:00a
TESTFILE     COM     25276     7-24-87    12:00a
             3 File(s)  232448 bytes free
```

The following DOS command illustrates that the DOS COPY command fully supports wildcard characters:

```
A> COPY  *.COM  *.EXE
```

This command directs COPY to copy all of the files that have the extension COM. The new copies have identical file names, but the extension is EXE. When this copy process is complete, issue the DIR command to view the list of files.

```
A> DIR
Volume in drive A has no label
Directory of  A:\

COMMAND       COM      25276    7-24-87   12:00a
COMMAND       NEW      25276    7-24-87   12:00a
TESTFILE      COM      25276    7-24-87   12:00a
COMMAND       EXE      25276    7-24-87   12:00a
TESTFILE      EXE      25276    7-24-87   12:00a
               5 File(s)   181248 bytes free
```

If you omit a file extension on your target file, as in the command

```
A> COPY  TESTFILE.EXE  NEWFILE
```

DOS will create the target file without an extension, as shown here:

```
A> DIR

Volume in drive A has no label
Directory of  A:\

COMMAND       COM      25276    7-24-87   12:00a
COMMAND       NEW      25276    7-24-87   12:00a
TESTFILE      COM      25276    7-24-87   12:00a
COMMAND       EXE      25276    7-24-87   12:00a
TESTFILE      EXE      25276    7-24-87   12:00a
NEWFILE                25276    7-24-87   12:00a
               6 File(s)   155648 bytes free
```

Later chapters will examine the COPY command in more detail.

Renaming Your DOS Files

Just as the DOS COPY command allows you to duplicate your files, the DOS RENAME command allows you to change a file name. The format of the DOS RENAME command is

    RENAME   current_name.ext   newname.ext

or

    REN   current_name.ext   newname.ext

You can enter the entire command name, RENAME, or its abbreviation, REN. For example, given the directory

```
A> DIR

Volume in drive A has no label
Directory of  A:\

COMMAND      COM     25276     7-24-87    12:00a
COMMAND      NEW     25276     7-24-87    12:00a
TESTFILE     COM     25276     7-24-87    12:00a
COMMAND      EXE     25276     7-24-87    12:00a
TESTFILE     EXE     25276     7-24-87    12:00a
NEWFILE              25276     7-24-87    12:00a
             6 File(s)  155648 bytes free
```

you can rename the COMMAND.NEW file as NEWFILE.DAT:

```
A> REN  COMMAND.NEW  NEWFILE.DAT
```

Invoking the DIR command will show that your directory listing now contains the following files:

```
A> DIR

Volume in drive A has no label
Directory of  A:\

COMMAND     COM     25276    7-24-87    12:00a
NEWFILE     DAT     25276    7-24-87    12:00a
TESTFILE    COM     25276    7-24-87    12:00a
COMMAND     EXE     25276    7-24-87    12:00a
TESTFILE    EXE     25276    7-24-87    12:00a
NEWFILE             25276    7-24-87    12:00a
          6 File(s)   155648 bytes free
```

RENAME also supports the DOS wildcard characters. For example, with this command you can rename all of the files with the extension EXE to files with the extension COM.

```
A> RENAME *.EXE *.COM
```

Later chapters will examine RENAME's capabilities again. This chapter gives you the foundation of the command's function.

> **Warning**: During normal operation, do not rename files with a COM or EXE file extension. If you do, DOS will not be able to find the files and will not be able to execute the programs included in the files.

Deleting Your Files When They Are No Longer Needed

Just as you can throw away the files in your office when they are no longer needed, DOS allows you to delete your files from disk. Using the DOS DEL command, you can delete one or more files from your directory when they are no longer required. For example, given the directory listing

```
A> DIR

Volume in drive A has no label
Directory of  A:\

COMMAND       COM       25276       7-24-87    12:00a
NEWFILE       DAT       25276       7-24-87    12:00a
TESTFILE      COM       25276       7-24-87    12:00a
COMMAND       EXE       25276       7-24-87    12:00a
TESTFILE      EXE       25276       7-24-87    12:00a
NEWFILE                 25276       7-24-87    12:00a
              6 File(s)  155648 bytes free
```

you can delete the NEWFILE.DAT file by using this command:

```
A> DEL  NEWFILE.DAT
```

A directory listing of your disk now displays

```
A> DIR

Volume in drive A has no label
Directory of  A:\

COMMAND       COM       25276       7-24-87    12:00a
TESTFILE      COM       25276       7-24-87    12:00a
COMMAND       EXE       25276       7-24-87    12:00a
TESTFILE      EXE       25276       7-24-87    12:00a
NEWFILE                 25276       7-24-87    12:00a
              5 File(s)  181248 bytes free
```

Once you delete a file, you cannot get it back. The information the file contained is lost; therefore, be careful when you issue the DOS DEL command. An errant DEL command can have devastating results on your files.

The DOS DEL command also supports the DOS wildcard characters. This command deletes all of the files with the extension EXE:

```
A> DEL *.EXE
```

The directory now contains

```
A> DIR

Volume in drive A has no label
Directory of  A:\

COMMAND     COM     25276     7-24-87     12:00a
TESTFILE    COM     25276     7-24-87     12:00a
NEWFILE             25276     7-24-87     12:00a
            3 File(s)  232448 bytes free
```

This command directs DEL to delete all files in your directory:

```
A> DEL *.*
```

Because this command can have devastating results if you invoke it in error, DOS will first prompt you with

```
A> DEL *.*
Are you sure (Y/N)?
```

before proceeding. If you really want to delete all of the files in your directory, type **Y** and then press ENTER. If you do not want to delete all of your files, type **N** and press ENTER.

What About Write-Protected Disks?

In Chapter 3 you learned that by placing a write-protect tab over your disk's write-protect notch, you can protect your disk from errant commands. In particular, write protecting your disks keeps DISKCOPY and FORMAT from overwriting their contents and DEL from erasing files contained on the disk. For example, if you attempt to format a disk that is write-protected, FORMAT will display

```
Attempted write-protect violation
Format failure
```

If you attempt to delete a file contained on a write-protected disk, DOS will display

```
Write protect error writing drive A
```

If you try to rename a file contained on a write-protected disk or copy a file to the disk, DOS will also display

```
Write protect error writing drive A
```

Therefore, you should not write protect disks whose contents you anticipate changing. However, you should always write protect your original program disks, such as the DOS Program disk.

Hands-On Practice

If you have your bootable disk that you created in Chapter 6, put it in drive A. If you do not have this disk, format a bootable disk with this command:

```
A> FORMAT  A:  /S
```

Issue the DOS DIR command to view the directory:

```
A> DIR

Volume in drive A has no label
```

```
Directory of  A:\

COMMAND        COM      25276      7-24-87     12:00a
               1 File(s)   283648 bytes free
```

COMMAND.COM is the first DOS file that you will copy, using this command:

```
A> COPY  COMMAND.COM  TESTFILE.COM
               1 File(s) copied

A>
```

Issue the DOS DIR command again. DOS has duplicated the file as desired. Next, issue this COPY command, followed by a DIR command:

```
A> COPY  TESTFILE.COM  NEWFILE.DAT
               1 File(s) copied.

A> DIR
Volume in drive A has no label
Directory of  A:\

COMMAND        COM      25276      7-24-87     12:00a
TESTFILE       COM      25276      7-24-87     12:00a
NEWFILE        DAT      25276      7-24-87     12:00a
               3 File(s)   232448 bytes free

A>
```

COPY fully supports the DOS wildcard characters. This command, for example, copies all of your files with the extension COM to matching file names with the extension EXE:

```
A> COPY  *.COM  *.EXE
```

When you then issue the DOS DIR command, DOS will display

```
A> DIR

Volume in drive A has no label
Directory of  A:\

COMMAND      COM      25276      7-24-87    12:00a
TESTFILE     COM      25276      7-24-87    12:00a
NEWFILE      DAT      25276      7-24-87    12:00a
COMMAND      EXE      25276      7-24-87    12:00a
TESTFILE     EXE      25276      7-24-87    12:00a
              5 File(s)  181248 bytes free
```

As you can see, by using the DOS COPY command you can duplicate one or more files.

Next, use the DOS RENAME command to change the names of your existing DOS files. For example, to change the extension on the TESTFILE.COM file, use the command

```
A> REN  TESTFILE.COM  TESTFILE.DAT
```

You could have also used the DOS wildcard * character to achieve the same result:

```
A> REN  TESTFILE.COM  *.DAT
```

Using DOS wildcard characters in the command, rename all your files that have the extension COM to files with the extension SAV.

```
A> REN  *.COM  *.SAV
```

A DOS directory listing displays

```
A> DIR

Volume in drive A has no label
Directory of  A:\

COMMAND      SAV      25276      7-24-87    12:00a
TESTFILE     DAT      25276      7-24-87    12:00a
```

```
NEWFILE      DAT      25276     7-24-87   12:00a
COMMAND      EXE      25276     7-24-87   12:00a
TESTFILE     EXE      25276     7-24-87   12:00a
             5 File(s)   181248 bytes free
```

Using the DOS DEL command, you can remove existing files from your directory. For example, when you issue the command

```
A> DEL  TESTFILE.EXE
```

a directory listing displays

```
A> DIR

Volume in drive A has no label
Directory of  A:\

COMMAND      SAV   25276    7-24-87   12:00a
TESTFILE     DAT   25276    7-24-87   12:00a
NEWFILE      DAT   25276    7-24-87   12:00a
COMMAND      EXE   25276    7-24-87   12:00a
             4 File(s)   206848 bytes free
```

The DOS DEL command fully supports DOS wildcard characters. Issue the command

```
A> DEL  *.*
```

which will delete all files from your directory. As a precaution, DOS displays the prompt

```
Are you sure (Y/N)?
```

Type **N** and press ENTER to cancel the command and retain the files in your directory.

Use DEL to erase from your disk all of the files with the extension EXE by issuing the following command.

```
A> DEL *.EXE
```

Your directory listing now contains these files:

```
A> DIR

Volume in drive A has no label
Directory of  A:\

COMMAND       SAV    25276    7-24-87   12:00a
TESTFILE      DAT    25276    7-24-87   12:00a
NEWFILE       DAT    25276    7-24-87   12:00a
              3 File(s)  232448 bytes free
```

DEL is an essential DOS command that you will use on a daily basis. You must take care when using this DOS command, however, because a DEL command issued in error will cause irreparable harm to your directories.

Summary

DOS allows you to copy the contents of your files, rename them, and later delete them when they are no longer needed.

Using the DOS COPY command, you can duplicate your files. COPY fully supports the DOS wildcard characters.

The DOS RENAME command allows you to rename existing DOS files. You can issue RENAME by typing in the complete command name or simply the abbreviation REN. RENAME fully supports the DOS wildcard characters.

You can erase your files from disk when they are no longer needed by using the DOS DEL command. Once you delete a file, the information that it contains is lost; therefore, take care when you issue the DOS DEL command. DEL fully supports the DOS wildcard characters.

8 *Getting Around On Your Disk Drive*

All of the commands that you have entered thus far have been either internal DOS commands (commands that DOS always keeps present in memory) or external commands that reside on the disk in drive A (such as DISKCOPY or FORMAT). In this chapter you will learn how to execute programs contained on disks other than drive A, how to select a different drive as your current drive, and how to manipulate files (using COPY, RENAME, or DEL) that are contained on different disks. This chapter assumes that your system has two floppy disk drives. Later chapters discuss systems with one floppy disk drive and a fixed disk.

Changing Your Default Drive

DOS defines your *current* or *default* disk drive as the drive that it searches by default when you issue an external command. For example, if at the DOS prompt you enter the command

```
A> TEST
Bad command or file name

A>
```

drive A's disk activation light will illuminate briefly as DOS looks for the command on that disk. DOS searches drive A because it is the

---

Default Disk Drive

DOS defines your current or default drive as the disk drive that it will search by default each time you enter an external command. You can recognize your default drive in the DOS prompt.

---

default disk drive. The DOS prompt tells you which drive is your default.

```
A>
↑
```
Default disk drive
is A

If your system has a second floppy disk drive, drive B, you can select that drive as your default drive by typing in the drive identification letter followed immediately by a colon (:), as shown here:

```
A> B:
```

DOS will acknowledge your change in default disk drives by modifying your system prompt.

```
A> B:
B>
```

Place a formatted disk in drive B and issue the command

```
B> TEST
Bad command or file name
```

You will now see drive B's disk activation light illuminate for a moment as DOS searches for the command. Drive B is now your default disk drive.

Listing Files on Another Disk

Leave the formatted disk in drive B and place your DOS Program disk in drive A. Your default drive should still be drive B, as indicated by the following prompt:

```
B>
```

If drive B is not your default disk drive, select drive B, as shown here:

```
A> B:
B>
```

With drive B as the default drive, list the files contained on drive A by issuing the command

```
B> DIR  A:
```

You are already familar with the DOS DIR command. The only thing that you are doing differently here is specifying the disk drive from which you want to list the files. In this case, the disk that you want is contained in drive A. If you are interested in a specific file, specify the file name immediately following the disk drive specifier, as shown here:

```
B> DIR  A:FORMAT.COM

Volume in drive B has no label
Directory of  B:\

FORMAT          COM     11671     7-24-87   12:00a
                1 File(s)  309248 bytes free
```

No matter what the default drive is, DOS fully supports its wildcard characters, as you can see when you issue the following command.

```
B> DIR A:*.SYS

Volume in drive A is MS330PP01
Directory of  A:\

ANSI        SYS      1647     7-24-87   12:00a
COUNTRY     SYS     11254     7-24-87   12:00a
DISPLAY     SYS     11259     7-24-87   12:00a
DRIVER      SYS      1165     7-24-87   12:00a
            4 File(s)  5120 bytes free

B>
```

Abort, Retry, Fail?

Now that you are expanding your use of multiple disk drives, there is a greater likelihood that you may commit the error of not closing the disk drive latch on the drive specified in the command. If this should occur, DOS will display an error message. For example, if you open the drive latch for drive A and then issue the command

Accessing Files on Other Disk Drives

DOS allows you to change your current or default disk drive by typing in the letter identification of the disk drive desired, followed immediately by a colon.

A>B:
B>

Commands such as DIR can be used to access files contained on a disk other than the current default by placing the disk drive letter in the command, as shown here:

A> DIR B:
A> DIR B: FORMAT.COM

```
B> DIR  A:
```

DOS will display this error message rather than the desired directory listing:

```
Not ready error reading drive A
Abort, Retry, Fail?
```

DOS is telling you that it cannot continue without your intervention. You need to press either A, R, or F, as defined here:

Keypress   **Effect**

A   Directs DOS to abort the command that was responsible for the error. If you select this option, DOS will terminate the command and redisplay its prompt.

R   Directs DOS to retry the command that caused the error. In most cases you will select this option after you have intervened to correct the problem that was causing the error (in this case, you would close the disk drive latch).

F   Directs DOS to ignore the error and attempt to continue processing. In some cases DOS will have an error when it reads a portion of a disk. You may (if you are lucky) be able to tell DOS to ignore the error allowing you to save other files on the disk.

In most cases you will simply close the disk drive latch and press R, directing DOS to retry the operation that caused the error.

Abort, Retry, Fail?

This error message is most common when you have either failed to put a disk in the disk drive specified or have failed to close the drive's latch. If this should occur, simply correct the problem and press R, directing DOS to retry the command that failed.

Executing a Command
Stored on Another Disk

As previously stated, all of the commands that you have entered thus far have been either internal commands or commands that reside on the default drive. This will not always be the case, however.

With your DOS Program disk in drive A and your formatted disk in drive B, select drive B as your default drive.

```
A> B:
B>
```

Next, type in the command

```
B> DISKCOPY
Bad command or file name

B>
```

This command fails because the DISKCOPY.COM file resides on the disk in drive A, not on your default disk in drive B. You must tell DOS where to look for external commands by specifying a disk drive identifier before the command name, as shown here:

```
B> A:DISKCOPY
```

Note that there are no spaces between the disk drive specifier and the command name. Assuming that your DOS Program disk is contained in drive A, DOS will respond with

```
B> A:DISKCOPY

Insert SOURCE diskette in drive A:

Press any key when ready . . .
```

> ### *Executing Commands Contained on a Disk Other Than the Default*
>
> By default, DOS always looks for external commands on the default drive. You can direct DOS to execute commands contained on disks other than the default by simply preceding the command name with the disk drive letter of the drive that contains the command, as shown here:
>
> B> A:FORMAT A:

Cancel this command by pressing CTRL-BREAK and, as another example, invoke the DOS FORMAT command that also resides on the disk in drive A.

```
B> A:FORMAT A:
Insert new diskette for drive A:
and strike ENTER when ready
```

Terminate the command by pressing CTRL-BREAK.

Issuing external commands that reside on other disks is that easy. You may be wondering why you issue the command

```
B> DIR A:
```

as opposed to

```
B> A:DIR
Bad command or file name

B>
```

Remember that DIR is an *internal* DOS command that resides in memory. You only specify disk drive identifiers before *external* commands that reside on a disk other than the default disk.

Moving Files
Among Your Disks

In this section you will learn how to copy, rename, and delete files that reside on a disk other than the default disk drive. Most seasoned DOS users know how to perform each of these processes; however, many of these users fail to save keystrokes by taking advantage of some simple rules that you will examine here. This is your next step to becoming a sophisticated DOS user!

In an earlier chapter you learned how to copy a file, placing the duplicate file on the same disk with a different name. In this section, you will learn how to copy files between disks.

Place a disk in drive B that is newly formatted and that contains either no files or only the COMMAND.COM file in its directory, as shown here:

```
B> DIR  B:

Volume in drive B has no label
Directory of  B:\

File not found

B>
```

Place your DOS Program disk in drive A and issue the command

```
B> COPY  A:FORMAT.COM  FORMAT.COM
          1 File(s) copied

B>
```

This command directs DOS to copy the file contents of the FOR-MAT.COM file from the disk in drive A to a file with the same name on the disk in drive B. This process is illustrated in Figure 8-1.

In a similar manner, the following command directs DOS to copy the DISKCOPY.COM file from drive A to drive B.

```
B> COPY A:DISKCOPY.COM DISKCOPY.COM
        1 File(s) copied

B>
```

If your current disk drive were drive A as opposed to drive B, you would copy the DISKCOPY.COM file to drive B, as shown here:

```
A> COPY DISKCOPY.COM B:DISKCOPY.COM
        1 File(s) copied

A>
```

and the FORMAT.COM file could be copied this way:

```
A> COPY FORMAT.COM B:FORMAT.COM
        1 File(s) copied

A>
```

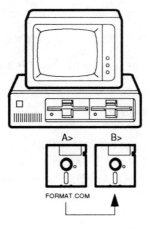

Figure 8-1. *Copying FORMAT.COM from drive A to drive B*

As you can see, the function of the COPY command has not changed. Now, however, you can include a disk drive identifier on either the source or target file name.

Using DOS Wildcard Characters

You can simplify the COPY commands you use to copy files between disks by using the DOS wildcard characters, just as you did when you copied files on the same disk. For example, if you issue the command

```
A> COPY DISKCOPY.COM B:*.*
```

DOS will copy the DISKCOPY.COM file from drive A to drive B, using the source file name (DISKCOPY.COM) for the file created on drive B. The command

```
A> COPY DISKCOPY.COM B:DISKCOPY.COM
```

is functionally the same, but using the DOS wildcard characters makes the input simpler, and the chance of error is reduced. This command, for example, copies all of the files contained on drive A to drive B.

```
A> COPY *.* B:*.*
```

DOS will display the names of each file as it copies it to drive B.

Another Shortcut

DOS provides one more shortcut that you can use when you copy files from one disk to another. If you do not specify a target file name when you transfer files from one disk to another, DOS uses the source file name by default. For example, consider the command

```
A> COPY DISKCOPY.COM B:
```

Because no file name is specified for the target file, COPY will, by default, use DISKCOPY.COM.

In a similar manner, this command copies the FORMAT.COM file to drive B.

```
A> COPY  FORMAT.COM  B:
```

If drive B were your default disk drive, you would issue this command, which is identical in function.

```
B> COPY  A:DISKCOPY.COM
```

As you can see, when you copy files across disk drives, you do not need to specify a file name for the target file. If you do not specify a file name, DOS will use the source file name.

Hands-On Practice

This section assumes that your system has two floppy disk drives. If your system has only one floppy disk drive, closely examine these commands to ensure that you understand how they work; you will use similar commands in later chapters that discuss fixed disks.

Place your DOS Program disk in drive A and a newly formatted disk in drive B. Type the command

```
A> TEST
```

and DOS will display

```
Bad command or file name

A>
```

Note that drive A's disk drive activation light illuminates briefly while DOS searches for the TEST command. DOS searched drive A for the command because drive A is your default drive.

Change your default drive to drive B.

```
A> B:
```

Note that DOS responds to your drive change command by modifying its prompt.

```
A> B:
B>
```

Issue the command

```
B> TEST
```

and again DOS will display

```
Bad command or file name

B>
```

DOS will unsuccessfully search your default disk drive for the TEST command. In this case, however, drive B is your default drive.

Next, open the disk drive latch for drive A. Issue the command

```
B> DIR  A:
```

Rather than displaying a directory listing of your files on drive A, DOS instead displays the error message

```
Not ready error reading drive A
Abort, Retry, Fail?
```

If you press A, DOS will abort the command and redisplay your system prompt. If you press R, DOS will retry the command that generated the error in the first place. If you press F, DOS will ignore the error and attempt to continue where it left off. In this case, close the disk drive latch for drive A and press R. DOS will retry the DIR command as originally desired.

Use the COPY command to move the FORMAT.COM file from the disk in drive A to the disk in drive B. Make sure that drive B is your default drive, and then issue the command

```
B> COPY  A:FORMAT.COM  B:FORMAT.COM
          1 File(s) copied
```

A directory listing of drive B now displays

```
B> DIR

Volume in drive B has no label
Directory of  B:\

FORMAT          COM      11671     7-24-87    12:00a
              1 File(s)  350208 bytes free

B>
```

To accomplish this interdisk copying procedure, there are two other commands you can use. (DOS will simply overwrite the previous file's contents.) Issue this command, which uses the * wildcard character.

```
B> COPY  A:FORMAT.COM  *.*
          1 File(s) copied
```

Copy FORMAT.COM again, this time by entering the command

```
B> COPY  A:FORMAT.COM
          1 File(s) copied
```

All three of these commands accomplish the same task—they each copy the FORMAT.COM file to drive B. (How many of you retyped all of the characters in those COPY commands as you issued them?

Remember, DOS buffers your previous command so that you can use your keyboard function keys to simplify your command entry.)

Change your default drive to drive A.

```
B> A:
A>
```

Copy the COMMAND.COM file to drive B. Each of the following commands perform that task:

```
A> COPY  COMMAND.COM  B:COMMAND.COM

A> COPY  COMMAND.COM  B:*.*

A> COPY  COMMAND.COM  B:
```

With drive A as your default disk drive, invoke commands that reside on drive B. First, issue the DOS FORMAT command.

```
A> B:FORMAT  A:
```

This command directs DOS to execute the FORMAT command that resides on the disk in drive B. The characters "A:" specify the disk drive containing the disk to format. For this example, when FORMAT prompts

```
Insert new diskette for drive A:
and strike ENTER when ready
```

terminate the command by pressing CTRL-C. Now invoke the DISK-COPY command that also resides on drive B.

```
A> B:DISKCOPY  A:  B:
```

Again, use CTRL-C to terminate the command.

The ability to access files that reside on disk drives other than the default disk drive is an important capability. Therefore, this chapter lays the foundation for many of the concepts that you will learn in later lessons.

Summary

DOS defines your default drive as the disk drive that it searches by default each time you enter an external DOS command. Your system prompt will tell you which drive is your current default, as shown here:

```
A>
↑
Default
disk drive
is A
```

DOS allows you to manipulate (using DIR, COPY, RENAME, or DEL) files that are contained on a disk other than the default disk by simply preceding the file name with the disk drive identification letter (for the drive containing the desired file) and a colon.

When DOS displays the message

```
Not ready error reading drive A
Abort, Retry, Fail?
```

it is telling you that it cannot continue without your intervention. If you press ͟ADOS will abort the command and redisplay your system prompt. If you press R, DOS will retry the command that generated the error in the first place. If you press F, DOS will ignore the error and attempt to continue where it left off.

To execute commands that are contained on a disk other than the current default, precede the command name with the letter identification of the disk that the command resides on, as shown here:

```
A> B:FORMAT  A:
```

Summary (continued)

To copy files from one disk drive to another, there are three ways to issue the command. First, you can specify complete DOS file names for the source and target files:

A> COPY COMMAND.COM B:COMMAND.COM

Second, you can use DOS wildcard characters:

A> COPY COMMAND.COM B:*.*

Third, you can omit the target file name.

A> COPY COMMAND.COM B:

If you either use the DOS wildcard characters or omit the file name, DOS will use the source file name for the target file name. In the examples just given, the source and target file names would both be COMMAND.COM.

Glossary

The *current* or *default* disk drive is the disk drive DOS searches (by default) when you issue an external command.

9 Creating and Displaying Your Files

By the end of this chapter you will have seen almost all of the DOS file manipulation commands that you will use on a daily basis. You will learn to create your own simple files and how to display their contents by using the DOS TYPE command. In addition, you will see that DOS does not allow you to display the contents of all of your files. Files that contain DOS commands or programs also contain unprintable characters that prevent display of the files. The files that you can display are normally called text files because they contain only standard characters.

Using the CON Keyboard Device

In this text you will examine names that DOS assigns to various devices. One such device name is CON, which DOS uses to reference either your keyboard or screen display. In so doing, DOS allows you to use CON to create your own files.

Consider the command

```
A> COPY COMMAND.COM B:*.*
```

which directs DOS to copy the COMMAND.COM file to drive B. The COMMAND.COM file is the source of the information that you want to copy. The destination of the information is a file named COM-

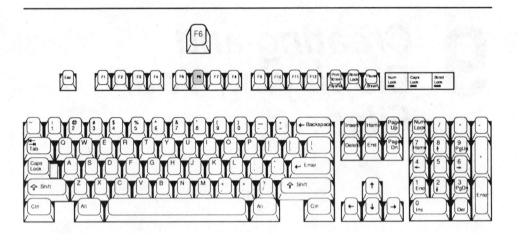

Figure 9-1.   *Location of F6 key*

MAND.COM on drive B. With this in mind, and knowing that DOS assigns the name CON to your keyboard device, you can see how the following command will create a file called TEST.DAT that contains the information that you type in from the keyboard:

```
A> COPY CON TEST.DAT
```

When you press ENTER to issue this command, nothing appears to happen. DOS is waiting for you to type in data from your keyboard. The data that you type in will become the contents of the TEST.DAT file. Below the command, type in the following:

```
This is line one.
Line two is here.
This is the last line.
```

You do not want to enter any more information after the third line. To inform DOS of this, press the F6 function key, located on the keyboard as shown in Figure 9-1. DOS will then display

```
A> COPY CON TEST.DAT
This is line one.
Line two is here.
This is the last line.
^Z
```

The character ^Z, called "control Z," signifies the end of your text files. DOS predefines the F6 function key as this character. Now press ENTER again, and DOS displays

```
A> COPY CON TEST.DAT
This is line one.
Line two is here.
This is the last line.
^Z
                1 File(s) copied

A>
```

DOS has successfully copied the information that you typed in from the keyboard into the TEST.DAT file. Your disk directory now displays your newly created file.

```
A> DIR

Volume in drive A has no label
Directory of  A:\

TEST          DAT     128    4-17-88   7:11p
              1 File(s)  361472 bytes free
```

CON

DOS allows you to copy information from your keyboard into a file by using the CON device, as shown here:

A> COPY CON FILENAME.EXT

Once you have entered all of the data desired, press F6 to notify DOS that you are done.

Using the CON device again, you can create a file called TWO.DAT, which contains several lines of two's, as seen in the following example display:

```
A> COPY  CON  TWO.DAT
2222
22
222
22222
^Z
                    1 File(s) copied

A>
```

Your directory listing now shows

```
A> DIR

Volume in drive A has no label
Directory of  A:\

TEST          DAT    128    4-17-88  7:11p
TWO           DAT    128    4-17-88  7:13p
              2 File(s)  360448 bytes free

A>
```

Using TYPE to Display
Your File's Contents

The files you created using the CON device now exist on disk, but you need a way to display their contents. The DOS TYPE command allows you to do just that.

Leave the disk that contains the TEST.DAT and TWO.DAT files in drive A, and issue the following DOS TYPE command to display the contents of the TEST.DAT file.

```
A> TYPE  TEST.DAT
This is line one.
Line two is here.
This is the last line.

A>
```

The DOS TYPE command is an internal command that directs DOS to display the contents of the file specified. As another example, use TYPE to display the contents of the TWO.DAT file.

```
A> TYPE  TWO.DAT
2222
22
222
22222

A>
```

In Chapter 8 you learned how to manipulate files that reside on disks other than the current default. Similarly, by placing a disk drive letter and a colon in front of a file name in the TYPE command, you can direct TYPE to display the contents of a file on any disk drive. This format of the TYPE command will display the contents of a file in disk drive B when the default drive is drive A.

```
A> TYPE  B:FILENAME.EXT
```

The DOS TYPE command does *not* support the DOS wildcard characters; therefore, if you enter the command

```
A> TYPE  *.*
```

the command will fail, and you will see this error message.

```
A> TYPE  *.*
Invalid filename or file not found

A>
```

What About Nontext Files?

TYPE only displays the contents of DOS text files. Files that contain DOS commands or programs are *not* text files. These files contain unprintable characters that prevent their display. For example, if you enter the command

```
A> TYPE COMMAND.COM
```

with your DOS Program disk in drive A, your screen will fill up with strange characters, your computer's bell will beep, and the TYPE command will fail.

Hands-On Practice

Place a newly formatted disk in drive A and issue the following DIR command:

```
A> DIR

Volume in drive A has no label
Directory of  A:\

File not found

A>
```

Enter the following command, directing DOS to copy the information that you type into a file called FIRST.DAT:

```
A> COPY CON FIRST.DAT
This is my first file!
It will have four lines.
This is the third line.
This is the last line!
```

When you have typed in the last line, press F6. DOS will display the end-of-file character on your screen, as shown here:

```
A> COPY  CON  FIRST.DAT
This is my first file!
It will have four lines.
This is the third line.
This is the last line!
^Z
```

Press ENTER, and DOS will create your file.

```
A> COPY  CON  FIRST.DAT
This is my first file!
It will have four lines.
This is the third line.
This is the last line!
^Z
                 1 File(s) copied

A>
```

Issue the DOS DIR command to verify that your newly created file exists:

```
A> DIR

Volume in drive A has no label
Directory of  A:\

FIRST          DAT     128    4-17-88   7:18p
               1 File(s)  361472 bytes free

A>
```

Repeat this process to create the NUMBERS.DAT file.

```
A> COPY  CON  NUMBERS.DAT
1
22
```

```
333
4444
55555
666666
7777777
88888888
999999999
^Z
                    1 File(s) copied

A>
```

Your directory of files should now contain

```
A> DIR

Volume in drive A has no label
Directory of  A:\

FIRST          DAT      128    4-17-88   7:18p
NUMBERS        DAT      128    4-17-88   7:19p
               2 File(s)  360448 bytes free

A>
```

With these new files on your disk, you can now use the DOS TYPE command to display their contents. Since you have multiple files, try using the DOS wildcard characters to display the contents of these files.

```
A> TYPE *.*
Invalid filename or file not found

A>
```

TYPE does not support the DOS wildcard characters, so you must view the contents of one file at a time, issuing a TYPE command at each prompt.

```
A> TYPE  FIRST.DAT
This is my first file!
It will have four lines.
This is the third line.
This is the last line!

A> TYPE  NUMBERS.DAT
1
22
333
4444
55555
666666
7777777
88888888
999999999

A>
```

Take your disk out of drive A and place it in drive B. Then issue the command

```
A> TYPE  B:NUMBERS.DAT
1
22
333
4444
55555
666666
7777777
88888888
999999999

A>
```

Remember, to manipulate files that are contained on disks other than the current default drive, precede each file name with the disk drive letter desired and a colon. Note that the DOS TYPE command works whether you have a disk in drive A or not, because TYPE is an internal DOS command that always resides in the computer's memory.

Summary

DOS predefines names for several of the devices found on your computer. One such device is CON, which DOS uses to reference your keyboard and screen device. Using CON, you can copy information from your keyboard into a file by entering a command in the following form:

A> COPY CON FILENAME.EXT

The DOS TYPE command allows you to display the contents of text files (files containing standard characters) to your screen device. The format of the command is

A> TYPE FILENAME.EXT

Files containing DOS commands or programs contain non-printable characters that prevent their display. If you attempt to display such a file using the DOS TYPE command

A> TYPE COMMAND.COM

your screen will fill with strange characters and your command will fail.

If your files reside on a disk other than the default, precede the file name with a disk drive letter and colon, as shown here:

A> TYPE B:FILENAME.EXT

The DOS TYPE command does not support DOS wildcard characters. If you attempt such a command, it will fail, and DOS will display

A> TYPE *.*
Invalid filename or file not found.

Glossary

Text files contain only standard keyboard characters.

Nontext files contain commands or programs that include unprintable characters. Therefore, nontext files cannot be created using the CON device, nor can they be displayed.

10 *Taking a Close Look at Your Disks*

By now you should feel fairly comfortable working with your floppy disks. In this chapter you will take a close look at how DOS stores information on your disk, some dos and don'ts for handling your floppy disks, and several DOS commands that inform you about your disks.

What Is a Disk?

You know that disks store programs and data. You have used disks in previous chapters of this book to manipulate files—creating, renaming, copying, displaying, and even deleting their contents. What you need to know is how DOS stores information on your disk.

For starters, take a look at the various parts of a standard 5 1/4-inch floppy disk, shown in Figure 10-1. One component of the disk that you have already used to protect your files from DOS commands is the *write-protect notch.* Another important part of the disk, the *storage media,* is a piece of plastic that has been specially coated so it can magnetically record information. When your disk drive writes information to the disk, it does so by magnetizing the information onto the storage media. Always keep your disks away from magnetic or powerful electronic devices, which can affect the information that is magnetized on your disk.

The *disk jacket* is the dark cardboard cover that surrounds your disk's storage media. When you are not using a disk, this jacket

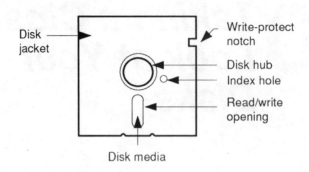

Disk
jacket

Write-protect
notch

Disk hub

Index hole

Read/write
opening

Disk media

Figure 10-1.   *Parts of a floppy disk*

protects the disk from dust, smoke, and fingerprints. When the disk
is in use, the jacket keeps the disk from being crushed as you insert
and remove the disk from the drive.

The *disk hub* is a reinforced portion of the disk that rotates the disk
in the drive. Whenever you insert a disk into the disk drive and close
the disk drive latch, the disk begins spinning at a fast rate. The drive
"grabs" the disk in order to spin it, and this is done at the disk hub.
Examine your floppy disk. The hub should have a reinforced metal
ring. If it does not, you should consider a different brand of disk, because this hub is a critical component that protects your disk.

If you grab the disk hub and carefully rotate your disk, you will
eventually find a small hole in the disk storage media that you can
see through. This hole, called the *index hole*, provides your disk drive
with a starting point for storing information. It is a timing mechanism
that your computer uses the first time a disk is formatted.

Without touching your disk storage media, locate the *read/write
opening*. DOS reads information from and writes information to disk,
directing the disk drive to access the storage media through this opening. If you touch the disk storage media through this opening, you
risk damaging the disk and losing all the information that it contains.

Users who are new to personal computers may want to sacrifice an
unused floppy disk to view the inner construction of the disk, shown

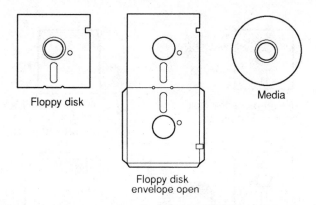

Floppy disk

Floppy disk
envelope open

Media

Figure 10-2.   *Inner construction of floppy disks*

in Figure 10-2. This gives you a chance to see how simple these storage devices really are.

Figure 10-3 illustrates several rules for handling your floppy disks.

Microfloppy Disks

With the advent of IBM's PS/2 line of computers, the use of microfloppy disks has grown tremendously. Figure 10-4 shows you what this type of disk looks like.

To the end user, microfloppy disks function identically to standard 5 1/4-inch floppy disks—both store programs and files. The differences are basically in packaging. Unlike floppy disks, which are flexible, microfloppy disks are made out of a hard plastic that better protects them from accidental damage.

Another difference between standard floppy disks and microfloppy disks is that microfloppy disks do not expose the disk storage media to dust, smoke, and fingerprints. This is a result of the unique construction. If you look at the top of the microfloppy disk, you will

Figure 10-3.   *Rules for handling floppy disks*

Figure 10-4. *Microfloppy disk*

notice a small metal portion called a *shutter*, shown in Figure 10-5. If you slide this shutter to the left, you can see the disk's storage media, as shown in Figure 10-6. If you turn the microfloppy disk over, you will find the *disk spindle* and *sector notch,* shown in Figure 10-7.

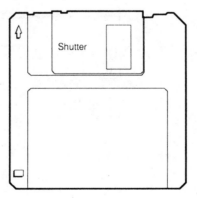

Figure 10-5. *Location of shutter*

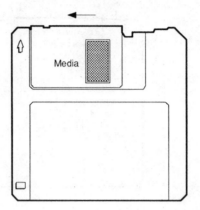

Figure 10-6.   *Disk media*

When you insert a microfloppy disk into the disk drive, it begins spinning, just as the standard floppy disk does. To rotate the microfloppy disk, the drive uses the disk spindle. Unlike a floppy disk that

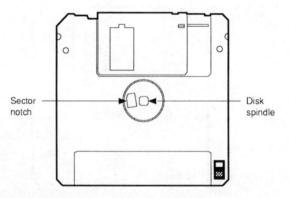

Figure 10-7.   *Sector notch and disk spindle on a microfloppy disk*

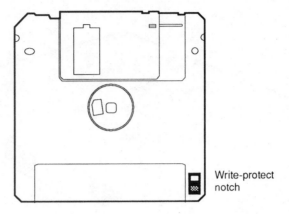

Write-protect
notch

Figure 10-8.   *Write-protect hole on microfloppy disk*

uses an index hole for timing, the microfloppy disk uses a disk sector notch. When you insert a microfloppy, the drive locates this notch and hence knows its orientation for recording information onto the disk.

There is one more difference between the two types of floppy disks worth noting: microfloppy disks do not have a write-protect notch. Instead, they use a *write-protect hole,* shown in Figure 10-8. When the hole is exposed and you can see through your disk, the drive is write-protected. When this hole is closed, DOS can update your disk in any way it requires.

Fixed Disks

Fixed disks are identical to floppy disks in the way they store information. The main differences are speed and storage capacity. Unlike the plastic storage media used by floppy and microfloppy disks, fixed disks use solid metal media. This means that more information can

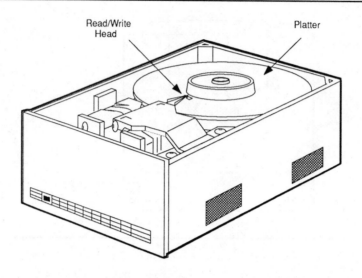

Figure 10-9.   *Fixed disk in sealed casing*

be written to the disk because the recording surface is more precise. Also, the disk access is much faster because the metal disk can rotate almost ten times as fast as the floppy disk.

A fixed disk is a sealed container for several metal platters on which your data is stored, as shown in Figure 10-9. Since the fixed disk has multiple platters for storing data, the amount of information that they can store is much greater than floppy disks.

Disk Storage Capabilities

Earlier in this text you performed directory listings of disks that contained one or two files, as shown here:

```
A> DIR

Volume in drive A has no label
Directory of  A:\

FORMAT        COM    11616    3-18-87   12:00p
CHKDSK        COM    9850     3-18-87   12:00p
               2 File(s)  339968 bytes free

A>
```

The last item DOS always displays in directory listings is the amount of space that is available for storing your files on disk.

```
2 File(s)   339968 bytes free
```

Remember that a byte is equivalent to a character of information; therefore, this disk still has 339,968 bytes of available space.

The amount of storage space on the disk depends on your disk type. Standard 5 1/4-inch disks, for example, provide storage space for 368,640 bytes. Microfloppy disks can store either 737,280 or 1,474,560 bytes, depending on the type of microfloppy disk. Finally, 5 1/4-inch quad-density disks can store 1,228,800 bytes. Table 10-1 compares the various types of floppy disks.

Disk Size	Disk Description	Storage	DOS Versions
5 1/4	360K	368,640 bytes	DOS 2.0 or greater
5 1/4	1.2MB	1,228,800 bytes	DOS 3.0 and greater
3 1/2	720K	737,280 bytes	DOS 3.2
3 1/2	1.44MB	1,474,560 bytes	DOS 3.3

Table 10-1.   *Storage Capacities of Disks*

Disk Type	Number of Files Supported
Single-sided	64
Double-sided	112
Quad-density	224
Hard disk	512

Table 10-2.   *Fixed Disks Versus Floppy Disks*

Fixed disks, on the other hand, can store more than ten times as much information as floppy disks, as shown in Table 10-2.

It is not important that you remember the exact number of bytes that your disks can store. It is important, however, to recognize that there are several types of disks, each capable of storing different amounts of information.

Tracks, Sectors, and Sides

Visualize your disk as containing many circular grooves, similar to a record album. These grooves on the disk are called tracks, as shown in Figure 10-10. DOS uses these tracks to locate and store information on your disk.

Each track contains several different sections, called sectors, which are shown in Figure 10-11. When DOS stores information on your disk, it does so by placing information into each sector.

The term "sides" refers to the number of sides of your disk (one or two) on which DOS stores information. In most cases, DOS uses both sides of your disk.

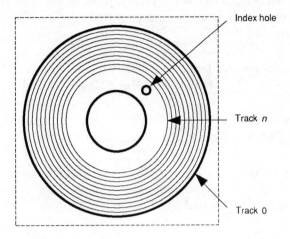

Figure 10-10. *Tracks that make up a disk*

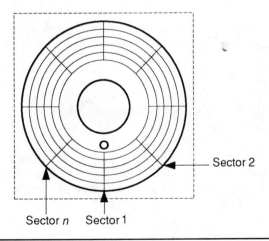

Figure 10-11. *Sectors that make up tracks*

Knowing these three terms—tracks, sectors, and sides—you can determine how much data your disk can store by using the following formula:

storage   = tracks per disk * sectors per track *
             bytes per sector * sides

Using a standard 5 1/4-inch floppy disk, for example, your storage capabilities can be determined like this:

storage   = tracks per disk * sectors per track *
             bytes per sector * sides
           = 40 * 512 * 9 * 2
           = 368,640 bytes

This information is not essential for everyday use of your computer. The computer industry uses these terms on a regular basis, however, so your understanding of them will be an asset.

Giving Your Disk a Name

Place your DOS Program disk in drive A. Issue the DIR command, as shown here:

```
A> DIR

Volume in drive A is MS330PP01
Directory of  A:\

4201          CPI    17089  7-24-87   12:00a
5202          CPI    459    7-24-87   12:00a
ANSI          SYS    1647   7-24-87   12:00a
APPEND        EXE    5794   7-24-87   12:00a
ASSIGN        COM    1530   7-24-87   12:00a
  .             .      .       .
  .             .      .       .
  .             .      .       .
  .
```

```
SYS            COM    4725   7-24-87   12:00a
               34 File(s) 5120 bytes free
```

Each time you issue a DIR command, DOS displays the name, or volume label, of the current disk.

```
Volume in drive A is MS330PP01
Directory of A:\
```

If your disk does not have a name, DOS will display

```
A> DIR

Volume in drive A has no label
Directory of  A:\
```

You may have already seen that the DOS FORMAT command provides you with an opportunity to label your disk.

```
A> FORMAT  A:  /V

Insert new diskette for drive A:
and strike ENTER when ready

Head:  1 Cylinder:   39

Volume label (11 characters, ENTER for none)?

362496 bytes total disk space
362496 bytes available on disk

Format another (Y/N)?
```

In most cases it is a good idea to assign a unique, meaningful name to your disks. As an example of why this is true, assume that you keep track of your monthly bills on your disk in the files shown here:

```
A> DIR

Volume in drive A has no label
Directory of  A:\

JAN          $$$    14   4-20-88   7:47a
FEB          $$$    14   4-20-88   7:47a
MAR          $$$    14   4-20-88   7:47a
APR          $$$    14   4-20-88   7:47a
MAY          $$$    14   4-20-88   7:47a
             5 File(s)   357376 bytes free
```

Each year you get a new disk and begin creating the same files again. After three years you will have accumulated the disks shown in Figure 10-12.

A problem occurs if you accidentally place the disk for the wrong year into your disk drive. Once you have done so, there is no easy way of knowing that the disk is correct if it has no volume label. The following is an example of a disk that is clearly labeled.

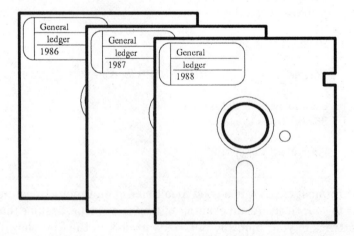

Figure 10-12. *Software company's general ledger system on disk*

```
A> DIR

Volume in drive A is BILLS-1988
Directory of  A:\

JAN            $$$    14    4-20-88   7:47a
FEB            $$$    14    4-20-88   7:47a
MAR            $$$    14    4-20-88   7:47a
APR            $$$    14    4-20-88   7:47a
MAY            $$$    14    4-20-88   7:47a
               5 File(s)  357376 bytes free
```

To help you label your disks, DOS provides the LABEL command.
With your DOS Program disk in drive A, issue the command

```
A> DIR  LABEL.COM

Volume in drive A is MS330PP01
Directory of  A:\

LABEL          COM   2346   7-24-87   12:00a
               1 File(s)  5120 bytes free
```

As you can see, LABEL is an external DOS command.
    With the disk that needs labeling in drive B, issue the command

```
A> LABEL  B:
```

DOS will acknowledge your command, displaying the current volume
label and prompting you to enter the disk volume label, as shown
here:

```
Volume in drive B has no label

Volume label (11 characters, ENTER for none)?
```

Type in **BILLS-1988** and press ENTER. Your display will now look like
this.

```
A> LABEL  B:

Volume in drive B has no label

Volume label (11 characters, ENTER for none)? BILLS-1988

A>
```

A directory listing of that disk now displays

```
A> DIR

Volume in drive A is BILLS-1988
Directory of  A:\

JAN            $$$     14   4-20-88   7:47a
FEB            $$$     14   4-20-88   7:47a
MAR            $$$     14   4-20-88   7:47a
APR            $$$     14   4-20-88   7:47a
MAY            $$$     14   4-20-88   7:47a
             5 File(s)   357376 bytes free
```

You can enter a desired disk name when you enter the command

```
A> LABEL  B:BILLS-1988
```

Next, DOS provides the VOL command, which displays the disk volume label for the drive specified. If your DOS Program disk is in drive A, the command

```
A> VOL
```

will display

```
A> VOL

Volume in drive A is MS330PP01

A>
```

If you enter the command

```
A> VOL B:
```

DOS displays the name of the disk that you just assigned.

```
A> VOL B:

Volume in drive B is BILLS-1988

A>
```

The DOS CHKDSK command allows you to find out if your disk contains any damaged locations or lost files. It is possible, though not very likely, that DOS will commit an error when it writes information to your disk. Depending on the error, you may not be aware of the fact that it has occurred. The DOS CHKDSK command allows you to examine your disk's structure. At the DOS prompt, enter the following command:

```
A> CHKDSK
```

CHKDSK will examine your disk and display the following information:

- Disk volume name (if one exists)
- Total disk space on the disk in bytes
- Disk space consumed by DOS hidden files in bytes
- Disk space consumed by DOS subdirectories in bytes
- Disk space consumed by user files in bytes
- Disk space consumed by damaged sectors in bytes
- Available disk space in bytes
- Total memory present in your computer
- Available memory (unused by DOS) in bytes

Here is an example of a CHKDSK command display:

```
A> CHKDSK

Volume MS330PP01   created Jul 24, 1987 11:28a

362496 bytes total disk space
53248 bytes in 3 hidden files
304128 bytes in 35 user files
5120 bytes available on disk

655360 bytes total memory
586912 bytes free

A>
```

You learned earlier in this text that for a disk to be bootable by DOS, the disk must contain the COMMAND.COM file and several hidden files. If these files are present on your disk, CHKDSK will tell you the amount of disk space these files consume. In the previous example, these numbers were

```
362496 bytes total disk space
53248 bytes in 3 hidden files
```

The next two entries

```
304128 bytes in 35 user files
5120 bytes available on disk
```

indicate the space that your files consume on disk. Later chapters will examine DOS subdirectories in detail. For now, think of subdirectories simply as a means of organizing your files on disk.

Previous chapters discussed how FORMAT prepares your disk for use under DOS. If FORMAT locates damaged locations on your disk, it marks them as unusable to prevent DOS from attempting to store information in them. If such locations exist on your disk, CHKDSK will display

```
nnnn bytes in bad sectors
```

where *nnnn* represents the number of damaged areas on the disk.

CHKDSK also displays the number of bytes available that you can use for your files. In the previous example, the display was

```
5120 bytes available on disk
```

Finally, CHKDSK displays the amount of memory present in your computer, and the amount that is available.

```
655360 bytes total memory
586912 bytes free
```

If, during its processing, CHKDSK displays a message similar to

```
nnn lost clusters found in n chains.
Convert lost chains to files  (Y/N)?
```

CHKDSK has located damaged files on your disk. If this occurs, turn to the CHKDSK command in the command reference section at the back of this text. Although this error message is important, it is fairly uncommon, and its discussion now would be more confusing than helpful.

Hands-On Practice

Place your DOS Program disk in drive A and issue the following command:

```
A> DIR  /P
```

As the following example shows, DOS will not only list the files on your disk, but also the volume label.

```
A> DIR  /P

Volume in drive A is MS330PP01
Directory of  A:\

4201          CPI    17089    7-24-87    12:00a
5202          CPI    459      7-24-87    12:00a
ANSI          SYS    1647     7-24-87    12:00a
APPEND        EXE    5794     7-24-87    12:00a
ASSIGN        COM    1530     7-24-87    12:00a
ATTRIB        EXE    10656    7-24-87    12:00a
```

Use the DOS VOL command to display the disk volume label.

```
A> VOL

Volume in drive A is MS330PP01

A>
```

If your system has two floppy disk drives, place a newly formatted disk in drive B. Issue the command

```
A> LABEL  B:
```

DOS will prompt you to enter a disk drive name, as shown here:

```
A> LABEL  B:

Volume in drive B has no label

Volume label (11 characters, ENTER for none)?
```

A disk volume name can contain up to 11 characters. All of the characters that are valid in DOS file names are valid disk volume names. In this case, type **NEWDISK** and press ENTER.

```
A> LABEL  B:

Volume in drive B has no label

Volume label (11 characters, ENTER for none)? NEWDISK

A>
```

A directory listing of this disk now displays

```
A> DIR  B:

Volume in drive B is NEWDISK
Directory of  B:\
```

To verify this disk label, use the DOS VOL command:

```
A> VOL  B:

Volume in drive B is NEWDISK

A>
```

Again use the DOS LABEL command to label the disk in drive B. In this case, however, specify the desired name on the same line as your command.

```
A> LABEL  B:MISC
```

Invoke the VOL command to verify that DOS has updated your disk as desired.

```
A> VOL  B:

Volume in drive B is MISC

A>
```

If your system has only a single floppy disk drive, you must swap disks. Place your DOS Program disk in drive A and issue the command

```
A> LABEL
```

When DOS displays the prompt

```
Volume in drive A is MS330PP01

Volume label (11 characters, ENTER for none)?
```

exchange your DOS Program disk with the disk that you want to label, as shown in Figure 10-13. Type in the name that you desire and press ENTER. DOS will now display

```
A> LABEL

Volume in drive A is MS330PP01

Volume label (11 characters, ENTER for none)? TESTDISK

A>
```

A directory listing of this disk reveals

```
A> DIR

Volume in drive A has no label
Directory of  A:\TESTDISK
```

If you make an error while naming a disk, or later decide that you do not want the disk named, simply invoke LABEL as before.

```
A> LABEL
```

DOS will display the prompt

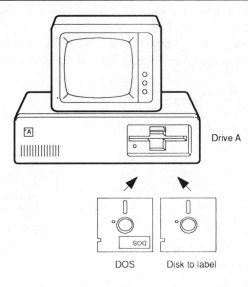

Drive A

DOS   Disk to label

Figure 10-13.   *Swapping disks for single-floppy drive system*

```
A> LABEL

Volume in drive A is MS330PP01

Volume label (11 characters, ENTER for none)?
```

If you want to rename the disk, type in the name that you desire. If you want to delete the disk's name, press ENTER. LABEL will then prompt

```
A> LABEL

Volume in drive A is MS330PP01

Volume label (11 characters, ENTER for none)?

Delete current volume label (Y/N)?
```

Type **Y** to delete the disk name or type **N** to leave the volume label unchanged.

Finally, take a look at the CHKDSK command. Place your DOS Program disk in drive A and issue the command

```
A> DIR  CHKDSK.COM

Volume in drive A is MS330PP01
Directory of  A:\

CHKDSK          COM     9819     7-24-87    12:00a
                1 File(s)  5120 bytes free
```

CHKDSK is an external DOS command that examines your disk structure. Use CHKDSK now to display the structure of your DOS Program disk.

```
A> CHKDSK

Volume MS330PP01   created Jul 24, 1987 11:28a

362496 bytes total disk space
53248 bytes in 3 hidden files
304128 bytes in 34 user files
5120 bytes available on disk

655360 bytes total memory
586912 bytes free

A>
```

Remember that your DOS Program disk is bootable, so it contains hidden system files.

If you have two floppy disk drives, place a newly formatted disk in drive B and issue the command

```
A> CHKDSK  B:
```

DOS will display

```
A> CHKDSK  B:

Volume MISC      created Apr 20, 1988 8:18a

362496 bytes total disk space
362496 bytes available on disk

655360 bytes total memory
586912 bytes free

A>
```

As long as you did not format the disk with the /S qualifier, it will not contain hidden system files.

Summary

Whether you are using standard 5 1/4-inch floppy disks, 3 1/2-inch microfloppy disks, or large fixed disks, DOS stores information on them in the same way.

Floppy disks are made up of several parts: the plastic storage media, which is specially coated to allow it to store magnetized information; the disk jacket, which protects your storage media; the write-protect notch, which allows you to prevent DOS from modifying your disk; the disk hub, which is used by the disk drive to rotate your disk in the drive; and the index hole, which provides your disk drive's starting reference point.

Microfloppy disks are very similar to floppy disks, except that microfloppy disks are made out of a solid plastic material that better protects them, and they do not expose the storage media to the environment. In addition, microfloppy disks use a write-protect hole, which can be easily opened and closed, as opposed to the write-protect notch found on floppy disks.

There are three factors in determining the amount of information that your disk can store—tracks, sectors, and sides:

$$storage = tracks\ per\ disk\ *\ sectors\ per\ track\ *$$
$$bytes\ per\ sector\ *\ sides$$

DOS allows you to assign a unique name, known as a volume label, to each of your disks. To assign a volume label, you use the DOS LABEL command. Likewise, the DOS VOL command allows you to display a disk volume label.

The DOS CHKDSK command provides you with information regarding your disk. When you invoke CHKDSK from the DOS prompt, CHKDSK will examine your disk and display the disk volume name; the total disk space; the disk space used by hidden files, subdirectories, user files, and damaged sectors; the available disk space; the total memory present in your computer; and the available memory.

Summary (continued)

Fixed disk drives are functionally very similar to floppy and microfloppy disk drives. The only real differences are speed and storage capabilities.

Glossary

Visualize your disk as containing many circular grooves similar to a record album. These grooves are called *tracks*. DOS uses these tracks to locate and store information on your disk.

Each track on your disk contains several different sections, called *sectors*. When DOS stores information on your disk, it does so by placing information into each sector.

You can assign a unique name, or *volume label,* to each of your disks. The DOS LABEL command allows you to assign a disk name, while the DOS VOL command will display the volume label. DOS volume labels can contain up to 11 characters. All of the characters valid in DOS file names are also valid in volume labels.

11 *Using Your System Printer*

So far you have examined many aspects of DOS by creating files or viewing information on your computer's screen. In this chapter you will learn how to access your printer from DOS. First, you will learn how to send basic screen copies to your printer. Second, you will learn how to send to your printer every character DOS writes to your screen. Third, you will learn how to print files by using the DOS PRINT command. When you complete this chapter, you will have something to show for your efforts—printed output.

Before You Get Started

If you have not used your printer yet, you may need to learn an additional DOS command—the MODE command—before you get started.

Printers are classified as either parallel or serial, depending on the cables that you use to connect your printer to your computer.

Serial

Parallel

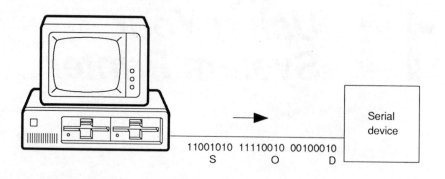

Figure 11-1. *Serial data communication*

A *serial device* uses one wire to transmit data. Each character of information sent to your printer is represented by eight bits, or binary digits, which are sent over this wire one bit at a time. Figure 11-1 shows how a serial printer operates.

A *parallel device,* on the other hand, uses eight wires to transmit data. This means that an entire character can be sent at one time, as shown in Figure 11-2.

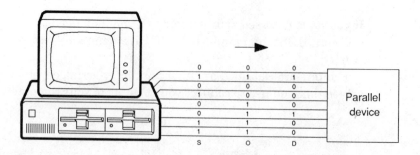

Figure 11-2. *Parallel data communication*

Because a parallel printer sends one complete character at a time, as opposed to a bit at a time, it is much faster than a serial printer. If your printer is a parallel device, you need not perform any other steps before using it.

If your printer is a serial device, however, you must issue the following command while your DOS Program disk is in drive A:

```
A> MODE  LPT1:=COM1:
```

DOS will display

```
A> MODE  LPT1:=COM1:

LPT1:  rerouted  to  COM1:

A>
```

Issue this command only when you are sure that your printer is a serial device. In later chapters you will examine the DOS MODE command in detail. It is used briefly in this chapter only to allow those users with serial printers to perform the exercises.

Printing the Contents of Your Screen Display

With your DOS Program disk in drive A, issue the DIR command

```
A> DIR
```

When the command completes make sure that your printer is on, and press the right or left SHIFT key. Without releasing the SHIFT key, press the PRINT SCREEN key. (The location of these keys on the keyboard is shown in Figure 11-3.) DOS will print your current screen contents, as shown in Figure 11-4.

In most cases, regardless of your screen contents, you can obtain a printed copy of your screen display by pressing the SHIFT- PRINT

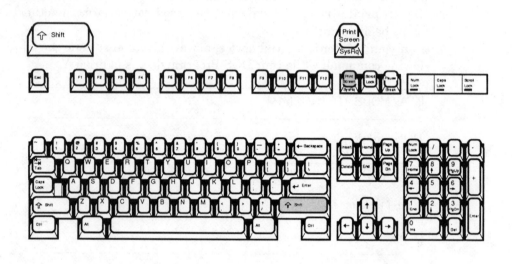

Figure 11-3.   *Location of* SHIFT *and* PRINT SCREEN *keys*

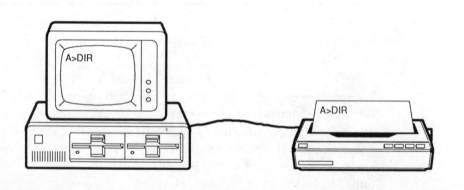

Figure 11-4.   *DOS printing screen contents*

Printing Your Screen Contents

The SHIFT-PRINT SCREEN key combination directs DOS to print the current contents of your screen display.

SCREEN key combination. The only exception is graphics images, as shown in Figure 11-5.

If you plan to copy graphics images to your printer, you must first issue the DOS GRAPHICS command. Issue this command any time your screen contains a graph or other picture image and the key combination SHIFT-PRINT SCREEN does not reproduce the image on your printer.

With your DOS Program disk in drive A, issue the command

```
A> DIR  GRAPHICS.COM

Volume in drive A is MS330PP01
Directory of  A:\

GRAPHICS      COM     13943     7-24-87     12:00a
              1 File(s)  5120 bytes free
```

Figure 11-5.   *Graphics images cannot be printed from screen*

As you can see, GRAPHICS is an external DOS command, and its sole function is to help DOS print graphics images. You only issue the GRAPHICS command once. After that DOS will know how to print graphics images until you restart your system. Once you issue the GRAPHICS command, you will be able to print graphics images by using SHIFT-PRINT SCREEN.

If your graphics image prints too dark, you may want to direct DOS to print the white images that appear on your screen as black, and vice versa. You can do this by invoking GRAPHICS with the /R (reverse image) qualifier, as shown here:

```
A> GRAPHICS  /R
```

The only time that you need to issue the GRAPHICS command is when you are using SHIFT-PRINT SCREEN to print graphics images. If you do not intend to do this, you will never need to issue the DOS GRAPHICS command.

Echoing Your Screen
Text to the Printer

The SHIFT-PRINT SCREEN key combination directs DOS to print the current contents of your screen display. Similarly, the CTRL-PRINT SCREEN key combination directs DOS to send to your printer each character it displays on the screen. To invoke this feature, issue the DOS DIR command, and then simultaneously press the CTRL and PRINT SCREEN keys, located on your keyboard as shown in Figure 11-6. Press ENTER to invoke the DIR command.

As DOS displays each character on your screen, it also sends it to your printer. DOS will continue to echo characters to your printer in this way for an indefinite period of time. The CTRL-PRINT SCREEN combination works like an on-off switch: when you first press it, DOS enables character echoing to your printer; the second time, DOS turns off character echoing.

Echoing Characters to Your Printer

The CTRL-PRINT SCREEN key combination directs DOS to send each character it writes to your screen display also to your system printer. This keyboard combination works as a toggle. The first time you press it, DOS enables character echoing. The second time disables character echoing.

Sending Files to Your Printer

You have just seen two ways to get information to your printer. Neither of these methods, however, is well suited for printing the complete contents of a file. For this reason, DOS provides the powerful PRINT command. The simplest form of the PRINT command is

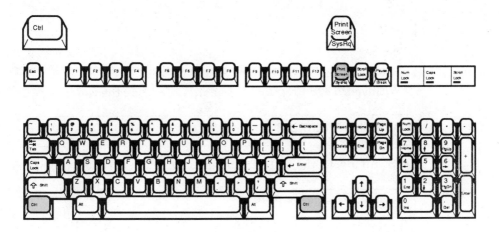

Figure 11-6. *Location of CTRL and PRINT SCREEN keys*

```
A> PRINT  FILENAME.EXT
```

With your DOS Program disk in drive A, issue the following command:

```
A> DIR  PRINT.COM

Volume in drive A is MS330PP01
Directory of  A:\

PRINT          COM     8995      7-24-87   12:00a
               1 File(s)  5120 bytes free
```

As you can see, PRINT is an external DOS command. To experiment with this command, you need to create a file that you can print. Use the CON device, discussed in Chapter 9, to do this.

```
A> COPY  CON  B:TEST.DAT
This is our printer test file.
The DOS PRINT command allows us
to send files to the printer.
^Z
                1 File(s) copied

A>
```

With your DOS Program disk in drive A, issue the command

```
A> PRINT  B:TEST.DAT
```

DOS will invoke the PRINT command, which in turn will prompt

```
Name of printer device [PRN]:
```

PRINT is asking you what device you want to print to. Usually you will want to use PRN, the default device. This is the case in this example, so press ENTER to accept the default device. PRINT will respond with

```
B:\TEST.DAT is currently being printed
```

The file that you just created will begin printing and DOS will redisplay the prompt.

You can repeat this command several times by pressing F3 and then ENTER. PRINT will print multiple copies of your file, displaying

```
B:\TEST.DAT is currently being printed
B:\TEST.DAT is in queue
```

Note the second line of this message. DOS is placing your files into a storage facility called a *queue*. A queue is nothing more than a waiting line. In this case, the queue is composed of files waiting to be printed. Each time you send a file to your printer by using the DOS PRINT command, if a file is currently being printed, PRINT will tell you that it is placing the file into the queue, as shown here:

```
B:\TEST.DAT is currently being printed
B:\TEST.DAT is in queue
B:\FILE.EXT is in queue
B:\TAXS.DAT is in queue
```

If you have several files waiting to be printed, you can issue the DOS PRINT command to see which files are in the queue.

```
A> PRINT

B:\TEST.DAT is currently being printed
B:\TEST.DAT is in queue
B:\FILE.EXT is in queue
B:\TAXS.DAT is in queue

A>
```

Not all files are printable. You cannot display the contents of all files on your screen because they contain unprintable characters, and the same is true for sending files to your printer. For example, if you issue the command

```
A> PRINT  COMMAND.COM
```

your printer will print many unrecognizable characters. Therefore, only send standard text files to your printer.

The DOS PRINT command allows you to send several files to your printer at one time by typing the name of each file in your command line, as shown here:

```
A> PRINT  MARCH.BIL  MAY.BIL  TOTAL.BIL
```

In this case, DOS will display

```
A> PRINT  MARCH.BIL  MAY.BIL  TOTAL.BIL

A:\MARCH.BIL is currently being printed
A:\MAY.BIL is in queue
A:\TOTAL.BIL is in queue

A>
```

Chapter 12 examines the advanced concepts of the DOS PRINT command. Practicing the basic use of this command now would be helpful.

Hands-On Practice

Place your DOS Program disk in drive A and issue the command

```
A> DIR  PRINT.COM
```

The following will be displayed by DOS.

```
A> DIR  PRINT.COM

Volume in drive A is MS330PP01
Directory of  A:\

PRINT           COM     8995      7-24-87   12:00a
                1 File(s)  5120 bytes free
```

Remember, PRINT is an external DOS command. Before you continue, make sure that your printer is turned on. With the directory listing of the PRINT.COM file still on your screen, press SHIFT-PRINT SCREEN to print the current contents of your screen display.

If nothing happens when you press SHIFT-PRINT SCREEN, make sure that your printer is turned on. If it is, you probably have a serial printer and you must issue the following command for printing to begin.

```
A> MODE LPT1:=COM1:
```

If your printer displays unrecognizable characters, you have a *baud rate* problem; that is, your computer and printer are not communicating at the same speed. If this occurs, refer back to your printer reference manual.

Next, type in the following command, but do not press ENTER.

```
A> DIR
```

Press CTRL-PRINT SCREEN, directing DOS to print all the characters that it simultaneously displays on your screen. Press ENTER now to invoke the DIR command, and DOS will send directory listings of your disk to both your screen and your printer. Press CTRL-PRINT SCREEN again to turn off this character echoing.

So that you have several files to print by using the DOS PRINT command, create the following files.

```
A> COPY CON B:PRINTER.DAT
The DOS PRINT command allows you
to send files to your system printer.
PRINT is an external DOS command.
^Z
                1 File(s) copied

A> COPY CON B:NUMBERS.DAT
1
22
333
4444
55555
666666
7777777
88888888
999999999
^Z
                1 File(s) copied

A> COPY CON B:DOS.TXT
DOS is GOOD!
^Z
                1 File(s) copied

A>
```

If you do not have two floppy disk drives on your system, place these files on the disk containing your working copy of DOS. Remember, if you have write protected this disk, you will need to remove the write-protect tab before you can copy files to it.

With your DOS Program disk in drive A, issue the command

```
A> PRINT B:PRINTER.DAT
```

or

```
A> PRINT PRINTER.DAT
```

Which command you use depends on the drive in which you placed the files when you created them. For convenience, the examples in the remainder of this section assume that you are using drive B.

When you press ENTER to invoke the DOS PRINT command, DOS will display

```
A> PRINT  B:PRINTER.DAT
Name of list device [PRN]:
```

Press ENTER to select the default printer device, PRN. The DOS prompt will return to your screen as your file begins printing, at which time you can use PRINT on your remaining files, as follows:

```
A> PRINT  B:NUMBERS.DAT  B:DOS.TXT
```

DOS will display

```
A> PRINT  B:NUMBERS.DAT  B:DOS.TXT

B:\PRINTER.DAT is currently being printed
B:\NUMBERS.DAT is in queue
B:\DOS.TXT is in queue

A>
```

PRINT is telling you that these files are in line for printing.

PRINT fully supports DOS wildcard characters. For example, if you issue the command

```
A> PRINT  B:*.DAT
```

DOS will place the following files into the queue for printing.

```
B:\PRINTER.DAT is currently being printed
B:\NUMBERS.DAT is in queue
B:\PRINTER.DAT is in queue
B:\NUMBERS.DAT is in queue
```

PRINT is a critical command that you will use on a regular basis.
Chapter 12 discusses its advanced capabilities.

Summary

Printers are classified as either serial or parallel, depending on the number of wires they use to receive data from your computer. Serial printers get data one bit at a time from your computer, while parallel printers receive a complete character. Parallel printers are, therefore, much faster than serial printers. If you are using a serial printer, you must issue the following command to use standard DOS printing operations:

```
A> MODE LPT1:=COM1
```

The SHIFT-PRINT SCREEN key combination directs DOS to print the current contents of your screen display. If your screen contains graphics images, however, you will have to issue the DOS GRAPHICS command in order for DOS to print your screen contents.

DOS uses the CTRL-PRINT SCREEN key combination as a toggle. The first time you press CTRL-PRINT SCREEN, DOS will send to your printer each character it displays on your screen. The second time you press CTRL-PRINT SCREEN, DOS stops echoing characters from your screen to your printer.

Using the DOS PRINT command, you can quickly and easily print the contents of text files. PRINT is an external DOS command that places files into a waiting line called a queue so that they can be printed. PRINT fully supports the DOS wildcard characters.

Glossary

A *serial device* sends information across one wire one bit at a time. A *parallel device* uses eight wires to transmit data.

Baud rate is the speed at which the computer and printer communicate with each other.

A *queue* is a waiting line. The DOS PRINT command places your files into a queue when they are printed. When PRINT finishes printing a file, it begins printing the next file in the queue.

12 *Getting the Most from PRINT*

Chapter 11 examined the DOS PRINT command and its basic capabilities. At that time you learned that PRINT uses a storage facility called a queue, which is simply a waiting line for files to be printed. You will see in this lesson that PRINT has several advanced qualifiers that give you complete control over the files in the print queue. These qualifiers also allow you to fine-tune PRINT to improve its performance and to meet your specific needs.

How PRINT Works

You can use the PRINT command to produce hardcopy (printed output) of your files. The first time you enter the DOS PRINT command, DOS performs several steps behind the scenes. Storage must be set aside in memory to hold the names of the queued files, and special software that is responsible for managing your printer output must be loaded to memory. Figure 12-1 illustrates the memory allocation involved with the PRINT command.

You can modify many of the standard attributes that PRINT uses to perform its processing, such as the maximum queue size. Qualifiers to the command, including those examined in this chapter—/D, /B, /Q, /M, /S, and /U—can only be issued the first time that you invoke PRINT.

When DOS displays the message

Resident part of PRINT installed

it is telling you that it has successfully loaded all of the software into memory that is required to manage your printer output, and that it has set aside the storage that PRINT will use for its queue of file names and to transfer data from disk to your printer, as shown here:

```
A> PRINT
Name of list device [PRN]:
Resident part of PRINT installed
PRINT queue is empty

A>
```

Alternative PRINT Devices

The first time that you invoke the PRINT command, PRINT prompts you for the desired printer device name.

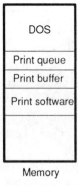

Figure 12-1. *Loading PRINT into memory*

```
A> PRINT
Name of list device [PRN]:
```

In most cases you will select the default device name PRN. In Chapter 11, if you were using a serial printer as opposed to a parallel printer, you had to also issue the command

```
A> MODE  LPT1:=COM1:
```

in order to complete the exercises in that chapter. However, if you do not anticipate using SHIFT-PRINT SCREEN or CTRL-PRINT SCREEN, as discussed in Chapter 11, you can direct PRINT to write to your serial printer by typing the device name **COM1:** at the prompt.

```
A> PRINT
Name of list device [PRN]: COM1:
```

You can also specify the device name the first time that you invoke the PRINT command by using the /D qualifier.

```
A> PRINT  /D:COM1:
```

When you issue this command, PRINT will use the printer connected to the serial port on the back of your computer. Since you have just specified the device, PRINT will not prompt you for one.

The device name COM1 is the name that DOS assigns to the first serial port on the back of your computer. DOS assigns the name LPT1 to the first parallel port on the back of your system.

Remember that if you elect to use the command

```
A> PRINT  /D:COM1:
```

as opposed to

```
A> MODE  LPT1:=COM1:
```

PRINT will write its output to the serial device, but the key combinations SHIFT-PRINT SCREEN and CTRL- PRINT SCREEN will not work.

Increasing Your Print Buffer

When you issue the DOS PRINT command, PRINT reads a portion of your file from disk into memory, prints that part of the file, and then reads some more of the file from disk. Figure 12-2 shows this function of PRINT.

The area of memory into which PRINT reads your file from disk is called the *print buffer*. By default, PRINT sets aside 512 bytes of memory for your print buffer. If you are printing a file that contains more than 512 characters (about half a page), your print buffer will fill quickly. Each time PRINT finishes printing only 512 characters of information from your file, it must read your disk for the next portion of the file. Compared to the electronic speed of your computer's memory, your mechanical disk drive is slow. Therefore, if you in-

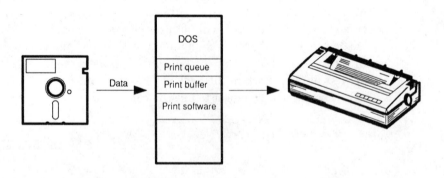

Figure 12-2.   *Use of the buffer by the PRINT command*

crease the number of times DOS must read information from your disk, you also increase the amount of time that command will take to complete.

PRINT offers a solution to this problem. You increase the size of your print buffer by using the /B qualifier. A typical setting for the print buffer size is 4096 bytes (about two pages), which you would indicate in the command as shown here:

```
A> PRINT /B:4096
```

The buffer size that you select must be a multiple of 512 (1024, 1536, 2048, and so on). The maximum buffer size you can specify is 16,386 bytes. If you use the maximum value, however, you may be guilty of overkill. Most of your files probably are not that large, and you would be consuming a significant amount of memory space that may never get used.

Building a Bigger Print Queue

Your printer can only print one file at a time. Thus, if you send multiple files to your printer by using the DOS PRINT command, PRINT must place the files that are not printing into a queue, as you can see in this example:

```
A:\TEST.DAT is currently being printed
A:\MAY.BIL is in queue
A:\INFO.TAX is in queue
```

By default, PRINT sets aside enough space in the queue for ten file names. If you attempt to print more than ten files, PRINT will display this message:

```
PRINT queue is full
```

If you anticipate sending many files to your printer at one time, you must use the /Q qualifier to direct PRINT to set aside more space for a larger Print queue. To create a queue large enough to hold 32 file names, for example, issue the following PRINT command:

```
A> PRINT /Q:32
```

The /Q qualifier is only valid the first time you issue the DOS PRINT command. If you have already invoked PRINT and need to resize your queue, you must restart DOS.

Printing as a Background Task

The DOS PRINT command is unique in that it need not finish everything it is doing before returning control to DOS. For example, if you have a 30-page report to print, you invoke PRINT, as shown here:

```
A> PRINT FILENAME.EXT
```

PRINT will start printing your document and immediately return control to DOS, which in turn redisplays its prompt. You are then free to issue any DOS command while your report prints. Your computer appears to be performing two tasks at once. Actually, DOS is rapidly switching between printing your report and whatever other task you are performing. Because DOS switches between these two tasks so quickly, it appears as if they are happening simultaneously. If, for example, you are printing a large report while issuing the DOS DIR command, DOS will pass control of the computer between PRINT and DIR in a round-robin fashion, as shown in Figure 12-3.

Three PRINT qualifiers relate directly to the amount of time that DOS allows PRINT to control the computer in this round-robin distribution. Keep in mind that these are advanced PRINT qualifiers, and to understand them completely requires a stronger PC and DOS foundation than you can establish in this book. Experiment with the

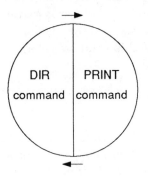

Figure 12-3.   *Exchange of control of the computer*

values suggested here until you are satisfied with the PRINT command's performance.

By using the /M qualifier, you can specify the amount of time PRINT retains control of the computer each time it gets control. The value is specified in terms of CPU clock ticks, which occur every 0.0549 seconds. The default number of clock ticks given to PRINT is 2, and the maximum value that you can specify is 255. If you want your files to print at a faster rate, increase this value to a number such as 64 by invoking the following command:

```
A> PRINT  /M:64
```

If you specify a value larger than 64, your overall system response may become sluggish.

The /S qualifier specifies how many times in one second DOS will switch control between PRINT and a second application. The default value for the /S qualifier is 8, and the maximum value that you can specify is 255. Increasing this value reduces the amount of time that PRINT actually gets to control the computer. Most users, therefore, use the default setting.

The /U qualifier tells PRINT how long, in clock ticks, it can wait to write a character if the printer is currently busy. The default waiting period is 1 clock tick, and the maximum value that you can specify is 255. To increase this value to 8 clock ticks, for example, use the following command:

```
A> PRINT  /U:8
```

In most cases your printer, because it is mechanical, is much slower than your computer. Therefore, you will probably want to set this value between 8 and 16. If you set the value larger than this, your overall system response may suffer.

Admittedly, this has been a quick look at several complex qualifiers. Most users should find that the command

```
A> PRINT  /B:4096  /M:64  /U:16
```

gives them good response from PRINT without adversely affecting their entire system.

Controlling the Files in Your Print Queue

Just as you can place files into a print queue, such as

```
A:\TEST.DAT is currently being printed
A:\MAY.BIL is in queue
A:\INFO.TAX is in queue
A:\DATA.DAT is in queue
A:\JUNE.BIL is in queue
A:\INCOME.TAX is in queue
```

the DOS PRINT command allows you to remove files from the queue that you decide you do not want to print. The /C qualifier directs PRINT to remove the file named before /C on the command line as well as any files named after /C. Here is the format for using the /C qualifier.

```
A> PRINT FILENAME.EXT /C
```

When you remove a file from the print queue, PRINT will display the message

```
File FILENAME.EXT canceled by operator
```

on your printer output instead of printing the file.

If, for example, you have

```
A:\TEST.DAT is currently being printed
A:\MAY.BIL is in queue
A:\INFO.TAX is in queue
A:\INCOME.TAX is in queue
```

on the print queue, you can remove two of the files by using /C, as shown here:

```
A> PRINT MAY.BIL /C INFO.TAX

A:\TEST.DAT is currently being printed
A:\INCOME.TAX is in queue

A>
```

When PRINT finds the /C in its command line, it performs the following processing:

- If a file name precedes the /C in the command line, PRINT removes the specified file from the PRINT queue.

- If one or more file names follow the /C in the command line, PRINT removes from the print queue files specified to the end of the specified command or to the next PRINT qualifier.

This command, for example, deletes the A.DAT, B.DAT, and C.DAT files from the print queue.

```
A> PRINT A.DAT /C B.DAT C.DAT
```

The PRINT command fully supports the DOS wildcard characters, even when you are using the /C qualifier. Consider the following queue, for example:

```
A:\TEST.DAT is currently being printed
A:\MAY.BIL is in queue
A:\INFO.TAX is in queue
A:\INCOME.TAX is in queue
```

Issuing the command

```
A> PRINT *.TAX /C
```

Controlling Files in Your Print Queue

PRINT supports three qualifiers that allow you to control the files in your print queue:

/C removes the files(s) specified from the queue. Example: PRINT *FILE.EXT* /C

/T terminates printing of the current file and removes *all* files from the print queue. Example: PRINT /T

/P allows you to place files into the print queue in the same command in which you are removing files with the /C qualifier. Example: PRINT *FILE.EXT* /C *FILE.NEW* /P will reduce the queue to this:

```
A:\TEST.DAT is currently being printed
A:\MAY.BIL is in queue
```

The /T qualifier directs PRINT to terminate printing of the current file and remove all of the files from the print queue. When you use this qualifier, as shown here,

```
A> PRINT /T
```

PRINT will stop printing the current file, remove all files from the print queue, and write the following message on your printed output:

```
All files canceled by operator
```

You can use the /P qualifier to add files to the PRINT queue in the same command in which you are using /C to remove files. For example, consider the command

```
A> PRINT A.DAT /C A.NEW /P
```

PRINT will remove the A.DAT file from the print queue as directed by the /C qualifier. The /P qualifer directs PRINT to add the A.NEW file to the queue. In a manner similar to /C, the /P qualifier works as follows:

- If a file name precedes the /P in the command line, PRINT adds the specified file to the print queue.

- If one or more file names follow the /P in the command line, PRINT adds to the print queue the files that are specified to the end of the command or that are specified up to the next PRINT qualifier.

Hands-On Practice

Make sure that your printer is turned on, and then restart DOS using the CTRL-ALT-DEL key combination so that you can create a new print queue. When DOS restarts, issue the following command if you are using a parallel printer:

```
A> PRINT /D:LPT1: /Q:32 /M:64 /U:16 /B:4096
```

Issue this command if you are using a serial printer.

```
A> PRINT /D:COM1: /Q:32 /M:64 /U:16 /B:4096
```

Here is what these commands accomplish:

- Define the printer device LPT1 or COM1, to which PRINT will output data
- Direct PRINT to set aside memory for 32 queue entries
- Allow PRINT to retain control of the system for 64 clock ticks once it begins processing
- Direct PRINT to retain control for 16 clock ticks in order to print a character if the printer is currently busy
- Direct PRINT to set aside memory for a print buffer of 4096 bytes (2 pages), which reduces the number of slow disk-read operations PRINT must perform

Note that because these commands specified the printer device desired, PRINT did not display the prompt

```
Name of list device [PRN]:
```

Create the files shown in Figure 12-4 so that you will have several files that you can send to your printer.

```
A> COPY CON B:LETTERS.DAT
AAAA
BBBB
CCCC
DDDD
EEEE
FFFF
GGGG
HHHH
IIII
^Z
              1 File(s) copied

A> COPY CON B:X.DAT
X
XX
XXX
XXXX
XXXXX
XXXXXX
XXXXXXX
XXXXXXXX
XXXXXXXXX
XXXXXXXXXX
^Z
              1 File(s) copied

A> COPY   CON  B:DOS.NTS
The DOS PRINT command has several advanced
qualifiers, namely /C, /T, and /P, that we
will use on a regular basis.
^Z
              1 File(s) copied

A>
```

Figure 12-4.   *Sample file*

The commands used in the remainder of this chapter assume that you have two floppy disk drives. If you do not, create the files and then place their contents on drive A.

Print all three of the files that you just created, using the command

```
A> PRINT  B:LETTERS.DAT  B:X.DAT  B:DOS.NTS

B:\LETTERS.DAT is currently being printed
B:\X.DAT is in queue
B:\DOS.NTS is in queue

A>
```

As soon as the DOS prompt returns, issue the command

```
A> PRINT  /T
```

Your printer should stop printing the current file and display this message on your printed output.

```
All files canceled by operator
```

Use the DOS wildcard characters to print all of the files that have the extension DAT. DOS will display

```
A> PRINT  B:*.DAT

B:\LETTERS.DAT is currently being printed
B:\X.DAT is in queue

A>
```

As soon as the DOS prompt returns to your screen, issue this command to cancel printing of the X.DAT file.

```
A> PRINT  B:X.DAT  /C
```

Now, rather than printing the X.DAT file, PRINT will display this message on your printed output.

```
File B:X.DAT canceled by operator
```

Next, enter the following command:

```
A> PRINT  B:X.DAT
```

Use the F3 function key to repeat this command several times, placing several copies of the X.DAT file into the print queue, which will look like this:

```
A> PRINT  X.DAT

B:\LETTERS.DAT is currently being printed
B:\X.DAT is in queue
B:\X.DAT is in queue
B:\X.DAT is in queue
B:\X.DAT is in queue
B:\X.DAT is in queue

A>
```

Using the /C qualifier, issue the command

```
A> PRINT  B:X.DAT  /C
```

PRINT will remove *every* file matching the name X.DAT from the queue, as shown in the following display:

```
A> PRINT  X.DAT  /C

B:\LETTERS.DAT is currently being printed

A>
```

Finally, just for fun, issue the following command:

```
A> PRINT B:X.DAT B:LETTERS.DAT B:LETTERS.DAT /C
```

What will this command print? First, the command directs PRINT to place the X.DAT and LETTERS.DAT files into the print queue. When PRINT locates the /C, however, it removes from the queue the file whose name precedes the qualifier, which in this case is LETTERS.DAT. As a result, only the X.DAT file is printed.

If you modify the previous command to

```
A> PRINT B:X.DAT B:LETTERS.DAT B:LETTERS.DAT /C B:LETTERS.DAT /P B:DOS.NTS
```

all of the files will print. The processing is similar to the previous command, which only printed the X.DAT file. In this case, however, the /P qualifier directs PRINT to place the LETTERS.DAT and DOS.NTS files into the print queue.

As you can see, PRINT provides you with several powerful qualifiers. You probably will not use most of them on a regular basis, but it is important that you know that they exist.

Summary

The DOS PRINT command provides several advanced qualifiers with which you control your print queue attributes and the files within the print queue.

The first time you issue the DOS PRINT command, DOS performs several steps behind the scenes in order to set aside storage space for your print queue and data transfer buffer. The first time PRINT is invoked, DOS assigns your print queue's attributes; therefore, if you need to modify the default queue attributes, you must do so the first time you invoke PRINT.

The PRINT /D qualifier allows you to specify the desired print device. For example, use the command PRINT /D:LPT1: if you have a parallel printer.

The PRINT /B qualifier allows you to specify the number of bytes that PRINT sets aside for your data transfer buffer. By default, PRINT sets aside a buffer large enough to store about one-half page of text. If your file is larger than this, PRINT will spend considerable time reading information from disk into this buffer area. Most users, therefore, realize better PRINT performance by increasing the buffer size to almost two pages with this command:

/B:4096

By default, PRINT creates a queue large enough to store ten file names. If you anticipate printing more files than this at one time, you must increase the size of your print queue by using the PRINT /Q qualifier. For example, the command PRINT /Q:32 will allow 32 files to be stored in the queue.

PRINT has three qualifiers that control the amount of time PRINT can use your computer to print your files while DOS is performing other commands. These qualifiers are based on CPU clock ticks, and their complete understanding requires a strong working knowledge of the PC and DOS. To avoid confusion with these qualifiers, most users will get optimal performance from

Summary (continued)

the command PRINT /M:64 /U:16. The /S qualifier is not used in this command, thus leaving it set at the default value of 8.

To provide you with complete control over the files in your PRINT queue, PRINT provides the /C, /T, and /P qualifiers. The /C qualifier allows you to remove a specific file or files from the queue. The general form for a command using this qualifier is PRINT *FILENAME.EXT* /C. The /T qualifier directs PRINT to stop printing the current file and remove *all* files from the print queue. PRINT /T is the form of the PRINT command using this qualifier. The /P qualifier allows you to add files to the print queue in the same PRINT command that you are using to remove files. The command would appear as PRINT *FILENAME.EXT* /C *NEWFILE.EXT* /P.

Glossary

Hardcopy is another term for printed output. If you send a file to your printer, the paper containing the printed result is your hardcopy.

The *print buffer* is the area of memory into which the PRINT command reads your files from disk before printing them. This buffer only holds 512 bytes of characters at a time—about half a page.

Getting the Most From DOS

Part Two

Congratulations! You have mastered all the DOS basics that you will need in order to perform your daily activities with your computer and to complete the exercises that follow in the remainder of this text. In Part Two of this book, you will learn how to create, display, and modify text files with EDLIN, the DOS text-line editor. The chapters in this part will examine several DOS device names (such as CON, LPT1, and PRN) along with how to customize these devices for your specific needs by using the DOS MODE command.

Also discussed in the following chapters are file and disk management by using DOS subdirectories, which lays the foundation you will need to install DOS on your fixed disk. Lastly, you will learn how to save time and keystrokes by combining multiple DOS commands into DOS batch files.

The topics that you examine in Part Two of this book are intermediate-level topics. Use of this information is a key step to your becoming a sophisticated DOS user. Follow the same procedures you did throughout the earlier chapters of this book—first read the introductory text and then perform the exercises in the "Hands-On" section. Once a week you should quickly browse the "Hands-On" sections that you have already performed. In so doing, you will keep all DOS concepts (such as the DOS function keys) fresh in your mind.

For fixed disk users, this section of the book will get you up and running with your fixed disk. More importantly, it will teach you how to correctly install DOS on your fixed disk while maximizing your system's performance and file organization. Part One of this book taught you how to get started with DOS. Part Two teaches you how to use DOS efficiently.

13 Creating Text Files with EDLIN

So far, each time you created a text file, you had to copy the file's contents from your keyboard device, using this command:

```
A> COPY CON FILENAME.EXT
```

DOS, however, provides a software program called EDLIN that allows you to create or modify text files. EDLIN is not a word processor. Instead, EDLIN allows you to perform basic text manipulation. If you have a word processor such as WordStar, WordPerfect, or Microsoft Word, you will not need to use EDLIN, and you can skip the next two chapters. However, if you do not have a word processing package yet, EDLIN should meet most of your text processing needs. By the end of this chapter you will be using EDLIN to quickly produce letters, memos, and reports or to record brief notes that you want to store on disk.

Getting Started with EDLIN

Place your DOS Program disk in drive A and then issue the following command.

```
A> DIR  EDLIN.COM

Volume in drive A is MS330PP01
Directory of  A:\

EDLIN           COM     7495   7-24-87   12:00a
                        1 File(s)  5120 bytes free
```

As you can see, EDLIN is an external DOS command that DOS loads
into memory when you want to edit files. When you invoke EDLIN
from the DOS prompt, you must specify the name of the file that you
want to edit.

```
A> EDLIN  FILENAME.EXT
```

If you do not specify a file name, EDLIN will display

```
A> EDLIN
File name must be specified

A>
```

Once EDLIN has loaded your file from disk into memory, the following messages will be displayed if you are editing a new file:

```
A> EDLIN  FILENAME.EXT
New file
*
```

This message will be displayed instead if you are editing a previously
existing file:

```
A> EDLIN  FILENAME.EXT
End of input file
*
```

For example, create a new file called TEXTFILE.NEW by entering

```
A> EDLIN  B:TEXTFILE.NEW
```

EDLIN will respond with

```
A> EDLIN  B:TEXTFILE.NEW
New file
*
```

The asterisk (*) is EDLIN's command prompt—EDLIN's way of asking you to enter one of the following single-letter commands:

Command	Function
A	Appends lines from disk into memory
C	Copies lines from one location in the file to another
D	Deletes a line or series of lines
E	Ends an editing session, saves the file's contents, and exits to DOS
I	Inserts a line or series of lines
L	Displays a line or series of lines
M	Moves a line or series of lines to a new location in the file
P	Displays a page (23 lines) of information
Q	Quits the editing session without saving changes
R	Replaces a word or phrase with a second word or phrase
S	Searches for a specific word or phrase
T	Transfers lines from a second file into this file
W	Writes lines from memory back to disk

You can enter each of these EDLIN commands in either uppercase or lowercase.

Since your file is empty, you can insert text by using the EDLIN Insert command, I.

```
A> EDLIN  B:TEXTFILE.NEW
New file
*I
            1:*
```

EDLIN is a *line editor*, which means that it allows you to create or modify files one line at a time. In this case, the characters "1:*" tell you that EDLIN is waiting for you to type in line 1. Type in the sentence **This is line one**, and press ENTER. Your screen now displays

```
A> EDLIN  B:TEXTFILE.NEW
New file
*I
                    1:* This is line one
                    2:*
```

EDLIN is ready for you to enter line 2 of the file. Type in the line **This is line two**, and press ENTER. The display is

```
A> EDLIN  B:TEXTFILE.NEW
New file
*I
                    1:* This is line one
                    2:* This is line two
                    3:*
```

Repeat this process for line 3, as shown here:

```
A> EDLIN  B:TEXTFILE.NEW
New file
*I
                    1:* This is line one
                    2:* This is line two
                    3:* This is line three
                    4:*
```

You have now inserted all the lines you need to place into the file. To notify EDLIN of this fact, press the CTRL-C keyboard combination, located on the keyboard as shown in Figure 13-1. EDLIN will exit Insert mode and redisplay its command prompt.

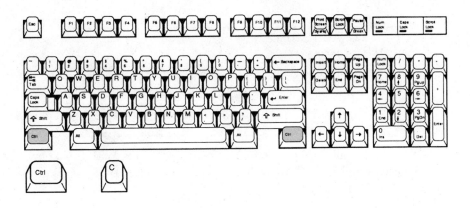

Figure 13-1. *Location of* CTRL *and* C *keys*

```
A> EDLIN  B:TEXTFILE.NEW
New file
*I
          1:* This is line one
          2:* This is line two
          3:* This is line three
          4:* ^C
*
```

Using the EDLIN Exit command, E, save your new file and return
to DOS.

```
A> EDLIN  B:TEXTFILE.NEW
New file
*I
          1:* This is line one
          2:* This is line two
          3:* This is line three
          4:* ^C
*E

A>
```

From DOS, display the contents of this file by using the DOS TYPE command.

```
A> TYPE  B:TEXTFILE.NEW
This is line one
This is line two
This is line three

A>
```

That's all it takes to create a file with EDLIN. With this knowledge, create the ALLSTAR.DAT file and then exit to DOS, as shown here:

```
A> EDLIN  B:ALLSTAR.DAT
New file
*I
                1:* L. BYRD
                2:* D. WILKINS
                3:* P. EWING
                4:* M. JORDAN
                5:* I. THOMAS
                6:* ^C
*E

A>
```

Again, using the TYPE command from DOS, display the new file's contents.

```
A> TYPE  B:ALLSTAR.DAT
L. BYRD
D. WILKINS
P. EWING
M. JORDAN
I. THOMAS

A>
```

Viewing a File with EDLIN

You can examine the contents of your TEXTFILE.NEW file by using the EDLIN command. Invoke the command

```
A> EDLIN  B:TEXTFILE.NEW
```

Because your file already exists, EDLIN will then display the message

```
A> EDLIN  B:TEXTFILE.NEW
End of input file
*
```

At the EDLIN command prompt (*), type the number 1 and press ENTER to view line 1. EDLIN will display

```
A> EDLIN  B:TEXTFILE.NEW
End of input file
*1
              1:* This is line one
              1:*
```

EDLIN is displaying the current contents of line 1. The second "1:*" is EDLIN's prompt for new text for line 1. You simply want to view line 1, so press ENTER, leaving the line unchanged. EDLIN will display

```
A> EDLIN  B:TEXTFILE.NWE
End of input file
*1
              1:* This is line one
              1:*
*
```

If you press ENTER again, EDLIN will repeat this process for line 2.

```
A> EDLIN  B:TEXTFILE.NEW
End of input file
*1
                1:* This is line one
                1:*
  *
                2:* This is line two
                2:*
  *
```

Perform the same steps for line 3:

```
A> EDLIN  B:TEXTFILE.NEW
End of input file
*1
                1:* This is line one
                1:*
  *
                2:* This is line two
                2:*
  *
                3:* This is line three
                3:*
  *
```

When you issue the EDLIN Exit command, E, EDLIN records all of your changes to disk. In this case, you have made no changes to the file, so you can use the EDLIN Quit command, Q.

```
A> EDLIN  B:TEXTFILE.NEW
End of input file
*1
                1:* This is line one
                1:*
  *
                2:* This is line two
                2:*
  *
                3:* This is line three
                3:*
  *Q
```

EDLIN will respond by displaying

```
A> EDLIN  B:TEXTFILE.NEW
End of input file
*1
                  1:* This is line one
                  1:*
*
                  2:* This is line two
                  2:*
*
                  3:* This is line three
                  3:*
*Q
Abort edit (Y/N)?
```

If you type **Y**, EDLIN will leave your file unchanged, returning you
to the DOS prompt. If instead you enter **N**, EDLIN will redisplay its
prompt, allowing you to continue editing the file. For now, type **N** to
continue editing, so that you can examine the EDLIN List command,
which is L.

At the EDLIN command prompt, select line 1 as the current line.

```
*1
                  1:* This is line one
                  1:*
*
```

Type **L** and press ENTER to list the contents of your file.

```
*L
                  1:* This is line one
                  2:  This is line two
                  3:  This is line three
*
```

The EDLIN List command allows you to display several lines of
your file with one command. By default, List displays 23 lines of your
file, starting at the current line. The EDLIN List command also al-

lows you to specify a range of numbers for display with the following command variables:

starting_line, ending_line L

For example, to display lines 2 and 3 of this file, you would enter the command

```
*2,3L
              2: This is line two
              3: This is line three

*
```

If you do not specify an ending line, EDLIN will simply display 23 lines from the starting line or the entire file, if the file is fewer than 23 lines long.

File Restrictions with EDLIN

Just as you cannot use the TYPE and PRINT commands to display the contents of files such as FORMAT.COM and COMMAND.COM, you can use EDLIN only to display or edit text files that contain letters and numbers.

Modifying Your File's Contents

You just saw that you can easily display your file contents by using EDLIN. In a similar manner, EDLIN allows you to change your file's contents.

The changes you will make to your sample file will be quite straightforward. You will simply replace the lines

```
This is line one
This is line two
This is line three
```

with

> This is line 1
> This is line 2
> This is line 3

To make these changes, you first invoke EDLIN with the TEXT-FILE.DAT file.

```
A> EDLIN  B:TEXTFILE.DAT
```

Type the number **1** to display line 1, as shown here:

```
A> EDLIN  B:TEXTFILE.NEW
End of input file
*1
                    1:* This is line one
1:*
```

EDLIN is ready for you to enter the new text for this line. Type the new line, **This is line 1**, and press ENTER. EDLIN now displays

```
A> EDLIN  B:TEXTFILE.NEW
End of input file
*1
                    1:* This is line one
                    1:* This is line 1
*
```

Repeat this process for lines 2 and 3.

```
A> EDLIN  B:TEXTFILE.NEW
End of input file
*1
                    1:* This is line one
                    1:* This is line 1
*2
                    2:* This is line two
                    2:* This is line 2
```

```
*3
                    3:* This is line three
                    3:* This is line 3
*
```

To save your changes, use the EDLIN Exit command, E.

```
A> EDLIN  B:TEXTFILE.NEW
End of input file
*1
                    1:* This is line one
                    1:* This is line 1
*2
                    2:* This is line two
                    2:* This is line 2
*3
                    3:* This is line three
                    3:* This is line 3
*E

A>
```

At the DOS prompt, display the contents of your updated file.

```
A> TYPE  B:TEXTFILE.NEW
This is line 1
This is line 2
This is line 3

A>
```

Next, issue the following DIR command:

```
A> DIR  B:TEXTFILE
```

DOS will display

```
A> DIR  B:TEXTFILE

Volume in drive B is EDLIN
Directory of B:\

TEXTFILE        BAK       60    4-25-88   4:10p
TEXTFILE        NEW       52    4-25-88   4:23p
                2 File(s)  195200 bytes free
```

Each time you use EDLIN to modify a file, EDLIN saves a copy of
the original file and gives it the extension BAK, for backup. If, after
editing a file, you decide you really wish you had not modified the file,
you still have the original copy.

Invoke EDLIN with the TEXTFILE.DAT file.

```
A> EDLIN  B:TEXTFILE.DAT
```

What if you want to add the line "This is line 0" to the beginning
of your file? You will again use the Insert command, but in this case,
because you want this line to be the first line in your file, you must
insert it before line 1. To do so, type in the command

```
A> EDLIN  B:TEXTFILE.NEW
End of input file
*I1
```

EDLIN will acknowledge your command, displaying

```
A> EDLIN  B:TEXTFILE.NEW
End of input file
*I1
                1:*
```

Type in **This is line 0**, and press ENTER. EDLIN will display

```
A> EDLIN  B:TEXTFILE.NEW
End of input file
*I1
                    1:* This is line 0
                    2:*
```

EDLIN has no way of knowing how many lines you want to insert; therefore, it will prompt you to type in a second line of text. Since you want to add only one line, press CTRL-C to return to the EDLIN command prompt:

```
A> EDLIN  B:TEXTFILE.NEW
End of input file
*I1
                    1:* This is line 0
                    2:* ^C
*
```

As you can see, the EDLIN Insert command can be used to place text before any line in a file. To do this, you must type in the number of the line before which you want to place the text, followed immediately by the letter "I."

Use the EDLIN Exit command to return to the DOS prompt and to save your updates, as shown here:

```
A> EDLIN  B:TEXTFILE.NEW
End of input file
*I1
                    1:* This is line 0
                    2:* ^C
*E

A>
```

With the DOS TYPE command, display the file's updated contents.

```
A> TYPE  B:TEXTFILE.NEW
This is line 0
This is line 1
This is line 2
This is line 3

A>
```

Next, use EDLIN's Delete command to remove several lines from the file. First, invoke EDLIN with the TEXTFILE.DAT file.

```
A> EDLIN  B:TEXTFILE.DAT
```

Display the first line of the file.

```
A> EDLIN  B:TEXTFILE.NEW
End of input file
*1
                    1:* This is line 0
                    1:*

*
```

At the EDLIN command prompt, type the letter **D** and press ENTER.

```
A> EDLIN  B:TEXTFILE.NEW
End of input file
*1
                    1:* This is line 0
                    1:*
*D
```

EDLIN will delete the first line, as you can see when you display the contents of the file by typing **L** and then pressing ENTER.

```
*L
                    1:* This is line 1
                    2:  This is line 2
                    3:  This is line 3

*
```

The EDLIN Delete command provides you with three options. First, you can delete the current line, as just shown. Second, you can delete a specific line by preceding the letter "D" with the number of the line to delete, as shown here:

```
*3D
```

Third, EDLIN allows you to delete a range of lines, as shown here:

```
*L
                1:* This is line 1
                2:  This is line 2
                3:  This is line 3
*2,3D
*L
                1:  This is line 1

*
```

In this case, the EDLIN Delete command deleted lines 2 and 3 from the file.

Issue the EDLIN Exit command, E, to return to DOS. Use the TYPE command to display the file's contents. With these basic fundamentals under your belt, you can practice using EDLIN.

Hands-On Practice

For this practice you will create a file containing the following spelled-out numbers:

ZERO
ONE
TWO

```
THREE
FOUR
FIVE
SIX
SEVEN
EIGHT
NINE
TEN
```

Invoke EDLIN with the NUMBERS.DAT file.

```
A> EDLIN  B:NUMBERS.DAT
```

Since this file is new, EDLIN will display

```
A> EDLIN  B:NUMBERS.TXT
New file
*
```

This file is empty, so you must use the EDLIN Insert command to add text to the file.

```
A> EDLIN  B:NUMBERS.TXT
New file
*I
```

At EDLIN's prompt for line 1, type **ZERO** and press ENTER.

```
A> EDLIN B:NUMBERS.TXT
New file
*I
                1:* ZERO
                2:*
```

EDLIN has prompted you to enter line 2. Enter the remaining numbers that comprise your file.

```
A> EDLIN  B:NUMBERS.TXT
New file
*I
            1:* ZERO
            2:* ONE
            3:* TWO
            4:* THREE
            5:* FOUR
            6:* FIVE
            7:* SIX
            8:* SEVEN
            9:* EIGHT
            10:* NINE
            11:* TEN
            12:*
```

After you have typed in the last line, press CTRL-C to return to the EDLIN command prompt, and you will see the following display:

```
A> EDLIN  B:NUMBERS.TXT
New file
*I
            1:* ZERO
            2:* ONE
            3:* TWO
            4:* THREE
            5:* FOUR
            6:* FIVE
            7:* SIX
            8:* SEVEN
            9:* EIGHT
            10:* NINE
            11:* TEN
            12:* ^C
     *
```

Use the EDLIN List command to display your file's contents.

```
*L
            1: ZERO
            2: ONE
            3: TWO
            4: THREE
            5: FOUR
            6: FIVE
            7: SIX
            8: SEVEN
            9: EIGHT
            10: NINE
            11: TEN
  *
```

Since many of the examples you will examine make more sense if each word in the file corresponds to the line number, delete the first line of the file by using the EDLIN Delete command.

```
*1D
```

A listing of your file's contents displays

```
*L
            1: ONE
            2: TWO
            3: THREE
            4: FOUR
            5: FIVE
            6: SIX
            7: SEVEN
            8: EIGHT
            9: NINE
            10: TEN
  *
```

Use the EDLIN Exit command to save your file contents and return control to DOS.

```
*E

A>
```

Invoke EDLIN once again to edit the NUMBERS.TXT file.

```
A> EDLIN  B:NUMBERS.TXT
End of input file
*
```

Delete lines 5 through 10, as shown here:

```
A> EDLIN  B:NUMBERS.TXT
End of input file
*5,10D
*L
                1: ONE
                2: TWO
                3: THREE
                4: FOUR

*
```

Replace the lines that you just deleted with the numbers 5 to 10.

```
*I
                5:* 5
                6:* 6
                7:* 7
                8:* 8
                9:* 9
                10:* 10
                11:* ^C
*E
```

Then exit to DOS using the Exit command, E, and issue the following DIR command.

```
A> DIR  B:NUMBERS

Volume in drive B is EDLIN
Directory of  B:\

NUMBERS       BAK      77      4-25-88    4:48p
NUMBERS       TXT      28      4-25-88    4:57p
              2 File(s)  151304 bytes free
```

As you can see, DOS has saved a copy of your previous file. Edit this file again, changing line 1 to "ONE ONE ONE," as shown here:

```
*1
              1: ONE
              1: ONE ONE ONE
*
```

Use the EDLIN Quit command to terminate this editing session. At the prompt, indicate your intention to end the session without modifying the contents of your file.

```
*1
              1: ONE
              1: ONE ONE ONE
*Q
Abort edit (Y/N)? Y

A>
```

Display the file's contents from DOS by invoking the TYPE command.

```
A> TYPE NUMBERS.TXT
ONE
TWO
THREE
FOUR
5
6
7
8
9
10

A>
```

You can see that EDLIN has indeed left your file unchanged.

Admittedly, the files that you have created in this chapter have been quite simple. There is no reason, however, for you not to use EDLIN to create reports or letters, as in the following example:

```
A> EDLIN JAY.LTR
New file
*I
                1:* Dear Jay,
                2:*
                3:* So how's Norway?  Things here are pretty much
                4:* the same as always. Nothing is going on at work.
                5:*
```

Summary

Prior to this chapter, you created a text file by copying the file's contents from your keyboard device, using the following command:

A> COPY CON FILENAME.EXT

DOS provides a program called EDLIN that allows you to create and edit text files. EDLIN is a line editor, which means that you must perform your text manipulation one line at a time.

When you invoke EDLIN, the program displays an asterisk (*), which is its command prompt. With EDLIN you use single-letter commands to perform such actions as appending, copying, deleting, inserting, displaying, or moving lines, as well as for searching text, replacing text, transferring lines between files, and quitting EDLIN. These commands can be uppercase or lowercase letters.

The EDLIN Insert command, I, allows you to place text into your file at a specific location. Once you issue the Insert command, EDLIN enters Insert mode. After you have entered your last text, you must press the CTRL-C key combination, which notifies EDLIN to return to its command prompt.

To stop editing and save your changes to disk, use the EDLIN Exit command, E. When you issue this command, EDLIN makes a backup copy of your original file and gives it the extension BAK. If you later wish that you had not edited the file, you still have the original.

The EDLIN List command, L, allows you to display a line or series of lines within your file. The EDLIN Delete command, D, allows you to delete one or more lines.

If you want to stop editing without saving your changes to disk, issue the EDLIN Quit command, Q. EDLIN will prompt you to verify that you really want to quit, and EDLIN will return you to DOS with your file unchanged.

Glossary

Text manipulation is the process of editing, adding, and deleting words, phrases, and paragraphs in a text file.

A *line editor* is a software program that allows you to perform basic text manipulation commands one line at a time. EDLIN is a line editor.

14 Advanced File Editing with EDLIN

In Chapter 13 you learned how to create, modify, and display files by using the EDLIN command. In this chapter you will expand on these basic capabilities and learn how EDLIN allows you to search for words or phrases, replace one word or phrase with another, and even move or copy text from one location in your file to another. Although EDLIN lacks the flair of a word processing system, it should provide you with a partial solution to most of your text processing problems.

Using the Current Line Number

Chapter 13 explained that when you type a line number at the EDLIN command prompt and press ENTER, the number that you enter is the line that is displayed as the current line.

```
A> EDLIN  B:NUMBERS.TXT
End of file found
*1
                  1:* ONE
                  1:*
```

To assist you in entering your editing commands, EDLIN defines the period (.) to represent the current line number. By itself, the period is not really significant; however, EDLIN allows you to use the period with plus or minus offsets, giving you the ability to list ranges of lines that precede or follow the current line number. For example, consider the following file:

```
*L
          1:*ONE
          2: TWO
          3: THREE
          4: FOUR
          5: 5
          6: 6
          7: 7
          8: 8
          9: 9
          10: 10
*
```

Select line 5 as the current line number.

```
*5
          5:*5
          5:*
```

You can now use the EDLIN List command to list lines 5 and 6, as shown here:

```
*.,+1L
          5:*5
          6: 6
*
```

To list lines 4 through 6, use the command

```
*-1,+1L
          4: 4
          5:*5
          6: 6
*
```

When line 5 is the current line number, the following expressions are true.

.	Refers to line 5
.-1	Refers to line 4
.+10	Refers to line 15
.-4	Refers to line 1

All EDLIN commands that allow you to specify line numbers support this notation.

EDLIN defines the pound sign (#) as the end of a file. To list the last three lines in the previous file, for example, use this command:

```
*#
*-3,L
           8: 8
           9: 9
          10: 10
*
```

As the size of your EDLIN files increases, your ability to specify ranges and offsets in this way will become quite convenient.

Looking at a Large File One Page at a Time

Assume for the moment that you are editing a large file, which contains more than 100 lines, consisting of consecutive Arabic numbers. In Chapter 13 you saw that the EDLIN List command allows you to display up to 23 lines of a file at one time. Used on your file, List would display

```
*L
          1:*1
          2: 2
          3: 3
```

```
              4: 4
              5: 5
              6: 6
              7: 7
              8: 8
              9: 9
             10: 10
             11: 11
             12: 12
             13: 13
             14: 14
             15: 15
             16: 16
             17: 17
             18: 18
             19: 19
             20: 20
             21: 21
             22: 22
             23: 23
   *
```

By continually modifying the range of numbers to be displayed, you could eventually display the entire file by using the EDLIN List command. Here, you select line 24 as your current line, and List displays the next 23 lines:

```
   *24L
             24: 24
             25: 25
             26: 26
             27: 27
             28: 28
             29: 29
             30: 30
             31: 31
             32: 32
             33: 33
             34: 34
             35: 35
             36: 36
             37: 37
```

```
                   38: 38
                   39: 39
                   40: 40
                   41: 41
                   42: 42
                   43: 43
                   44: 44
                   45: 45
                   46: 46
  *
```

You could continue invoking List until you had seen the entire file.

EDLIN provides you with a more convenient method of traversing a file with the Page command, P. Like the List command, Page displays up to 23 lines of your file at a time. When used on your file, Page displays

```
*P
                    1:*1
                    2: 2
                    3: 3
                    4: 4
                    5: 5
                    6: 6
                    7: 7
                    8: 8
                    9: 9
                   10: 10
                   11: 11
                   12: 12
                   13: 13
                   14: 14
                   15: 15
                   16: 16
                   17: 17
                   18: 18
                   19: 19
                   20: 20
                   21: 21
                   22: 22
                   23: 23
  *
```

Unlike List, when Page completes, it sets the current line number to the last line number displayed. Given your file, you can quickly view the first 46 lines by repeating the Page command, as shown here:

```
*P
                1:*1
                2: 2
                3: 3
                4: 4
                5: 5
                6: 6
                7: 7
                8: 8
                9: 9
               10: 10
               11: 11
               12: 12
               13: 13
               14: 14
               15: 15
               16: 16
               17: 17
               18: 18
               19: 19
               20: 20
               21: 21
               22: 22
               23:*23
*P
               24: 24
               25: 25
               26: 26
               27: 27
               28: 28
               29: 29
               30: 30
               31: 31
               32: 32
               33: 33
               34: 34
               35: 35
               36: 36
```

```
        37: 37
        38: 38
        39: 39
        40: 40
        41: 41
        42: 42
        43: 43
        44: 44
        45: 45
        46: 46
   *
```

If your files are large, the Page command is an efficient way to view their contents.

Editing Large Files With EDLIN

When EDLIN was first written, most of the personal computers in use were running with 64K to 128K of memory. If you were lucky, your system had 256K of memory. EDLIN is, therefore, used to working in cramped quarters. Some of these early experiences still influence EDLIN's processing today. If you are editing a file that is bigger than your available memory, EDLIN will load as much of your file into memory as it can while ensuring that 25% of memory remains unused. The extra memory is available for you to insert or copy text within the file.

When EDLIN cannot load your entire document into memory, the EDLIN prompt is displayed.

```
A> EDLIN  LARGE.DAT
*
```

In order to continue editing your file, you will have to use the EDLIN Write and Append commands.

Assume that your file contains 1000 lines and only 800 of them fit into memory. Once you have edited the first 800 lines, you must write them from memory back to disk in order to make space for the last 200 lines. This is done by invoking the EDLIN Write command, W, as shown here:

```
*800W
*
```

The number before the EDLIN Write command specifies the number of lines EDLIN is to write to disk.

To edit the last 200 lines, you must use the EDLIN Append command, A, to bring in the last 200 lines of the file from disk.

```
*200A
*
```

The number that precedes the Append command tells EDLIN how many lines to read into memory from disk. If you omit the number of lines, EDLIN will read in lines until either the end of the file is found or memory is 75% full.

Using Another File's Contents

Many times when editing a file, you will need to include the contents of another file by invoking the EDLIN Transfer command, T. For example, assume that you are working on a monthly summary of your company revenues. You have asked your sales department to provide you with its sales figures in a file called SALES.MAY, which looks like this:

```
A> TYPE  B:SALES.MAY
DISKETTES    4,000
PAPER          500
PRINTERS     1,200
KEYBOARDS      440
SOFTWARE       144

A>
```

As you prepare your report, you reach the point where you need to insert the sales information.

```
115:* Sales for the month were as shown:
116:*
117:* ^C
*
```

Use the EDLIN Transfer command, T, whose format is

[*line number*] T *FILENAME.EXT*

Here, *line number* specifies the line number within your file at which you want the new file inserted. The processing of your file becomes

```
115:* Sales for the month were as shown:
116:*
117:* ^C
*117TSALES.MAY
```

Listing that section of your file now reveals

```
115:* Sales for the month were as shown:
116:*
117:* ^C
*117TSALES.MAY
*115L
```

```
115: Sales for the month were as shown:
116:
117:* DISKETTES    4,000
118: PAPER           500
119: PRINTERS      1,200
120: KEYBOARDS       440
121: SOFTWARE        144

 *
```

In the "Hands-On Practice" section of this chapter, you will use the EDLIN Transfer command to build one file out of several smaller files.

Moving Text Within Your File

When you prepare a report, you may decide that you need to rearrange one or two paragraphs to increase the report's readability. A "brute-force" solution to this problem is to delete the original lines of text and retype them at the correct location. EDLIN, however, provides you with a more efficient solution—the Move command, M. Move allows you to move a single line or range of lines to a new location. Here are a few examples of how the MOVE command can be used:

Command	Effect
*,,10M	Moves the current line to line 10
*1,1,4M	Moves line 1 to line 4
*1,5,20M	Moves lines 1 through 5 to line 20

Consider the NUMBERS.TXT file you created in Chapter 13. During an editing session, the lines of your file become disordered, as shown here.

```
*L
            1:* ONE
            2: TWO
            3: FOUR
            4: FIVE
            5: THREE
            6: SIX
            7: SEVEN
            8: EIGHT
            9: NINE
           10: TEN
    *
```

Use the EDLIN Move command to quickly restore the file to its desired contents, moving lines 3 and 4 to line 6.

```
*3,4,6M
*L
            1:* ONE
            2: TWO
            3: THREE
            4: FOUR
            5: FIVE
            6: SIX
            7: SEVEN
            8: EIGHT
            9: NINE
           10: TEN
    *
```

Duplicating the Text in Your File

Just as it is not uncommon to move text in your file from one location to another, in many cases you must duplicate a line or range of lines and place them in another location in your file. The EDLIN Copy command, C, allows you to do just that. The format of this command is [*first line*], [*last line*], *destination line*, [*number of copies*] C

Here, *first line* and *last line* specify the range of lines that EDLIN is to copy; *destination line* is the line number in your file to which lines are copied; and *number of copies* specifies how many copies of the lines will be placed at the destination. Consider these EDLIN Copy commands and what they do:

Command	Effect
*1,1,10,C	Copies line 1 to line 10
*1,5,10,C	Copies lines 1 through 5 to line 10
*1,5,10,2C	Makes two copies of lines 1 through 5 and places them at line 10

For example, if your file contains

```
*L
             1:* ONE
             2: TWO
             3: THREE
             4: FOUR
             5: FIVE
             6: SIX
             7: SEVEN
             8: EIGHT
             9: NINE
            10: TEN
*
```

the EDLIN Copy command

```
*3,4,6C
```

will result in

```
*L
             1: ONE
             2: TWO
             3: THREE
             4: FOUR
```

```
          5: FIVE
          6:* THREE
          7: FOUR
          8: SIX
          9: SEVEN
         10: EIGHT
         11: NINE
         12: TEN
   *
```

The powerful EDLIN Copy and Move commands can save you considerable time and effort as the complexity of your files increases.

Searching for Words and Phrases

If you have a large file, you could spend considerable time and effort finding a specific location within the file that you want to display or edit. In some instances the EDLIN Search command, S, can simplify this task by directing EDLIN to examine a range of lines for a specific word or phrase. The format of the EDLIN Search command is

[*first line*],[*last line*][?]S*word or phrase*

Here, *first line* and *last line* specify the range of lines in the file that Search is to examine. If you omit these lines, EDLIN will search from the current line to the end of the file. By default, EDLIN will stop searching the first time it encounters a match of the word or phrase. The question mark directs EDLIN to continue its search until either the end of the file is found or the user types **Y** at EDLIN's prompt

```
   O.K.?
```

EDLIN displays this prompt each time it finds a match.

Here are a few examples of the Search command

Command	Effect
*1,STEN	Searches the entire file for the word "TEN"
*1,5SDear	Searches lines 1 through 5 for the word "Dear"
*1,?SMr	Searches the entire file for the word "Mr," and each time the word is found, prompts the user with "O.K.?"

Assume that the file you are editing contains the following:

```
*L
            1:* DOS is the Disk Operating System for
            2: the IBM PC and PC compatibles.  There
            3: are two well known versions of DOS, MS-DOS
            4: and PC DOS. MS-DOS is Microsoft's DOS, while
            5: PC DOS is IBM's.  Regardless of which DOS you
            6: are using, the commands in this book are valid.
*
```

The EDLIN Search command 1,SDOS results in

```
*1,SDOS
            1: DOS is the Disk Operating System for
*
```

Likewise, the command 1,SOS/2 results in

```
*1,SOS/2
Not found
*
```

because the word "OS/2" does not appear in the file.

When searching for the word "DOS," if you know that it appears several times throughout the file, you can direct EDLIN to prompt with the following message:

```
O.K.?
```

with each match of the word by including the question mark in your Search command. This allows you to continue the search by typing **N**, as shown here:

```
*1,?SDOS
                    1:* DOS is the Disk Operating System for
O.K.? N
                    3:  are two well known versions of DOS, MS-DOS
O.K.? N
                    4:  and PC DOS.  MS-DOS is Microsoft's DOS, while
O.K.? N
                     5:  PC DOS is IBM's.  Regardless of which DOS you
O.K.? N
Not found
*
```

If at any time you had wanted to stop the search, you would have typed **Y** at the prompt.

Replacing One Word or Phrase with Another

Just as the EDLIN Search command allows you to look up specific words and phrases within your file, the EDLIN Replace command, Ŕ, allows you to locate a specific word or phrase and replace it with another throughout your entire document. The format of the EDLIN Replace command is

[*first line*],[*last line*]R*word or phrase*<F6>*word or phrase*

The symbol <F6> in the command format tells you that you must press the F6 function key after you have typed in the letters of the phrase that you want to replace. For example, consider these commands and what they do.

Command	Effect
*1,RArizona\<F6\>AZ	Replaces the first occurrence of the word "Arizona" with the letters "AZ"
*1,RMister\<F6\>Mr.	Replaces the first occurrence of the word "Mister" with "Mr."
*5,10?Rshould\<F6\>	Deletes each occurrence of the word "should" in lines 5 through 10 of the file, prompting you at each occurrence with "OK?"

For example, assume that you have just written the following memo:

```
A> EDLIN B:MEMO.TXT
*L
                1:* Dear John,
                2:
                3: Just got the word from our Chicago office
                4: that sales for the month are at record highs!
                5: John, I want you to know how much your efforts
                6: are appreciated.
                7:
                8: KAJ
    *
```

You decide that you also want to send this memo to Ted, your vice president of production. You can use the EDLIN Replace command to modify the file, as shown here:

```
*1,?RJohn^ZTed
                1:* Dear Ted,
    O.K.?
                5: Ted, I want you to know how much your efforts
    O.K.?
    *
```

Your memo is now ready to go out.

```
*L
            1:* Dear Ted,
            2:
            3:  Just got the word from our Chicago office
            4:  that sales for the month are at record highs!
            5:  Ted, I want you to know how much your efforts
            6:  are appreciated.
            7:
            8:  KAJ
            9:  ^C
 *
```

This chapter has presented quite a bit of difficult material in a small number of pages. When you complete the "Hands-On Practice" section, take a few extra minutes to write a letter or memo with EDLIN. You should find it easy to use.

Hands-On Practice

With your DOS Program disk in drive A, use EDLIN to create the following file:

```
A> EDLIN  B:LETTERS.TXT
New file
*I
            1:* AAAAA
            2:* BBBBB
            3:* CCCCC
            4:* DDDDD
            5:* EEEEE
            6:* FFFFF
            7:* GGGGG
            8:* HHHHH
            9:* IIIII
           10:* ^C
 *
```

Type **5** and press ENTER to select line 5 as the current line.

```
*5
                5:* EEEEE
                5:*
    *
```

Enter the command offsets **+2** and **-2** to display lines 3 through 7, as shown here:

```
*-2,+2L
                3: CCCCC
                4: DDDDD
                5:*EEEEE
                6: FFFFF
                7: GGGGG
    *
```

Remember that EDLIN defines the period (.) as the current line number. The following command, therefore, is functionally identical to the previous one:

```
*.-2,.+2L
                3: CCCCC
                4: DDDDD
                5:*EEEEE
                6: FFFFF
                7: GGGGG
    *
```

If you specify a plus or minus offset without the period in an EDLIN command, EDLIN defaults to the current line number.

Experiment with offsets some more to delete lines 3 through 8 of this file.

```
*-2,+3D
*L
                1: AAAAA
                2: BBBBB
```

```
                3: IIIII
*
```

Probably the most common use of offsets is to display the text that immediately surrounds the current line number. For example, this command displays the three lines before and after the current line 5.

```
*-3,+3L
                2: BBBBB
                3: CCCCC
                4: DDDDD
                5:*EEEEE
                6: FFFFF
                7: GGGGG
                8: HHHHH
*
```

Using the EDLIN Quit command, Q, stop editing this file and return to DOS without saving the file's contents.

```
*Q
Abort edit (Y/N)? Y
```

Invoke EDLIN to create the following file:

```
A> EDLIN B:NUMBERS.NEW
*I
                1:* 11
                2:* 22
                3:* 33
                4:* 66
                5:* 77
                6:* 44
                7:* 55
                8:* 88
                9:* 99
                10:* ^C
*
```

Make sure that you type the numbers in exactly as they appear here.
   Use the EDLIN Move command, M, to get the numbers into the
correct order:

```
*6,7,4M
*L
            1: 11
            2: 22
            3: 33
            4: 44
            5: 55
            6: 66
            7: 77
            8: 88
            9: 99
    *
```

Move line 1 to the end of the file, as shown here:

```
*1,1,#M
*L
            1: 22
            2: 33
            3: 44
            4: 55
            5: 66
            6: 77
            7: 88
            8: 99
            9: 11
    *
```

Remember that the pound sign (#) represents the end of the file.
   Again using the EDLIN Move command, move line 9 back to its
original position as line 1.

```
*9,9,1M
*L
            1: 11
            2: 22
            3: 33
            4: 44
            5: 55
            6: 66
            7: 77
            8: 88
            9: 99
*
```

Rearranging the text in your file is that easy.

Quit editing this file and return to DOS without saving the contents of the file.

```
*Q
Abort edit (Y/N)? Y

A>
```

Using EDLIN, type in the following letter:

```
A> EDLIN  B:PARTY.LTR
New file
*I
            1:* Dear Jay,
            2:*
            3:* I just wanted to let you know that
            4:* our party is still on for this
            5:* weekend.  I hope that you and Sue will
            6:* be able to make it.
            7:*
            8:* KAJ
            9:* ^C
*
```

Exit to DOS, saving the file so that you can print it.

```
*E

A> PRINT  B:PARTY.LTR
```

Edit this file so that you can send it to Jim. First, you must replace all occurrences of "Jay" with "Jim."

```
A> EDLIN  B:PARTY.LTR
End of file found
*L
            1: Dear Jay,
            2:
            3: I just wanted to let you know that
            4: our party is still on for this
            5: weekend.  I hope that you and Sue will
            6: be able to make it.
            7:
            8: KAJ
*1,RJay^ZJim
            1: Dear Jim,

*
```

Listing your file displays

```
*L
            1: Dear Jim,
            2:
            3: I just wanted to let you know that
            4: our party is still on for this
            5: weekend.  I hope that you and Sue will
            6: be able to make it.
            7:
            8: KAJ

*
```

You still have a problem: Jim doesn't have a wife named Sue, so you need to have EDLIN delete each occurrence of the phrase "and Sue" throughout the document.

```
*1,Rand Sue^Z
                5: weekend. I hope that you  will
   *
```

The letter is now ready for printing.

```
*L
                1: Dear Jim,
                2:
                3: I just wanted to let you know that
                4: our party is still on for this
                5: weekend.  I hope that you  will
                6: be able to make it.
                7:
                8: KAJ
   *
```

Using EDLIN again, create the following three files, A, B, and C:

```
A> EDLIN  B:A
New file
*I
                1:* AAAAA
                2:* AAAAA
                3:* ^C
   *E

A> EDLIN  B:B
New file
*I
                1:* BBBBB
                2:* BBBBB
                3:* ^C
   *E

A> EDLIN  B:C
New file
*I
                1:* CCCCC
                2:* CCCCC
                3:* CCCCC
```

```
*E

A>
```

Invoke EDLIN to create file D.

```
A> EDLIN  B:D
New file
*
```

Using the EDLIN Transfer command, T, read the contents of file A
into file D, as shown here:

```
A> EDLIN  B:D
New file
*TA
*L
                1:* AAAAA
                2: AAAAA
*
```

Repeat this process to transfer files B and C into file D.

```
A> EDLIN B:D
New file
*TA
*L
                1:* AAAAA
                2: AAAAA
*#
*TB
*#
*TC
*
```

Your file now contains

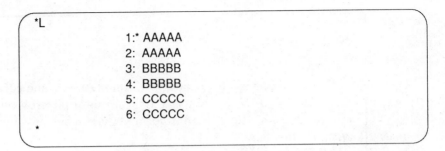

```
*L
            1:* AAAAA
            2: AAAAA
            3: BBBBB
            4: BBBBB
            5: CCCCC
            6: CCCCC
*
```

Using the EDLIN Transfer command to include other files within your document is that simple.

Eventually, most of you will end up with a word processor of some type. For those of you who do not yet have one, EDLIN can satisfy many of your text processing needs.

Summary

EDLIN allows you to do more than simply create and edit text files. Using EDLIN, you can search for words or phrases, replace one word or phrase with another, and even move or copy text within your file.

EDLIN uses the period (.) to represent the current line number. EDLIN also allows you to specify plus or minus offset values from the current line number in order to manipulate a range of text lines. EDLIN defines the pound sign (#) as the line immediately following your last line of text in a file.

The EDLIN Page command, P, is very similar to the List command, L, in that it allows you to display up to 23 lines of a file at one time. Unlike the List command, however, Page sets the current line number to the number of the last line displayed. By so doing, EDLIN makes paging through a file very easy.

If you edit a large file, EDLIN may not be able to load the entire file into memory. When this occurs, you must edit the portion of the document that is present in memory, use the EDLIN Write command, W, to save that portion of the file to disk, and then load the next portion of your file with the EDLIN Append command, A.

When you are editing, it is not uncommon to include the contents of a second file with your current file. The EDLIN Transfer command, T, allows you to include the file that you specify at either the current line number or the line number that precedes the Transfer command.

In many cases you may need to restructure reports or documents by moving paragraphs or sentences from one location to another. The EDLIN Move command, M, simplifies this process.

You may frequently need to duplicate text within your documents. The EDLIN Copy command, C, allows you to copy a line or range of lines within your file.

As your files grow in length, you may spend considerable time looking for a specific word or phrase in your document. The EDLIN Search command, S, provides you with a convenient way to look for specific text within your file.

Summary (continued)

The EDLIN Replace command, R, allows you to replace a word or phrase in your document with a second word or phrase. If you omit replacement text, the Replace command will delete each occurrence of the specified text.

EDLIN lacks the flair of a word processing system, but it does provide you with most of the capabilities you need to produce simple reports, letters, and memos.

15 *Understanding DOS Device Names*

In earlier chapters you have used the following names that DOS assigns to devices:

Name	Device
CON	Keyboard or screen display
COM1	First serial port on your computer
LPT1	First parallel port on your computer
PRN	Also the first parallel port on your computer

This chapter will give you more details on each of these devices, along with a few others. Also, you will examine the DOS MODE command, which allows you to specify the characteristics of many of these devices.

CON: The DOS Keyboard or Screen Display

Prior to Chapter 14, which focused on EDLIN, you created DOS text files by copying files from your keyboard.

```
A> COPY CON NUMBERS.DAT
1
22
333
4444
```

```
55555
666666
7777777
88888888
999999999
^Z
                    1 File(s) copied

A>
```

In Chapter 9 you learned that DOS uses the device name CON to refer to your keyboard or to your screen display.

When you use the CON device name in a command, DOS asks itself the question, "Is CON the source or target destination for the command?" If CON is the source for the command, as indicated in the command

```
A> COPY  CON  FILENAME.EXT
```

DOS assigns CON to point to your keyboard device, as shown here:

A> COPY CON FILENAME.EXT

If CON is the target destination for the command as indicated in the command

```
A> COPY  FILENAME.EXT  CON
```

DOS assigns CON to point to your screen display.

A> COPY FILENAME.EXT CON

In other words, when you use CON for input, CON points to your keyboard device. When you use CON for output, CON points to your screen display.

COMn *and* LPTn

In Chapter 11 you learned that your printer is either a parallel or a serial device. A parallel device can send one character of information at a time, as shown in Figure 15-1. A serial device, on the other hand, sends one bit of information over a single wire, as shown in Figure 15-2. As a result, a parallel device is much faster than a serial device.

Most computers come with at least one parallel and one serial connection. These are called *ports* and are shown in Figure 15-3.

The name of the DOS serial port is COM1, because most data communications modems allow two computers to exchange information serially. The DOS parallel port is called LPT1 because this port is normally used for line printers.

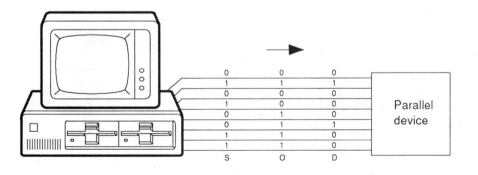

Figure 15-1. *Parallel data commuication*

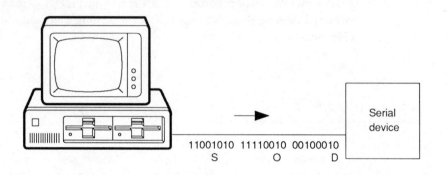

Figure 15-2.   *Serial data communication*

You are not restricted to just one serial or parallel port on your system. DOS version 3.3 fully supports the following device names: COM1, COM2, COM3, COM4, LPT1, LPT2, and LPT3.

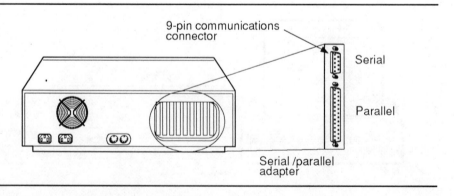

Figure 15-3.   *Serial and parallel ports*

What Are PRN and AUX?

In most cases you will connect your parallel printer to the first parallel port, LPT1. DOS makes this port the default printing port and assigns it the name PRN. When the DOS PRINT command prompts

```
A> PRINT
Name of list device [PRN]:
```

PRINT is telling you that if you press ENTER, PRINT is going to use the PRN device as the destination for all of your printed output. Because PRN points to your first parallel device, this default setting is normally correct.

DOS assigns the device name AUX to your first serial device, COM1. You can use this name for any command for which you previously used COM1.

How Can You Reference Devices?

You just saw that you can copy files from your keyboard by using the CON device in this way.

```
A> COPY  CON  NUMBERS.DAT
1
22
333
4444
55555
666666
7777777
88888888
999999999
^Z
              1 File(s) copied
```

You can also use the CON device to copy files to your screen display, as shown here:

```
A> COPY NUMBERS.DAT CON
1
22
333
4444
55555
666666
7777777
88888888
999999999

A>
```

In a similar manner, DOS allows you to copy files to COM*n* and LPT*n*, where *n* is the number attached to your printer's device name. If you have a parallel printer, use this COPY command.

```
A> COPY FILENAME.EXT LPT1:
```

If you have a serial printer, use this COPY command.

```
A> COPY FILENAME.EXT COM1:
```

Admittedly, you *could* copy all of your files to your printer, thus bypassing the DOS PRINT command. However, if you do this, two problems arise. First, the PRINT command automatically starts each new file on its own page. If you copy files to the device instead, all your files will run together on the printed output. Second, and more importantly, PRINT is a background command that allows you to work on other tasks while your files are printing. If you copy files to your printer, you must wait for the entire document to print before you can continue.

It is useful to know that the ability to copy files to devices exists; however, it is more efficient and convenient to use the DOS PRINT command.

Using MODE to Specify Device Characteristics

With your DOS Program disk in drive A, issue the command

```
A> DIR  MODE.COM

Volume in drive A is MS330PP01
Directory of  A:\

MODE          COM     15440     7-24-87   12:00a
              1 File(s)  5120 bytes free
```

MODE is an external DOS command that allows you to change the attributes of your screen display, printer, and serial communications ports (COM1 through COM4).

Video Display

Just as there are several types of computers—PC, PC XT, PC AT, and so on—there are several video display types, as shown in Table 15-1.

Software developers must ensure that their programs will execute successfully on each of these display types. Some programmers, therefore, will attach two monitors to their system. The first is a monochrome (noncolor) display, while the second is color. Figure 15-4 shows this type of system.

Monitor Type	Name	Function
Monochrome	MONO or MDA	Text only in green or amber
Color graphics	CGA	Text and graphics in up to 16 colors
Enhanced graphics	EGA	Text and graphics in up to 64 colors
Video graphics array	VGA	Text and graphics in up to 256 colors

Table 15-1.   *Types of Monitors*

When DOS starts, it uses the monochrome monitor. When you are ready to use the color display, issue the DOS MODE command. In its simplest form, the format of the MODE command is

MODE *n*

where *n* specifies one of the following display attributes:

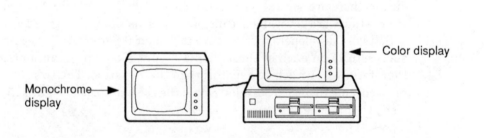

Figure 15-4.   *Two-monitor system*

n	Effect
MONO	Selects the monochrome display system when two display screens are attached to your system
40	Selects 40-column mode for your color display
80	Selects 80-column mode for your color display
BW40	Selects 40-column mode for your color display with color disabled
BW80	Selects 80-column mode for your color display with color disabled
CO40	Selects 40-column mode for your color display with color enabled
CO80	Selects 80-column mode for your color display with color disabled

For example, if you have a color display, the command

```
A> MODE  40
```

sets your display to 40-column mode, doubling your character size, as shown here:

```
A>
```

To restore the screen to 80 columns, use MODE as shown here:

```
A> MODE  80
```

DOS will clear your screen display and reset your display to 80 columns per line.

In rare instances, some displays do not correctly align the rows and columns on your screen display. If this occurs, you can use the DOS MODE command to correct the misalignment. To move the characters left, invoke MODE as

```
A> MODE , L , T
```

To move the characters right, invoke the command

```
A> MODE , R , T
```

which results in this screen display:

```
012345678901234567890123456789012345678901234567890123456789012345678901234567890123456789
Do you see the leftmost 0 (Y/N)?
```

If you type **Y**, DOS will leave your display screen unchanged. If you type **N**, DOS will move your characters to the right one character location. Using MODE in this way is usually not required.

Customizing Your Printer

In addition to allowing you to customize your screen display, MODE lets you customize your printer output. You have already seen one example of MODE's printer manipulation capabilities with the command

```
A> MODE LPT1:=COM1:
```

which directs DOS to use your serial printer for printed output instead of the default parallel printer device LPT1. To customize your output, you can use MODE to specify the number of characters per line (80 or 132) and also the vertical spacing per inch (6 or 8). The format of the MODE command you invoke to do this is

```
MODE [ cpl ] , [ lpi ] , [ P ]
```

where *cpl* specifies your desired characters per line and *lpi* specifies the number of lines per inch. The qualifier P, if present, directs DOS to continually retry printer operations if a timeout error occurs. For example, the command

```
A> MODE LPT1: 132
```

directs DOS to send information to the printer based on 132 characters per line. This command selects 132 characters per line and 8 lines per inch.

```
A> MODE  LPT1: 132,8
```

By default, your printer uses 80 characters per line and 6 lines per inch.

Specifying Your Serial Port Attributes

Using MODE, you can specify your serial port communication characteristics. When you use your serial port to communicate with a device, your port and the device must agree on how fast they will communicate (known as the *baud rate*) and also the format in which information will be specified (either *parity, data bits,* or *stop bits*). The DOS MODE command allows you to specify these items for your serial port, as shown here:

MODE COM1: *baud* [, *parity* [, *data bits* [, *stop bits* [, P]]]]

As before, all of the items specified within brackets ([ ]) are optional. If you do not specify values for these optional parameters, DOS will use the default values, as defined here.

Parameter	Effect
Baud	Specifies the baud rate or speed at which your port will communicate. Valid speeds include 110, 150, 300, 600, 1200, 2400, 4800, 9600, and 19,200. MODE requires you to enter only the first two digits of your desired baud rate. The default baud rate is 2400.
Parity	Specifies the type of parity the devices will use. E is even parity, O is odd, and N is no parity. The default parity is E.
Data bits	Specifies the number of data bits in each transmission, either 7 or 8. The default value is 7.

Parameter	Effect
Stop bits	Specifies the number of stop bits in each transmission, either 1 or 2. The default for 110 baud is 2. For all other baud rates, the default is 1.
P	P if present directs DOS to continually retry printer operations if a timeout error occurs.

For example, this command sets your COM1 serial port to 4800 baud and even parity.

```
A> MODE  COM1: 4800 , E
```

Because MODE requires only the first two digits of the baud rate, this command is functionally identical.

```
A> MODE  COM1: 48 , E
```

Note that in both commands several of the command options were not specified. For the parameters not specified, MODE used its default values.

Unless you are using your serial port for a laser printer or modem, you probably will not have to worry about using the MODE command in this manner.

Hands-On Practice

With your DOS Program disk in drive A, issue the DIR command:

```
A> DIR  MODE.COM

Volume in drive A is MS330PP01
Directory of  A:\

MODE            COM     15440    7-24-87   12:00a
                1 File(s)  5120 bytes free
```

Remember that MODE is an external DOS command. At the DOS prompt, issue the following MODE command:

```
A> MODE 40
```

If you have a color monitor, DOS will respond by setting your screen to 40-column mode, as shown here:

```
A>
```

To restore your screen to 80-column mode, issue the command

```
A> MODE 80
```

DOS will clear your screen display and redisplay its prompt in the upper left corner of the screen in 80-column mode.

```
A>
```

If you are using a parallel printer, experiment with its capabilities by directing it to use 132 columns per line.

```
A> MODE LPT1: 132
```

Next, create this file so you will have a file to print.

```
A> COPY CON LETTERS.TST
AAAAAAAAAA
BBBBBBBBBBBBBBBBBBBBB
CCCCCCCCCCCCCCCCCCCCCCCCCCCCCCCCCC
DDDDDDDDDDDDDDDDDDDDDDDDDDDDDDDDDDDDDDDDDDDDDDDDD
DDD
^Z
          1 File(s) copied
```

Print the file.

```
A> PRINT LETTERS.TST
```

Compress your printer output to an even greater extent by specifying 8 lines per inch spacing, as shown here:

```
A> MODE LPT1: 132 , 8
```

Print the file again to compare your results. Compare the output of
80 characters per line.

```
AAAAAAAAAA
BBBBBBBBBBBBBBBBBBBBB
CCCCCCCCCCCCCCCCCCCCCCCCCCCCCCCCCCCC
DDDDDDDDDDDDDDDDDDDDDDDDDDDDDDDDDDDDDDDDDDDDDDDDDDDD
```

with 132 characters per line.

```
AAAAAAAAAA
BBBBBBBBBBBBBBBBBBBBB
CCCCCCCCCCCCCCCCCCCCCCCCCCCCCCCCCCCC
DDDDDDDDDDDDDDDDDDDDDDDDDDDDDDDDDDDDDDDDDDDDDDDDDDDD
```

Finally, compare both of the previous outputs with this one that has
132 characters per line and 8 lines per inch.

```
AAAAAAAAAA
BBBBBBBBBBBBBBBBBBBBB
CCCCCCCCCCCCCCCCCCCCCCCCCCCCCCCCCCCC
DDDDDDDDDDDDDDDDDDDDDDDDDDDDDDDDDDDDDDDDDDDDDDDDDDDD
```

To restore your printer to its original settings, issue the command

```
A> MODE LPT1: 80 , 6
```

Summary

DOS provides several unique names for hardware devices on your computer. The names DOS assigns are defined here:

Name	Device
CON	Keyboard or screen display
COM1 to COM4	Serial ports on your computer
LPT1 to LPT3	Parallel ports on your computer
PRN	First parallel port on your computer
AUX	First serial port on your computer

Under DOS version 3.3, your computer can have up to four serial ports. Because these ports are often used for data communications, DOS names them COM1 through COM4.

Your primary serial port is COM1. DOS provides a second name for this port, AUX, which is short for auxiliary.

Your computer can have up to three parallel ports. Because parallel ports are normally used for line printers, DOS names these three ports LPT1 through LPT3.

Most users attach their printer to their first parallel port, LPT1. DOS provides a second name for this port, PRN. In most cases, PRN will be your default printer device.

Just as you can copy files from you keyboard by using the CON device, DOS also allows you to copy files to your screen display by specifying CON as the output destination, as shown here:

```
A> COPY FILENAME.EXT CON
```

The DOS MODE command is an external command that allows you to set the attributes of your screen display, printer, and serial ports.

For your screen display, MODE allows you to select the number of columns per line and hence the character size. MODE also

Summary (continued)

helps you correct misalignment of rows and columns if your screen is displaying errors.

The following MODE command allows you to use your serial printer instead of your parallel device for output:

```
A> MODE  LPT1:=COM1:
```

If you are using a parallel printer, MODE allows you to specify the number of characters per line (80 or 132) and lines per inch (6 or 8) on the printed output.

Finally, devices that communicate serially must agree on their transmission or baud rate as well as the format of the data. If you are attaching a laser printer to your serial port or are using a serial modem, the DOS MODE command allows you to specify your serial port's data communication parameters.

Glossary

Ports are connections through which devices—or other computers—can be attached to your computer.

The *baud rate* is the speed at which data is communicated. *Parity* is the manner in which a computer checks communication between the computer and other devices or with another computer. *Data bits* are the number of bits involved in each transmission of information. *Stop bits* are the number of bits used to stop the transmission of information.

16 *Organizing Your Files*

All of the files that you have created so far have been on newly formatted disks. As your use of your computer increases, you will begin to create files with word processors, spreadsheets, and other countless applications. In this chapter you will learn how to best organize your files. Whether you are using a floppy- or fixed-disk-based system, the lessons you will learn in this chapter are critical to your success not only with DOS, but also with all the other applications that you will use in the future.

The Importance of File Organization

In Chapters 13 and 14 you learned how to create text files with EDLIN, the DOS line editor. Using EDLIN, you can track your weekly expenses, income, and important meetings, as shown here:

```
A> TYPE 01-01-89.MTG
09:30 Meet with finance to discuss merger
10:00 Call New York with sales results
11:00 Lunch with software developers
13:00 Call San Diego for cost seminar
14:00 Dinner reservations at Hugo's
15:00 Order pictures for Friday's meeting
```

```
A> TYPE  01-01-89.EXP
$10.00 Parking downtown
$45.00 Lunch at the Garden with software developers
$55.00 Dinner at Hugo's

A> TYPE  01-01-89.INC
Commission Sales From MicroDat $500.00
Bonus for Sales $100.00


A>
```

If you have an active schedule, you can quickly generate a long list of
files, such as these:

```
Volume in drive A is TEST
Directory of  A:\

.                   <DIR>          5-04-88   5:34p
..                  <DIR>          5-04-88   5:34p
01-01-89            EXP      3     5-04-88   5:35p
01-01-89            INC      3     5-04-88   5:35p
01-01-89            MTG      3     5-04-88   5:35p
01-08-89            EXP      3     5-04-88   5:35p
01-08-89            MTG      3     5-04-88   5:35p
01-08-89            INC      3     5-04-88   5:35p
01-15-89            EXP      3     5-04-88   5:35p
01-15-89            MTG      3     5-04-88   5:35p
01-15-89            INC      3     5-04-88   5:35p
01-22-89            EXP      3     5-04-88   5:35p
01-22-89            MTG      3     5-04-88   5:35p
01-22-89            INC      3     5-04-88   5:35p
            14 File(s)    292704 bytes free
```

Because you have used meaningful file names and file extensions,
you can easily identify the contents of each file. However, as the number of files in your directory increases, so too does the difficulty of
locating a specific file.

If you are using floppy disks, a second problem exists. By default,
DOS provides space for only 112 files on your floppy disk, regardless
of the size of each file. If you create 112 files that are each one byte
long, over 360,000 bytes remain available on disk.

```
110                 1    5-04-88   5:35p
111                 1    5-04-88   5:35p
112                 1    5-04-88   5:35p
          112 File(s)  360322 bytes free
```

DOS will still display the following message when you attempt to create the 113th file:

```
File creation error
```

Those of you using fixed disks are not free from this error. The only difference is that DOS allows you to place more files onto the fixed disk before the directory becomes full.

One solution to this problem (and one that is strongly recommended) is to logically separate your files onto multiple disks. Your set of files containing weekly expenses, income, and meetings can be put on three disks, as shown in Figure 16-1.

When you start creating files with EDLIN or a word processor, you might want separate disks for letters, memos, and reports. Not only

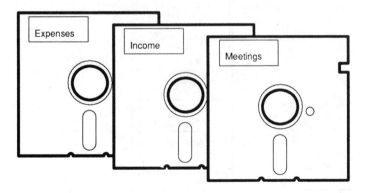

Figure 16-1.   *Files on separate disks*

does this allow you to fit all of your files on disk, but it also helps you keep your files organized.

Putting your files on separate disks does increase your file organization, but you are still left with the problem that DOS only allows a fixed number of files in each disk's directory. Also, those of you who purchased a fixed disk did so because you wanted to be able to place all of your files onto it. If you can't do so, the speed and storage capabilities that the fixed disk offers are wasted.

DOS does offer a way to increase file organization while supporting a virtually unlimited number of files on your disk by allowing you to create directories.

Before looking at how to use DOS directories, take a step back to determine what directories are. Compare your disk to a filing cabinet that might be in your office. Just as your filing cabinet exists to store information, so too does your disk.

If you were to file your sample set of files, you would want the drawers of your filing cabinet to be labeled "EXPENSES," "INCOME," and "MEETINGS." If you recorded an expense on paper, you would place it into the drawer labeled "EXPENSES" (as shown in Figure 16-2).

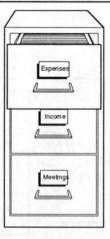

Figure 16-2.   *Placing EXPENSES files in filing cabinet*

DOS directories work in the same way by logically dividing up your disk so that you can separate your files on the disk, as illustrated here:

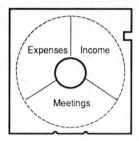

Remember that DOS keeps track of the files on your disk in a list, as shown here:

```
A> DIR

Volume in drive A has no label
Directory of  A:\

01-01-89        EXP    3     5-04-88    5:35p
01-01-89        INC    3     5-04-88    5:35p
01-01-89        MTG    3     5-04-88    5:35p
01-08-89        EXP    3     5-04-88    5:35p
01-08-89        MTG    3     5-04-88    5:35p
01-08-89        INC    3     5-04-88    5:35p
01-15-89        EXP    3     5-04-88    5:35p
01-15-89        MTG    3     5-04-88    5:35p
01-15-89        INC    3     5-04-88    5:35p
01-22-89        EXP    3     5-04-88    5:35p
01-22-89        MTG    3     5-04-88    5:35p
01-22-89        INC    3     5-04-88    5:35p
                12 File(s)    350208 bytes free
```

When you divide your disk into multiple storage locations, you are actually dividing your list into sublists, or directories.

Creating Directories with MKDIR

Just as you can add files to your filing cabinet, you can create directories by using the DOS MKDIR command (which stand for make directory). Begin by placing a newly formatted disk in drive A. Issue the DOS DIR command.

```
A> DIR

Volume in drive A has no label
Directory of  A:\

File not found

A>
```

There are no files on the disk. Now you want to create the following directories in order to increase your file organization:

Directory Name	Function
EXPENSES	Stores the files that contain your weekly expenses
INCOME	Stores the files that contain your weekly income
MEETINGS	Stores the files that contain your weekly appointments

To create these directories, you will use the DOS MKDIR command. First make the EXPENSES directory, as shown here:

```
A> MKDIR  EXPENSES
```

A directory listing of drive A now reveals

```
A> DIR

Volume in drive A has no label
Directory of  A:\

EXPENSES          <DIR>     5-04-88  6:10p
             1 File(s)  361472 bytes free
```

DOS has just created your first directory. Think of this process as similar to labeling the top drawer of your filing cabinet.

Again issue the MKDIR command, this time to create a directory called INCOME.

```
A> MKDIR  INCOME
```

The directory listing now displays

```
A> DIR

Volume in drive A has no label
Directory of  A:\

EXPENSES          <DIR>    5-04-88  6:10p
INCOME            <DIR>    5-04-88  6:11p
           2 File(s)   360448 bytes free
```

Because the MKDIR command is used so frequently, DOS allows you to use the abbreviation MD. Using this form of the command, create the third directory, MEETINGS.

```
A> MD  MEETINGS
```

The DOS DIR command now displays all three directories.

```
A> DIR

Volume in drive A has no label
Directory of  A:\

EXPENSES          <DIR>    5-04-88  6:10p
INCOME            <DIR>    5-04-88  6:11p
MEETINGS          <DIR>    5-04-88  6:11p
           3 File(s)   359424 bytes free
```

You now have three DOS directories into which you can place your files.

MKDIR

The DOS MKDIR command allows you to create subdirectories on your disk. Because you will use this command on a regular basis, DOS allows you to abbreviate this command as MD.

Selecting Directories with CHDIR

To use a specific DOS directory, you must use the DOS CHDIR command (which stands for change directory). CHDIR allows you to select a directory of files to work with, just as you would open a specific drawer in your filing cabinet. Use the CHDIR command now to select the EXPENSES directory.

```
A> CHDIR  EXPENSES
A>
```

As you can see, DOS simply redisplays its system prompt. To verify that you have actually selected the EXPENSES directory, issue the DOS DIR command.

```
A> DIR

Volume in drive A has no label
Directory of  A:\EXPENSES

 .                <DIR>     5-04-88   6:38p
 ..               <DIR>     5-04-88   6:38p
         2 File(s)   359424 bytes free
```

DOS predefines two subdirectories that exist in every directory you create and to which it assigns the period and double period. These subdirectories will be discussed in detail in Chapter 17.

Try using the DOS CHDIR command to select the directory named INCOME.

```
A> CHDIR  INCOME
Invalid directory

A>
```

Unless you tell DOS otherwise, it will search for the directory that you specify within the directory that you are currently using, called the current directory. In this example, the current directory is EX-PENSES. INCOME, however, is a directory that resides not within EXPENSES, but rather within the main DOS directory. You must specifically tell DOS that INCOME resides in the main directory when you issue the CHDIR command by typing a backslash (\) before typing **INCOME**, as shown here:

```
A> CHDIR  \INCOME
```

Every DOS disk has, by default, one directory built in. Throughout this text you have created your files in this main directory, called the root directory. When you are in this directory you will see only a backslash where the directory name should appear, as shown here:

```
A> DIR

Volume in drive A has no label
Directory of  A:\
```

CHDIR

The DOS CHDIR command allows you to select your current working directory. Because you will use this command on a regular basis, DOS allows you to abbreviate CHDIR as CD.

In order to access a file or directory that resides in the root directory, you must precede the name with a backslash, as shown here:

```
A> CHDIR \EXPENSES
A> CHDIR \INCOME
A> CHDIR \MEETINGS
```

Knowing this, you can quickly change from one DOS directory to
another. Start with the EXPENSES directory.

```
A> CHDIR \EXPENSES
A> DIR

Volume in drive A has no label
Directory of  A:\EXPENSES

    .              <DIR>     5-04-88   6:10p
    ..             <DIR>     5-04-88   6:10p
          2 File(s)   359424 bytes free

A>
```

The CHDIR command is used so frequently that DOS allows you
to use the abbreviation CD. Use this form of the command to select
the INCOME directory.

```
A> CD \INCOME
A> DIR

Volume in drive A has no label
Directory of  A:\INCOME

    .              <DIR>     5-04-88   6:10p
    ..             <DIR>     5-04-88   6:10p
          2 File(s)   359424 bytes free

A>
```

Select the MEETINGS directory.

```
A> CD \MEETINGS
A> DIR

Volume in drive A has no label
Directory of  A:\MEETINGS

.                      <DIR>     5-04-88   6:10p
..                     <DIR>     5-04-88   6:10p
             2 File(s)  359424 bytes free

A>
```

Using only the backslash, select the root as your current directory:

```
A> CD \
A> DIR

Volume in drive A has no label
Directory of  A:\

EXPENSES               <DIR>     5-04-88   6:10p
INCOME                 <DIR>     5-04-88   6:11p
MEETINGS               <DIR>     5-04-88   6:11p
             3 File(s)  359424 bytes free

A>
```

Selecting your DOS directories is that easy!
    Select MEETINGS as your current directory, and create this file:

```
A> CD \MEETINGS
A> COPY CON 01-01-88.MTG
10:00 Call for lunch reservation
12:00 Lunch at Huey's
14:00 Basketball at the University
^Z
             1 File(s) Copied
A>
```

A directory listing of MEETINGS now displays

```
A> DIR

Volume in drive A has no label
Directory of  A:\MEETINGS

.                        <DIR>     5-04-88   6:11p
..                       <DIR>     5-04-88   6:11p
01-01-88            MTG       54   5-04-88   6:20p
                 3 File(s)  358400 bytes free
```

Do the same for EXPENSES. A directory listing of EXPENSES now
displays

```
A> DIR

Volume in drive A has no label
Directory of  A:\EXPENSES

.                        <DIR>     5-04-88   6:11p
..                       <DIR>     5-04-88   6:11p
01-01-88            EXP       54   5-04-88   6:20p
                 3 File(s)  358400 bytes free
```

Select the root directory as your current working directory.

```
A> CD \
```

A directory listing of your files reveals

```
A> DIR

Volume in drive A has no label
Directory of  A:\

EXPENSES             <DIR>     5-04-88   6:10p
INCOME               <DIR>     5-04-88   6:11p
MEETINGS             <DIR>     5-04-88   6:11p
                 3 File(s)  358400 bytes free

A>
```

The files that you created are in the MEETINGS and EXPENSES directories and are therefore not included in this display of the root directory. Directory listings are thus kept free of clutter, and it is much easier for you to locate a specific file.

Removing Directories with RMDIR

The DOS RMDIR command allows you to remove a directory. For example, consider this directory listing:

```
A> DIR

Volume in drive A has no label
Directory of  A:\

EXPENSES          <DIR>     5-04-88   6:10p
INCOME            <DIR>     5-04-88   6:11p
MEETINGS          <DIR>     5-04-88   6:11p
          3 File(s)   358400 bytes free

A>
```

The following command fails:

```
A> DEL  EXPENSES.DIR
```

This error message is displayed:

```
File not found
```

This error occurs because DOS treats subdirectories differently from files; the DEL command that you use to delete files does not work for directories. If you want to remove a directory, you must use the DOS RMDIR command. Invoke this command to remove the INCOME directory. Because INCOME resides in the root directory, you must precede the name with the backslash (\).

RMDIR

The DOS RMDIR command allows you to remove a DOS subdirectory from your disk. Because you will use this command on a regular basis, DOS allows you to abbreviate RMDIR as RD.

```
A> RMDIR \INCOME
```

A directory listing of your root directory now displays

```
A> DIR

Volume in drive A has no label
Directory of  A:\

EXPENSES          <DIR>     5-04-88   6:10p
MEETINGS          <DIR>     5-04-88   6:11p
           2 File(s)   359424 bytes free
```

As you can see, DOS has removed the INCOME directory as desired.

DOS allows you to use the abbreviation RD for the frequently used RMDIR command. Remove the INCOME directory by using this abbreviation.

```
A> RD \EXPENSES
Invalid path, not directory,
or directory not empty

A>
```

As you can see, DOS does not allow you to remove a directory that contains files. You must delete all of the files in the directory before you can remove the directory.

Creating Subdirectories

Earlier in this chapter you created several directories within your root directory. Picture these directories appearing as follows:

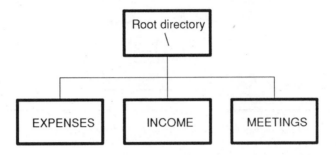

To increase your file organization to an even greater extent, DOS allows you to create subdirectories within your directory. For example, you might want to separate the meetings in your MEETINGS directory by month, as shown here:

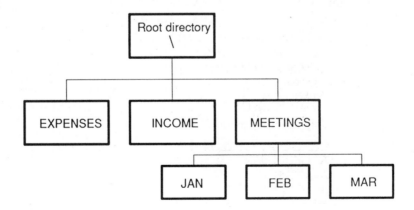

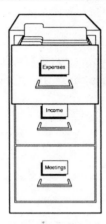

Figure 16-3. *Placing several files in drawer of filing cabinet*

This is similar to placing several files into one drawer of your filing cabinet in order to improve your file organization, as in Figure 16-3.

You create these subdirectories using MKDIR and specifying the name of the new subdirectory in one of two ways. First, if you are not in the MEETINGS directory (the working directory of the newly created subdirectories), you must specify the names of your subdirectories, starting with the name of the root directory, as follows:

```
A> MKDIR \MEETINGS\JAN
A> MKDIR \MEETINGS\FEB
A> MKDIR \MEETINGS\MAR
```

If the MEETINGS directory is also your current directory, you can simply specify the subdirectory name:

```
A> MKDIR JAN
A> MKDIR FEB
A> MKDIR MAR
```

When you examine a DOS subdirectory name, ask yourself the following question: "Does the directory name begin with a backslash (\)?" If so, as in the case of the directory name \MEETINGS\JAN, the directory name begins with the name of root directory. If not, as in the case of JAN, the new subdirectory is created in the working directory.

Given the directory structure,

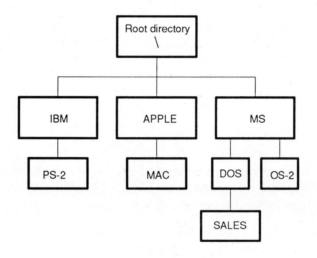

the following are valid DOS directory and subdirectory names:

    \
    \IBM
    \IBM\PS-2
    \APPLE
    \APPLE\MAC
    \MS
    \MS\DOS

\MS\OS-2
\MS\DOS\SALES

Rules for Naming Your
Directories and Subdirectories

DOS directories and subdirectories follow the same naming conventions as DOS files. The following characters are valid in both DOS directory and subdirectory names:

~ ! @ # $ % ^ & ( ) - _ { } '

The following rules will guide you as you create your DOS directories and subdirectories:

■ Unless you start the name at the root directory by placing a backslash (\) before the name, DOS will create the directory or subdirectory within the current directory.

■ Including a disk drive specifier allows you to create a directory on a disk other than the current default disk, as shown here:

```
A> MKDIR B:\TEST
```

■ Do not create a DOS directory or subdirectory with the same name as a file that will reside in that directory.

■ Do not create a directory called \DEV. DOS uses a hidden internal directory called \DEV to perform input and output operations to such devices as your printer.

■ The longest directory or subdirectory name that DOS will support is 63 characters.

■ The maximum number of files that you can place on your disk when you do *not* use subdirectories is shown in Table 16-1.

Disk Space	Maximum Number of Subdirectories in the Root Directory
160K	64
180K	
320K	112
360K	
1.2MB	224
Fixed disk	Based on partition size

Table 16-1. *Subdirectories Supported by Root Directory*

Displaying the Current Directory with CHDIR

The DOS CHDIR command (or its abbreviation, CD) allows you to change or display the current directory name. If you become uncertain about which directory you are using while working, invoke CHDIR at the DOS prompt without a directory name.

```
A> CHDIR
```

DOS will display the current directory name on your screen, as shown here:

```
A> CHDIR
A:\
A>
```

If you want to know the current directory for the disk in drive B, for example, use this CD command.

```
CD B:
B:\EXPENSES
A>
```

Why Can My Disk Store More Files Now?

You know that DOS restricts your disk to a specific number of files. In the case of floppy disks, for example, the number of files is restricted to 112. Actually, DOS restricts your *root directory* to a limited number of files. If you create a directory under the root directory, DOS will allow you to place virtually unlimited files in that directory. The reason for this is beyond the scope of this book. The point to remember now is that the root directory can contain a limited number of files. If you are going to place a large number of files on disk, you must use DOS directories.

How Many Default Directories Are There?

So far you have actually worked only with directories that reside on one disk. The current directory (the one that you have most recently selected with CHDIR) is also known as your default directory. This directory is so named because, by default, it is the directory that DOS searches for your files and commands, unless you tell it otherwise. Most people have no problem understanding how DOS uses the current directory once they begin to issue commands or access files that reside within directories.

The point you must remember is that DOS keeps track of a current directory for each disk on your system. Therefore, if you have a two-floppy-drive system, you have a default directory for drive A and a default directory for drive B. So far you have used only the root directory as the default for each. There is no reason, however, that you couldn't be working in the root directory of your DOS Program disk in drive A, while the current directory in drive B is EXPENSES. Here is how this is done:

```
A> CHDIR
A:\
A> CHDIR  B:
B:\EXPENSES
A>
```

Don't panic if you find this introduction to directories confusing. Directories are a powerful and complex subject. That's why there are three chapters dealing with them. By the end of Chapter 18, this will all be old hat!

Hands-On Practice

Place a newly formatted disk in drive A. With the DOS directory command, identify the fact that you are listing the files contained in the disk's root directory.

```
A> DIR

Volume in drive A has no label
Directory of  A:\

File not found

A>
```

Next, use the DOS MKDIR command to create the subdirectory ONE, as shown here:

```
A> MKDIR  ONE
```

Another listing of the files on drive A displays

```
A> DIR

Volume in drive A has no label
Directory of  A:\

ONE                 <DIR>    5-04-88   6:38p
                1 File(s)  361472 bytes free
```

Now create the directories TWO and THREE, remembering that
DOS allows you to abbreviate MKDIR as MD.

```
A> MKDIR  TWO
A> MD  THREE
```

Your disk now contains

```
A> DIR

Volume in drive A has no label
Directory of  A:\

ONE                 <DIR>    5-04-88   6:38p
TWO                 <DIR>    5-04-88   6:38p
THREE               <DIR>    5-04-88   6:38p
                3 File(s)  359424 bytes free
```

Using the DOS CHDIR command, display your current directory.

```
A> CHDIR
A:\
A>
```

Use CHDIR to select the ONE directory as your default directory.

```
A> CHDIR  ONE
```

Verify that ONE is now your current directory with either the DIR
or CHDIR command.

```
A> CHDIR
A:\ONE
A>
```

Next, issue the command

```
A> CHDIR  TWO
Invalid directory
A>
```

Why did this command fail? Remember, if you do not precede your directory name with a backslash (\), DOS will look for the directory in the current directory. Because the TWO directory resides in your root directory, not the ONE directory, you must use the backslash when selecting it, as shown here:

```
A> CHDIR  \TWO
```

A directory listing of your disk now reveals the contents of TWO—the two subdirectories automatically created with every new directory.

```
A> DIR

Volume in drive A has no label
Directory of  A:\TWO

   .                  <DIR>     5-04-88  6:38p
   ..                 <DIR>     5-04-88  6:38p
           2 File(s)  359424 bytes free
```

Using the abbreviated form of the CHDIR command, and remembering that the THREE subdirectory resides in your root directory, select THREE as your default directory:

```
A> CD  \THREE
```

Next, create a file named 3.3 in this directory.

```
A> COPY  CON  3.3
3
33
333
^Z
                    1 File(s) copied

A>
```

A directory listing of your disk now displays

```
A> DIR

Volume in drive A has no label
Directory of  A:\THREE

.                   <DIR>    5-04-88  6:38p
..                  <DIR>    5-04-88  6:38p
3           3         12     5-04-88  6:41p
              3 File(s)  358400 bytes free
```

Using CHDIR, select the root directory as your current directory.

```
A> CHDIR  \
```

Use the DOS DIR command to list the files in this directory.

```
A> DIR

Volume in drive A has no label
Directory of  A:\

ONE                 <DIR>    5-04-88  6:38p
TWO                 <DIR>    5-04-88  6:38p
THREE               <DIR>    5-04-88  6:38p
              3 File(s)  358400 bytes free
```

Note that the 3.3 file does not appear. When DOS lists the files in a directory, it only displays the files contained in that specific directory.

The 3.3 file resides in THREE, not in the root directory. In this way, DOS removes much of the clutter from your directory listings.

Using the DOS RMDIR command, remove the ONE directory.

```
A> RMDIR \ONE
```

In the same manner, remove the THREE directory.

```
A> RMDIR \THREE
Invalid path, not directory,
or directory not empty

A>
```

DOS does not allow you to remove this directory because it contains files. Use the DEL command to delete the files, but keep this directory—you will be using it later.

Using CHDIR, select the TWO as the current directory.

```
A> CHDIR \TWO
```

Next, use RMDIR to remove this directory.

```
A> CHDIR \TWO
A> RMDIR \TWO
Invalid path, not directory,
or directory not empty

A>
```

As you can see, DOS also does not allow you to delete the current directory. To remove the TWO directory, select THREE as the current directory.

```
A> CHDIR \THREE
```

When you issue the RMDIR command

```
A> RMDIR \TWO
```

the directory is removed. You can confirm this by listing your root
directory with the DOS DIR command.

Summary

As the use of your computer grows, so too will the number of files that you have on disk. If you are using floppy disks, one solution to the problem of file management is to logically separate your files onto several floppy disks. As a result, when you must locate a specific file, your search is significantly reduced.

By default, DOS restricts the number of files that can be placed in your root directory. If you are going to place a large number of files on your disk, you must create DOS directories under the root directory.

Just as you can organize files within a filing cabinet by grouping them in a logical manner, DOS allows you to organize the files on your disk. To do so, you simply divide your directory into several subdirectories. The DOS CHDIR, MKDIR, and RMDIR commands deal specifically with DOS directories.

The DOS MKDIR command allows you to create a DOS directory. Because of its frequent use, this command can be abbreviated as MD.

The DOS CHDIR command (abbreviated as CD) allows you to select your current directory. DOS defines the current directory as the directory that you have most recently selected with the DOS CHDIR command. By default, and unless told to do otherwise, DOS always looks in your current directory for files and commands. Therefore, the current directory is also referred to as the default directory. Each of your disks has a current directory that DOS keeps track of.

The DOS RMDIR command (abbreviated as RD) allows you to remove a directory when it is no longer needed. Before removing a directory, you must ensure that it contains no files and is not the current directory.

Glossary

DOS maintains a list of all of the files on your disk. This list is a *directory*. Each time you issue the DOS DIR command, DOS displays the files in your directory.

DOS defines the *current directory* as the directory that you have most recently selected with the DOS CHDIR command. By default, and unless told to do otherwise, DOS always looks in your current directory for files and commands. Therefore, your current directory is also referred to as your *default directory*.

Each time your system starts, DOS places you into the *root directory*. This directory is so named because all of your other directories actually grow out of it. DOS represents the root directory with the backslash (\).

17 *Using DOS Directories*

In Chapter 16 you learned how to organize your files by creating DOS directories. In this chapter you will learn how to manipulate files that are contained in directories, execute external commands that reside in directories, and list all of the files on your disk.

Standard File Operations

In Chapters 7 and 8 you learned how to display, copy, rename, and delete files from your disk by using the DOS TYPE, COPY, REN, and DEL commands. You can easily apply these commands to files that reside in DOS directories as well.

To get started, place a newly formatted disk in drive A and create the following directories:

```
A> MKDIR \FOOTBALL
A> MKDIR \BASEBALL
```

Using the DOS CHDIR command, select FOOTBALL as your current directory.

```
A> CHDIR \FOOTBALL
```

Next, create the TEAM.DAT file, as shown here:

```
A> COPY  CON  TEAMS.DAT
Seahawks
Raiders
Broncos
Bears
Browns
Bills
^Z
                1 File(s) copied

A>
```

Use the DOS TYPE command to display this file's contents.

```
A> TYPE  TEAMS.DAT
Seahawks
Raiders
Broncos
Bears
Browns
Bills

A>
```

The DOS TYPE command works here because the TEAMS.DAT file resides in the current directory.

Using the CHDIR command, select the root directory as your current directory.

```
A> CHDIR  \
```

A listing of that directory displays

```
A> DIR

Volume in drive A has no label
Directory of  A:\
```

```
FOOTBALL          <DIR>    5-05-88  9:06a
BASEBALL          <DIR>    5-05-88  9:06a
              2 File(s)  359424 bytes free
```

Use DIR to list the files contained in the FOOTBALL directory.

```
A> DIR \FOOTBALL

Volume in drive A has no label
Directory of  A:\FOOTBALL

.                    <DIR>    5-05-88  9:06a
..                   <DIR>    5-05-88  9:06a
TEAMS        DAT   102    5-05-88  9:06a
              3 File(s)  359424 bytes free
```

As you can see, when you specify a directory name in the DOS DIR
command, DOS displays the files residing in that directory. Using
this technique, list the files contained in the BASEBALL directory.

```
A> DIR \BASEBALL

Volume in drive A has no label
Directory of  A:\BASEBALL

.                    <DIR>    5-05-88  9:06a
..                   <DIR>    5-05-88  9:06a
              2 File(s)  359424 bytes free
```

You have not placed any files into that directory yet; the only files
displayed are those designated with a period and double period, which
DOS automatically includes in every directory you create.

   Return now to the FOOTBALL directory, this time using the DOS
wildcard characters in the DIR command to display the files in the
directory.

```
A> DIR \FOOTBALL\*.*
```

DOS will display

```
A> DIR \FOOTBALL\*.*

Volume in drive A has no label
Directory of A:\FOOTBALL

.                    <DIR>     5-05-88   9:06a
..                   <DIR>     5-05-88   9:06a
TEAMS        DAT       102 5-05-88   9:06a
             3 File(s)  359424 bytes free
```

If you are interested in one specific file, simply precede the file name desired with the directory name, as shown here:

```
A> DIR \FOOTBALL\TEAMS.DAT
```

DOS will display

```
A> DIR \FOOTBALL\TEAMS.DAT

Volume in drive A has no label
Directory of A:\FOOTBALL

TEAMS        DAT   102 5-05-88   9:06a
             1 File(s)  359424 bytes free
```

When you place a directory name in front of a file name in this manner, you create a path name. A path name is simply the path of directories that DOS must follow to locate a command or file. For example, given the path name

    \FOOTBALL\TEAMS.DAT

DOS must start at the root directory (\), locate the FOOTBALL directory, and within that directory find the TEAMS.DAT file. Even a complex path name such as

    \FOOTBALL\COACHES\WINNING\WEST\KNOX.SEA

is nothing more than a list of directories that DOS will go through to locate a file or command.

Given the directory structure shown here, for example,

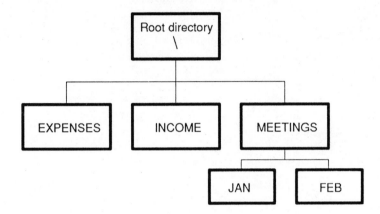

the following DOS path names are valid:

```
\
\EXPENSES
\INCOME
\MEETINGS
\MEETINGS\JAN
\MEETINGS\FEB
```

Don't be intimidated by DOS path names. Think of them as road maps to your files and commands.

Path Names

If you place a DOS directory name in front of a DOS file name, you create a DOS path name. In general, a DOS path name is a list of directories that DOS must go through to locate a file or command.

Using your knowledge of path names, invoke the DOS TYPE command to display the contents of the TEAMS.DAT file.

```
A> TYPE \FOOTBALL\TEAMS.DAT
```

DOS will display

```
A> TYPE \FOOTBALL\TEAMS.DAT
Seahawks
Raiders
Broncos
Bears
Browns
Bills

A>
```

Working with files in your subdirectories is that easy!

You also use path names to copy files from your keyboard. For example, to copy the contents of the PLAYERS.DAT file into the BASEBALL, invoke this command and enter the information that is shown here:

```
A> COPY CON \BASEBALL\PLAYERS.DAT
MAYS
SEAVER
BLUE
BRETT
JACKSON
DAVIS
RIPKEN
^Z
                    1 File(s) copied

A>
```

Your command line in this example is actually quite straightforward: COPY is the DOS command that you are executing; CON (the keyboard) is the source of the information; and the DOS path name

\BASEBALL\PLAYERS.DAT tells DOS the name of the file into which to copy the information.

A directory listing of the BASEBALL directory now reveals

```
A> DIR \BASEBALL

Volume in drive A has no label
Directory of  A:\BASEBALL

.                    <DIR>    5-05-88  9:06a
..                   <DIR>    5-05-88  9:06a
PLAYERS      DAT       51     5-05-88  9:16a
             3 File(s)   358400 bytes free
```

You can use the DOS TYPE command to display the contents of the PLAYERS.DAT file.

```
A> TYPE \BASEBALL\PLAYERS.DAT
MAYS
SEAVER
BLUE
BRETT
JACKSON
DAVIS
RIPKEN

A>
```

So that you have a third file to manipulate, create the NOTES.DAT file in the FOOTBALL directory, as shown here:

```
A> COPY  CON  \FOOTBALL\NOTES.DAT
A touchdown is worth 6 points
An extra point is worth 1 point
A field goal is worth 3 points
Baseball uses 9 players at a time
Each team gets three outs per inning
^Z
             1 File(s) copied
```

A directory listing of FOOTBALL now displays

```
A> DIR \FOOTBALL

Volume in drive A has no label
Directory of  A:\FOOTBALL

.                  <DIR>     5-05-88  9:06a
..                 <DIR>     5-05-88  9:06a
TEAMS       DAT      102 5-05-88  9:06a
NOTES       DAT      170 5-05-88  9:19a
                 4 File(s)  357376 bytes free
```

Next, use this DOS COPY command to copy the NOTES.DAT file
from the FOOTBALL subdirectory to BASEBALL.

```
A> COPY \FOOTBALL\NOTES.DAT  \BASEBALL\NOTES.DAT
```

In Chapters 7 and 8 of this book, you learned that if you do not specify
a target file name when you are copying files between two disk drives,
as shown here,

```
A> COPY  FILENAME.EXT  B:
```

or if you use the DOS wildcard characters, as shown here,

```
A> COPY  FILENAME.EXT  B:*.*
```

DOS, by default, will use the source file name. This fact also holds
true for DOS directories. Therefore, these three commands function
identically:

```
A> COPY  \FOOTBALL\NOTES.DAT  \BASEBALL\NOTES.DAT
A> COPY  \FOOTBALL\NOTES.DAT  \BASEBALL\*.*
A> COPY  \FOOTBALL\NOTES.DAT  \BASEBALL
```

DOS thus allows you to save time and keystrokes when you enter
your commands.

Use the DOS COPY command now to copy the NOTES.DAT file to the BASEBALL directory. This time, however, change the file name to RULES.TXT, as shown here:

```
A> COPY \FOOTBALL\NOTES.DAT \BASEBALL\RULES.TXT
```

A listing of the BASEBALL subdirectory now displays

```
A> DIR \BASEBALL

Volume in drive A has no label
Directory of  A:\BASEBALL

.                  <DIR>     5-05-88   9:06a
..                 <DIR>     5-05-88   9:06a
PLAYERS     DAT      51    5-05-88   9:16a
NOTES       DAT      170   5-05-88      9:19a
RULES       TXT      170   5-05-88   9:19a
          5 File(s)   356352 bytes free
```

The DOS DEL command works in a manner similar to TYPE and COPY. To delete a file that resides in a DOS directory, you must specify a complete path name when you issue the command. For example, to delete the RULES.TXT file from the BASEBALL directory, issue this command:

```
A> DEL \BASEBALL\RULES.TXT
```

DOS will delete your file, as shown here:

```
A> DIR \BASEBALL

Volume in drive A has no label
Directory of  A:\BASEBALL

.                  <DIR>     5-05-88   9:06a
..                 <DIR>     5-05-88   9:06a
PLAYERS     DAT   51     5-05-88   9:16a
NOTES       DAT   170    5-05-88      9:09a
          4 File(s)   357376 bytes free
```

You can also delete files in two steps, first selecting the directory and then deleting the file, as shown here:

```
A> CHDIR \BASEBALL
A> DEL  RULES.TXT
```

However, since DOS allows you to accomplish this task in one command by specifying a complete path name, why issue two commands?

If you want to delete all of the files in a DOS directory, specify the subdirectory name followed by the DOS wildcard characters *.*, using this form of the Delete command:

```
A> DEL  \DIR_NAME\*.*
```

DOS will prompt you with

```
Are you sure (Y/N)?
```

before continuing.

If there is one command that you will have difficulty with when you are working with DOS directories, it will most likely be the RENAME command. If you specify a disk drive identifier in the target name of a file that you are renaming, as shown here,

```
A> REN  B:FILENAME.EXT B:NEWFILE.EXT
```

the command will fail and DOS will display

```
Invalid parameter
```

This occurs because RENAME does not move files, it renames them. The correct command is

```
A> REN  B:FILENAME.EXT NEWFILE.EXT
```

Because you have specified the disk drive identifier in the source file name, DOS knows the disk for the target file.

Renaming Files That Reside in DOS Directories

To rename a file that resides in a DOS directory, do not specify a directory name in your target file name. The DOS RENAME command only renames files—it does not move them. Therefore, you cannot rename a file from one DOS directory to another.

The RENAME command works the same way for DOS directories. If, for example, you want to rename the NOTES.DAT file that resides in the FOOTBALL directory to RULES.DAT, issue the command

```
A> REN \FOOTBALL\NOTES.DAT  RULES.DAT
```

DOS will rename the file, leaving it in the same directory. If you place a DOS backslash (\) path name in front of the RULES.DAT file, as shown here,

```
A> REN \FOOTBALL\NOTES.DAT  \FOOTBALL\RULES.DAT
```

the command fails and DOS displays

```
Invalid parameter
```

Given the directory structure

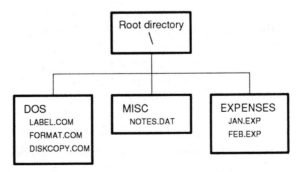

the following DOS commands are valid:

```
A> TYPE \MISC\NOTES.DAT
A> PRINT \EXPENSES\JAN.EXP
A> COPY \MISC\NOTES.DAT B:
A> COPY  CON \EXPENSES\MAR.EXP
```

What Are . and .. ?

Every DOS directory that you create contains two subdirectories, as shown here:

```
A> DIR

Volume in drive A is TEST
Directory of  A:\DIRECTORYNAME

.                  <DIR>     5-05-88   9:54a
..                 <DIR>     5-05-88   9:54a
         2 File(s)   19787776 bytes free
```

DOS defines the period and double period as follows:

.   An abbreviation for the current directory
..   An abbreviation for the directory immediately above
           the current directory

For example, if your current directory is FOOTBALL, DOS defines the period and double period as follows:

.   The FOOTBALL directory
..   The root directory, because it is immediately above
           FOOTBALL

If the FOOTBALL\SCORES subdirectory is the current directory, DOS will define the period and double period as follows:

    .   The FOOTBALL\SCORES subdirectory

    ..   The FOOTBALL directory, because it is the directory immediately above the current directory

You can verify these definitions by selecting the FOOTBALL directory as the current directory.

```
A> CHDIR \FOOTBALL
```

A listing of this directory displays

```
A> DIR

Volume in drive A has no label
Directory of  A:\FOOTBALL

.                   <DIR>     5-05-88   9:06a
..                  <DIR>     5-05-88   9:06a
TEAMS      DAT      102 5-05-88   9:06a
NOTES      DAT      170 5-05-88   9:19a
       4 File(s)  357376 bytes free
```

Now use the period to display the files in the current directory.

```
A> DIR .

Volume in drive A has no label
Directory of  A:\FOOTBALL

.                   <DIR>     5-05-88   9:06a
..                  <DIR>     5-05-88   9:06a
TEAMS      DAT      102 5-05-88   9:06a
NOTES      DAT      170 5-05-88   9:19a
       4 File(s)  357376 bytes free
```

Replacing the name of the current directory, FOOTBALL, with the period abbreviation for the current directory resulted in a functionally equivalent command.

Use the double period to display the files in the root directory (because the root is immediately above the FOOTBALL directory).

```
A> DIR ..

Volume in drive A has no label
Directory of  A:\

FOOTBALL          <DIR>     5-05-88   9:06a
BASEBALL          <DIR>     5-05-88   9:06a
             2 File(s)  357376 bytes free
```

Again using the double period, select the root directory as your current directory, and verify your selection by invoking DIR.

```
A> CD ..
A> DIR

Volume in drive A has no label
Directory of A:\

FOOTBALL          <DIR>     5-05-88   9:06a
BASEBALL          <DIR>     5-05-88   9:06a
             2 File(s)  357376 bytes free
```

Most users don't use these two abbreviations often. You should know what these abbreviations are, however, because they will appear in all your directories.

Examining Your Disk Structure

You have already seen that DOS directories allow you to organize your files by logically grouping them into specific locations. You have also seen that once you do so, DOS displays only the names of the files that reside in the current directory or the directory specified when you issue the DIR command. If your disk contains a large number of directories, it may seem that locating a specific file is harder now than it was when all of your files were stored in a single directory.

To solve this problem, DOS provides you with the TREE command, which displays the names of all of the directories on your disk and, optionally, the files that each directory contains. The name "TREE" is appropriate, because many people think of a directory structure as a tree that grows up from the root directory.

Assume, for example, that your disk in drive B contains this directory structure:

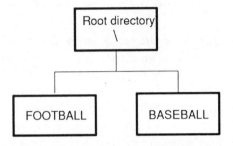

The command

```
A> TREE  B:
```

will display

```
A> TREE  B:

DIRECTORY PATH LISTING
Path: \FOOTBALL
Sub-directories:  None

Path: \BASEBALL
Sub-directories:  None

A>
```

To display the files that reside in each directory, add the /F qualifier.

```
A> TREE  B:  /F
```

TREE is an external DOS command, and it will become more useful as the structure of your directory increases in complexity.

Executing Commands That Reside in DOS Directories

Thus far all of the commands that you have entered at the DOS prompt have been either internal commands that reside in your computer's memory (such as CLS, TYPE, and DIR) or external commands whose files are in the current directory (such as DISKCOPY, LABEL, and FORMAT). Eventually, as your use of DOS directories increases, you will have to execute a command that resides in a directory other than the current default. To do so, simply precede the command name with a complete path name, as shown here:

```
A>  \SUBDIR\COMMAND
```

For example, if you are given the directory structure

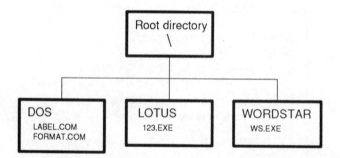

> ### Executing DOS Commands That Reside in Other Directories
>
> To execute a DOS command that resides in a directory other than the current default, use a complete path name for the command.
>
> A> \DIRECTORYNAME\COMMAND

the following DOS commands are valid:

```
A> \DOS\LABEL
A> \DOS\FORMAT A:
A> \LOTUS\123
A> \WORDSTAR\WS
```

Remember, a DOS path name is simply a list of directories that DOS must go through to locate a file or command. If your commands reside in a directory other than the current directory, simply tell DOS where a command resides by using a DOS path name.

Hands-On Practice

Place a newly formatted disk in drive A and then create the following directories:

```
A> MKDIR  ONE
A> MKDIR  TWO
A> MKDIR  DOS
```

A directory listing of your disk now displays

```
A> DIR

Volume in drive A has no label
Directory of  A:\

ONE              <DIR>     5-05-88   10:03a
TWO              <DIR>     5-05-88   10:04a
DOS              <DIR>     5-05-88   10:04a
         3 File(s)   359424 bytes free
```

Using the DOS COPY command, create the following files:

```
A> COPY  CON  \ONE\ONE.DAT
1
^Z
                 1 File(s) copied

A> COPY  CON  \TWO\TWO.DAT
2
22
^Z
                 1 File(s) copied

A> COPY  CON  \DOS\DOS.NTS
A DOS path name is simply a list of
directories DOS must traverse in order
to locate a file or command.
^Z
                 1 File(s) copied

A>
```

A directory listing of your root directory still displays

```
A> DIR

Volume in drive A has no label
Directory of A:\

ONE              <DIR>     5-05-88    10:03a
TWO              <DIR>     5-05-88    10:04a
DOS              <DIR>     5-05-88    10:04a
              3 File(s)  359424 bytes free
```

Use the DOS COPY command to copy the DOS.NTS file from your DOS directory into the ONE directory, as shown here:

```
A> COPY \DOS\DOS.NTS \ONE\DOS.NTS
              1 File(s) copied

A>
```

Remember that the following commands are functionally identical:

```
A> COPY \DOS\DOS.NTS \ONE\DOS.NTS
A> COPY \DOS\DOS.NTS \ONE\*.*
A> COPY \DOS\DOS.NTS \ONE
```

With this fact in mind, copy the DOS.NTS file into TWO directory.

```
A> COPY \DOS\DOS.NTS \TWO
```

Verify that your file copies occurred by listing the files in directory called ONE.

```
A> DIR \ONE

Volume in drive A has no label
Directory of  A:\ONE

.                    <DIR>     5-05-88   10:03a
..                   <DIR>     5-05-88   10:03a
ONE          DAT       3     5-05-88   10:04a
DOS          NTS      107   5-05-88   10:05a
             4 File(s)  354304 bytes free
```

Then display the contents of the TWO directory.

```
A> DIR \TWO

Volume in drive A has no label
Directory of  A:\TWO

.                    <DIR>
..                   <dir>
TWO          DAT       7     5-05-88   10:04a
DOS          NTS      107  5-05-88   10:05a
             4 File(s)  354304 bytes free
```

Using complete DOS path names, display the contents of the files
ONE.DAT and TWO.DAT as shown here:

```
A> TYPE \ONE\ONE.DAT
1

A> TYPE \TWO\TWO.DAT
2
22

A>
```

DOS path names tell DOS the list of subdirectories that it must go
through to locate a command or file. With this in mind, use the DOS
DEL command to delete the DOS.NTS file from the TWO directory.

```
A> DEL \TWO\DOS.NTS
```

A directory listing of TWO now displays

```
A> DIR \TWO

Volume in drive A has no label
Directory of  A:\TWO

.                    <DIR>
..                   <DIR>
TWO          DAT      7    5-05-88   10:04a
             3 File(s)  355328 bytes free
```

Use the DOS wildcard character to delete all of the files in the ONE
directory.

```
A> DEL \ONE\*.*
```

When DOS prompts

```
Are you sure (Y/N)?
```

type **N** to stop the file deletion.

```
DEL \ONE\*.*
Are you sure (Y/N)? N

A>
```

Use the RENAME command to change the name of the ONE.DAT
file to 1.DAT, as shown here:

```
A> RENAME \ONE\ONE.DAT 1.DAT
```

Listing the directory for ONE now displays

```
A> DIR \ONE

Volume in drive A has no label
Directory of  A:\ONE

.                <DIR>     5-05-88  10:03a
..               <DIR>     5-05-88  10:03a
1           DAT    3       5-05-88  10:04a
DOS         NTS    107 5-05-88  10:05a
            4 File(s)  355328 bytes free
```

Again using RENAME, change the name of the TWO.DAT file to
2.DAT by specifying a complete path name on the target file, as shown
here:

```
A> RENAME \TWO\TWO.DAT \TWO\2.DAT
```

This command will fail, however, and DOS will display

```
Invalid parameter
```

Remember, RENAME does not move files, it only renames them.
When using RENAME, therefore, you can only specify a file name as
the target, not a DOS path name.

Using the DOS CHDIR command, select the subdirectory ONE as
your current directory.

```
A> CHDIR \ONE
```

List all of the files in this directory by using the period.

```
A> DIR .

Volume in drive A has no label
Directory of  A:\ONE

.                   <DIR>     5-05-88   10:03a
..                  <DIR>     5-05-88   10:03a
1            DAT    3         5-05-88   10:04a
DOS          NTS    107 5-05-88   10:05a
             4 File(s)  355328 bytes free
```

Remember, DOS defines the period as the current directory and the double period as the directory immediately above the current directory. Use the double period now to display the contents of the root directory.

```
A> DIR ..

Volume in drive A has no label
Directory of  A:\

ONE                 <DIR>     5-05-88   10:03a
TWO                 <DIR>     5-05-88   10:04a
DOS                 <DIR>     5-05-88   10:04a
             3 File(s)  355328 bytes free
```

For those of you with two floppy disk drives, place your DOS Program disk in drive B and issue these commands:

```
A> COPY  B:TREE.COM  \TREE.COM
A> COPY  B:LABEL.COM  \DOS\LABEL.COM
```

Next, use CHDIR to select the root directory as the current directory.

```
A> CHDIR \
```

Issue the DOS TREE command to display your disk's directory structure.

```
A> TREE

DIRECTORY PATH LISTING
Path: \ONE
Sub-directories:  None

Path: \TWO
Sub-directories:  None

Path: \DOS
Sub-directories:  None
```

Remember, by adding the /F qualifier you can direct TREE to display all of the files contained in each directory of your disk, as shown here:

```
A> TREE  /F
```

For those who want to print out a listing of the tree structure, use the CTRL-PRINT SCREEN key combination.

Select the ONE subdirectory as your current directory.

```
A> CHDIR  \ONE
```

Again, issue the TREE command.

```
A> TREE
Bad command or file name

A>
```

The TREE.COM file resides in your root directory; therefore, you must tell DOS the complete path name to this command, as follows:

```
A> \TREE
```

Using the DOS LABEL command, label this disk TESTDISK. Remember that the LABEL command currently resides in the DOS directory.

```
A> \DOS\LABEL

Volume in drive A has no label

Volume label (11 characters, ENTER for none)? TESTDISK

A>
```

\DOS\LABEL is the complete path name for the LABEL command. As you can see, to execute DOS commands that reside in directories other than the current directory, you must precede the command name with a complete DOS path name.

Summary

When you place a directory name in front of a file name in a command, you create a path name, which is the path of directories that DOS must follow to locate a command or file.

The DOS commands DIR, TYPE, DEL, COPY, and RENAME fully support DOS path names. Given the directory structure shown here,

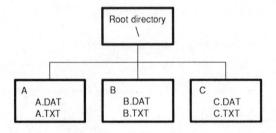

the following DOS commands are valid:

```
A> TYPE \A\A.DAT
A> DEL \A\A.TXT
A> PRINT \B\B.*
A> COPY \C\C.TXT B:
A> COPY \C\C.TXT \A\NEWFILE.TXT
```

Summary (continued)

It is not uncommon for DOS commands to reside in directories other than the current default. To execute DOS commands that reside in directories other than the current directory, you must precede the command name with a complete DOS path name. Given the directory structure shown here,

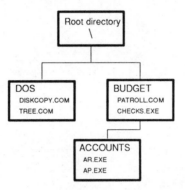

the following DOS commands are valid:

```
A> \DOS\DISKCOPY A: B:
A> \DOS\TREE /F
A> \BUDGET\PAYROLL
A> \BUDGET\CHECKS
A> \BUDGET\ACCOUNTS\AR
A> \BUDGET\ACCOUNTS\AP
```

To help you issue directory manipulation commands, DOS defines the period and double period as follows:

.	An abbreviation for the current directory
..	An abbreviation for the directory immediately above the current directory

The DOS TREE command is an external command that displays your directory structure and, optionally, all of the files that each directory contains.

Glossary

When you place a directory name in front of a file name, you create a *path name*, which is the path of directories that DOS must follow to locate a command or file.

18 *Placing DOS on Your Fixed Disk*

If you have not been using your fixed disk so far, this chapter will get you up and running with your fixed disk. If you have been using your fixed disk, this chapter will help ensure that your files are properly installed on your fixed disk to optimize your computer's performance. Even if you don't have a fixed disk, you will benefit from reading this chapter because fixed disks are used frequently, and you should have a working knowledge of how DOS treats them.

What Makes a Fixed Disk Different?

Fixed and floppy disks both exist for the same reason: to store programs and files. Unlike floppy disks, which are removable, fixed disks are built into the computer's chassis, as shown in Figure 18-1.

Floppy disks use a thin plastic disk for their recording media, but fixed disks use solid metal platters that are more precise and can therefore store more information than a floppy disk (see Table 18-1).

In addition to offering greater storage capacity, fixed disks are much faster than floppy disks for read and write operations.

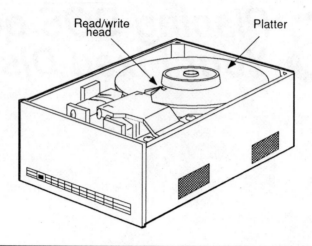

Figure 18-1. *Fixed disk*

To the end user, there is no difference in the way DOS treats files and directories in the fixed and floppy disk systems. If you have been working with DOS on floppy disks, your transition to a fixed disk will be easy.

Fixed Disk	Equivalent Number of Floppy Disks
10MB	29 double-sided, double-density, 360K floppies
10MB	9 quad-density, 1.2MB floppies
20MB	58 double-sided, double-density, 360K floppies
20MB	18 quad-density, 1.2MB floppies

Table 18-1. *Comparison of Fixed Disks and Floppy Disks*

How Much Preparation
Does a Fixed Disk Need?

Depending on your computer retailer, much of your fixed disk preparation may have already been done for you. For the benefit of those
users whose disks have not yet been prepared, this discussion will
start at square one.

With your DOS Program disk in drive A, issue the command

```
A> DIR  C:
```

As stated in Chapter 1, DOS assigns your fixed disk the drive letter
C. If DOS displays the message

```
A> DIR  C:
Invalid drive specification

A>
```

in response to your Directory command, DOS has never been told that
your fixed disk exists. You must execute the DOS FDISK command,
as explained in the Command Reference section (Part Four) of this
book. When you have completed the FDISK procedure, you can continue your disk preparation.

If DOS responds to your DIR command with

```
General Failure error reading drive C:
Abort, Retry, Fail?
```

DOS knows about your fixed disk, but your disk has never been formatted. You need to issue the following command:

```
A> FORMAT  C:/S
```

Remember, your goal is to build a bootable fixed disk. You must therefore include the /S qualifier on the FORMAT command so that DOS

will format your fixed disk in the same way that it formats your floppy disks.

DOS may respond to your Directory command by displaying files in the root directory on drive C. This indicates that someone has already formatted your fixed disk for you, but you need to verify that the disk is bootable.

Open the disk drive latch on drive A and press the CTRL-ALT-DEL key combination to restart DOS. If DOS is installed correctly on your fixed disk, your computer will boot using drive C. If DOS is not installed correctly, your computer will display the built-in BASIC program. If someone else has installed DOS on your fixed disk and your computer does not boot, tell them that you plan to reformat the disk to make it bootable. Ask them to verify that you can do this without losing critical files. If possible, have them perform the DOS installation with you.

For those of you who *do not have* DOS on your fixed disk *yet*, issue the command

```
A> FORMAT C:/S
```

When this command completes, use the DOS MKDIR command to create a directory called DOS on drive C.

```
A> MKDIR C:\DOS
```

Copy all the files from your DOS Program disk to this directory, as shown here:

```
A> COPY *.* C:\DOS
```

In order for DOS to boot, you must have the COMMAND.COM file in the root directory of drive C. Copy this file from your DOS Program disk to the root.

```
A> COPY COMMAND.COM C:\
```

Place your DOS Supplemental Programs disk in drive A, and copy the files that it contains to the DOS directory.

```
A> COPY *.* C:\DOS
```

Open the disk drive latch for drive A and press CTRL-ALT-DEL to re-start DOS. Your system should now boot from your fixed disk, displaying the DOS DATE and TIME commands and the C> prompt.

```
Current date is Fri 05-05-1988
Enter new date (mm-dd-yy):
Current time is 7:01:03:96
Enter new time:


Microsoft(R) MS-DOS(R) Version 3.30
                (C)Copyright Microsoft Corp 1981-1987
C>
```

From here on out you can use your fixed disk for all the commands that you will issue in the remainder of this text.

What Should Be in Drive C's Root Directory?

You have just created a directory called DOS on your fixed disk to store all your DOS commands. If you will be placing files onto your fixed disk for the first time by following the examples in this chapter, your disk will be properly configured. If your disk already had files on it, however, you may need to move several of them into DOS directories other than the root.

To find out what files are on your fixed disk, issue the following DIR command:

```
C> DIR \
```

If you have been using DOS directories correctly, you should have *at most* the following three files in drive C's root directory:

- AUTOEXEC.BAT
- CONFIG.SYS
- COMMAND.COM

Later chapters will examine the AUTOEXEC.BAT and CONFIG.SYS files in detail. If these files are not on your fixed disk, you will create them later. If you have more than these files in your root directory, it's time to create DOS directories to organize your files. Start with the DOS directory. Once you move files into the correct directories by using the COPY command, delete the files from the root.

How Do You Issue DOS Commands?

Now that all of your external DOS commands reside in the DOS directory, you simply specify a complete path name to execute a DOS command, as shown here:

```
C> \DOS\FORMAT A:
C> \DOS\DISKCOPY A: B:
```

This command processing is identical to that for the commands you issued in Chapter 17.

Why Does the Computer Always Look on Drive A First?

Each time your system boots, you see the disk activation light for drive A illuminate as your computer searches for DOS in drive A. Your computer searches drive A first for two reasons. First, not all computers have a fixed disk. To maintain a standard, drive A is always examined first. Second, and more importantly, if your fixed disk becomes damaged, you need a way to boot your computer. Since your computer always examines drive A first, you can always boot DOS with a floppy disk if the fixed disk is damaged.

Hands-On Practice

If someone has already installed DOS on your fixed disk for you, there is no way that you can tell how your fixed disk is configured. As long as your disk boots, just make sure that you have cleaned up your root directory by moving all of the files except AUTOEXEC.BAT, CON-FIG.SYS, and COMMAND.COM into DOS directories. To do this correctly may require the assistance of the individual who originally configured your disk.

For those of you with a new fixed disk, issue the command

```
A> DIR  C:
```

and note the response. If DOS displays the message

```
A> DIR  C:
Invalid drive specification

A>
```

you will need to turn to the FDISK command in the Command Reference section (Part Four) of this book. When the FDISK command completes, you are ready to continue the process of preparing your fixed disk for use.

If DOS responds to the DIR command with

```
General Failure error reading drive C
Abort, Retry, Fail?
```

you must issue the following FORMAT command:

```
A> FORMAT  C:  /S
```

When the FORMAT command completes, create the DOS directory
and copy the contents of your DOS Program disk to it.

```
A> MKDIR  C:\DOS
A> COPY  *.*  C:\DOS
```

Remember that the COMMAND.COM file must reside in the root
directory in order for your disk to be bootable, so copy it now.

```
A> COPY  COMMAND.COM  C:\
```

Insert your DOS Supplemental Programs disk in drive A and copy
all of the files it contains into your DOS subdirectory.

```
A> COPY  *.*  C:\DOS
```

Your fixed disk is now ready for use.
   To execute DOS external commands, use a complete path name.

```
C> \DOS\LABEL
```

Summary

Fixed disks can store more information and are faster than floppy disks. The end user, however, can recognize no difference in the way DOS treats fixed and floppy disks.

Depending on your computer retailer, much of your fixed disk preparation may have already been done for you. If your disk is brand new, you will have to follow these steps:

1. Issue the DOS FDISK command to inform DOS about the fixed disk.

2. Format your fixed disk with the FORMAT /S command to create a bootable disk.

3. Create the DOS directory on your fixed disk and copy the files on your DOS Program disk and Supplemental Programs disk to the DOS directory.

4. Copy the COMMAND.COM file from your DOS Program disk to the root directory of your fixed disk.

Regardless of how DOS was installed on your fixed disk, you must organize all your files into DOS directories. The only files that should reside in your root directory are AUTOEXEC.BAT, CONFIG.SYS, and COMMAND.COM. All other files should be in DOS subdirectories.

When you have placed your DOS external commands into the DOS directory, you can issue DOS commands by specifying a complete path name, as shown here:

```
C> \DOS\TREE
```

Even if your system has DOS installed on a fixed disk, your computer will first examine floppy disk drive A for DOS before booting DOS from your fixed disk. This means that if your fixed disk ever becomes damaged, you have a means of booting DOS by using your floppy disk.

19 Saving Keystrokes and Time with DOS

Throughout this text, each time you have issued a DOS command, you have had to wait for that command to complete before you could invoke a second command. In most cases the commands that you have been issuing complete fast enough to avoid your having to wait a considerable amount of time before issuing subsequent commands. As you will see, however, this is not always the case. In this chapter you will learn how to develop DOS batch files, which are text files that contain one or more DOS commands. Once you create a batch file, DOS can execute the commands that the file contains without your intervention, thus saving you time and keystrokes.

Getting Started with Batch Files

Having to wait for a command to complete before you can issue a subsequent command demands that you be in constant interaction with your computer to perform your processing. Processing of this type is called interactive processing, and it is the most common type of processing performed on computers today.

In many cases, however, your processing will not require constant interaction. For example, consider an application that calculates employee salaries, sorts the salaries by amount, and then prints employee paychecks. To perform this processing, you must issue three commands, which are contained in your general ledger software package:

Command	Function
PAYROLL.EXE	Calculates employee salaries
SORTPAY.EXE	Sorts salaries by amount
PRINTPAY.EXE	Prints employee paychecks

First, from the DOS prompt, issue the command

```
A> PAYROLL
```

When that command completes, issue the SORTPAY command, as shown here:

```
A> PAYROLL

A> SORTPAY
```

Once SORTPAY has sorted your salaries, invoke the PRINTPAY command to print employee paychecks, as shown here:

```
A> PAYROLL

A> SORTPAY

A> PRINTPAY
```

The PRINTPAY command will begin printing employee paychecks, and you are free to leave your computer in order to perform other tasks. However, because you performed all of these commands interactively, waiting for one command to complete before issuing another command, you had to stay at your computer until the checks began printing. Depending on the size of your company, you may have wasted considerable time doing nothing but waiting to issue the next command.

None of the commands in this example program required your presence at the computer either to answer questions or to change disks. Therefore, this application is an excellent candidate for batch processing, in which DOS allows you to group several commands into a file with the extension BAT (for batch). Once you do this you can later simply type in the name of the batch file at the DOS prompt, and DOS will begin executing the commands that the file contains without your intervention. This not only saves you keystrokes, but also can save you a tremendous amount of time, depending on your application. Figure 19-1 contrasts batch processing with interactive processing.

Use the previous example to create a batch file called DOPAY.BAT, which contains the batch file commands shown here:

```
A> COPY CON DOPAY.BAT
PAYROLL
SORTPAY
PRINTPAY
^Z
            1 File(s) copied

A>
```

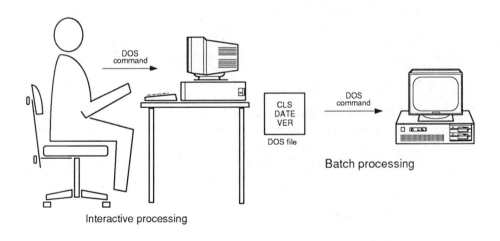

Figure 19-1. *Comparison of interactive and batch processing*

You can now simply type in the name of the batch file at the DOS prompt in order to execute all three commands.

```
A> DOPAY
```

Once DOS recognizes the fact that DOPAY is a batch file, it will begin executing all the commands that the file contains. By default, DOS will display the name of each command on your screen as it is executed.

```
A> DOPAY

A> PAYROLL

A> SORTPAY

A> PRINTPAY
```

By grouping these commands into a single BAT file, you have saved a significant amount of time that you would otherwise have spent waiting at the keyboard for one command to complete so that you could execute subsequent commands. You may have several commands that will always be executed sequentially. By placing these commands into a batch file, you ensure that they are always executed in the correct order while also reducing your typing.

Creating Your Own Batch Files

The best way to understand how batch files work is to try one. Create a simple batch file called DATETIME.BAT that does the following:

1. Clears your screen display with CLS

2. Prompts you to enter a new system date with DATE

3. Prompts you to enter a new system time with TIME

To create this file, either use EDLIN or copy the file from your keyboard, as shown here:

```
A> COPY CON DATETIME.BAT
CLS
DATE
TIME
^Z
            1 File(s) copied
```

Execute this batch file by typing **DATETIME** at the DOS prompt, as shown here:

```
A> DATETIME
```

When DOS recognizes DATETIME as a batch file (by the BAT extension), it begins executing the commands that the batch file contains, displaying the following:

```
A> DATE
Current date is Fri  5-06-1988
Enter new date (mm-dd-yy):

A> TIME
Current time is 14:54:10.23
Enter new time:

A>
```

As you create your batch files, keep the following guidelines in mind:

- Do not create a batch file with the same name as a DOS internal command (such as CLS, TYPE, DIR) or external command (such as FORMAT or DISKCOPY). If you were to do this, DOS would never be able to locate your batch file.

- DOS batch files must have the extension BAT.

■ During the batch file's processing, if you must remove the floppy disk that contains your batch file, DOS will prompt you to replace the disk in the drive if it is required for processing to continue.

With these guidelines in mind, create the following batch file, which clears the screen display, lists all of the files in the current directory, and then displays the disk volume label:

```
A> COPY  CON  SHOWDISK.BAT
CLS
DIR
VOL
^Z
            1 File(s) copied

A>
```

When you invoke SHOWDISK, DOS will first clear the screen, display the files in the directory, and then display the volume label, as shown here:

```
A> DIR

Volume in drive A has no label
Directory of  A:\

SHOWDISK     BAT     23     5-06-88   2:56p
             1 File(s)   361472 bytes free

A> VOL

Volume in drive A has no label

A>
```

Grouping commands into DOS batch files is that easy.

Suppressing Display of Command Names with ECHO OFF

As you just saw, when you invoke a DOS batch file, DOS displays the names of each command as they are executed.

```
A> DOPAY

A> PAYROLL

A> SORTPAY

A> PRINTPAY
```

You may not always want the user to know the sequence of commands that DOS is executing. You can direct DOS to suppress the display of command names by placing the ECHO OFF command at the beginning of your batch files, as shown here:

```
A> COPY CON DOPAY.BAT
ECHO OFF
PAYROLL
SORTPAY
PRINTPAY
^Z
            1 File(s) copied

A>
```

When you later execute this batch file, DOS will display

```
A> DOPAY

A> ECHO OFF

A>
```

Although DOS executes the commands PAYROLL, SORTPAY, and PRINTPAY within the batch file, the end user is unaware of that fact.

@ Versus ECHO OFF

If you are using DOS version 3.3, you have a second method of suppressing the display of command names as your batch file executes: precede each command in your batch file with the @ character, as shown here:

```
A> COPY  CON  DOPAY.BAT
@PAYROLL
@SORTPAY
@PRINTPAY
^Z
            1 File(s) copied

A>
```

When you later invoke the procedure, DOS will display

```
A> DOPAY

A>
```

The most common use of this character is to prevent the message "A> ECHO OFF" from appearing at the start of a batch file, as shown here:

```
@ECHO OFF
```

Using ECHO to Display Messages

You can provide the user with more information by invoking the DOS ECHO command to display messages within your batch file. Place the ECHO command at the beginning of your batch file, followed immediately by the message that you want to display to the end user.

Here, the ECHO command is used along with ECHO OFF:

```
A> COPY  CON  DOPAY.BAT
ECHO OFF
ECHO About to execute the PAYROLL program to generate salaries
PAYROLL
ECHO Payroll is complete, sorting salaries
SORTPAY
ECHO Salaries sorted, printing checks
PRINTPAY
^Z
                1 File(s) copied

A>
```

When you later execute this batch file, DOS will display

```
A> ECHO  OFF
About to execute the PAYROLL program to generate salaries
Payroll is complete, sorting salaries
Salaries sorted, printing checks
A>
```

The ECHO command allowed you to tell the user what was happening as each command in your batch file was executed. The actual name of each command was suppressed by ECHO OFF, thus making your batch file more readable.

Documenting Your Batch Files with REM

One of the most important steps in programming is documentation. You have learned that DOS batch files exist to help you save time and keystrokes. It is possible, however, to create a DOS batch file that performs a specific task, and then, several weeks later, forget what that task was. To prevent this occurrence, DOS provides the REM command (for remark), which allows you to leave remarks or comments within your batch files. Given your previous batch file, for example, you might use REM as follows:

```
ECHO OFF
REM ********************************************************
REM *         D O P A Y                           *
REM * Written by Kris Jamsa 06/01/88              *
REM * This procedure executes the programs        *
REM * PAYROLL, SORTPAY, and PRINTPAY, which *
REM * generate employee payroll, sort the        *
REM * salaries by amount, and lastly,            *
REM * print the employee checks.                 *
REM ************************************************ ****
ECHO About to execute the PAYROLL program to generate salaries
PAYROLL
ECHO Payroll is complete, sorting salaries
SORTPAY
ECHO Salaries sorted, printing checks
PRINTPAY
```

When you later edit or type this file's contents, you will know exactly who wrote it and why. Therefore, placing one or two lines at the top of all your batch files that tell when they were written, by whom, and why is a good habit to get into.

NOTE: Using the ECHO OFF command in the DOPAY batch procedure prevents DOS from displaying each remark in the batch file when it is executed. If you omit the ECHO OFF command, each remark will be displayed, as in this batch file.

```
A> COPY CON DATETIME.BAT
REM Written by Kris Jamsa 06-01-88
REM This procedure issues both the DATE and TIME commands
DATE
TIME
^Z
                1 File(s) copied

A> DATETIME

A> REM Written by Kris Jamsa 06-01-88

A> REM This procedure issues both the DATE and TIME commands

A> DATE
Current date is Fri 5-06-1988
Enter new date (mm-dd-yy):

A> TIME
Current time is 15:02:05.17
Enter new time:

A>
```

Getting the User's Attention With PAUSE

In many cases you may have to stop your batch processing and wait for the user to perform a specific action, such as turning on the printer or placing a new disk in drive A. The DOS PAUSE command allows you to display a message to the end user and then waits until the user presses a key to continue.

For example, this batch file displays the volume label and files for the disk in drive B. Before the procedure displays the volume label and directory listing, it prompts the user as follows:

```
A> PAUSE Place the diskette desired in drive B
Strike a key when ready . . .
```

This procedure implements SHOWDISK.

```
PAUSE Place the diskette desired in drive B
VOL B:
DIR B:
```

You can now modify your DOPAY batch file to ensure that the user has checks in the printer before the PRINTPAY command executes.

```
ECHO OFF
REM ******************************************************
REM *          D O P A Y                              *
REM * Written by Kris Jamsa 06/01/88                  *
REM * This procedure executes the programs            *
REM * PAYROLL, SORTPAY, and PRINTPAY which *
REM * generate employee payroll, sort the            *
REM * salaries by amount, and lastly,                *
REM * prints the employee checks.                    *
REM ******************************************* ***************
ECHO About to execute the PAYROLL program to generate salaries
PAYROLL
ECHO Payroll is complete, sorting salaries
SORTPAY
ECHO Place checks into the printer and place the printer on-line
PAUSE
ECHO Salaries sorted, printing checks
PRINTPAY
```

As you can see, the DOS PAUSE command gives you considerable control over your batch files.

Terminating a Batch File

In Chapter 5 you learned that one way to terminate DOS commands is to press the CTRL-C key combination. As it turns out, CTRL-C also gives you a means of terminating DOS batch files. If, while your batch file is executing, you press CTRL-C, DOS will display

```
Terminate batch job (Y/N)?
```

To terminate the batch file, type **Y** and press ENTER. If you want the batch file to continue, type **N** and press ENTER.

For example, when the DOPAY batch file displays the message

```
Place checks into the printer and place the printer on-line
```

if the user realizes that there are no checks that can be used for printing, he or she can press CTRL-C to terminate the command.

Hands-On Practice

Start by creating this batch file, which clears your screen display and prompts you for the current system time.

```
A> COPY  CON  T.BAT
CLS
TIME
^Z
                1 File(s) copied

A>
```

With this batch file you can abbreviate the DOS TIME command to T. At the DOS prompt, type **T** to execute this batch file.

```
A> T
```

DOS will respond by clearing your screen display and prompting you for the current system time.

```
Current time is 15:02:05.17
Enter new time:
```

Write another batch file, but this time create it to perform the following tasks:

1. Clear your screen display

2. Prompt you for the system date

3. Again clear the screen display

4. Prompt you for the system time

```
A> COPY  CON  DATETIME.BAT
CLS
DATE
CLS
TIME
^Z
            1 File(s) copied

A>
```

To invoke this procedure, type **DATETIME** at the DOS prompt.

Using the DOS REM command, document the first batch file that you created.

```
A> COPY  CON  T.BAT
REM Written By Kris Jamsa 06/01/88
REM This procedure abbreviates the DOS TIME command as T
CLS
TIME
^Z
            1 File(s) copied

A>
```

When you invoke this procedure, DOS will display all of your remarks on the screen. To suppress these comments, add the ECHO OFF command at the first line of the batch file.

```
A> COPY  CON  T.BAT
ECHO OFF
REM Written By Kris Jamsa 06/01/88
REM This procedure abbreviates the DOS TIME command as T
CLS
TIME
^Z
                 1 File(s) copied


A>
```

If you are using DOS 3.3, place the @ character in front of the ECHO OFF command to suppress its display.

Now when you invoke the batch file, it will suppress command names, clear the screen display, and finally prompt you to enter the current time. The screen display is

```
Current time is 15:02:05.17
Enter new time:
```

As a final practice, create this simple batch procedure.

```
A> COPY  CON  DT.BAT
DATE
TIME
^Z
                 1 File(s) copied
```

Invoke the batch file by typing **DT** at the DOS prompt.

```
A> DT
```

DOS will respond by issuing the DOS DATE command, as shown here:

```
A> DT
Current date is Fri  5-06-1988
Enter new date (mm-dd-yy):
```

Rather than typing in a date, press CTRL-C to terminate the batch file. DOS then displays

```
A> DT
Current date is Fri  5-06-1988
Enter new date (mm-dd-yy): ^C

Terminate batch job (Y/N)?
```

Type **Y** and press ENTER. DOS will redisplay its prompt, as shown here:

```
A> DT
Current date is Fri  5-06-1988
Enter new date (mm-dd-yy): ^C

Terminate batch job (Y/N)? Y

A>
```

Once again, invoke DT.

```
A> DT
```

Again press CTRL-C at the prompt for the current date.

```
A> DT
Current date is Fri  5-06-1988
Enter new date (mm-dd-yy): ^C
```

When DOS prompts

```
A> DT
Current date is Fri  5-06-1988
Enter new date (mm-dd-yy): ^C

Terminate batch job (Y/N)?
```

type **N** and press ENTER. DOS will continue executing the next command in the batch file.

```
A> DT
Current date is Fri  5-06-1988
Enter new date (mm-dd-yy): ^C

Terminate batch job (Y/N)? N

Current time is 15:02:05.17
Enter new time:
```

Believe it or not, you are actually programming DOS! DOS batch processing is so powerful and convenient that discussion of the subject will continue in Chapters 20 and 21.

Summary

Most of the commands computers execute today are interactive commands—the user enters one command, waits for that command to complete, and then types in the next command.

In addition to supporting interactive processing, DOS allows you group commands into a text file with the extension BAT. When you type in the name of this batch file at the DOS prompt, DOS will begin executing the commands that the file contains.

As you create your batch files, keep the following guidelines in mind:

- Do not create a batch file with the same name as a DOS internal or external command. If you were to do this, DOS would never be able to locate your batch file.

- DOS batch files must have the extension BAT.

- If you must remove the floppy disk that contains your batch file during the batch file's processing, DOS will prompt you to replace the disk in the drive necessary for processing to continue.

By default, each time DOS executes a command contained in a batch file, the command's name is displayed on your screen. In some cases you may want to suppress the display of command names. To do so, place the ECHO OFF command at the first line of your batch file. If you are using DOS version 3.3, you can also precede each command name in the batch file with the @ character. When DOS encounters this character, it will suppress the name of the command that it is executing.

A very important step in creating any batch file is to add comments that help you remember why you created the batch file in the first place. You should at least include who wrote the file, when it was written, and why. The DOS REM command allows you to place such remarks in your batch files.

The CTRL-C key combination terminates the execution of a DOS batch file just as it allowed you to terminate programs.

Glossary

Processing in which the computer receives all of its commands from the user is called *interactive processing*. Most of the processing performed on computers today is interactive processing.

Processing in which DOS obtains its input from a file as opposed to the user is called *batch processing*. In this type of processing, DOS allows you to group several commands into a text file with the extension BAT, called a *batch file*. When you type in the name of the file containing the commands at the DOS prompt, DOS recognizes the BAT and begins executing the commands that the file contains.

20 Creating Intelligent Batch Commands

In Chapter 2, a program was defined as a list of instructions for the computer to perform. You actually began programming DOS in Chapter 19, when you grouped lists of DOS commands into batch files for DOS to execute.

In this chapter you will take a look at three DOS commands that exist specifically for batch processing—IF, GOTO, and FOR. You will also examine a special batch file called AUTOEXEC.BAT.

Decision Making Within Your Batch Files

In Chapter 19, all of the batch files that you created executed their commands sequentially, from the first command in the file to the last, as in this batch file.

```
DOPAY
PAYROLL
SORTPAY
PRINTPAY
```

As your batch files become more complex, you will often want to design them so that, under certain conditions, you can decide whether or not a command should be executed. The DOS IF command is called a *conditional batch command* because it allows batch files to perform decision making based on one of three conditions.

For example, the following batch file clears your screen display and checks to see if the TEST.BAT file exists in your current directory. If the file exists, the batch file will use the TYPE command to display the file's contents. If not, the batch file will terminate.

```
CLS
IF  EXIST  TEST.BAT  TYPE  TEST.BAT
```

Take a close look at this DOS IF command. IF is the DOS command you are executing. EXIST tells you that DOS will test if the file whose name immediately follows the command exists on disk as specified. In this example, TEST.BAT is the file DOS will search for. TYPE TEST.BAT is the command that DOS will execute if the file is found. If TEST.BAT does not exist as specified, DOS will do nothing.

Using this technique, write the following batch file, which tests if the NUMBERS.DAT file exists on the disk in drive B. If it does, the batch file will display its contents.

```
CLS
IF  EXIST  B:NUMBERS.DAT  TYPE  B:NUMBERS.DAT
```

This batch file works in a similar manner to the first. The only difference is that in this case you are searching for a different file name. This test, IF EXIST, is the first of three conditions that you can test for within your batch files.

The second condition that you will examine uses the completion status of the command that executed immediately before the IF command. Several DOS commands help your batch files make decisions by specifying values when they complete that indicate their level of success. These values are called *exit status values*. For example, the DOS BACKUP command (which is examined in detail in Chapter 30) returns one of the following values based on its processing.

Value	Meaning
0	BACKUP successfully completed
1	BACKUP did not find any files to back up
2	BACKUP did not complete due to file-sharing conflicts
3	BACKUP was terminated by a user CTRL-C
4	BACKUP was terminated by an error

The format of the second condition, which uses exit status values, is shown here:

```
IF ERRORLEVEL VALUE DOS_command
```

IF is the command that you are executing. ERRORLEVEL tells you that DOS will compare the exit status value of the previous command to the value that immediately follows. If the exit status value is greater than or equal to *VALUE,* DOS will execute *DOS_command.* For example, the command line

```
IF ERRORLEVEL 3 DOS_command
```

directs DOS to compare the exit status value of the previous command to the value 3. If the exit status value is *greater than or equal to* 3, DOS will execute *DOS_command.* If the exit status value is less than 3, DOS will do nothing.

Not all programs provide exit status values; therefore, you will not use this form of the IF command as often as IF EXIST. If you see this command in a DOS batch file, however, it is important that you understand its function.

The last condition that you will examine compares the characters in two strings. The format of the condition is

```
IF STRING1==STRING2 DOS_command
```

In this case, DOS will perform a letter-by-letter comparison of the words contained in *STRING1* and *STRING2.* If the letters match identically, DOS will execute the specified command. For example, when you execute the batch file

```
@ECHO OFF
CLS
IF FIRSTSTRING==FIRSTSTRING ECHO STRINGS ARE IDENTICAL
```

DOS displays the message

```
STRINGS ARE IDENTICAL
```

The strings must match letter for letter; for example, these two strings are not equal.

```
CLS
IF FIRSTSTRING==firststring ECHO STRINGS ARE IDENTICAL
```

You will use this form of the IF command quite often in Chapter 24, which discusses advanced DOS batch processing.

Repeating a Command For Several Files

Frequently during your batch processing, you will want DOS to repeat a specific command for several files. The DOS FOR command is known as an *iterative command* because it allows you to do just that. For example, assume that you want DOS to display the contents of the JUN.EXP, JUN.MTG, and JUN.INC files. The following DOS batch file clears your screen display and then uses the DOS FOR command to display the contents of each file:

```
CLS
FOR %%F IN (JUN.EXP JUN.MTG JUN.INC) DO TYPE %%F
```

Here is how the DOS FOR command works. The characters "%%F" are the name of a DOS variable to which DOS can assign a file name.

In the example FOR command just shown, DOS first assigns the file name JUN.EXP to %%F. Therefore, when DOS issues the command

```
TYPE %%F
```

DOS actually performs the command

```
TYPE JUN.EXP
```

When this command completes, DOS assigns the next file in the list of files, JUN.MTG, to %%F, resulting in the command

```
TYPE JUN.MTG
```

Likewise, the third loop results in the command

```
TYPE JUN.INC
```

DOS looks for the next file but does not find one, so the FOR command completes.

This FOR command displays the contents of the ONE, TWO, THREE, and FOUR files.

```
CLS
FOR %%F IN (ONE TWO THREE FOUR) DO TYPE %%F
```

The DOS FOR command also supports DOS wildcard characters. For example, you can change this FOR command from

```
FOR %%F IN (JUN.EXP JUN.MTG JUN.INC) DO TYPE %%F
```

to the following:

```
FOR %%F IN (JUN.*) DO TYPE %%F
```

When the wildcard character is used in this way, DOS continues to display the contents of all files with the file name JUN until no additional files exist.

Few users take advantage of the benefits of the FOR command. In Chapter 24, you will see how FOR can be used to create convenient batch files.

Moving Around in Your Batch Files

Even though the DOS IF statement allows you to execute one command only if a specific condition exists, you are still executing all of the commands in the batch file sequentially. As the complexity of your batch files increases, there may be times when you want DOS to perform a specific set of commands if one condition exists, and another set if that condition fails.

The DOS GOTO command gives you the ability to jump from one location in a batch file to another. The format of this command is

```
GOTO label_name
```

where *label_name* is the location in the batch file to which you want to branch. For example, consider this batch file:

```
:LOOP
DIR
GOTO LOOP
```

The line ":LOOP" is simply a DOS label name. All DOS label names begin with the colon, and when DOS encounters that colon, it knows that the line contains a label that requires no action. Here are some guidelines for creating DOS labels:

■ DOS reads only the first eight characters of a DOS label name. For example, DOS will consider the label names DOS_LABEL1 and DOS_LABEL2 as identical.

■ Despite the limit on how many characters DOS will recognize, DOS label names can be virtually any length. This allows you to create labels that are meaningful.

After reading the LOOP line, DOS encounters the DIR command and executes it. DOS then executes the GOTO statement, which sends you back to the LOOP line at the top of the batch file. DOS will again execute the DIR command and then the GOTO command, and then will continue to list the files in your current directory until you press CTRL-C to cancel the command. By using the DOS GOTO command in this manner, you can repeat any series of DOS commands forever.

Using the DOS GOTO command in conjunction with the IF command, you can perform a series of commands or skip several commands based on a specific condition. This batch file, for example, checks to see if the TEST.BAT file resides on the disk in drive B. If it does, the procedure completes. If the file does not exist there but rather in drive A, the batch file copies it from drive A to drive B.

```
IF EXIST B:TEST.BAT GOTO DONE
COPY TEST.BAT B:
:DONE
```

Using the DOPAY batch file discussed in Chapter 19, add the assumption that if the PAYROLL command does not successfully complete its processing, it returns an error status value of 1. If the command successfully completes, it will return the value 0. If PAYROLL fails, there is no reason for SORTPAY and PRINTPAY to execute. To provide this additional control, use the IF ERRORLEVEL condition in conjunction with the DOS GOTO command.

```
PAYROLL
IF ERRORLEVEL 1 GOTO ERROR
SORTPAY
PRINTPAY
GOTO DONE
:ERROR
ECHO ERROR IN PAYROLL PROCESSING
:DONE
```

As you can see, by using the IF and GOTO commands, you can increase the complexity of your batch files tremendously.

Using NOT to Enhance Your Control of the IF Command

You have seen several examples of batch files that perform a command or series of commands when a specific condition is *true*. In many cases however, you will want to issue a series of commands or skip commands when a condition *fails*. For this purpose DOS provides the NOT operator, which you place in front of the condition that you want to examine. This batch file, for example, displays the message "FILE DOES NOT EXIST" if the TEST.BAT file does not reside in the current directory.

```
CLS
IF NOT EXIST TEST.BAT ECHO FILE DOES NOT EXIST
```

Using the NOT operator can save you time and keystrokes. For example, the batch file

```
IF EXIST B:TEST.BAT GOTO DONE
COPY TEST.BAT B:
:DONE
```

can be simplified from three lines to one by using the NOT operator as follows:

```
IF NOT EXIST B:TEST.DAT COPY TEST.DAT B:
```

As you can see, using IF, FOR, GOTO, and NOT gives you unlimited batch processing capabilities.

AUTOEXEC.BAT, a Special Batch File

In Chapter 18 you learned only three files should be in the root directory of your fixed disk: CONFIG.SYS, AUTOEXEC.BAT, and COMMAND.COM. By the use of the BAT extension, you should know that AUTOEXEC.BAT is a DOS batch file. Thus, you can place DOS commands into AUTOEXEC.BAT just as you would into any batch file.

AUTOEXEC.BAT is not just any batch file, however. Each time DOS boots, it searches the root directory for the AUTOEXEC.BAT file. If DOS finds this file, it executes the commands that AUTO-EXEC.BAT contains. If DOS does not find this file, it executes the familiar DATE and TIME commands that you respond to each time DOS boots.

AUTOEXEC.BAT gives you a means of executing a set of commands automatically each time your system boots. For example, if your computer has a built-in clock that remembers the current date and time, you do not need to execute the DATE and TIME commands. When you place a command like CLS in the AUTOEXEC.BAT file,

```
A> COPY CON AUTOEXEC.BAT
CLS
^Z
              1 File(s) copied

A>
```

DOS will find AUTOEXEC.BAT in your root directory when your system boots and execute the commands that it contains in place of the DATE and TIME commands.

Hands-On Practice

This chapter contains several difficult concepts. It is, therefore, especially important that you perform all of the commands in this practice section.

To give you some files to manipulate, create A, B, and C, as shown here:

```
A> COPY  CON  A
A
AA
AAA
^Z
                1 File(s) copied

A> COPY  CON  B
B
BB
BBB
^Z
                1 File(s) copied

A> COPY  CON  C
C
CC
CCC
^Z
                1 File(s) copied

A>
```

Next, create this batch file called DISPLAY.BAT.

```
A> COPY  CON  DISPLAY.BAT
IF EXIST A TYPE A
IF EXIST B TYPE B
IF EXIST C TYPE C
IF EXIST D TYPE D
^Z
                    1 File(s) copied

A>
```

When DOS executes this batch file, it will display

```
A> DISPLAY

A> IF  EXIST  A  TYPE  A
A
AA
AAA

A> IF  EXIST  B  TYPE  B
B
BB
BBB

A> IF  EXIST  C  TYPE  C
C
CC
CCC

A>
```

The first three lines are fairly straightforward: if the files A, B, and C exist in your current directory, DOS will display their contents. The last line, however,

```
IF  EXIST  D  TYPE  D
```

illustrates the fact that if the condition fails, DOS does nothing. That explains why DOS does not display the error message

```
File not found
```

The TYPE D command will never execute because the condition IF EXIST D always fails.

Use the DOS FOR command to display the contents of files A, B, and C, as shown here:

```
CLS
FOR %%F IN (A B C) DO TYPE %%F
```

When you invoke this batch file, it will display

```
A> FOR %F IN (A B C) DO TYPE %F

A> TYPE A
A
AA
AAA

A> TYPE B
B
BB
BBB

A> TYPE C
C
CC
CCC

A>
```

Use this DOS GOTO command to repeatedly display the contents of the A file.

```
:LOOP
TYPE A
GOTO LOOP
```

When you invoke this batch file, DOS will continue to display the contents of A until you press CTRL-C to terminate its processing.

Using the DOS NOT command, as shown here, test to see if the files A, B, and C reside on the disk in drive B (or drive C if you have a fixed disk). If they do not, copy the files to the disk.

```
IF NOT EXIST B:A COPY A B:
IF NOT EXIST B:B COPY B B:
IF NOT EXIST B:C COPY C B:
```

Select the root directory as your current directory by using the DOS CHDIR command.

```
A> CHDIR \
```

Next, issue the following DIR command.

```
A> DIR AUTOEXEC.BAT
```

If the file exists, display its contents by using the DOS TYPE command. If it does not, create the following file:

```
A> COPY CON AUTOEXEC.BAT
CLS
VOL
^Z
                1 File(s) copied

A>
```

Using the CTRL-ALT-DEL key combination, restart DOS. Instead of displaying the familar DATE and TIME commands, DOS will now clear your screen and display your disk volume label.

Summary

Most batch files execute sequentially, from the first command to the last. As your batch files increase in complexity, there may be instances when you need your batch files to execute a command or series of commands if a specific condition is met. The DOS IF command allows batch files to perform this kind of decision making.

There may be instances when you want your batch files to repeat a command. The DOS FOR command allows you to repeat a specific DOS command for a given set of files.

The DOS GOTO command gives you the flexibility to branch from one location in your batch file to another. You can use GOTO in conjunction with the DOS IF command to maximize control of your batch files.

Just as there are instances when you want DOS to perform a specific command when a given condition is true, you also may want DOS to execute a command when the condition is false. DOS allows you to perform such processing when you place the NOT operator in front of the condition you are testing.

Each time DOS boots, it examines the root directory for the AUTOEXEC.BAT file. If DOS finds this file, it executes the commands that the file contains. If DOS does not find the AUTOEXEC.BAT file, it executes the familiar DATE and TIME commands. AUTOEXEC.BAT thereby gives you the capability to direct DOS to execute a specific set of commands each time your computer starts.

Glossary

A *conditional batch command* is a command that executes a specific DOS command when a condition is met. The DOS IF command allows you to place conditional commands in your batch files.

An *iterative command* is a command that repeats itself until a given condition is met. The DOS FOR command allows you to perform iterative processing within your batch files.

21 Controlling DOS Input and Output

The commands you have issued so far in this book have written their output to your screen display. Although you have learned several tricks, such as using SHIFT-PRTSC and CTRL-PRTSC to obtain printouts of your output, the command-line operators you will learn about in this chapter will give you greater control over your program's output. In addition, you will learn about three DOS commands. The MORE command allows you to display a command's output one screen at a time, the SORT command sorts information, and the FIND command allows you to display lines in a file that contain a specific word or phrase.

The command-line operators used in this chapter are called *DOS I/O redirection operators*. These operators allow you to redirect the output of a command from your screen to a file or a device such as your printer.

Getting Started with DOS I/O Redirection

At the DOS prompt, issue the command

```
A> DIR
```

As always, DOS displays the output of the DIR command on your screen display. Turn your system printer on and issue the command

```
A> DIR  >  PRN:
```

Your printer should begin printing the directory listing, and no new information appears on your screen display. Rather than displaying the output of the DIR command to your screen, DOS has redirected it to your system printer.

The greater-than symbol (>) is the DOS *output redirection operator*. You can use this operator to instruct DOS to redirect output from the screen display to a file or device. In the previous command you used this operator to redirect output to the printer. Figure 21-1 shows how this process works.

You can also use the output redirection operator to redirect the output of the DOS DIR command from your screen to a file. Here, the file's name is DIR.DAT.

```
A> DIR  >  DIR.DAT
```

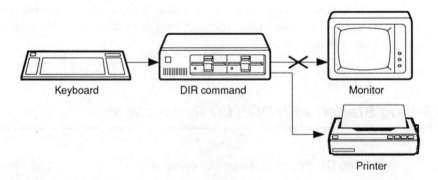

Keyboard   DIR command   Monitor

                                       Printer

Figure 21-1. *Redirecting output to the printer*

Output Redirection Operator (>)

The DOS output redirection operator (>) allows you to tell DOS to redirect the output of a command from your screen display to a file or device.

A> DIR > PRN:
A> DIR > DIR.DAT

Again, rather than displaying your directory listing on the screen, DOS creates a file called DIR.DAT, which contains the directory listing. Figure 21-2 illustrates this process.

You can use the DOS output redirection operator with all of your DOS commands, like the ones shown here.

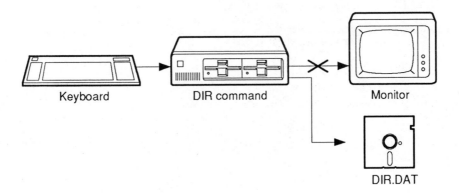

Figure 21-2. *Redirecting output to a file*

```
A> TREE /F > PRN:
A> VOL > NAME.DSK
A> CHKDSK > PRN:
```

DOS provides a second redirection operator called the *append redirection operator,* which is the double greater-than sign (>>). Given the command line

```
A> DIR >> DIR.LST
```

DOS will perform the following processing:

1. Create the DIR.LST file if it does not exist

2. Append the contents of the DIR command to either the newly created file or a previously existing DIR.LST

Assume that you have files named START, MIDDLE, and END, which contain the following:

```
A> TYPE START
This is line 1 of the file
This is line 2 of the file

A> TYPE MIDDLE
This is the middle of the
file that you are building.

A> TYPE END
These are the last two
lines of the file.
```

Using the DOS append redirection operator, >>, give the command

```
A> TYPE START >> WHOLE
```

DOS will create the WHOLE file, putting into it the contents of START.

```
A> TYPE  WHOLE
This is line 1 of the file
This is line 2 of the file

A>
```

Next, append the contents of the MIDDLE file to the WHOLE file, as shown here:

```
A> TYPE  MIDDLE  >>  WHOLE
```

Using the DOS TYPE command, display the current contents of WHOLE.

```
A> TYPE  WHOLE
This is line 1 of the file
This is line 2 of the file
This is the middle of the
file that we are building

A>
```

Repeat this process to append the END file to the WHOLE file.

```
A> TYPE  END  >>  WHOLE
```

The WHOLE file is now complete.

```
A> TYPE  WHOLE
This is line 1 of the file
This is line 2 of the file
This is the middle of the
file that we are building
This is the last two
lines of the file.

A>
```

Append Redirection Operator (>>)

The DOS append redirection operator (>>) allows you to tell DOS to redirect the output of a command from your screen display, appending it to a previously existing file. Here is the format of a DIR command that uses >>:

A> DIR >> FILENAME.EXT

If the specified file does not exist, DOS will create it.

The > and >> operators both tell DOS to redirect the output of a command from the screen display to a file or device. This is why > and >> are classified as *output* redirection operators. DOS also provides you with an *input redirection operator,* <, which instructs DOS to obtain a program's input from a file as opposed to the keyboard. Figure 21-3 shows how this is done.

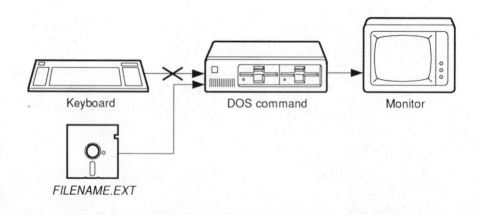

Keyboard   DOS command   Monitor

FILENAME.EXT

Figure 21-3.   *Redirecting input from file instead of keyboard*

Input Redirection Operator (<)

The DOS input redirection operation (<) allows you to tell DOS to redirect the source of input for a command from your keyboard to a file or device. Here is the format of the MORE command using <:

A> MORE < FILENAME

The input redirection operator does not work the same way as DOS batch files. From batch files, DOS obtains the command it is to execute, not the command's input. To better understand input redirection, consider the DOS MORE command, which displays a file's output one screen at a time.

To start, create the DIR.LST file, which contains the directory listing of your files.

A> DIR > DIR.LST

Invoke the following DOS MORE command:

A> MORE < DIR.LST

MORE is an external DOS command; therefore, it must reside in the the current directory of drive A for this example. MORE will display the contents of the DIR.LST file one screen at a time. Each time MORE displays a screenful of information, MORE will pause and prompt

--MORE--

If you want to display the next screenful of information, press ENTER. If you want to cancel the command, press CTRL-C.

With the DIR.LST file, the output of the MORE command would be as follows.

```
A> MORE  <  DIR.LST

Volume in drive A is MS330PP01
Directory of  A:\

4201          CPI   17089   7-24-87   12:00a
5202          CPI   459     7-24-87   12:00a
ANSI          SYS   1647    7-24-87   12:00a
APPEND        EXE   5794    7-24-87   12:00a
ASSIGN        COM   1530    7-24-87   12:00a
ATTRIB        EXE   10656   7-24-87   12:00a
CHKDSK        COM   9819    7-24-87   12:00a
COMMAND       COM   25276   7-24-87   12:00a
COMP          COM   4183    7-24-87   12:00a
COUNTRY       SYS   11254   7-24-87   12:00a
DISKCOMP      COM   5848    7-24-87   12:00a
DISKCOPY      COM   6264    7-24-87   12:00a
DISPLAY       SYS   11259   7-24-87   12:00a
DRIVER        SYS   1165    7-24-87   12:00a
EDLIN         COM   7495    7-24-87   12:00a
EXE2BIN       EXE   3050    7-24-87   12:00a
FASTOPEN      EXE   3888    7-24-87   12:00a
FDISK         COM   48919   7-24-87   12:00a
FIND          EXE   6403    7-24-87   12:00a
FORMAT        COM   11671   7-24-87   12:00a
-- More --
```

As you can see, once MORE displays a screenful of information, it pauses and prompts you with "--MORE--." Press ENTER to display the next screen.

```
GRAFTABL      COM   6136    7-24-87   12:00a
GRAPHICS      COM   13943   7-24-87   12:00a
JOIN          EXE   9612    7-24-87   12:00a
KEYB          COM   9041    7-24-87   12:00a
LABEL         COM   2346    7-24-87   12:00a
MODE          COM   15440   7-24-87   12:00a
MORE          COM   282     7-24-87   12:00a
NLSFUNC       EXE   3029    7-24-87   12:00a
PRINT         COM   8995    7-24-87   12:00a
RECOVER       COM   4268    7-24-87   12:00a
SELECT        COM   4132    7-24-87   12:00a
```

SORT	EXE	1946	7-24-87	12:00a
SUBST	EXE	10552	7-24-87	12:00a
SYS	COM	4725	7-24-87	12:00a

34 File(s)   5120 bytes free

If several screens of information remain, MORE will display each in this fashion. If only a partial screenful of information exists, MORE will display the information and terminate.

Figure 21-4 illustrates processing with MORE.

Displaying Sorted Output

The DOS SORT command allows you to write sorted output to your screen display. SORT is an external DOS command, which means that it must reside in the current directory in order for the command to successfully execute.

Assume that the LETTERS.DAT file contains

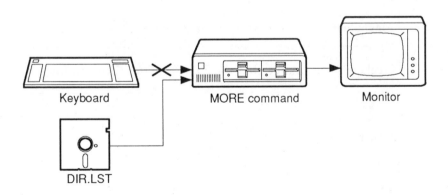

Keyboard   MORE command   Monitor

DIR.LST

Figure 21-4.   *Processing with MORE*

```
A> COPY  CON  LETTERS.DAT
C
E
D
A
B
F
^Z
                1 File(s) copied

A>
```

The input redirection operator causes the command

```
A> SORT < LETTERS.DAT
```

to display

```
A> SORT < LETTERS.DAT
A
B
C
D
E
F

A>
```

Likewise, assuming that the STATES.DAT file contains

```
A> COPY  CON  STATES.DAT
Washington
Colorado
Nevada
Arizona
California
New York
^Z
                1 File(s) copied
```

the command

```
A> SORT < STATES.DAT
```

will display

```
A> SORT < STATES.DAT
Arizona
California
Colorado
Nevada
New York
Washington

A>
```

The format of the DOS SORT command is

```
SORT [/+column] [/R]
```

Two optional parameters are supported by this command. The first parameter allows you to specify a column number within the file that you want the data in the file sorted on. For example, assume that the ADDRESS.DAT file contains the following company names, cities, and states where they are located:

```
A> TYPE ADDRESS.DAT

Logitech       Fremont        California
McGraw-Hill    New York       New York
Microsoft      Redmond        Washington
Borland        Scotts Valley  California

A>
```

To sort this data by state (column 33), use the SORT column qualifier as shown.

```
A> SORT /+33 < ADDRESS.DAT
Borland          Scotts Valley  California
Logitech         Fremont        California
McGraw-Hill      New York       New York
Microsoft        Redmond        Washington

A>
```

Likewise, to sort the information by city (column 17), use the following command:

```
A> SORT /+17 < ADDRESS.DAT
Borland          Scotts Valley  California
Logitech         Fremont        California
McGraw-Hill      New York       New York
Microsoft        Redmond        Washington

A>
```

The second optional qualifier in the SORT command, /R, allows you to direct SORT to sort the data in reverse order (highest to lowest). Given the LETTERS.DAT file, the command

```
A> SORT /R < LETTERS.DAT
```

will display

```
A> SORT /R < LETTERS.DAT
F
E
D
C
B
A

A>
```

Searching for a Key Word or Phrase

The third command that will be examined in conjunction with DOS I/O redirection is the FIND command. FIND allows you to easily search for words and phrases within a file. Assume, for example, that the GRADES.DAT file contains

```
A> TYPE  GRADES.DAT
Test One
                Jim Byrd       88
                Mark Kozak     93
                Rich Neal      94
                Mark Pellerin  92

Test Two
                Jim Byrd       98
                Mark Kozak     92
                Rich Neal      91
                Mark Pellerin  79

Test Three
                Jim Byrd       83
                Mark Kozak     44
                Rich Neal      87
                Mark Pellerin  45

A>
```

If you need to list all of the grades for Jim Byrd, issue the command

```
A> FIND  "Jim Byrd"  <  GRADES.DAT
                Jim Byrd       88
                Jim Byrd       98
                Jim Byrd       83

A>
```

If your monthly expense file contains

```
A> TYPE  JUNE.EXP
06-01-88 Beer at Murphy's     $10.00
06-02-88 Rent                 $500.00
06-03-88 Beer at ball game    $15.00
06-04-88 Groceries            $45.00
06-06-88 Beer at Shenigans    $10.00

A>
```

you can determine how much money you are investing in beer as
shown here:

```
A> FIND  "Beer"  <  JUNE.EXP
06-01-88 Beer at Murphy's     $10.00
06-03-88 Beer at ball game    $15.00
06-06-88 Beer at Shenigans    $10.00

A>
```

Chapter 22 will continue this discussion with advanced DOS I/O
redirection concepts. You will take a closer look at the DOS FIND
command at that time. For now, simply remember that FIND allows
you to quickly locate a word or phrase within a file.

Multiple Redirection Operators

All of the redirection examples that you have examined so far in this
chapter have used only one redirection operator per command. As you
will see, however, this doesn't have to be the case. If, for example, you
want a printed sorted listing of the file named GRADES.DAT, enter
the command

```
A> SORT  <  GRADES.DAT  >  PRN:
```

SORT will obtain its input from the GRADES.DAT file, as shown in
Figure 21-5. After SORT has sorted the data, the operator > PRN:

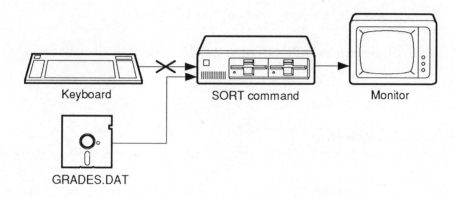

Figure 21-5. *SORT obtaining input from GRADES.DAT*

directs DOS to send the sorted output to the printer as opposed to the screen display. Figure 21-6 illustrates this process.

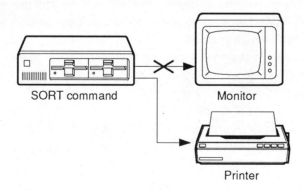

Figure 21-6. *Sending sorted output to a printer*

You can perform similar commands with FIND, as shown here:

```
A> FIND "Jim Byrd" < GRADES.DAT > BYRD.DAT
```

All references to Jim Byrd in the GRADES.DAT file will be written to the BYRD.DAT file.

Hands-On Practice

With a newly formatted disk in drive B (or drive A if you are using a fixed disk), place your DOS Program disk in drive A (or select the subdirectory C:\DOS). Next, issue the following command:

```
A> DIR
```

DOS will display your DOS files on your screen. Turn on your system printer, and modify the command to redirect output to the printer as opposed to the screen, as shown here:

```
A> DIR > PRN:
```

Your printer should begin printing, and no new information should be displayed on your screen. As you specified, DOS has redirected the output from your screen display to your printer.

Repeat this process and use the DOS TREE command.

```
A> TREE /F > PRN:
```

Just as DOS allows you to redirect your output to a device such as your printer, DOS also lets you redirect output to a file. Issue the following command:

```
A> TREE /F > B:TREE.DAT
```

Listing the files on the corresponding floppy disk displays

```
A> DIR  B:

Volume in drive B has no label
Directory of  B:\

TREE    DAT    1138  5-10-88  10:04a
                 1 File(s)  362000 bytes free
```

Using the DOS TYPE command, display the contents of the file named TREE.DAT:

```
A> TYPE  B:TREE.DAT
```

Because this file contains more than a screenful of information, its contents may scroll past you on the screen faster than you can read them. Use the DOS MORE command, as shown here:

```
A> MORE  <  B:TREE.DAT
```

MORE displays the first screen of the file and the "--MORE--" prompt, as shown here:

```
A> MORE  <  B:TREE.DAT

DIRECTORY PATH LISTING FOR VOLUME MS330PP01
Files: 4201    .CPI
5202           .CPI
ANSI           .SYS
APPEND         .EXE
ASSIGN         .COM
ATTRIB         .EXE
CHKDSK         .COM
COMMAND        .COM
COMP           .COM
COUNTRY        .SYS
DISKCOMP       .COM
DISKCOPY       .COM
DISPLAY        .SYS
```

```
DRIVER        .SYS
EDLIN         .COM
EXE2BIN       .EXE
FASTOPEN      .EXE
FDISK         .COM
FIND          .EXE
FORMAT        .COM
GRAFTABL      .COM
-- More --
```

To view the second screenful of information, press ENTER.

```
GRAPHICS      .COM
JOIN          .EXE
KEYB          .COM
LABEL         .COM
MODE          .COM
MORE          .COM
NLSFUNC       .EXE
PRINT         .COM
RECOVER       .COM
SELECT        .COM
SORT          .EXE
SUBST         .EXE
SYS           .COM
```

If you had wanted to cancel the command, you could have pressed CTRL-C at the "--MORE--" prompt.

Using the DOS output redirection operator, create a file called DIR.LST that contains the files in your directory.

```
A> DIR  > B:DIR.LST
```

Next, use the DOS SORT command to display a sorted listing of your files:

```
A> SORT  < B:DIR.LST
```

Repeat this process and use the /R qualifier to display the directory listing in reverse order.

```
A> SORT /R < B:DIR.LST
```

You can place multiple redirection operators in your command line; therefore, repeat the previous command, and send the output to your printer.

```
A> SORT /R < B:DIR.LST > PRN:
```

So that you have a file to manipulate with the DOS FIND command, create the following file:

```
A> COPY CON BIRTHDAY.LST
April          2        Aunt Sandie
August         23       Dad
July           14       Alice
May            6        Grandma
June           14       Tim
April          11       Mom
December       8        Debbie
July           9        John
June           19       Margie
^Z
               1 File(s) copied

A>
```

Using this file, display all of the birthdays that occur in June.

```
A> FIND "June" < BIRTHDAY.DAT
```

Repeat this command, this time redirecting the output of the FIND command to your printer.

```
A> FIND "June" < BIRTHDAY.LST > PRN:
```

Write the birthdays that occur in July to the JULY.DAT file.

```
A> FIND "July" < BIRTHDAY.LST > JULY.DAT
```

Use the DOS SORT command to sort the contents of this file.

```
A> SORT < BIRTHDAY.LST
April        11      Mom
April        2       Aunt Sandie
August       23      Dad
December     8       Debbie
July         14      Alice
July         9       John
June         14      Tim
June         19      Margie
May          6       Grandma

A>
```

Summary

By default, DOS writes the output of your commands to the screen display. By using DOS I/O redirection, you can direct DOS to send the output of a command to a file or device and even to provide the input for a command from a file or device.

The DOS output redirection operator, >, tells DOS to redirect a command's output from the screen display to a file or device. For example, the > operator can be used to send a disk's directory listing to a specific file. The format of such a command is

```
A> DIR > FILENAME.EXT
```

If a file with the name specified as the destination already resides on disk, DOS will overwrite it. If it does not exist, DOS will create it.

The DOS append redirection operator, >>, directs DOS to append the output of a command to a file or device. When DOS encounters the append operator, as in the command

```
A> DIR >> FILENAME.EXT
```

DOS will perform the following processing:

1. Create the *FILENAME.EXT* file if it does not exist

2. Append the contents of the DIR command to either the newly created file or a previously existing file named *FILENAME.EXT*

Several commands allow you to redirect their input away from the keyboard to a device or file using the DOS input redirection operator, <.

One such command, MORE, allows you to display the contents of a file one screen at a time.

```
A> MORE < FILENAME.EXT
```

Summary (continued)

After MORE displays a screenful of information, MORE will prompt you with the message

--MORE--

To display the next screenful of information, press ENTER. To terminate the command, press CTRL-C.

The DOS SORT command allows you to sort a file's contents, as shown here:

A> SORT < FILENAME.EXT

The optional /+*column* and /R qualifiers allow you to direct SORT to sort the file based upon a specific column in the file or in reverse order (highest to lowest).

The DOS FIND command allows you to quickly locate a word or phrase within a file. The format of this command is

A> FIND "word or phrase" < FILENAME.EXT

Although most of the redirection examples you have examined here used only one redirection operator, DOS allows you to place multiple redirection operators in your command line, as shown here:

A> SORT < DIR.LST > PRN:

In this example, SORT will obtain its input from the DOS.LST file. Once SORT has sorted this information, it will write the result to your printer.

Glossary

I/O redirection, allows you to direct DOS to send the output of a command to a file or device and to provide the input for a command from a file or device. By default, DOS writes the output of your commands to the screen display.

Advanced Commands

Part Three

Believe it or not, you have essentially learned the DOS commands you will use on a daily basis. At the start of this book, you were told that not only would you get started with DOS, but that you would become a sophisticated DOS user. This section examines all of the advanced DOS commands. Although you will not use all of these commands on a daily basis, knowledge of their existence will make you more confident and productive with your computer.

Although these last chapters are grouped under the heading "Advanced Commands", you do not have to worry. All of the material is presented in just the same manner as the chapters before and you will pick up on the information just as fast. You've made it this far. Don't quit now! Just think how far you've come since Chapter 1.

22 Getting the Most From DOS I/O Redirection

In Chapter 21, you learned about the DOS I/O redirection operators >, >>, and <. At that time you learned that DOS allows you to redirect a command's output from your screen display to either a device or a file. For example, this command will print a directory listing.

```
A> DIR > PRN:
```

You also found that DOS allows you to redirect the source of input for a command from the keyboard to an existing file, as shown here:

```
A> MORE < FILENAME.EXT
```

In this chapter you will examine the final DOS redirection operator, called the DOS pipe (|). First, however, take another look at the DOS FIND command.

Expanding on the FIND Command

In Chapter 21, you used the DOS FIND command exclusively with the DOS input redirection operator, <.

```
A> FIND "word or phrase" < FILENAME.EXT
```

FIND also allows you to specify in your command line one or more files that it is to examine in search of the specified word or phrase. The format for this type of FIND command is

```
A> FIND "word or phrase" FILE1.EXT FILE2.EXT FILE3.EXT
```

FIND will first search the *FILE1.EXT* file for the specified word or phrase. Once FIND has examined that file, it will next search the *FILE2.EXT* and *FILE3.EXT files,* in that order.

Assume, for example, that the FOOTBALL.DAT and BASE-BALL.DAT files contain

```
A> TYPE FOOTBALL.DAT
Falcons -- Atlanta
Seahawks -- Seattle
Cardinals -- Phoenix
Raiders -- Los Angelos
Bills -- Buffalo

A> TYPE BASEBALL.DAT
Dodgers -- Los Angelos
Twins -- Minnesota
Cubs -- Chicago
Cardinals -- St Louis
A's -- Oakland

A>
```

The command

```
A> FIND "Cardinals" FOOTBALL.DAT BASEBALL.DAT
```

will display

```
---------- FOOTBALL.DAT
Cardinals -- Phoenix

---------- BASEBALL.DAT
Cardinals -- St Louis
```

FIND displays the name of each file it is searching before displaying whether or not the word or phrase was found.

If you invoke FIND in this manner, you can still use the DOS output redirection operator, as shown here:

```
A> FIND "Cardinals" FOOTBALL.DAT BASEBALL.DAT > PRN:
```

For example, if you want to have a printout showing how much money you spent on beer during the summer, you can issue the command

```
A> FIND "Beer" JUNE.EXP JULY.EXP AUGUST.EXP > PRN:
```

Qualifying Your FIND Commands

In addition to supporting DOS I/O redirection and multiple files on your command line, the DOS FIND command also supports the following command-line qualifers:

- /C directs FIND to display the total number of lines containing the specified word or phrase for the current file.

- /N directs FIND to display the line number associated with each occurrence of the word or phrase within the file. If you specify this qualifier in conjunction with /C, FIND will ignore /N.

- /V Directs FIND to display all of the lines that *do not* contain the specified word or phrase. If you use this qualifier in conjunction with /C, FIND will ignore /V.

The complete format for the DOS FIND command becomes

```
FIND  [/C] [/V] [/N]  "word or phrase"  [FILENAME [...]]
```

The three periods (...) in the FIND command format tell you that FIND allows you to place multiple file names in the command line.

Also note that the /C, /V, and /N qualifiers must precede the word or phrase that you are searching for.

Using the JUNE.EXP file from Chapter 21, shown here,

```
A> TYPE JUNE.EXP
06-01-88 Beer at Murphy's    $10.00
06-02-88 Rent                $500.00
06-03-88 Beer at ball game   $15.00
06-04-88 Groceries           $45.00
06-06-88 Beer at Shenigans   $10.00

A>
```

you can list the number of lines that contain the word "Beer" in the file, as shown here:

```
A> FIND  "Beer" JUNE.EXP

---------- JUNE.EXP
06-01-88 Beer at Murphy's    $10.00
06-03-88 Beer at ball game   $15.00
06-06-88 Beer at Shenigans   $10.00

A>
```

To list expenses other than beer, use the /V qualifier.

```
A> FIND /V "Beer" JUNE.EXP

---------- JUNE.EXP
06-02-88 Rent                 $500.00
06-04-88 Groceries            $45.00

A>
```

If you use the /N qualifier, FIND will display the line number of each occurrence of the word "Beer".

```
A> FIND /N "Beer" JUNE.EXP

---------- JUNE.EXP
[1]06-01-88 Beer at Murphy's     $10.00
[3]06-03-88 Beer at ball game    $15.00
[5]06-06-88 Beer at Shenigans    $10.00

A>
```

FIND supports each of these qualifiers even if you are using DOS I/O redirection, as shown here:

```
A> FIND /N "Beer" < JUNE.EXP

[1]06-01-88 Beer at Murphy's     $10.00
[3]06-03-88 Beer at ball game    $15.00
[5]06-06-88 Beer at Shenigans    $10.00

A>
```

Using the DOS Pipe

The last I/O redirection operator that you will examine is called the DOS pipe (|). The keyboard key associated with the DOS pipe is found along the middle-right side of your keyboard, as in Figure 22-1.

With a non-write-protected DOS Program disk in drive A, issue the following command:

```
A> DIR | MORE
```

DOS will display your directory listing one screen at a time. Rather than redirecting the listing to a file or device, the DOS pipe makes the output of one DOS command (in this case, DIR) become the input of a second command (MORE), as shown in Figure 22-2.

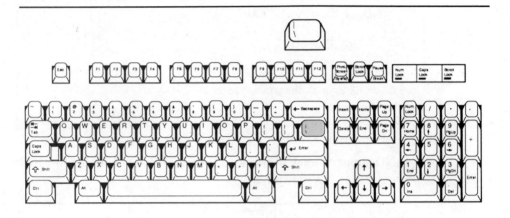

Figure 22-1.   *Location of pipe operator*

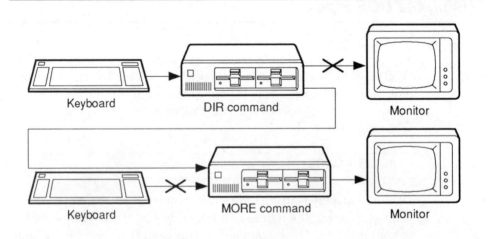

Figure 22-2.   *Piping the DIR command's output to MORE*

With each screenful of information, MORE will again display its familiar "--MORE--" prompt. To display the next screenful of information, press ENTER. To terminate the command, press CTRL-C.

With your DOS Program disk still in drive A, issue the command

```
A> DIR | SORT
```

DOS will respond by displaying a sorted listing of your directory.

```
A> DIR | SORT

                 34 File(s)    5120 bytes free
Directory of  A:\
Volume in drive A is MS330PP01
4201        CPI     17089     7-24-87     12:00a
5202        CPI       459     7-24-87     12:00a
ANSI        SYS      1647     7-24-87     12:00a
APPEND      EXE      5794     7-24-87     12:00a
ASSIGN      COM      1530     7-24-87     12:00a
ATTRIB      EXE     10656     7-24-87     12:00a
CHKDSK      COM      9819     7-24-87     12:00a
COMMAND     COM     25276     7-24-87     12:00a
COMP        COM      4183     7-24-87     12:00a
COUNTRY     SYS     11254     7-24-87     12:00a
DISKCOMP    COM      5848     7-24-87     12:00a
DISKCOPY    COM      6264     7-24-87     12:00a
DISPLAY     SYS     11259     7-24-87     12:00a
DRIVER      SYS      1165     7-24-87     12:00a
EDLIN       COM      7495     7-24-87     12:00a
EXE2BIN     EXE      3050     7-24-87     12:00a
FASTOPEN    EXE      3888     7-24-87     12:00a
FDISK       COM     48919     7-24-87     12:00a
FIND        EXE      6403     7-24-87     12:00a
FORMAT      COM     11671     7-24-87     12:00a
GRAFTABL    COM      6136     7-24-87     12:00a
GRAPHICS    COM     13943     7-24-87     12:00a
JOIN        EXE      9612     7-24-87     12:00a
KEYB        COM      9041     7-24-87     12:00a
LABEL       COM      2346     7-24-87     12:00a
MODE        COM     15440     7-24-87     12:00a
MORE        COM       282     7-24-87     12:00a
```

```
NLSFUNC     EXE     3029     7-24-87   12:00a
PRINT       COM     8995     7-24-87   12:00a
RECOVER     COM     4268     7-24-87   12:00a
SELECT      COM     4132     7-24-87   12:00a
SORT        EXE     1946     7-24-87   12:00a
SUBST       EXE     10552    7-24-87   12:00a
SYS         COM     4725     7-24-87   12:00a

A>
```

Figure 22-3 illustrates how this command works.

Using the DOS pipe, you gain considerable flexibility, as shown in the following commands:

```
A> TYPE  FILENAME.EXT  |  MORE
A> TYPE  JUNE.EXP  |  SORT
A> TYPE  JUNE.EXP  |  FIND  "Beer"
```

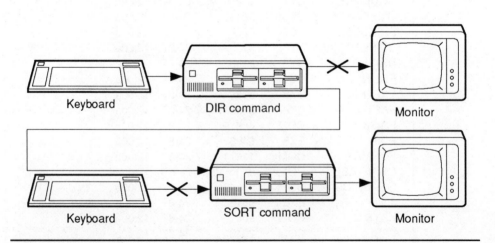

Figure 22-3. *Piping the DIR command's output to SORT*

Multiple Redirection Operators

Just as DOS allows you to place multiple input and output redirection operators on the same command line, as in the command

```
A> SORT < FILENAME.EXT > PRN:
```

DOS also allows you to combine these operators with the DOS pipe operator, as shown here:

```
A> SORT < FILENAME.EXT | MORE
A> FIND "Beer" < JUNE.EXP | SORT > PRN:
A> FIND "Beer" < JUNE.EXP | SORT | MORE
A> TYPE JUNE.EXP | FIND "Beer" | MORE
```

Write-Protected Disks and the DOS Pipe

You used a non-write-protected disk in drive A in a previous example because each time you use the DOS pipe, DOS must create one or more temporary files on your disk. If your disk is write-protected, DOS will not be able to create the files and will display

```
A> DIR | SORT
Write protect error writing drive A
Abort, Retry, Fail?

A>
```

To complete the exercises in the rest of this chapter, you must remove the write-protect tab from your disk.

A Word of Warning

Whenever you use the DOS pipe or redirection operators to manipulate a file, *always* make sure that you change either the file's name or its extension if you are redirecting output back to a file.

```
A> SORT < FILENAME.EXT > NEWFILE.EXT
```

If you use the same file name, as in

```
A> SORT < FILENAME.EXT > FILENAME.EXT
```

DOS will become mixed up as it reads from and writes to the file. You will very likely lose the information that the file contains.

Additional Terminology: stdin and stdout

If you discuss DOS I/O redirection with another user, two terms that often come up are "stdin" and "stdout." These two words are simply abbreviations for "standard input" and "standard output," respectively. Every DOS command has a source of input and output, as shown in Figure 22-4. By default, your keyboard is the source of input, and is thus called stdin. Your monitor, as the default source of output, is called stdout. When you use the DOS I/O redirection operators, DOS modifies the source and destination for stdin and stdout, as shown in Figure 22-5.

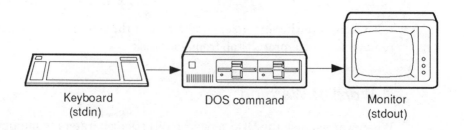

Keyboard   DOS command   Monitor
(stdin)   (stdout)

Figure 22-4.   *Standard input (stdin) and standard output (stdout)*

A> DIR > PRN:

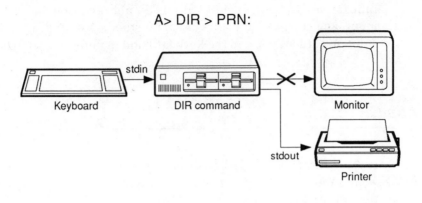

A> MORE <JUNE.EXP

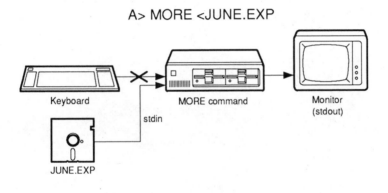

A> DIR | SORT

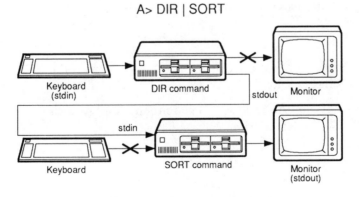

Figure 22-5. *Processing with stdin and stdout*

How DOS does this redirection is not important. What is important for you to know is that stdin is an abbreviation for standard input, and stdout is an abbreviation for standard output. By default, stdin and stdout point to the keyboard and monitor, respectively.

Hands-On Practice

If your DOS Program disk in drive A is write-protected, remove the write-protect tab for this exercise. Reinsert the disk in drive A, and then create the following files:

```
A> COPY  CON  ONE.DAT
ONE.DAT
This file is ONE.DAT
ONE ONE ONE
TWO MINUS ONE is ONE
^Z
                    1 File(s) copied

A> COPY CON TWO.DAT
TWO.DAT
This file is TWO.DAT
It is different from ONE.DAT
ONE Plus ONE is TWO
^Z
                    1 File(s) copied

A>
```

Using the DOS FIND command, display each occurrence of the word "ONE" in the ONE.DAT file.

```
A> FIND  "ONE"  ONE.DAT

---------- ONE.DAT
ONE.DAT
This file is ONE.DAT
```

```
ONE ONE ONE
TWO MINUS ONE is ONE

A>
```

Repeat this command to display each occurrence of the word "ONE" in the TWO.DAT file.

```
A> FIND "ONE" TWO.DAT

---------- TWO.DAT
It is different from ONE.DAT
ONE Plus ONE is TWO

A>
```

Remember, FIND allows you to place both files in the same command line, as shown here:

```
A> FIND "ONE" ONE.DAT TWO.DAT

---------- ONE.DAT
ONE.DAT
This file is ONE.DAT
ONE ONE ONE
TWO MINUS ONE is ONE

---------- TWO.DAT
It is different from ONE.DAT
ONE Plus ONE is TWO

A>
```

Next, use the /C qualifier to display the number of lines containing the word "ONE" in the ONE.DAT file.

```
A> FIND /C "ONE" ONE.DAT

---------- ONE.DAT: 4
```

Using /N, direct FIND to precede each line that contains the word
"ONE" with a line number, as shown here:

```
A> FIND /N "ONE" ONE.DAT

---------- ONE.DAT
[1]ONE.DAT
[2]This file is ONE.DAT
[3]ONE ONE ONE
[4]TWO MINUS ONE is ONE

A>
```

Using the /V qualifier, direct FIND to display each line in the
TWO.DAT file that does not contain the word "ONE".

```
A> FIND /V "ONE" TWO.DAT

---------- TWO.DAT
TWO.DAT
This file is TWO.DAT

A>
```

As you can see, using these qualifiers with FIND gives you most of
the text-lookup capabilities you will require.

From the DOS prompt issue the following commmand:

```
A> DIR | MORE
```

DOS will display your directory listing one screen at a time. Using
the same technique, display a sorted listing of your files:

```
A> DIR | SORT
```

Combine the SORT and MORE commands to display a sorted directory listing one screenful at a time.

```
A> DIR | SORT | MORE
```

Modify this command slightly to print a sorted directory listing of
your files, as shown here:

```
A> DIR | SORT > PRN:
```

Remember that the DOS FIND command supports I/O redirection,
including the DOS pipe. Display all of the SYS files on your disk.

```
A> DIR | FIND "SYS"
ANSI         SYS    1647     7-24-87   12:00a
COUNTRY      SYS    11254    7-24-87   12:00a
DISPLAY      SYS    11259    7-24-87   12:00a
DRIVER       SYS    1165     7-24-87   12:00a

A>
```

Keep in mind that the letters in the phrase must match exactly.
Given the previous FIND command, FIND would not display lines
containing the word "system" since "sys" appears in lowercase.

If you have several DOS subdirectories, you can use the DOS FIND
command to display only the names of your DOS subdirectories.

```
A> DIR | FIND "<DIR>"
```

Summary

In addition to supporting DOS I/O redirection, as in

A> FIND "word or phrase" < FILENAME.EXT

the DOS FIND command allows you to specify on the command line one or more files that FIND will search in order to locate a word or phrase.

A> FIND "word or phrase" FILE.1 FILE.2 FILE.3

To support all of your word search requirements, FIND provides three qualifiers. /C displays the total number of lines containing the word or phrase specified for the current file. /N displays the line number associated with each occurrence of the word or phrase within the file. /V displays all of the lines that *do not* contain the specified word or phrase.

In addition to the input and output redirection operators <, >, and >> that you examined in Chapter 21, DOS also provides the DOS pipe operator (|). Unlike other redirection operators, which redirect input or output to a file or device, the DOS pipe redirects the output of one command so that it becomes the input to a second command. For example, when you invoke the command

A> DIR | MORE

DOS will display your directory listing one screenful at a time.

Summary (continued)

DOS allows you to place multiple redirection operators, including the DOS pipe, in your command line, as shown here:

A> DIR | SORT | MORE

A> DIR | SORT > PRN:

A> SORT < FILENAME.EXT | MORE

If you are using a floppy-disk-based system, you must ensure that your default drive contains a non-write-protected disk when you issue the commands that use the DOS pipe. This is because DOS must create one or more temporary files on the disk. If the disk is write-protected, DOS cannot create these files, and your command fails.

If you are using the DOS I/O redirection operators to modify a file's contents, make sure that you specify a new name for the file in your redirected output.

A> SORT < FILENAME.EXT > NEWFILE.EXT

If you use the same file name for input and output, as in

A> SORT < FILENAME.EXT > FILENAME.EXT

DOS will become confused, and as a result you will lose the information that the file contained.

Glossary

The *DOS pipe* is an input/output redirection operator (similar to >, >>, and <) that instructs DOS to make the output of one command become the input of a second command.

23 More DOS Commands

This chapter examines a collection of commands that you probably won't use on a daily basis, but they are, however, still important enough that you should understand their functions. Because you won't use these commands regularly, you won't be spending much time on them here. If you need more information on each command, refer to the Command Reference section (Part Four) of this book.

Using BREAK to Improve CTRL-C Response

Throughout this text you have used the CTRL-C and CTRL-BREAK key combinations extensively to terminate DOS commands. The amount of time that DOS takes to respond to a CTRL-C depends on the program that you are running. By default, DOS checks for a CTRL-C each time it reads from the keyboard or writes information to your screen display or printer. If the program that you are running does not perform any of these operations on a regular basis, DOS may not acknowledge a CTRL-C for a considerable amount of time.

The DOS BREAK command allows you to increase the number of times that DOS will check for a CTRL-C. The format of the BREAK command is

```
BREAK [ON | OFF]
```

where the command

```
A> BREAK  ON
```

enables extended CTRL-C checking and the command

```
A> BREAK  OFF
```

disables it. When you type **BREAK** and press ENTER, DOS will display the current state of CTRL-C checking (on or off), as shown here:

```
A> BREAK
Break is off

A>
```

You may be wondering why DOS doesn't perform extended CTRL-C checking all of the time. The answer is speed. Once you enable extended CTRL-C checking, you increase the number of times that DOS will check for a user-entered CTRL-C. Entering the command

```
A> BREAK  ON
```

causes DOS to spend a significant amount of time checking for CTRL-C. Everything else that DOS has to do must wait. In other words, extended CTRL-C checking improves your CTRL-C response time, but it does so at the cost of overall system performance.

Comparing Two Floppy Disks with DISKCOMP

One of the first things that you learned how to do with DOS was to copy the contents of one floppy disk to another by using the DISK-COPY command.

```
A> DISKCOPY  A:  B:
```

The DOS DISKCOMP command allows you to compare the contents of two floppy disks.

```
A> DIR  DISKCOMP

Volume in drive A is MS330PP01
Directory of  A:\

DISKCOMP      COM      5848   7-24-87   12:00a
              1 File(s)  5120 bytes free

A>
```

In instances where it is essential to ensure that DISKCOPY has successfully copied the contents of one floppy disk to another, you may want to issue a DISKCOMP command immediately following the DISKCOPY operation.

```
A> DISKCOMP  A:  B:
```

If the disks are identical, DISKCOMP will display

```
Compare OK
```

If differences exist, however, DISKCOMP will display

```
Compare error on side 0, track 0
```

If this message occurs, you should repeat your DISKCOPY command with a new floppy disk in the target drive.

Many people are confused about how two disks can differ even though they contain identical files. In Chapter 10, you learned that DOS records information on your disk by dividing your disk into tracks and placing data into storage locations called sectors. Even though two disks contain the same files, if you use the COPY command to place the files on disk, as shown here,

```
A> COPY *.*  B:
```

there is no way to ensure that DOS used the same sector locations. If the information resides in different sectors, DISKCOMP will flag this fact as a difference. The only way to ensure that DOS places information into the same sectors is to use DISKCOPY.

If you have only one floppy disk drive, invoke the DISKCOMP command as follows:

```
A> DISKCOMP
```

DISKCOMP will prompt you to enter the disks to compare.

```
Insert FIRST diskette in drive A:

Press any key when ready . . .
```

Determining Your DOS Version with VER

DOS was originally released for the IBM PC in 1981. Since that time, user needs have changed, disk technology has increased, and local area networks have come into the limelight. DOS has had to change in order to meet the needs of our ever-changing computer industry.

Each time the DOS developers have enhanced DOS, Microsoft and IBM have assigned a new version number to it. Table 23-1 summarizes the changes MS-DOS has experienced since 1981.

DOS version numbers are composed of two parts: one major version number and one minor version number. Given DOS version 3.2, for example, 3 is the major version number and 2 is the minor number.

When software developers upgrade a program, they normally follow these guidelines.

Version	Date	Function
1.0	1981	Original disk operating system
1.25	1982	Support for double-sided disks
2.0	1983	Support for subdirectories
2.01	1983	Support for international symbols
2.11	1983	Bug corrections
2.25	1983	Extended character set support
3.0	1984	Support for 1.2MB floppy disk
		Support for larger hard disk
3.1	1984	Support for PC networks
3.2	1986	Support for microfloppies
3.3	1987	Support for IBM Personal
		System/2 computers

Table 23-1. *History of MS-DOS*

1. If the upgrade is a significant enhancement in terms of function and capabilities, the major version number is incremented. For example, DOS 3.3 would become DOS 4.0.

2. If the upgrade provides minor enhancements and corrects one or two previous errors, the minor version number is incremented. For example, DOS 3.3 would become DOS 3.4.

Understanding this number system can help you determine whether or not you should upgrade your current version of DOS when a new version number is announced. Most users choose to upgrade only for major version number changes.

The DOS VER command allows you to display your current version of DOS, as shown here:

```
A> VER
MS-DOS Version 3.30

A>
```

The information VER displays depends on your specific version of DOS.

Verifying the Accuracy Of Your Disk Output

It is possible (although very unusual) that your disk may not properly record the information that DOS sends to it. Depending on the nature of the error, DOS may not even be aware of the fact that this error has occurred. The DOS VERIFY command provides you with a means of double-checking the information that DOS stores on disk. If an error occurs, DOS is more likely to detect it when the VERIFY command is used.

The format of the VERIFY command is

```
VERIFY [ON | OFF]
```

where the command

```
A> VERIFY  ON
```

enables disk verification (double-checking), and the command

```
A> VERIFY  OFF
```

disables it. As with the DOS BREAK command, when you type **VERIFY** and press ENTER, DOS will display its current state of disk verification (on or off).

```
A> VERIFY
VERIFY is off

A>
```

You may be asking yourself, "Why not enable disk verification all of the time?" The answer lies in performance, just as it did with the DOS BREAK command. When DOS enables disk verification, it rereads each piece of information that it writes to disk, comparing it to the information that should have been recorded. Depending on how often and how much information you write to disk, the overhead for this procedure can be tremendous.

Since disk errors of this kind are very rare, most users choose the default setting of

```
A> VERIFY  OFF
```

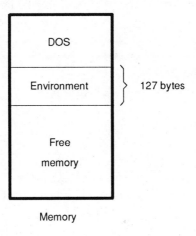

Figure 23-1. *Memory allocation for environment*

What Is the DOS Environment?

Each time DOS boots it sets aside an area in memory, called the DOS environment, for the storage of such items as the current DOS prompt and the directory containing the COMMAND.COM file. You can use the DOS environment to provide information to DOS, your batch files, and even programs. In Chapters 24 and 25, you will examine several uses for the DOS environment.

By default, DOS sets aside 127 bytes for your environment storage space, as shown in Figure 23-1. As long as you do not install any memory-resident software (the DOS GRAPHICS command, for example),DOS will allow your environment to grow in size as your needs require.

The DOS SET command allows you to display the contents of or add items to your environment. To display the environment, type **SET** and press ENTER.

```
A> SET
```

DOS will display the items that reside in your environment, as shown here:

```
A> SET
PATH=
COMSPEC=A:\COMMAND.COM

A>
```

By default, DOS places these two entries into your environment each time it starts. The COMMSPEC= entry tells DOS which subdirectory the COMMAND.COM file resides in. In Chapter 25, you will examine the PATH= entry in detail.

If you want to add an item to the DOS environment, use the following format:

```
SET entry=value
```

For example, to add an entry called FILE that contains the value CHAPTER.23, invoke this command.

```
A> SET  FILE=CHAPTER.23
```

When you again issue the command

```
A> SET
```

DOS will display

```
A> SET
PATH=
COMSPEC=A:\COMMAND.COM
FILE=CHAPTER.23

A>
```

As you can see, DOS has successfully added your entry to the environment. Repeat this process to create an entry called BOOK, whose contents are "Using MS-DOS."

```
A> SET  BOOK=Using MS-DOS
```

The SET command displays

```
A> SET
PATH=
COMSPEC=A:\COMMAND.COM
FILE=CHAPTER.23
BOOK=Using MS-DOS

A>
```

You can also use SET to remove items from your DOS environment. For example, to remove the BOOK entry, type the following:

```
A> SET  BOOK=
```

DOS will remove the entry, as shown here:

```
A> SET
PATH=
COMSPEC=A:\COMMAND.COM
FILE=CHAPTER.23

A>
```

The reasons why you want to place items into the environment will become much clearer in Chapters 24 and 25. You will see how DOS, your batch files, and even programs can access the entries stored in the environment.

Changing Your DOS Prompt

Every chapter should have at least one fun command; for this chapter it is PROMPT. The DOS PROMPT command allows you to define the prompt that DOS displays whenever it is ready for you to enter a command.

By default, DOS uses the current disk drive as a prompt.

```
A>
```

The DOS PROMPT command allows you to set your DOS prompt to virtually anything you want. For example, the command

```
A> PROMPT  YES?
```

changes your prompt to

```
YES?
```

If you press ENTER several times, DOS will repeat the prompt display.

```
YES?
YES?
YES?
```

If at this prompt you were to issue the command

```
YES? PROMPT COMMAND
```

your prompt would change to

```
COMMAND
```

To help you to create sophisticated DOS prompts, DOS predefines the following character combinations:

$b	The pipe character (	)
$d	The current date
$e	The ASCII escape character
$g	The greater-than character (>)
$h	The backspace character (good for erasing)
$l	The less-than character (<)
$n	The default drive letter
$p	The current directory and drive letter
$q	The equal-sign character (=)
$t	The current time
$v	The current version number
$$	The dollar-sign character
$_	The carriage-return and linefeed characters

For example, to set your prompt to YES>, use the $g character as shown here:

```
A> PROMPT YES$g
YES>
```

To set your prompt to the current version number of DOS, use

```
A> PROMPT $v
```

DOS will respond with

```
A> PROMPT  $v
MS-DOS Version 3.30
```

Many people who use complex prompts often combine them with the carriage-return and linefeed characters as well as another prompt. For example, the command

```
A> PROMPT  $v$_$n$g
```

results in

```
A> PROMPT  $v$_$n$g
MS-DOS VERSION 3.30

A>
```

The most useful prompt that you can use is the current directory, which is set with the following command:

```
A> PROMPT  [$p]
[A:\]
```

Your prompt will change as your directory changes.

```
[A:\] CD  DOS
[A:\DOS] CD  COMMANDS
[A:\DOS\COMMANDS] CD  \
[A:\] B:
[B:\]
```

This prompt will help you keep track of where you are on your disk.

To reset your prompt to the current default value, type **PROMPT** and press ENTER.

```
[A:\] PROMPT
A>
```

You should use the current directory prompt on a daily basis; there-fore, place the command

```
PROMPT [$p]
```

in your AUTOEXEC.BAT file, as discussed in Chapter 20. DOS will set your prompt to your current directory every time your system starts.

Hands-On Practice

At the DOS prompt, issue the command

```
A> BREAK
```

DOS will display the current state of extended CTRL-C checking, as shown here:

```
A> BREAK
BREAK is off

A>
```

Remember, by default DOS only checks for a CTRL-C after reading from your keyboard or after writing to your screen display. When you enable extended CTRL-C processing, DOS will acknowledge a CTRL-C much faster. This faster CTRL-C response time, however, is at the cost of overall system performance. Because DOS must now spend addi-tional time checking for CTRL-C, the other functions DOS performs must wait. This may make your system appear sluggish; therefore, most users will retain the default value of

```
A> BREAK  OFF
```

Next, issue the DOS VERIFY command to display the current disk verfication status (on or off).

```
A> VERIFY
VERIFY is off

A>
```

Most users choose to leave disk verification disabled to minimize their system overhead. Remember, when disk verification is on, DOS must reread each piece of information that it writes to disk to ensure that the information is correctly recorded. This processing adds significant system overhead. Because disk errors of this type are rare, most users keep the default value of

```
A> VERIFY  OFF
```

Using the DOS DISKCOPY command, make a copy of your DOS Program disk.

```
A> DISKCOPY  A:  B:
```

To verify that the copy is successful, leave your DOS Program disk in drive A and issue the command

```
A> DISKCOMP  A:  B:
```

DOS will respond with

```
Compare OK
```

This means that your disks are identical.

Leave your DOS Program disk in drive A and place your Supplemental Programs disk in drive B. Repeat the DISKCOMP command

```
A> DISKCOMP  A:  B:
```

DISKCOMP will immediately begin to display differences.

```
Compare error on side 1, track 0
```

Using the CTRL-C key combination, cancel the command.

If you have only one floppy disk drive on your system, you can still perform this exercise by typing

```
A> DISKCOMP
```

Place the correct disks in drive A when DISKCOMP prompts you for them.

```
A> DISKCOMP

Insert FIRST diskette in drive A:

Press any key when ready . . .
```

Using the DOS SET command, display all of the entries in the DOS environment.

```
A> SET
PATH=
COMSPEC=A:\COMMAND.COM
```

Use the SET command to add an entry called FILE whose contents are JUNE.EXP.

```
A> SET FILE=JUNE.EXP
```

A display of the environment contents now shows

```
A> SET
PATH=
COMSPEC=A:\COMMAND.COM
FILE=JUNE.EXP
```

To remove this entry, type the following:

```
A> SET FILE=
```

Invoking SET reveals

```
A> SET
PATH=
COMSPEC=A:\COMMAND.COM

A>
```

Type in the command

```
A> PROMPT TEST
```

DOS will respond by changing your system prompt. Again invoke SET.

```
A> PROMPT TEST
TEST SET
PATH=
COMSPEC=A:\COMMAND.COM
FILE=JUNE.EXP
PROMPT=TEST

TEST
```

As you can see, when you modify your system prompt, DOS places a PROMPT= entry in your DOS environment. Use the SET command to modify your prompt to "YES?" as shown here:

```
TEST SET PROMPT=YES?
YES?
```

DOS responds to the SET command by modifying your prompt.

It is strongly recommended that you change your DOS prompt to the current directory by using the command

```
A> PROMPT  [$p]
[A:\]
```

Therefore, you should place the entry

```
PROMPT  [$p]
```

in your AUTOEXEC.BAT file.

Summary

As you know, the CTRL-C and CTRL-BREAK key combinations allow you to terminate a DOS command. By default, DOS checks for a CTRL-C each time it reads from the keyboard or writes to your screen or printer. The DOS BREAK command allows you to increase the number of times that DOS checks for CTRL-C. DOS is thus more apt to recognize a CTRL-C sooner; however, it must spend a considerable amount of time checking for CTRL-C instead of performing other functions. Your overall system performance may suffer. Most users, therefore, prefer the default value of

A> BREAK OFF

In rare instances, it is possible for your disk drive to incorrectly record the information on disk. DOS may not even be aware that an error has occurred. The DOS VERIFY command directs DOS to double-check all information that it writes to disk by rereading the information and comparing it to the original data. If an error then occurs, DOS is far more likely to catch it. Rereading and comparing the information is a time-consuming process, and such errors are rare; therefore, most users leave disk verification turned off.

Just as the DOS DISKCOPY command allows you to copy the contents of one floppy disk to another, the DOS DISKCOMP command allows you to compare the contents of two disks. If the disks are not identical, DOS will display the side and track numbers of the disks that differ.

The DOS VER command allows you to display the current version of DOS. DOS version numbers are comprised of two parts: major and minor version numbers. Given DOS version 3.2, 3 is the major version number and 2 is the minor number.

Summary (continued)

The major version number is incremented if the upgrade is a significant enhancement in terms of function and capabilities; the minor version number is incremented if the upgrade provides minor enhancements and corrects one or two previous errors.

Each time DOS boots, it sets aside a region in memory called the DOS environment. The DOS SET command allows you to display or add items to the environment. In later chapters you will learn how DOS, your batch files, and even programs can utilize the information contained in the environment.

The DOS PROMPT command allows you to set your system prompt to something other than the default disk drive. To support sophisticated user prompts, the PROMPT command defines several character combinations. Most users should use the command

A> PROMPT [$p]

which directs DOS to use the current directory as the system prompt. This prompt will help you keep track of where you are on disk.

24 Advanced Batch Processing Techniques

In Chapters 19 and 20, you learned that DOS allows you to group logically related commands into text files with the BAT extension. These are called batch files. When you type in the batch file name at the DOS prompt, DOS begins executing the commands contained in the file. You learned that DOS batch files can save you significant time and keystrokes. By the end of Chapter 20, you were actually using batch files to program DOS.

In this chapter you will examine three more batch concepts: how to invoke one batch file from within another, how to pass values (called parameters) into a batch file to increase the number of applications the batch file can support, and how to use the DOS environment to increase the usefulness of your batch file.

By the end of this chapter, you will have all the batch processing tools readily available to become a sophisticated DOS user.

Invoking a Batch File from Within a Different Batch File

So far, all the batch files that you have examined have contained only a few DOS commands. In many cases, however, it is not uncommon to want to invoke one of your commonly used batch procedures from within another batch file. Although this technique seems straightforward, there is one trick involved.

First, if the batch file that you want to invoke (called the nested batch file) is the last statement in another batch file, you have no problem. Assume that the TEST.BAT file contains the following:

```
DATE
TIME
BATFILE
```

Assume that the BATFILE.BAT batch file contains

```
VOL
VER
```

Invoking TEST.BAT results in

```
A> TEST

A> DATE
Current date is Thu  5-12-1988
Enter new date (mm-dd-yy):

A> TIME
Current time is 18:07:37.30
Enter new time:

A> BATFILE

A> VOL

Volume in drive A is DOS

A> VER

MS-DOS Version 3.30

A>
```

As you can see from this example, all the commands in both batch files execute completely.

Rule 1 for Nested Batch Files

If the last command in your batch file invokes a second batch file, you do not have to perform any other processing. Simply specify the second batch file name.

```
CLS
DATE
BATFILE
```

If, however, the nested batch file is not the last command in the other batch file, you must precede the nested batch file name with COMMAND /C. For example, here are the contents of the TEST.BAT batch file when BATFILE is the second command:

```
DATE
COMMAND /C BATFILE
TIME
```

Remember, COMMAND.COM is an external DOS command. As such, it must either reside in the current directory or you must specify a complete path name to the command, as shown here:

```
CLS
B:\DOS\COMMAND /C BATFILE
DATE
```

Given the batch files

```
A> TYPE BATFILE.BAT
VOL
VER

A> TYPE TEST.BAT
DATE
COMMAND /C BATFILE
TIME
```

DOS will display the following upon invocation:

```
A> TEST

A> DATE
Current date is Thu  5-12-1988
Enter new date (mm-dd-yy):

A> COMMAND  /C  BATFILE

A> VOL

Volume in drive A is DOS

A> VER

MS-DOS Version 3.30

A> TIME
Current time is 18:07:37.30
Enter new time:
```

Rule 2 for Nested Batch Files

If you are invoking a second batch file from the middle of a batch file, you must precede the batch file name with COMMAND /C, as shown here:

```
DATE
COMMAND /C BATFILE
TIME
```

For DOS 3.3 users, DOS provides the CALL command, which allows you to invoke one batch file from within another. The format of the command is

```
CALL BATFILE
```

Given the batch file just shown, the procedure under DOS 3.3 becomes

```
DATE
CALL BATFILE
TIME
```

Supporting Several Applications With the Same Batch File

Assume that the T.BAT batch file contains the following:

```
A> COPY  CON  T.BAT
TYPE  TESTFILE.DAT
^Z
              1 File(s) copied
```

This batch file allows you to abbreviate the command

```
A> TYPE  TESTFILE.DAT
```

as simply

```
A> T
```

This batch file, therefore, can save you keystrokes. However, it is only useful when you want to display the contents of the TESTFILE.DAT file. A more useful batch file is one that allows you to abbreviate the TYPE command for all files, as shown here:

```
A> T  TESTFILE.DAT
A> T  AUTOEXEC.BAT
A> T  JUNE.EXP
```

The file names that you are specifying in the command line are called batch parameters. Given the batch file invocation

```
A> T  TEST.EXT
```

the letter "T" is your batch command file name, while TEST.EXT is the first batch parameter. Inside of the T.BAT file, your processing is

```
        TYPE %1
```

The characters "%1" refer to the first batch parameter in the command line. Given the command

```
  A> T  BASEBALL.DAT
```

DOS assigns the file name BASEBALL.DAT to %1. Therefore, the command

```
    TYPE  %1
```

actually becomes

```
    TYPE  BASEBALL.DAT
```

when the command executes.

In a similar manner, given the command

```
  A> BATFILE  A  B  C
```

DOS will specify the batch file parameters as follows:

    A is %1
    B is %2
    C is %3

DOS allows you to specify up to nine parameters in this manner, %1 to %9. Consider this example:

```
  A> BATFILE  A  B  C  D  E  F  G  H  I
```

DOS always defines %0 as the name of the batch file that is currently executing. Therefore, the batch command results in

%0 is BATFILE	%5 is E
%1 is A	%6 is F
%2 is B	%7 is G
%3 is C	%8 is H
%4 is D	%9 is I

Viewing Batch File Parameters

You can use the DOS ECHO command to display the values of each batch parameter. This may help you make some sense out of batch parameters.

Assume that the SHOWPAR.BAT batch file contains:

```
@ECHO %0 %1 %2 %3 %4 %5 %6 %7 %8 %9
```

Invoking SHOWPAR with no parameters results in

```
A> SHOWPAR
SHOWPAR

A>
```

If you specify batch parameters, as in

```
A> SHOWPAR  A  B  C
```

the procedure will display

```
A> SHOWPAR  A  B  C
SHOWPAR A B C
```

Likewise, the command

```
A> SHOWPAR Using MS-DOS taught me DOS
```

results in

```
A> SHOWPAR Using MS-DOS taught me DOS
SHOWPAR Using MS-DOS taught me DOS
```

Testing the Contents
Of Batch Parameters

You learned earlier that DOS batch files support the condition IF *string1==string2*. This condition will make more sense now that you have examined DOS batch parameters. Here's how it works.

Assume that you have three files named BASEBALL.DAT, FOOTBALL.DAT, and HOCKEY.DAT. Rather than having to remember the file name for each when invoking a command, as in

```
A> TYPE BASEBALL.DAT
A> TYPE FOOTBALL.DAT
A> TYPE HOCKEY.DAT
```

you might want to create a batch file that allows you to simply enter

```
A> SHOWME HOCKEY
```

or

```
A> SHOWME BASEBALL
```

When you do so, your batch file (SHOWME) will determine the corresponding file and display its contents.

```
IF %1==BASEBALL TYPE BASEBALL.DAT
IF %1==FOOTBALL TYPE FOOTBALL.DAT
IF %1==HOCKEY TYPE HOCKEY.DAT
```

When you invoke this procedure with

```
A> SHOWME  BASEBALL
```

the condition

```
IF  %1==BASEBALL  TYPE  BASEBALL.DAT
```

evaluates as true, and your batch file will display the contents of the BASEBALL.DAT file. Note that the test for the desired name is case-sensitive.

Testing for a Nonexistent Parameter

In some cases you may need to ensure that the user has specified a batch parameter in the command line. To do so, you must know that if a parameter such as %1 does not exist. The test

```
IF  '%1'==''  DOS_command
```

will evaluate as true. To determine whether or not the user specified at least three batch parameters, you would use

```
IF  '%3'==''  GOTO ERROR
```

Note that you can modify the SHOWME.BAT batch file as follows:

```
IF  '%1'=='' ECHO Specify BASEBALL, FOOTBALL, or HOCKEY
IF  %1== BASEBALL  TYPE BASEBALL.DAT
IF  %1== FOOTBALL  TYPE FOOTBALL.DAT
IF  %1== HOCKEY  TYPE HOCKEY.DAT
```

Handling More Than Nine Batch Parameters

You just learned that DOS provides the parameters %1 to %9, which allows you to handle up to nine batch parameters. In rare instances, however, you may need to specify more than nine parameters. The DOS SHIFT command allows you to do just that. The format of the SHIFT command is simply

```
SHIFT
```

Each time DOS encounters the SHIFT command within a batch file, it slides each parameter one position to the left. In other words, %1 becomes %0, and %2 becomes %1.

Assuming that the SHIFTTST.BAT file contains

```
ECHO OFF
ECHO %0 %1 %2 %3 %4 %5 %6 %7 %8 %9
SHIFT
ECHO %0 %1 %2 %3 %4 %5 %6 %7 %8 %9
```

the command

```
A> SHIFTTST  A  B  C
```

displays

```
A> SHIFTTST  A  B  C
SHIFTTEST  A  B  C
A B C
```

Likewise, given the command

```
A> SHIFTTST  1  2  3  4  5
```

the batch file will display

```
A> SHIFTTST  1  2  3  4  5
SHIFTTEST 1 2 3 4 5
1 2 3 4 5
```

If you add a second SHIFT statement, DOS moves each parameter one location to the left with the SHIFT command. For example, consider the following batch file:

```
ECHO  OFF
ECHO  %0  %1  %2  %3  %4  %5  %6  %7  %8  %9
SHIFT
ECHO  %0  %1  %2  %3  %4  %5  %6  %7  %8  %9
SHIFT
ECHO  %0  %1  %2  %3  %4  %5  %6  %7  %8  %9
```

The command

```
A> SHIFTTST  1  2  3  4  5
```

now displays

```
A> SHIFTTST  1  2  3  4  5
SHIFTTEST 1 2 3 4 5
1 2 3 4 5
2 3 4 5
```

The SHIFT command is convenient when you have more than nine batch parameters, as shown here:

```
A> BATFILE  1  2  3  4  5  6  7  8  9  10  11  12  13
```

Each time you issue the SHIFT command, DOS shifts a new value into %9 if more than nine batch parameters exist. If no value exists, DOS simply leaves the parameter %9 empty. Because it supports more than nine batch parameters, your batch processing can become very sophisticated.

A Complex Example

You just saw that the DOS SHIFT command allows you to place many batch parameters on your command line. Each time DOS executes the SHIFT command, it checks to see if more than nine batch parameters exist. If they do, it assigns a new value to %9. If they do not, DOS leaves %9 empty.

With this in mind, consider the following batch file called ECHO-TEST.BAT, which combines the SHIFT and GOTO commands to display all of the batch parameters on the command line:

```
ECHO OFF
:LOOP
IF '%1'=='' GOTO DONE
ECHO %1
SHIFT
GOTO LOOP
:DONE
```

The command line

```
A> ECHOTEST A B C D E
```

will display

```
A> ECHOTEST A B C D E
A
B
C
D
E
```

This batch file displays the %1 parameter until it is empty. Even if your command line contains more than nine batch parameters, this file will display all of them.

Using this processing, you can increase the capabilities of the T.BAT file.

```
ECHO OFF
:LOOP
IF '%1'=="  GOTO DONE
IF EXIST %1 TYPE %1
SHIFT
GOTO LOOP
:DONE
```

By looping through the batch parameters in this manner, you can issue commands such as

```
A> T JUNE.EXP JULY.EXP AUGUST.EXP
```

In this example, the batch file will first display the contents of the JUNE.EXP file, followed by JULY.EXP and AUGUST.EXP, in that order. If one of the files you specify does not exist, the batch file will ignore it.

As you can see, batch parameters bring out the true power of batch processing.

Using the DOS Environment

In Chapter 23, you learned that you can use the DOS environment in conjunction with your DOS batch files. To do this you must have DOS version 3.3, which supports the concept of named parameters.

Earlier, you used %1 to abbreviate the DOS TYPE command, as shown here:

```
A> COPY CON T.BAT
TYPE %1          .
^Z
                 1 File(s) copied
```

Using a named parameter, T.BAT becomes

```
A> COPY CON T.BAT
TYPE %FILE%
^Z
                    1 File(s) copied
```

When DOS encounters %FILE% in the batch file, it knows by the percent signs that FILE is a named parameter. When DOS recognizes a
named parameter, it searches the DOS environment for a matching
entry. In this example, your entry will take the form FILE=.

Using the DOS SET command, display the current contents of your
environment.

```
A> SET
PATH=
COMSPEC=A:\COMMAND.COM
```

Assuming that the JUNE.EXP file exists in your current directory,
issue the command

```
A> SET FILE=JUNE.EXP
```

DOS will add the entry to the environment, as shown here:

```
A> SET
PATH=
COMSPEC=A:\COMMAND.COM
FILE=JUNE.EXP

A>
```

When you later invoke the T.BAT file, DOS will recognize FILE as
a named parameter, locate the associated entry in your environment,
and display the contents of the JUNE.EXP file.

Hands-On Practice

DOS has difficulty executing batch files that are invoked from within another batch file. If you need to do this, simply precede the batch file name with COMMAND /C, as shown here:

```
CLS
COMMAND  /C  BATFILE
DATE
```

To verify this, first make sure that the COMMAND.COM file resides in the current directory.

```
A> DIR  COMMAND.COM

Volume in drive A is MS330PP01
Directory of  A:\

COMMAND        COM      25276    7-24-87   12:00a
               1 File(s)  5120 bytes free

A>
```

Next, create the batch files ONE.BAT and TWO.BAT.

```
A> COPY  CON  ONE.BAT
VER
COMMAND  /C  TWO.BAT
DATE
VOL
^Z
                1 File(s) copied

A> COPY  CON  TWO.BAT
ECHO  BATCH  FILE  TWO.BAT
^Z
                1 File(s) copied
```

When you invoke ONE.BAT, DOS will display

```
A> ONE

A> VER

MS-DOS Version 3.30

A> COMMAND  /C  TWO

A> ECHO  BATCH  FILE  TWO.BAT
BATCH FILE TWO.BAT

A> DATE
Current date is Thu  5-12-1988
Enter new date (mm-dd-yy):

A> VOL

Volume in drive A is DOS

A>
```

As you can see, both batch files run to completion. They only complete, however, because you have included COMMAND /C. If you are using DOS 3.3, replace COMMAND /C in the previous batch file with the CALL command.

Next, create the SHOWZERO.BAT file, as shown here:

```
A> COPY  CON  SHOWZERO.BAT
ECHO %0
^Z
                 1 File(s) copied

A>
```

Remember that DOS defines the parameters %0 to %9 to support your batch processing. By default, %0 contains the name of the batch file. Invoking the SHOWZERO.BAT file displays

```
A> SHOWZERO

A> ECHO  SHOWZERO
SHOWZERO

A>
```

You can examine several batch parameters by using the DIS-PLAY.BAT file, as shown here:

```
A> COPY  CON  DISPLAY.BAT
ECHO  OFF
ECHO  %1  %2  %3  %4  %5  %6  %7  %8  %9
^Z
                1 File(s) copied

A>
```

Invoke this batch file with the command

```
A> DISPLAY  A  B  C
A B C

A>
```

and the command

```
A> DISPLAY  1  2  3  4  5  6  7  8  9  10
1 2 3 4 5 6 7 8 9

A>
```

As you can see, in the first command, DISPLAY shows all of the batch parameters. In the second, however, DISPLAY only shows the first nine parameters. DOS supports only nine batch parameters unless you use the SHIFT command.

Using the DOS SHIFT command, modify DISPLAY.BAT so that it handles any number of parameters.

```
ECHO  OFF
:REPEAT
IF  '%1'=='  GOTO  DONE
ECHO  %1
SHIFT
GOTO  REPEAT
:DONE
```

Invoking DISPLAY with the command

```
A> DISPLAY  ONE  TWO  THREE  FOUR  FIVE
```

displays the following:

```
A> DISPLAY  ONE  TWO  THREE  FOUR  FIVE

A> ECHO  OFF
ONE
TWO
THREE
FOUR
FIVE

A>
```

Using the first batch parameter, %1, abbreviate the DOS TYPE
command, as shown here:

```
A> COPY  CON  T.BAT
TYPE %1
^Z
            1 File(s) copied

A>
```

You can now easily execute commands such as

```
A> T T.BAT
A> T JUNE.EXP
```

Taking advantage of the DOS FOR command, you can create a powerful T.BAT file, as shown here:

```
A> COPY CON T.BAT
FOR %%F IN (%1) DO IF EXIST %1 TYPE %1
^Z
                1 File(s) copied

A>
```

Using the FOR command in this manner, you can now issue commands such as

```
A> T T.BAT
A> T *.BAT
A> T *.*
```

Remember, the DOS TYPE command does not support wildcard processing.

Combine FOR, SHIFT, IF, and GOTO to create a more powerful T.BAT.

```
ECHO OFF
:REPEAT
IF '%1'=='' GOTO DONE
FOR %%F IN (%1) DO IF EXIST %1 TYPE %1
SHIFT
GOTO REPEAT
:DONE
```

You can now issue commands such as

```
A> T  JUNE.EXP  JULY.EXP  AUGUST.EXP
A> T  *.EXP  *.INC
A> T  *.BAT  *.DAT
```

Using the DOS SET command, display the contents of your DOS environment.

```
A> SET
PATH=
COMSPEC=A:\COMMAND.COM

A>
```

Create an environment entry called FILE that contains ONE.DAT:

```
A> SET  FILE=ONE.DAT
```

Verify your entry by again issuing the SET command.

```
A> SET
PATH=
COMSPEC=A:\COMMAND.COM
FILE=ONE.DAT
```

Next, create the ONE.DAT file, as shown here:

```
A> COPY  CON  ONE.DAT
1
11
111
1111
^Z
              1 File(s) copied

A>
```

Using DOS named parameters, create the NAMEDPAR.BAT batch file, which contains

```
A> COPY  CON  NAMEDPAR.BAT
CLS
TYPE %FILE%
^Z
                 1 File(s) copied

A>
```

Invoking NAMEDPAR results in

```
A> TYPE  ONE.DAT
1
11
111
1111

A>
```

Remove the environment entry FILE.

```
A> SET  FILE=
```

Invoking NAMEDPAR now results in

```
A> TYPE
Invalid number of parameters
```

As you can see, because NAMEDPAR cannot locate a named parameter called FILE in the environment, the command fails.

Summary

When trying to invoke one batch file from within another batch file, DOS may have difficulty. To accomplish this, you must specify COMMAND /C before the batch file name. If you are using DOS 3.3, DOS provides the CALL command, which allows you to invoke one batch file from within another.

To increase the number of applications that your batch files support, DOS provides batch parameters, which are simply values that you pass to your batch procedure. By default, DOS provides support for nine batch parameters, named %1 to %9.

Given the command line

A> BATFILE A B C

DOS would assign the batch parameters as shown here:

%1 contains the letter A
%2 contains the letter B
%3 contains the letter C

Within your batch files, you can manipulate these parameters as shown here:

TYPE %1
ECHO %2
REN %1 %3

In some cases your batch files may require the user to specify at least one batch parameter. Using the DOS IF command, you can test for a nonexistent parameter, as shown here:

IF '%1'==" ECHO NO PARAMETER SPECIFIED

When you need more than nine batch parameters, the DOS SHIFT command allows you to rotate each of your parameters one location to the left with each invocation. In other words, %1 becomes %0, %2 becomes %1, and so on. If more than nine batch

Summary (continued)

parameters exist on the command line, DOS rotates a new value into %9 with each **SHIFT** invocation. Once no additional parameters exist, DOS leaves %9 empty.

In addition to the batch parameters %1 to %9, DOS version 3.3 supports named parameters. You specify a named parameter within your batch file by enclosing the parameter within percent signs, as shown here:

TYPE %FILE%

When DOS encounters the named parameter (in this example, FILE), it searches your environment for a matching entry. Given the previous example, DOS would search the environment for an entry in the form

FILE=

Assuming that DOS finds

FILE=AUTOEXEC.BAT

the previous batch file directs DOS to display that file's contents.

Glossary

A *nested batch file* is a batch file that is invoked within a different batch file, as shown here:

```
DATE
COMMAND /C NESTED
TIME
```

To invoke a nested batch file from within the middle of a batch file, you must use COMMAND /C as shown.

A *batch file parameter* is a value that is passed in the command line to a batch file. DOS provides support for nine batch file parameters, assigning them to the variables %1 to %9. Within the batch file, you can manipulate these variables just as you would files. Given the command

```
A> BATFILE X Y Z
```

DOS would assign the parameters %1 to %3 as follows:

```
%1 contains X
%2 contains Y
%3 contains Z
```

DOS version 3.3 supports *named parameters*, which are batch file parameters that appear in a batch file surrounded by percent signs, as shown here:

```
CLS
TYPE %CHAPTER%
```

When DOS encounters a named parameter, it searches the DOS environment for a matching entry. In this example, DOS would be looking for an entry in the form

```
CHAPTER=CHAPTER.24
```

Glossary (continued)

If DOS finds a matching entry, it substitutes the corresponding value in place of the named parameter. In this case, the net result would be

```
CLS
TYPE CHAPTER.24
```

25 Advanced DOS Directory Commands

In Chapters 16 and 17, you learned how to organize your files logically with DOS directories. At that time you learned about the MKDIR, CHDIR, and RMDIR commands, along with how to manipulate files that reside in directories other than the current default. In this chapter you will learn four DOS commands—PATH, APPEND, SUBST, and JOIN—that increase the effectiveness of your directory manipulation. This chapter is geared more toward fixed disk users because these commands are most commonly used for fixed disks.

Take your time as you examine these commands. Although you will be working with only four commands, they are quite powerful. Your involvement in the "Hands-On Practice" section is therefore critical to your understanding.

Helping DOS Find Your Commands

You learned how to use DOS directories to enhance your file organization in Chapters 16 and 17. At that time you found that in order to execute a command that resides in a directory other than the current default, you have to specify a complete path name, as shown here:

```
C> \DOS\FORMAT A:
C> \DOS\DISKCOPY A: B:
```

Although this processing is fairly straightforward, you can reduce your keystrokes by using the DOS PATH command.

As you know, if you type in a command name without a path name before it, DOS first checks to see if the command is an internal command that resides in the computer's memory, such as CLS, DATE, and TIME. If DOS locates the command in memory, it executes it. If not, DOS checks to see if the command is an external command residing in the current directory. Again, if DOS finds the command, it executes it. Otherwise, DOS displays the message

```
Bad command or file name
```

When DOS fails to locate the command as an external command, it examines the PATH= entry in your DOS environment, as shown here:

```
C> SET
PATH=
COMSPEC=A:\COMMAND.COM

C>
```

In this way DOS determines if you have specified any other directories that it should examine in search of the command. If, for example, the PATH= entry contains

```
PATH=C:\DOS;C:\MISC
```

DOS first searches the \DOS directory on drive C, and then continues the search to the \MISC directory if the file has still not been found. If DOS locates the command in either of these directories, it executes it. Otherwise, DOS continues searching all the directories in the command path, eventually displaying the message

```
Bad command or file name
```

if the command is not found.

The DOS PATH command allows you to specify one or more directories that DOS should examine if it fails to locate an external command. The format of the PATH command is

```
PATH    [pathname [; ...]]
```

or simply

```
PATH ;
```

where *pathname* is the name of a directory that DOS should search for the command. The ";..." characters tell you that PATH allows you to specify multiple directories in the command but that each must be separated by a semicolon, as shown here:

```
C> PATH  C:\DOS
C> PATH  C:\DOS;C:\MISC
C> PATH  C:\DOS;C:\MISC;C:\LOTUS
```

Given the command

```
C> PATH  C:\DOS
```

each time DOS fails to locate your commands in the current directory or the specified directory, it will examine the \DOS directory on drive C in search of the command.

Consider this command:

```
C> PATH  C:\DOS;C:\MISC
```

If DOS fails to locate a command in the specified directory, it will first search the \DOS directory on drive C for the command. If DOS still fails to locate the command, it will search the \MISC directory. If DOS locates the command in either of these directories, it will execute the command. If DOS fails to locate the command in both directories, it will display

```
Bad command or file name
```

If you type **PATH** and press ENTER, DOS will display your current command path, as shown here:

```
C> PATH
PATH=C:\DOS;C:\MISC

C>
```

If you issue the PATH command followed immediately by a semicolon, as in

```
C> PATH ;
```

DOS will erase all of the subdirectories from the command search path. DOS will now search only for commands in the current directory or the directory specified in the command's path name. If you are using a fixed disk, you should place at least the DOS directory that contains your DOS commands in the command path, as shown here:

```
C> PATH  C:\DOS
```

You will probably want to place this PATH command in your AUTO-EXEC.BAT file so that it will be defined each time your system boots.

Many users ask, "Why not just place all of my directories into the command path?" The answer is that this creates too much system overhead, which in turn makes your system slower. Each time you issue an invalid DOS command, DOS must search all of the directories in your command path. If you place all of your directories into the path, DOS may waste considerable time searching all of your files for a command. Therefore, only place the directories that are likely to contain your commands into your DOS command path.

Defining a Search Path for Your Data Files

If you are using DOS version 3.3, DOS provides the APPEND command, which allows you to define a list of directories that DOS will examine in search of your data files. Assume, for example, that your fixed disk contains the directories EXPENSES, INCOME, and MEETINGS. Select the root as your current directory.

```
C> CD \
```

When you invoke the command

```
C> TYPE JUNE.EXP
File not found

C>
```

it fails because DOS cannot find the JUNE.EXP file in the current directory. However, if you include EXPENSES in the data file search path, as shown here,

```
C> APPEND C:\EXPENSES
```

the TYPE command now results in

```
C> TYPE JUNE.EXP
06-01-88 Beer at Murphy's        $10.00
06-02-88 Rent                   $500.00
06-03-88 Beer at ball game       $15.00
06-04-88 Groceries               $45.00
06-06-88 Beer at Shenigans       $10.00

C>
```

The command now succeeds because DOS searches each directory in the data file search path. When you include all three of the direc-

---

APPEND /X /E

Not all DOS commands support data file search paths by default. To increase the number of applications that support data file search paths, use the /X qualifier the *first* time you invoke APPEND.

Likewise, by default, APPEND does not place an entry containing your data file search path in your DOS environment. If one is desired, use the /E qualifier the first time you invoke APPEND.

Remember, APPEND is a DOS version 3.3 command.

---

tories—EXPENSES, INCOME, and MEETINGS—your APPEND command becomes

```
C> APPEND  C:\EXPENSES;C:\INCOME;C:\MEETINGS
```

Just as with the PATH command, if you type **APPEND** and press ENTER, DOS will display your current data file search path.

```
C> APPEND
APPEND=C:\EXPENSES;C:\INCOME;C:\MEETINGS

C>
```

To delete your data file search path, type **APPEND** followed immediately by a semicolon.

```
C> APPEND ;
```

Not all DOS commands recognize the data file search path by default. If you want to expand the number of applications that use the data file search path, you must use the /X qualifier the first time you invoke APPEND, as shown here:

```
C> APPEND /X
```

APPEND also does not place an entry in your DOS environment by default.

```
C> SET
PATH=
COMSPEC=A:\COMMAND.COM

C>
```

To do so (although it is not required for the command to work), use the /E qualifier the first time you invoke APPEND.

```
C> APPEND /E
```

The complete format for the APPEND command is

APPEND [/X] [/E] [*pathname* [; ...]]

or simply

APPEND ;

Some people are concerned that if they create a data file search path, DOS might inadvertnetly delete a file, given a command such as the following:

```
C> DEL FILENAME.EXT
```

DOS, however, has already taken this into account. If you attempt to delete a file that does not reside in the current directory or specified directory, and DOS locates that file in the data file search path, DOS will display the message

```
Access Denied
```

instead of deleting the file. Your files, therefore, are protected from erroneous commands.

If you have a directory of data files that you use on a regular basis, you may want to include the directory in a data file search path. Remember, however, if you place too many directories in the data file search path, DOS will spend more time searching through files than performing useful tasks.

Making Your Directories Appear as a Disk

If you follow the recommendations in Chapters 16 and 17 and logically divide your files into DOS directories, your directory names may become quite long, depending on the number of files on your disk.

```
C> CD \EXPENSES\ JUNE\FOOD
C> TYPE \BUSINESS\TRIPS\ JULY\BOSTON\TRIP.LTR
C> DEL \WORDPROC\LETTERS\AUGUST\DAILY.RPT
```

If you use several such directories on a regular basis, you may end up spending most of your time typing directory names.

Because the DOS developers want you to fully exploit DOS directories, they have provided you with the DOS SUBST command, which allows you to reference DOS path names by specifying a disk drive letter. For example, to abbreviate the directory name \EXPENSES\JUNE\FOOD simply as drive E, enter the command

```
C> SUBST E: \EXPENSES\JUNE\FOOD
```

Each time you refer to drive E for a command such as

```
C> DIR E:
```

or

```
C> TYPE E:FRUITS.CST
```

DOS accesses the \EXPENSES\JUNE\FOOD directory, thus saving you a considerable number of keystrokes.

If you type **SUBST** and press ENTER, DOS will display its current substitutions.

```
C> SUBST
E: => D:\EXPENSES\ JUNE\FOOD

C>
```

If the directory that you are abbreviating contains additional DOS directories, you can access them by specifying the path name immediately following the disk drive abbreviation, as shown here:

```
C> CD  E:\SUBDIR
C> RMDIR  E:\OLDDIR
C> TYPE  E:\MISC\NOTES.DAT
```

To delete a DOS directory abbreviation, type in the disk drive letter followed by /D, as shown here:

```
C> SUBST  E:  /D
```

Invoking SUBST without any parameters illustrates that DOS has removed the substitution as desired.

```
C> SUBST

C>
```

The complete format of the SUBST command is

SUBST [*drive: path name*]

or simply

SUBST *drive:* /D

Many older software packages require that files reside in the root directory of your disk. By using the DOS SUBST command as just shown, you can place these files in any DOS directory, later substituting a disk drive identification for the directory name. The files will end up residing in the root directory of the substituted disk.

Making Multiple Disks Appear as One

If you are using a floppy-disk-based system, there may be times when your programs require more files than you can fit on your floppy disk. The DOS JOIN command allows you to make two disks appear as one.

To use the DOS JOIN command, you must create an empty directory on your primary disk, as shown here:

```
A> MKDIR \JOINDIR
```

Join drive B to this directory, as shown here:

```
A> JOIN B: \JOINDIR
```

When you join a disk to a directory in this manner, several things happen. First, when you reference the joined directory, as in

```
A> DIR \JOINDIR
```

DOS will not only display the files that you have placed into that directory since you issued the JOIN command, but also all of those contained on the joined disk. Second, if you attempt to specifically reference the joined disk, as in

```
A> DIR  B:
```

DOS will display the message

```
Invalid drive specification
```

As far as DOS is concerned, that disk no longer exists. To reference that disk drive, you must use the joined directory:

```
A> DIR \ JOINDIR
```

If you type **JOIN** and press ENTER, DOS will display the current joins.

```
A> JOIN
B: => A:\ JOINDIR

A>
```

To remove the join, type the command

```
A> JOIN  B:  /D
```

Invoke JOIN with no parameters to verify that DOS has indeed removed the join.

```
A> JOIN

A>
```

Most users will not use the JOIN and SUBST commands. However, it is important that you know that they exist and understand their functions.

SUBST and JOIN Restrictions

Although DOS provides the SUBST and JOIN commands for your
convenience, they also make your disk structure appear differently
than it actually is to DOS. For this reason they should not be used
with the following commands:

BACKUP	CHKDSK
DISKCOMP	DISKCOPY
FDISK	FORMAT
LABEL	RECOVER
RESTORE	SYS

Hands-On Practice

At the DOS prompt, type **PATH** and press ENTER. DOS will display
your current command path.

```
A> PATH
No Path

A>
```

If you are using a floppy-disk-based system, issue the command

```
A> PATH A:\
```

If you are using a fixed disk and your DOS commands are stored in
a directory called \DOS, issue the command

```
C> PATH C:\DOS
```

Issue the PATH command to display your current command search
path.

```
A> PATH
```

If you have a floppy-disk-based system, place a formatted disk in drive B and select drive B as your current default disk.

```
A> B:
B>
```

If you are using a fixed disk, select the root directory as your default directory.

```
C> CD \
```

Issue the following DIR command:

```
A> DIR  LABEL
File not found

A>
```

Remember, LABEL is an external DOS command. As you can see, the command does not exist in the current directory; therefore, leaving your DOS Program disk in drive A, issue the command

```
A> LABEL
```

or

```
C> LABEL
```

depending upon your drive configuration. In either case, DOS will respond with

```
A> LABEL

Volume in drive A is DOS

Volume label (11 characters, ENTER for none)?
```

Use CTRL-C to terminate the command. Since DOS did not find the LABEL command in your current directory, it searched the directories specified in your command path. Because you included the directory containing your DOS files, DOS was able to locate the LABEL.COM file.

To remove the command search path, type **PATH** followed by a semicolon.

```
A> PATH ;
```

Invoking the LABEL command again results in

```
Bad command or file name
```

DOS no longer has a command search path to traverse in search of the command.

If you are using DOS version 3.3, and if you have been experimenting with the DOS APPEND command, reboot DOS. If you don't have DOS version 3.3, skip this section on APPEND.

When DOS restarts, enter the command

```
A> APPEND /X /E
```

Remember, you can only specify the /X and /E qualifiers the first time that you invoke APPEND. That is why those of you who had been experimenting with APPEND had to reboot DOS.

Next, create the TEMP directory on your current disk.

```
A> MKDIR \TEMP
```

Copy the FIVE.DAT file to the TEMP directory.

```
A> COPY  CON  FIVE.DAT
5
55
555
5555
55555
^Z
                    1 File(s) copied

A>
```

Select the root directory as your current default.

```
A> CD \
```

Without specifying a complete path name, issue the following
TYPE command:

```
A> TYPE  FIVE.DAT
File not found

A>
```

This command fails because the FIVE.DAT file does not reside in the
current directory. Use the APPEND command to create a data file
search path.

```
A> APPEND  \TEMP
```

If you type **APPEND** and press ENTER, DOS will display your current data file search path.

```
A> APPEND
APPEND=\TEMP

A>
```

Repeat the previous TYPE command.

```
A> TYPE  FIVE.DAT
5
55
555
5555
55555

A>
```

This time the command succeeds—DOS has located the FIVE.DAT file in the TEMP subdirectory.
   Try to delete the FIVE.DAT file.

```
A> DEL  FIVE.DAT
Access Denied

A>
```

Remember, DOS does not allow you to delete a file contained in the data file search path without specifying a complete path name, as shown here:

```
A> DEL  \TEMP\FIVE.DAT
```

Use the DOS SUBST command to abbreviate the directory name \TEMP as drive E.

```
A> SUBST  E:  C:\TEMP
```

Invoke SUBST to display the current substitutions.

```
A> SUBST
E: => C:\TEMP
```

Display the contents of the FIVE.DAT file, as shown here:

```
A> TYPE  E:FIVE.DAT
```

DOS will display

```
A> TYPE  E:FIVE.DAT
5
55
555
5555
55555

A>
```

Again using drive E, list the files contained in the TEMP directory.

```
A> DIR  E:

Volume in drive E is DOS
Directory of  E:\

.                 <DIR>      5-13-88  6:14p
..                <DIR>      5-13-88  6:14p
FIVE         DAT      25   5-13-88  6:14p
            3 File(s)  1976 bytes free
```

To remove this substitution, issue the command

```
A> SUBST  E:  /D
```

The command

```
A> DIR  E:
```

now results in

```
A> DIR  E:
Invalid drive specification
```

Create an empty directory, as shown here:

```
A> MKDIR \ JOINDIR
```

Using the DOS JOIN command, join the disk in drive B to the \JOINDIR directory.

```
A> JOIN  B: \JOINDIR
```

If you are using a fixed disk drive, you may want to join the disk in drive A to the directory, as shown here:

```
A> JOIN  A: \JOINDIR
```

If you select JOINDIR as your current directory with

```
A> CD  \JOINDIR
```

and issue a directory command, DOS will display the files that reside on the disk in drive B. To display the current joins, type **JOIN** and press ENTER.

```
A> JOIN
B: => C:\JOINDIR

A>
```

To remove this join, use the /D qualifier.

```
A> JOIN B: /D
```

Summary

Each time you issue a command from the DOS prompt, DOS first searches its list of internal commands for your command. If DOS finds the command as an internal command, DOS executes it. If DOS does not find the command, it searches the current directory for the command as an external command. Again if DOS finds the command it executes it. If not, DOS checks to see if you have defined a command search path with the DOS PATH command. If so, DOS begins traversing the list of directories contained in your command path.

At a minimum, fixed disk users should include the directory that contains their DOS commands in their command path.

In a similar manner to the DOS command search path, the APPEND command provided by DOS version 3.3 allows you to define a data file search path that contains a list of directories. DOS will examine these directories in search of your data files if it cannot locate the file in the current directory or the specified directory.

By default, not all DOS commands support the APPEND data file search path. To increase the number of applications that support APPEND, issue the APPEND command with the /X qualifier the first time that you invoke it.

As your use of DOS directories increases, so too will the length of your DOS path names. The DOS SUBST command allows you to abbreviate a path name as a single-letter disk drive identification. Instead of typing in the long path name, you can then simply refer to the disk drive letter.

If you are using a floppy-disk-based system, there may be times when your application requires more disk space than you can provide with a single floppy disk. The DOS JOIN command allows you to make two disks appear as one. To use JOIN, you must create an empty directory on your primary disk and then join the disk drive to it.

A> JOIN B: \JOINDIR

Summary (continued)

When you join a disk to a directory in this manner, several things happen. First, when you reference the joined directory with DIR, DOS will not only display the files that you have placed into that directory since you issued the JOIN command, but also all of those contained on the joined disk. Second, if you attempt to specifically reference the joined disk, as in DIR B:, DOS will display the message

Invalid disk drive specified

As far as DOS is concerned, that disk no longer exists. To reference that disk drive, you must use the joined directory.

The following DOS commands should not be used in conjunction with SUBST and JOIN:

BACKUP	CHKDSK
DISKCOMP	DISKCOPY
FDISK	FORMAT
LABEL	RECOVER
RESTORE	SYS

Glossary

A DOS *command path* is simply the list of DOS directories that DOS will examine in search of a command. The DOS PATH command allows you to define the DOS command path.

A *data file search path* is the list of DOS directories that DOS will examine in search of a command. DOS version 3.3 provides the APPEND command, which allows you to define the DOS data file search path.

26 *Advanced File Manipulation*

This chapter introduces you to four DOS file manipulation commands: ATTRIB, COMP, FASTOPEN, and FC. Rather than trying to teach you all of the idiosyncrasies of each command, the chapter introduces you to the basic functions of each command. (The specifics can be found in the Command Reference section of this book.)

You will learn in this chapter that each DOS file has unique characteristics, called *attributes,* that you can use to enhance your processing. You will also learn how to compare two files by using two different commands, COMP and FC. You will also examine the DOS FAST-OPEN command, which can improve your system response time if you are using the same files on your fixed disk repeatedly.

Keep in mind that all of the commands discussed in this chapter are external DOS commands, which means that you must load them from your DOS Program disk.

Setting and Displaying File Attributes

Each time you create or modify a DOS file, DOS assigns a date and time stamp to the file. This appears in your directory listings.

```
A> DIR

Volume in drive A is MS330PP01
Directory of  A:\

4201         CPI    17089    7-24-87    12:00a
5202         CPI      459    7-24-87    12:00a
ANSI         SYS     1647    7-24-87    12:00a
APPEND       EXE     5794    7-24-87    12:00a
ASSIGN       COM     1530    7-24-87    12:00a
ATTRIB       EXE    10656    7-24-87    12:00a
```

DOS also assigns an attribute field to the file. You can access this field, using the DOS ATTRIB command, in order to mark the file as follows:

Read-only   DOS commands that do not modify a file,
                   such as TYPE, COPY, and PRINT, have
                   complete access to a file marked Read-only.
                   Commands that attempt to modify or delete
                   a file marked Read-only will fail.

File Archived   Indicates that this file exists on a DOS backup
                   disk as described in Chapter 30.

Archive   Indicates that this file was created or modified
Required   since the last system backup. The next time
                   backups are performed, a copy of this file
                   needs to be archived.

When you create or modify a file, DOS changes the file's attribute field to reflect the fact that the file needs to be backed up or archived. Chapter 30 discusses the DOS BACKUP command in detail. At that time, the rationale for setting a file's attribute to Archive Required will make more sense. For now, however, understand that each file has a unique attribute field, and the DOS ATTRIB command allows you modify a file's attributes.

To display the current attributes for the files in the current directory, type the command

```
A> ATTRIB *.*
```

DOS will respond by displaying

```
A> ATTRIB *.*
A     A:\4201.CPI
A     A:\5202.CPI
A     A:\ANSI.SYS
A     A:\APPEND.EXE
A     A:\ASSIGN.COM
A     A:\ATTRIB.EXE
A     A:\CHKDSK.COM
A     A:\COMMAND.COM
A     A:\COMP.COM
A     A:\COUNTRY.SYS
A     A:\DISKCOMP.COM
A     A:\DISKCOPY.COM
A     A:\DISPLAY.SYS
A     A:\DRIVER.SYS
A     A:\EDLIN.COM
A     A:\EXE2BIN.EXE
A     A:\FASTOPEN.EXE
A     A:\FDISK.COM
A     A:\FIND.EXE
A     A:\FORMAT.COM
A     A:\GRAFTABL.COM
A     A:\GRAPHICS.COM
A     A:\JOIN.EXE
A     A:\KEYB.COM
A     A:\LABEL.COM
A     A:\MODE.COM
A     A:\MORE.COM
A     A:\NLSFUNC.EXE
A     A:\PRINT.COM
A     A:\RECOVER.COM
A     A:\SELECT.COM
A     A:\SORT.EXE
A     A:\SUBST.EXE
A     A:\SYS.COM
```

If a file requires archiving, DOS will display the letter "A" next to the file, as shown. If your files do not require archiving, DOS will not display the letter "A." Also, if you have set a file to Read-only, DOS will display the letter "R."

Setting a File to Read-only

The +R qualifier allows you to set a file to Read-only:

A>ATTRIB +R FILENAME.EXT

To later reset the file to read/write access, use the -R qualifier:

A> ATTRIB -R FILENAME.EXT

Just as write protecting your disks is a good practice, so too is setting your EXE and COM files to Read-only. Setting them in this manner ensures that an errant DOS command such as

A> DEL *.COM

will result in

Access Denied

To set a file to Read-only, use the DOS ATTRIB command, as shown here:

A> ATTRIB +R FILENAME.EXT

For example, to set the COMMAND.COM file to Read-only, issue the command

A> ATTRIB +R COMMAND.COM

If you later attempt to delete or rename COMMAND.COM, DOS will display

Access Denied

Thus, to protect all of your files, you would issue the command

```
A> ATTRIB +R *.*
```

To once again modify or delete a file marked Read-only, you would use -R instead of +R in the ATTRIB command.

The +A and -A qualifiers allow you to control whether or not a file needs to be backed up. By default, each time DOS creates or modifies a file, DOS flags it as needing to be backed up or archived. If you want to mark a file as requiring a backup yourself, enter the command

```
A> ATTRIB +A FILENAME.EXT
```

If you want to direct DOS *not* to back up a file, enter

```
A> ATTRIB -A FILENAME.EXT
```

In Chapter 27, when you examine the XCOPY command, the rationale for modifying a file's archive flag will become much clearer.

The complete format of the ATTRIB command is

```
ATTRIB [+A | -A][+R | -R] FILENAME.EXT [/S]
```

The optional /S qualifer at the end of the command directs ATTRIB to perform the command for files contained in directories below the current directory or specified directory. If you have a fixed disk, you

---

Setting a File's Archive Flag

Many DOS commands base their processing on the file's archive flag in the attribute field. The archive flag specifies whether or not the file needs to be backed up. The following command allows you to set a file's archive flag:

```
A> ATTRIB +A FILENAME.EXT
```

This command clears a file's archive flag:

```
A> ATTRIB -A FILENAME.EXT
```

can display the attributes of all of the files on your disk by issuing the command

```
C> ATTRIB \*.* /S
```

Comparing the Contents
Of Two Files

Just as the DOS COPY command allows you to copy the contents of one file to another, the DOS COMP command allows you to compare two or more files. When you first start using the COMP command, you will probably only use it to ensure that the DOS COPY command has successfully copied the contents of one file to another, as shown here:

```
A> COPY  FIRST.EXT  SECOND.EXT
          1 File(s) copied

A> COMP  FIRST.EXT  SECOND.EXT
```

If the file was copied successfully, COMP will display the message

```
Files compare ok
```

If a difference exists, COMP will display either the message

```
Compare error at OFFSET n
File 1 = nn

File 2 = mm
```

or the message

```
Files are different sizes, do you wish to
continue (Y/N)?
```

   The difficult aspect of the COMP command is that if two files are different, COMP displays the values that differ in hexadecimal form (that is, the base 16 numbering system). If COMP encounters more than ten differences, it will display the message

```
10 Mismatches - ending compare
```

and terminate the command.

   Like the DOS COPY command, COMP fully supports DOS wildcard characters. Therefore, if you issue the command

```
A> COMP  A:*.*  B:*.*
```

COMP will compare files that exist on both drive A and drive B.

   Consider the files ONE.1 and TWO.2, as shown here:

```
A> COPY  CON  ONE.1
11
11
111
111
11
11
^Z
                1 File(s) copied

A> COPY  CON  TWO.2
22
22
222
222
22
22
^Z
                1 File(s) copied

A>
```

When you issue the command

```
A> COMP  ONE.1  TWO.2
```

DOS will display the following information:

```
A> COMP  ONE.1  TWO.2

A:ONE.1 and A:TWO.2

Compare error at OFFSET 0
File 1 = 31

File 2 = 32

Compare error at OFFSET 1
File 1 = 31

File 2 = 32

Compare error at OFFSET 4
File 1 = 31

File 2 = 32

Compare error at OFFSET 5
File 1 = 31

File 2 = 32

Compare error at OFFSET 8
File 1 = 31

File 2 = 32

Compare error at OFFSET 9
File 1 = 31

File 2 = 32

Compare error at OFFSET A
File 1 = 31

File 2 = 32
```

```
Compare error at OFFSET D
File 1 = 31

File 2 = 32

Compare error at OFFSET E
File 1 = 31

File 2 = 32

Compare error at OFFSET F
File 1 = 31

File 2 = 32

10 Mismatches - ending compare
```

As previously stated, most users will only use the COMP command to ensure that a DOS COPY command was successful.

Improving the Speed
Of DOS File References

Each time you issue a DOS command such as

```
A> TYPE FILENAME.EXT
```

DOS must locate the specified file on disk, open it, and then display its contents. Because they are mechanical, disk drives are slow; therefore, the file-open operation can take a considerable amount of time. If you are repeatedly using the same files (in a database application, for instance), DOS version 3.3 provides the FASTOPEN command to improve your system performance. FASTOPEN does not support floppy disk drives, so it is for hard disk users only.

If you invoke FASTOPEN, DOS begins to keep track of the locations of your files on disk as you open them. If you later have to reopen a previously opened file, DOS knows exactly where the file resides on disk, making your file-open operations much faster.

The format of the FASTOPEN command is

FASTOPEN [*drive:* [=*number_of_files*]]

where *drive* specifies the disk drive that you want DOS to record files for, and *number _ of _ files* specifies the number of files that DOS should track. By default, FASTOPEN tracks ten files.

This FASTOPEN command, for example, directs DOS to store the locations of up to 40 files for your fixed disk (drive C).

```
C> FASTOPEN C:=40
```

It would make sense to track the locations of files on disk that you will be exchanging in and out of the drive quite often. FASTOPEN allows you to track up to 999 files per disk. Tracking this many files, however, would degrade your overall system performance, because DOS would spend a considerable amount of time searching your list of 999 file names with each file opening. Therefore, if you are running a database application or another program that uses the same files on a regular basis, you might consider setting FASTOPEN to approximately 30 files, as shown here:

```
C> FASTOPEN C:=30
```

Once you install file tracking, the only way to remove it is to reboot.

Displaying File Differences

Earlier in this chapter you learned that the DOS COMP command allows you to display the first ten differences between two files. Although COMP can be used to inform you that a file copy did not complete successfully, it is less useful when you are trying to determine the actual differences between two files. DOS version 3.3 provides the FC command to accomplish this task.

With FC you can compare standard text files, called *ASCII files*, or the executable EXE and COM files, called *binary files*. The format of the FC command is

```
A> FC  FILE1.EXT FILE2.EXT
```

If the files are identical, FC will display

```
fc: no differences encountered
```

If lines in the files differ, FC will display the differences.

For example, assume that the NOTES.DAT file contains the following notes:

```
A> TYPE  NOTES.DAT
Notes for June

Watch IBM stock for possible split.

Lawsuit will not affect Microsoft's earnings for the
quarter.  (watch trade releases) Apple?

Delay of spreadsheet packages is very likely for
OS/2 products.

What's going on with new word processors?
WORD, WordPerfect, Sprint? Any others?

Watch out for Borland programming languages migrating to OS/2.

A>
```

Also assume that the OLDNOTES.DAT file contains

```
A> TYPE  OLDNOTES.DAT
Notes for June

Watch IBM stock for possible split.
```

Lawsuit will not affect Microsoft's earnings for the
quarter. (watch trade releases)

Delay of spreadsheet packages is very likely for
OS/2 products.

What's going on with new word processors?
WORD, WordPerfect, Sprint?

Watch out for Borland products migrating to OS/2.

When you issue the command

A> FC NOTES.DAT OLDNOTES.DAT

DOS will display the following:

A> FC NOTES.DAT OLDNOTES.DAT

***** notes.dat
Lawsuit will not affect Microsoft's earnings for the
quarter. (watch trade releases) Apple?

***** oldnotes.dat
Lawsuit will not effect Microsoft's earnings for the
quarter. (watch trade releases)

*****

***** notes.dat
What's going on with new word processors?
WORD, WordPerfect, Sprint? Any others?

Watch out for Borland programming languages migrating to OS/2.

***** oldnotes.dat
What's going on with new word processors?
WORD, WordPerfect, Sprint?
Watch out for Borland products migrating to OS/2.

You are thus quickly able to locate the differences between these two files.

If your files are very large and very different, FC may display the message

```
resynch failed. Files are too different
```

FC is telling you that your files differ so much that it cannot find a location in the files similar enough for it to resume the comparison.

If you type **FC** and press ENTER, FC will display its format, as shown here:

```
A> FC
usage: fc [/a] [/b] [/c] [/l] [/lbNN] [/w] [/t] [/n] [/NNNN] file1 file2

A>
```

As you can see, FC supports several command-line qualifiers. In the Command Reference section of this book (Part Four), you will examine each qualifier in detail. For now, take a look at the most commonly used qualifiers:

- /A tells FC that the files are standard text files (ASCII files).

- /B tells FC that the files are executable files such as FC.EXE (binary files).

- /N directs FC to display line numbers before the differences in standard text files.

For example, consider the following file:

```
A> TYPE DAYS.DAT
Sunday
Monday
Tuesday
Wednesday
Thursday
Friday
Saturday
```

```
A> TYPE  WORKDAYS.DAT
Monday
Tuesday
Wednesday
Thursday
Friday

A>
```

When you invoke the command

```
A> FC  DAYS.DAT  WORKDAYS.DAT
```

DOS will display the following:

```
A> FC  DAYS.DAT  WORKDAYS.DAT
***** days.dat
Sunday
Monday
Tuesday
***** workdays.dat
Monday
Tuesday
*****

***** days.dat
Friday
Saturday
***** workdays.dat
Friday

A>
```

If you use FC to display the differences between two binary files, as in

```
A> FC  /B  COMMAND.COM  FC.EXE
```

FC will display the differences between the files in the form

> *AAAAAAAA B C*

where *AAAAAAAA* specifies the byte address that differ between the files, and *B* and *C* are the hexadecimal values of the bytes that differ.

Hands-On Practice

With your DOS Program disk in drive A, issue the command

```
A> ATTRIB *.*
```

DOS will respond to the ATTRIB command by displaying the attribute field of each file. If ATTRIB displays the letter "A" next to a file, the file has not been backed up since it was created or last modified. If ATTRIB displays the letter "R," the file has been marked as Read-only.

If your disk is write-protected, remove the write-protect tab for the remainder of this chapter. Use the ATTRIB command to set each file in your current directory to Read-only.

```
A> ATTRIB +R *.*
```

Verify that ATTRIB has updated the files by issuing this command.

```
A> ATTRIB *.*
```

In addition to the letter "A," for Archive Required, ATTRIB now precedes each file name with the letter "R," for Read-only.

Assume that the TEST.DAT file contains the following:

```
A> COPY CON TEST.DAT
This is a test file.
^Z
              1 File(s) copied
```

Protect this file by setting it to Read-only.

```
A> ATTRIB +R  TEST.DAT
```

Using the DOS DEL command, delete the TEST.DAT file.

```
A> DEL  TEST.DAT
```

The DOS DEL command fails, displaying

```
Access Denied
```

DEL cannot delete the TEST.DAT file because you have marked the file as Read-only. Again using the ATTRIB command, set the file to read or write access.

```
A> ATTRIB -R  TEST.DAT
```

The DEL command

```
A> DEL  TEST.DAT
```

succeeds this time because the file is no longer write-protected.

If you do not anticipate changing a file's contents, set the file to Read-only by using the ATTRIB command. Read-only files are one more level of protection against errant DOS commands.

Next, create the following files:

```
A> COPY  CON  LETTERS.DAT
A
B
C
D
E
^Z
                    1 File(s) copied

A> COPY  CON  VOWELS.DAT
```

```
A
E
I
O
U
^Z
                        1 File(s) copied
```

Using the DOS COMP command, compare the contents of each file.

```
A> COMP  LETTERS.DAT VOWELS.DAT

C:LETTERS.DAT and C:VOWELS.DAT

Compare error at OFFSET 3
File 1 = 42

File 2 = 45

Compare error at OFFSET 4
File 1 = 20

File 2 = 0D

Compare error at OFFSET 5
File 1 = 0D

File 2 = 0A

Compare error at OFFSET 6
File 1 = 0A

File 2 = 49

Compare error at OFFSET 7
File 1 = 43

File 2 = 0D

Compare error at OFFSET 8
File 1 = 0D
```

```
File 2 = 0A

Compare error at OFFSET 9
File 1 = 0A

File 2 = 4F

Compare error at OFFSET A
File 1 = 44

File 2 = 0D

Compare error at OFFSET B
File 1 = 0D

File 2 = 0A

Compare error at OFFSET C
File 1 = 0A

File 2 = 55

10 Mismatches - ending compare

A>
```

Issue the following COPY command:

```
A> COPY  LETTERS.DAT  LETTERS.NEW
          1 File(s) copied

A>
```

Verify that it was successful by using COMP.

```
A> COMP  LETTERS.DAT  LETTERS.NEW

C:LETTERS.DAT and C:LETTERS.NEW

Files compare ok
```

Most users only use the DOS COMP command to ensure that a file copy was successful.

If you have a fixed disk and are using DOS version 3.3, issue the DOS command

```
C> FASTOPEN C:=30
```

DOS will track the names of up to 30 files. If you later need to reopen a previously opened file that DOS contains in its list of file names, the file opening will occur much faster. Remember, if you make the number of files FASTOPEN is to track too large, you may adversely affect your system performance—DOS must spend considerable time searching its list of files with each file opening.

If you try to execute the FASTOPEN command for a floppy disk drive, as in

```
A> FASTOPEN  A:=30
```

DOS will display

```
A> FASTOPEN  A:=30

Cannot use FASTOPEN for drive A:

A>
```

If you are working with a database program that uses the same set of files repeatedly, you may want to place a FASTOPEN entry in your AUTOEXEC.BAT file.

If you are using floppy disks and MS-DOS version 3.3, locate the DOS FC command, which should reside on your Supplemental Programs disk. Then create the following files:

```
A> COPY  CON  NUMBERS.DAT
1
2
3
4
5
```

```
5
4
3
2
1
^Z
                 1 File(s) copied

A> COPY  CON  NUMBERS.NEW
1
2
3
4
55
55
4
3
2
1
^Z
                 1 File(s) copied

A>
```

Issue the command

```
A> FC  NUMBERS.DAT  NUMBERS.NEW
```

FC will display the differences between each file.

```
A> FC  NUMBERS.DAT  NUMBERS.NEW
***** numbers.dat
4
5
5
4
***** numbers.new
4
55
55
4
```

Use FC to compare the FC.EXE file to another EXE or COM file on the Supplemental Programs disk.

```
A> FC /B FC.EXE LINK.EXE
```

Because you are comparing two binary files, FC will display the differences in the form

AAAAAAAA B   C

where *AAAAAAAA* specifies the byte address in the files that differs, and *B* and *C* are the hexadecimal values of the bytes that differ.

Summary

DOS assigns an attribute field to each file in your directory. You can access this field, using the DOS ATTRIB command, in order to mark the file's characteristics. A file marked as Read-only can be accessed by DOS commands such as TYPE, COPY, and PRINT, which do not modify the file, but commands that attempt to modify or delete the file will fail. A file marked as File Archived exists on a DOS backup disk. A file marked as Archive Required was created or modified since the last system backup; the next time backups are performed, a copy of this file needs to be archived.

Each time you create or modify a file, DOS changes the file's attribute field to reflect the fact that the file needs to be backed up or archived.

If you use the ATTRIB command with +R to set a file to Read-only and later issue a command such as DEL, DOS will display the message

Access Denied

because DOS is unable to modify or delete a read-only file. It is a good practice to set all of your EXE and COM files to Read-only.

Just as the DOS COPY command allows you to copy the contents of one file to another, the DOS COMP command allows you to compare two files. If the files are identical, COMP displays the message

Files compare ok

If differences exist, COMP displays the location of the difference along with the values that differ. COMP displays these values in hexadecimal, which is the base 16 numbering system. Most users only use the COMP command when they have to ensure that a file copy was successful.

If you have a fixed disk and are using DOS version 3.3, the FASTOPEN command may improve your file access response

Summary (continued)

time. Each time DOS opens a file, it must search your disk for the specified file, so the file-open operation may take a considerable amount of time. If you are repeatedly using the same files (for example, in a database application), you may want to issue the FASTOPEN command, which directs DOS to keep track of the locations of your files on disk as you open them. If you must later reopen a previously opened file, DOS knows exactly where the file resides, and your file-open operations are much faster. FASTOPEN does not support floppy disk drives.

MS-DOS version 3.3 also offers the FC command, which allows you to quickly locate and display differences between two files. Unlike COMP, which only displays the hexadecimal offset and the first ten differences of the file, FC displays the actual lines in a text file that differ.

Three of the most commonly used qualifiers for FC are /A, which tells FC that the files are standard text files (ASCII files); /B, which tells FC that the files are executable files such as FC.EXE (binary files); and /N, which directs FC to display line numbers before the differences in standard text files.

Glossary

A *read-only file* is a file that DOS commands such as TYPE, PRINT, and COPY can read, but that commands such as DEL, REN, or COPY cannot modify. The DOS ATTRIB command allows you to set a file to Read-only, which protects the file from errant DOS commands.

Archiving a file means making a duplicate copy of the file's contents on another disk for safekeeping. The DOS BACKUP command allows you to archive your fixed disk to floppy disks. Each time you create or modify a file, DOS marks the file as requiring archiving, because you do not have a current duplicate copy of the file.

27 *Continuing with Advanced File Manipulation*

In this chapter you will take a look at four more DOS commands that deal specifically with file manipulation: RECOVER, SHARE, RE-PLACE, and XCOPY. Although you will examine the function of each command, it is most important that you understand XCOPY. As you will learn in this chapter, XCOPY gives you many "eXtensions" to the DOS COPY command.

Recovering Portions Of a Damaged File or Disk

Although it is not common, disks can become damaged by smoke, fingerprints, misuse, and sometimes even by old age. When this occurs, DOS may lose several sectors on the disk that contained parts of a file, as shown in Figure 27-1.

When this kind of damage occurs, you may want to save as much of the undamaged portions of the file as possible. The DOS RECOVER command allows you to do this.

WARNING: Just as the DOS RECOVER command can *salvage* parts of a damaged file or disk when it is used correctly, RECOVER can just as quickly *destroy* a file or disk that is not damaged. Therefore, only use RECOVER as a last resort.

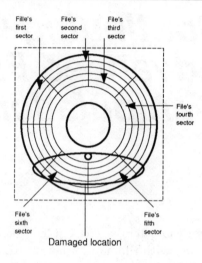

Figure 27-1.   *Lost sectors on a disk*

Assume, for example, that when you issue the command

```
A> TYPE JUNE.EXP
```

DOS starts writing unrecognizable characters as it begins displaying the contents of your file. When this occurs, the file may have become damaged. Repeat the command to see if the error goes away. If it does not, issue the command

```
A> RECOVER JUNE.EXP
```

RECOVER is an external DOS command that attempts to save as much of the undamaged portion of the file as possible. When the command completes, you may have to edit the file to restore some of its previous contents, but that is better than losing the entire file.

NOTE: Do not use RECOVER to recover an EXE or COM file. Remember, such files are programs that contain lists of instructions for the computer to perform. If some of the instructions are missing from the recovered program, you can destroy files and possibly even your disk by executing it.

If you have an entire disk that once contained programs and files that DOS can no longer access, you may be able to recover some of the files on the disk by specifying the RECOVER command with just a disk drive identification. For example, use drive B.

```
A> RECOVER  B:
```

When you use RECOVER in this manner to recover an entire disk, RECOVER places the files that it recovers into the root directory with names in the form

    FILE*nnnn*.REC

where FILE0001.REC is the first file recovered, FILE0002.REC is the second, and so on. A directory listing appears as follows:

```
A> DIR  B:

Volume in drive B has no label
Directory of  B:\

FILE0001       REC      1024      5-15-88    2:26p
FILE0002       REC      1024      5-15-88    2:26p
FILE0003       REC      1024      5-15-88    2:26p
               3 File(s)  359424 bytes free

A>
```

When RECOVER completes, use the DOS TYPE command to see if you can locate familiar text files. Again, do not execute recovered programs.

NOTE: Although the DOS RECOVER command can sometimes save a damaged file or disk, it does not replace good backup procedures. In Chapter 30, you will examine the DOS BACKUP command in detail. At that time you need to establish proper backup procedures to ensure that you always have duplicate copies of your files.

Replacing Specific
Files on Your Disk

If you are using DOS version 3.2 or later, DOS provides the REPLACE command to allow you to selectively copy files from a source to a target disk. By default, REPLACE works very much like the DOS COPY command, copying all the files from the source disk to the target.

Assuming that none of (or only a portion of) the files on the source disk reside on the target disk, you must use the REPLACE /A qualifier to direct REPLACE to add files found on the source disk to the target, as shown here:

```
A> REPLACE *.*  B:  /A
```

This command directs REPLACE to add all of the files that reside on drive A to drive B. If files exist with the same name on both disks, REPLACE will ignore them.

Since REPLACE is an external DOS command, floppy-disk-based system users must start with the DOS Supplemental disk in drive A in order to issue the REPLACE command. REPLACE provides the /W (Wait) qualifier, which is used as shown here:

```
A> REPLACE *.*  B:  /W
```

This qualifier allows you to issue the REPLACE command with your DOS Program disk in drive A and then insert your source disk in drive A when REPLACE prompts

```
Press any key to begin replacing file(s)
```

For example, if the disk in drive A contains

```
A> DIR

Volume in drive A is DOS
Directory of  A:\

ONE          DAT     6     5-15-88  2:27p
TWO          DAT     6     5-15-88  2:27p
THREE        DAT     6     5-15-88  2:27p
FOUR         DAT     6     5-15-88  2:27p
FIVE         DAT     6     5-15-88  2:27p
             5 File(s)  359392 bytes free

A>
```

and the disk in drive B contains

```
A> DIR  B:

Volume in drive B is TEST
Directory of  B:\

ONE          DAT     6     5-15-88  2:27p
TWO          DAT     6     5-15-88  2:27p
THREE        DAT     6     5-15-88  2:27p
             3 File(s)  359792 bytes free

A>
```

when you issue the command

```
A> REPLACE  *.*  B:
```

REPLACE will replace each file found on drive B with its counterpart
from drive A.

```
A> REPLACE *.* B:

Replacing B:\ONE.DAT

Replacing B:\TWO.DAT

Replacing B:\THREE.DAT

3 file(s) replaced
```

To add the files that are not present on drive B, use the /A qualifier, as shown here:

```
A> REPLACE *.* B: /A

Adding B:\FOUR.DAT

Adding B:\FIVE.DAT

2 file(s) added
```

Assume that you have the same files located in several directories on the target disk. By specifying the REPLACE /S qualifier, as shown here,

```
A> REPLACE *.* B: /S
```

REPLACE will locate every occurrence of the replacement files on the target disk, regardless of the directory in which files reside.

You cannot use REPLACE to completely upgrade DOS from one version to another. Although REPLACE allows you to move all of your external files to the correct directory, you must use the SYS command, as explained in Chapter 28, to update the DOS hidden files. The Command Reference section of this book (Part Four) examines each of REPLACE's qualifiers in detail.

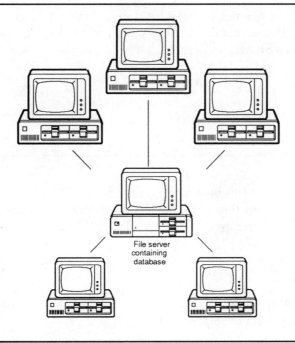

Figure 27-2. *File sharing and local area networks*

Sharing Files in a
Local Area Network

The DOS SHARE command exists specifically for computers that are part of a local area network, as shown in Figure 27-2. If your computer is part of a local area network, the SHARE command helps DOS perform the coordination necessary for computers to share files. The individual who installed your network should have already ensured that the SHARE command has been executed correctly if it is required for your system.

If you are not using a local area network, do not use the DOS SHARE command. The Command Reference section (Part Four) examines SHARE in detail.

Using XCOPY's Extended File-Copy Capabilities

Throughout this book you have used the DOS COPY command extensively to copy files from one disk or directory to another. DOS provides a second file-copy command, called XCOPY, which allows you to

- Selectively copy files based on the file's creation and modification date

- Selectively copy files based on the file's archive attribute flag, as discussed in Chapter 26

- Copy files contained in directories below the current directory to the target disk, creating an identical directory structure on the target disk

Unlike COPY, which is an internal DOS command, XCOPY is an external command. In its most basic form, XCOPY works just like COPY.

```
A> XCOPY  XCOPY.EXE  B:
              1 File(s) copied
```

Because XCOPY is an external DOS command, if you are a floppy disk user you will need to place your DOS Program disk in drive A to execute the command. Since the data you want to copy probably resides on another disk, you need to invoke XCOPY with the /W (Wait) qualifier.

```
A> XCOPY  *.*  B:  /W
```

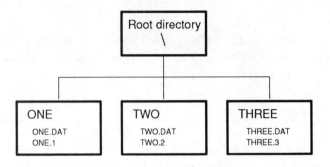

Figure 27-3. *Sample directory structure*

When XCOPY later prompts you with

```
Press any key to begin copying file(s)
```

remove the DOS Program disk from drive A and replace it with the disk containing your source files.

Assuming that your source disk contains the directory structure shown in Figure 27-3 and that your target disk in drive B is unused, the command

```
A> XCOPY \*.* B: /S /W
```

will copy all of the files found on the disk in drive A to the disk in drive B, creating an identical directory structure.

```
A> DIR  B:

Volume in drive B has no label
Directory of  B:\

ONE             <DIR>    5-15-88    2:35p
TWO             <DIR>    5-15-88    2:35p
```

```
THREE            <DIR>    5-15-88    2:35p
                 3 File(s)  359424 bytes free
```

In some cases you may want to selectively copy files from your source disk or directory to the target. To do so, use the /P qualifier, as shown here:

```
A> XCOPY *.*  B:  /P
```

With each new file, XCOPY will prompt you to determine whether or not the file should be copied to the target location, as shown here:

```
FILENAME.EXT (Y/N)?
```

To copy the file, type **Y**, and to exclude the file, type **N**. XCOPY will repeat this process for all of the remaining files.

When you only want to copy files that you have created since a specific date, use the XCOPY /D (Date) qualifier, as shown here:

```
A> XCOPY *.*  B:  /D:12:25:88
```

In this example, XCOPY will only copy the files that have been created or modified since December 25, 1988, from the source location to drive B

Remember that XCOPY allows you to selectively copy files based on the value of the archive flag in the file's attribute field. To support this processing, XCOPY provides the /A and /M qualifiers as defined here:

■ /A directs XCOPY to copy all files marked as Archive Required to your target disk.

■ /M directs XCOPY to copy all files marked as Archive Required to your target disk. Upon successful completion of a file copy, XCOPY will clear the file's archive flag, setting the file to No Archive Required.

If you have a fixed disk system, you may have already received this error message when you tried to copy files from your fixed disk to a floppy disk.

```
Insufficient disk space
```

You have no easy way of continuing the copy operation where you left off once you insert a new floppy disk. However, there is a solution to this problem: use XCOPY in conjunction with the DOS ATTRIB command. First, using the DOS ATTRIB command, set all of your files to Archive Required, as shown here:

```
A> ATTRIB +A *.*
```

Next, place a floppy disk in drive A and issue the command

```
C> XCOPY *.* A: /M
```

XCOPY will begin copying files to your target disk. Each time a file is copied successfully, XCOPY marks the file as No Archive Required. When your floppy disk fills, insert a new floppy disk in drive A and again issue the command

```
C> XCOPY *.* A: /M
```

XCOPY has been marking each file it copies as No Archive Required, so it can pick up exactly where it left off, with the first file set to Archive Required.

As you can see, XCOPY provides you with tremendous processing capabilities.

Hands-On Practice

With a blank disk in drive A, create the following files:

```
A> COPY  CON  ONE.DAT
1
1
^Z
                    1 File(s) copied

A> COPY  CON  TWO.DAT
2
2
^Z
                1 File(s) copied

A> COPY  CON  THREE.DAT
3
3
^Z
                1 File(s) copied

A>
```

Place your DOS Program disk in drive A, and use the /W (Wait) qualifier with the DOS REPLACE command, as shown here:

```
A> REPLACE  *.*  B:  /W  /A
```

When REPLACE prompts

```
Press any key to begin adding file(s)
```

remove your DOS Program disk and insert the disk containing your newly created files. REPLACE will add all three files to the disk in drive B, as shown here:

```
A> REPLACE *.* B: /W /A

Press any key to begin adding file(s)

Adding B:\ONE.DAT

Adding B:\TWO.DAT

Adding B:\THREE.DAT

3 file(s) added

A>
```

Using the DOS MKDIR command, create a subdirectory called \TEMP on drive B.

```
A> MKDIR B:\TEMP
```

Copy the ONE.DAT file into TEMP, as shown here:

```
A> COPY ONE.DAT B:\TEMP
              1 File(s) copied

A>
```

Again insert your DOS Program disk in drive A and issue the command

```
A> REPLACE *.* B: /S /W
```

When REPLACE displays the prompt

```
Press any key to begin replacing file(s)
```

exchange your DOS Program disk with the disk containing the
ONE.DAT, TWO.DAT, and THREE.DAT files, and press ENTER.
REPLACE will respond with

```
A> REPLACE *.*  B:  /S  /W

Press any key to begin replacing file(s)

Replacing B:\ONE.DAT

Replacing B:\TWO.DAT

Replacing B:\THREE.DAT

Replacing B:\TEMP\ONE.DAT

4 file(s) replaced

A>
```

As you can see, when the REPLACE command includes the /S
qualifier, REPLACE searches every directory on the target disk for
files matching the replacement files on the source disk.

Place your DOS Program disk into drive A and issue the command

```
A> XCOPY *.*  B:  /W
```

When XCOPY prompts you with

```
Press any key to begin copying file(s)
```

place your previous source disk back into drive A and press ENTER.
XCOPY will respond with

```
A> XCOPY *.*  B:  /W

Press any key to begin copying file(s)

Reading source file(s)...
ONE.DAT
```

```
TWO.DAT
THREE.DAT
3 File(s) copied

A>
```

When XCOPY completes, repeat this command. This time, however, direct XCOPY to copy all of the files that have an archive flag set to Archive Required. Use the /M qualifier to tell XCOPY to mark each file successfully copied as No Archive Required. Your new command is

```
A> XCOPY *.* B: /M /W
```

XCOPY responds with

```
A> XCOPY *.* B: /W /M

Press any key to begin copying file(s)
Reading source file(s)...
ONE.DAT
TWO.DAT
THREE.DAT
3 File(s) copied

A>
```

Repeat the previous command.

```
A> XCOPY *.* B: /M /W
```

This time XCOPY displays the message

```
A> XCOPY *.* B: /W /M
Press any key to begin copying file(s)

0 File(s) copied

A>
```

This response should make sense, because your last XCOPY command cleared the Archive Required flag for each of the files on the disk. Therefore, XCOPY found no files that required archiving.

Place your source disk back in drive A and issue these commands:

```
A> MKDIR  ONE
A> MKDIR  TWO
A> COPY *.* \ONE
ONE.DAT
TWO.DAT
THREE.DAT
            3 File(s) copied

A> COPY *.* \TWO
ONE.DAT
TWO.DAT
THREE.DAT
            3 File(s) copied

A>
```

Insert your DOS Program disk into drive A and issue the command

```
A> XCOPY *.*  B:  /S
```

Because you have included the /S qualifier, XCOPY will copy all the files contained in directories below the current directory and create an identical directory structure on drive B, as shown here:

```
A> DIR  B:

Volume in drive B has no label
Directory of  B:\

ONE          DAT    6    5-15-88  2:27p
TWO          DAT    6    5-15-88  2:27p
THREE        DAT    6    5-15-88  2:27p
ONE               <DIR>      5-15-88  2:46p
TWO               <DIR>      5-15-88  2:46p
        5 File(s)  357376 bytes free
```

Summary

If one of your disks or files becomes damaged during the course of your work, the DOS RECOVER command may allow you to recover the undamaged section. To recover a single file on drive B, for example, you would enter

A> RECOVER B:FILENAME.EXT

DOS would recover all of the data in the file up to the damaged location.

If your entire disk was damaged, you could simply enter

A> RECOVER B:

If RECOVER can recover any files, it will place the files into the root directory with the names FILE*nnnn*.REC, where FILE-0001.REC is the first file recovered. Using the DOS TYPE command, display the contents of these files in search of familiar text files. RECOVER cannot recreate a deleted file.

Do not execute recovered EXE or COM files. If these programs are missing sections following a recovery, executing them could damage your files or even your disk.

Using the DOS REPLACE command, you can easily update the contents of one disk with the files contained on another. Using various REPLACE qualifiers, you can add missing files to the target, or you can replace all files contained on the target disk with the updated versions from your source disk. REPLACE requires that you have DOS version 3.2 or greater.

If you are using a local area network, you may have to invoke the DOS SHARE command. SHARE helps DOS perform the file coordination required to share files among several computers. If you are not using a local area network, you will not need the SHARE command.

The DOS XCOPY command provides you with capabilities beyond those offered by the DOS COPY command. XCOPY, which is an external DOS command, enables you to copy files

Summary (continued)

selectively based on the file's creation and modification date or on the file's archive attribute flag. It also lets you copy files contained in directories below the current directory to the target disk, creating an identical directory structure on the target disk.

If you have a fixed disk, you will probably want to use XCOPY on a regular basis; the XCOPY.EXE file is easily accessible.

28 DOS System Commands

This chapter will examine the last four DOS commands that affect your system—ASSIGN, CTTY, EXIT, and SYS. You may never have to issue these commands; therefore, this chapter covers only the basic function of each. (You can find the specifics of each command in the Command Reference section.)

You should read each section presented here. You probably won't have to use these commands on a daily basis, but someday you may have a problem that one of these commands can solve. If you don't know that the command exists, your problem may go unsolved.

Convincing DOS That One Disk Is Another

Some older software packages require that all of their programs and data files reside on drive A. If you have a floppy-disk-based system, this is no problem. However, if you are using a fixed disk, you should place your files in a DOS directory on your fixed disk instead of always having to use drive A.

If you place your files onto your fixed disk, but DOS continues to search for them on drive A, you haven't accomplished anything. The ASSIGN command allows you to trick DOS into believing that one disk drive is really another.

For example, assume that you have placed your files into a directory on your fixed disk. You want DOS to look to drive C instead of A; therefore, you issue the command

```
C> ASSIGN C=A
```

This forces any command that references drive A, such as

```
C> DIR  A:
```

or

```
C> TYPE  A:FILENAME.EXT
```

to be routed by DOS to drive C. If your files are on your fixed disk and you want to invoke a program that always looks to drive A, type **AS-SIGN C=A** at the C> prompt immediately before executing the program. When the program completes, you can resume normal disk drive operations by typing **ASSIGN** at the C> prompt.

Although you may see the ASSIGN command used in this manner, Microsoft recommends that you issue the DOS SUBST command instead of ASSIGN. The following commands function identically:

```
C> ASSIGN  C=A
C> SUBST  A:  C:\
```

Getting Commands
From a Connected Terminal

In the past, some software developers connected terminals to their computer's auxiliary port during their software testing, as shown in Figure 28-1. In order to use the terminal's screen and keyboard in place of the computer's, the programmers had to issue the command

```
A> CTTY AUX:
```

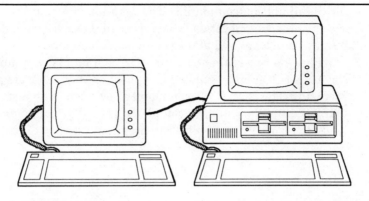

Figure 28-1.   *Connecting a terminal to an auxiliary port*

The DOS CTTY command allowed them to direct DOS to obtain its commands and to direct its output to the specified device. (In the command just shown, DOS used the AUX device.) When the software developers completed their testing and wanted to resume normal operations, they entered this command from their terminal keyboard.

```
A> CTTY  CON:
```

You may never require the CTTY command. If you invoke CTTY without a terminal attached to your system, you will have to reboot DOS to continue.

Exiting DOS Back to an Application Program

Several application programs, such as your word processor, database package, or spreadsheet, provide a menu option that allows you to temporarily suspend what you are doing, branch to DOS, and execute file manipulation commands. The manner in which this is done is specific to each application. The net result, however, is that DOS will display its prompt and allow you to issue commands.

When you have finished your DOS commands, you must have a way to exit DOS and resume the application that you were previously executing. The DOS EXIT command allows you to do just that.

If, for example, you have completed your DOS commands and are ready to resume your application program, type

```
A> EXIT
```

The DOS prompt will disappear, and you will be right back where you left off in your application.

If you have not yet branched to DOS from within an application program, you still issue the DOS EXIT command. DOS will ignore your command and redisplay its prompt.

```
A> EXIT
A>
```

Transferring Hidden Files to a Disk

In Chapter 6, you learned how to create a bootable disk by using the DOS FORMAT command, as shown here:

```
A> FORMAT  B:  /S
```

At that time, you found that in order for a disk to be bootable, it must contain the COMMAND.COM file along with DOS hidden operating system files. Examine your DOS Program disk with CHKDSK to verify the existence of the hidden files.

```
A> CHKDSK  B:

362496 bytes total disk space
53248 bytes in 2 hidden files
25600 bytes in 1 user files
283648 bytes available on disk

655360 bytes total memory
581392 bytes free

A>
```

If you are using a fixed disk, you certainly do not want to reformat your disk with each version of DOS if you can help it. DOS provides the SYS command so that you can transfer the hidden operating system files to your fixed disk, as shown here:

```
A> SYS  C:
```

For example, if you are using DOS version 3.2 on your fixed disk and you want to upgrade to DOS version 3.3, you first must boot the new version of DOS (version 3.3) in your floppy drive. Using the DOS SYS command

```
A> SYS  C:
```

you can transfer the hidden files to your fixed disk. If SYS is successful, DOS displays the message

```
System transferred
```

You can now copy the COMMAND.COM file from your floppy disk to drive C, and copy the DOS external command files to the directory on drive C that contains your DOS commands.

If the SYS command fails, DOS will display

> No room for the system on destination disk

You must reformat your disk in order to upgrade DOS. Before you do so, however, read Chapter 30, which discusses the DOS BACKUP and RESTORE commands. These commands allow you to save all of the files on your fixed disk to floppy disks before reformatting, and then later place the files back onto the fixed disk.

Hands-On Practice

If you have a floppy-disk-based system, place a formatted disk in drive B and your DOS Program disk in drive A. Issue the command

> A> SET A=B

to direct DOS to route all requests for drive B to the disk contained in drive A. If you then issue the command

> A> DIR B:

DOS will not display the files contained on the disk in drive B, but rather the files on drive A.

If you are using a fixed disk, issue the following commands:

> C> ASSIGN C=A
> C> DIR A:

Again, instead of displaying the files contained on drive A, DOS will display the files contained on drive C.

In either case, to resume normal operations, type **ASSIGN** and press ENTER. If you then invoke either the command

> A> DIR B:

or the command

```
C> DIR  A:
```

DOS will display the files on the correct disk.
    Format a disk for use by DOS, but do not make the disk bootable:

```
A> FORMAT  B:
```

Using the DOS CHKDSK command, verify that the newly formatted
disk does not contain hidden system files.

```
A> CHKDSK  B:

362496 bytes total disk space
362496 bytes available on disk

655360 bytes total memory
581392 bytes free

A>
```

Use the SYS command to transfer the hidden files to the new disk.

```
A> SYS  B:
```

Again using CHKDSK, verify the existence of the hidden files.

```
A> CHKDSK  B:

362496 bytes total disk space
53248 bytes in 2 hidden files
309248 bytes available on disk

655360 bytes total memory
581392 bytes free
A>
```

Remember, before you can boot the disk, you must copy the COM-
MAND.COM file to it.

```
A> COPY COMMAND.COM B:
```

Your new disk is now a bootable DOS disk.

Summary

Some older software packages always look for their program files and data files on drive A. If you are using a fixed disk and want to place these files in a DOS directory on the fixed disk, you must trick DOS into looking for the files on a disk other than the one in drive A. The DOS ASSIGN command allows you to route disk input/output requests from one disk to another.

If you have a program that always looks to drive A, you can redirect disk request to the new disk by using ASSIGN immediately before invoking the program. You can restore normal operations when the program completes by typing **ASSIGN** and pressing ENTER.

In the past, some program developers connected terminals to their auxiliary port during software development and testing. To use the terminal screen and keyboard instead of the computer's screen and keyboard, these programmers had to tell DOS to send its output and get its input from the AUX device. They achieved this by using the CTTY command. When the programmers were done using the terminal, they invoked the command from their terminal keyboard, and normal operations resumed. Most of you will never have to issue the CTTY command. If you do so without a terminal connected to your computer, you will have to reboot DOS to continue.

Several application programs allow you to temporarily branch to DOS in order to perform file manipulation commands. When you have completed your DOS commands and are ready to resume the application program, you must type **EXIT** at the DOS prompt. The DOS prompt will disappear, and you will resume your application program where you left off.

The DOS SYS command allows you to transfer to a target disk the hidden system files that DOS requires in order for a disk to be bootable. If you are upgrading from one version of DOS to the next on your fixed disk, you may be able to issue the DOS SYS command to transfer the hidden system files to disk instead of having to reformat.

Summary (continued)

If the DOS SYS command successfully transfers the hidden system files, you can then copy COMMAND.COM and the external DOS commands to your disk. If the SYS command fails, you will probably have to reformat your disk in order for it to be bootable under the new DOS version.

29 Customizing DOS For Enhanced Performance

Each time DOS boots, it searches your root directory for a file named CONFIG.SYS, which allows you to configure several DOS parameters and thereby achieve better system performance. CONFIG.SYS is a standard text file that you can create by using this command:

```
A> COPY CON CONFIG.SYS
```

CONFIG.SYS can contain several one-line entries that define different DOS characteristics. In this chapter you will examine each of the CONFIG.SYS entries in detail, and you will learn the guidelines you should follow to get the best possible performance from DOS. As you read about each parameter, keep in mind that each entry directly affects a specific aspect of DOS. Erroneous entries, therefore, can significantly decrease your system's performance.

DOS uses the contents of the CONFIG.SYS file to configure itself in memory. Each time you modify the file's contents, you must reboot DOS for the changes to take effect.

Enabling Extended CTRL-C Checking At System Start Up with BREAK

In Chapter 23, you learned that DOS, by default, only checks for a user-entered CTRL-C after reading from your keyboard or writing to your screen display or printer. By issuing the command

```
A> BREAK  ON
```

you can direct DOS to increase the number of times that it will test for a CTRL-C. Usually DOS will recognize the fact that you have pressed CTRL-C much sooner if you have extended checking. However, this additional checking adds overhead that may reduce your overall system performance.

By default, therefore, DOS leaves extended CTRL-C checking turned off. If you want DOS to enable CTRL-C checking each time it boots, place the following entry in CONFIG.SYS:

```
BREAK=ON
```

DOS will enable extended CTRL-C checking as soon as your system becomes active.

Reducing Your Disk Input/Output Operations with BUFFERS

By now you are familiar with the mechanical nature of both floppy and fixed disk drives, which causes disk drive references to be inherently slow. To reduce the number of disk input/output operations that it must perform, DOS provides large storage regions in memory called disk buffers. Each disk buffer can store 512 bytes of data, as shown in Figure 29-1.

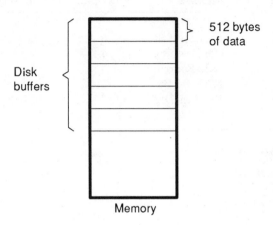

Figure 29-1. *Storage space of a disk buffer*

As stated in Chapter 10, DOS divides your disks into storage regions called sectors, which are also 512 bytes in size, as shown in Figure 29-2.

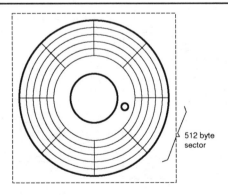

Figure 29-2. *Disk sectors as storage regions*

Name	Address	Pay Grade	Dependents
Jones	1327 First St.	5	2
Kent	926 Downing	4	5
Lowry	1822 Fourth Ave.	4	1
Smith	173 Fifth St.	5	5
Wilson	19 Jones Dr.	7	3

Table 29-1.   *Payroll Employee Records*

When DOS reads information from or writes information to disk, the smallest amount of information that DOS can transfer is 512 bytes. Assume, for example, that you have a payroll program that reads employee records like those in Table 29-1. Each record contains a name, address, pay grade, and number of dependents, and each record is 128 bytes in length.

When your program reads the first record in the file from disk, DOS must read 512 bytes (the disk sector size) from disk instead of the 128 bytes that are required for the first record. The 512 bytes that DOS reads are put into a disk buffer, and only the first 128 requested bytes are returned to the program. Figure 29-3 illustrates this process.

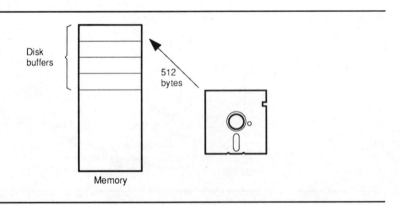

Figure 29-3.   *DOS reading a sector from a disk*

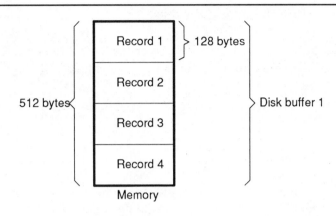

Figure 29-4. *DOS storing record information in memory*

You benefit from DOS reading data in this manner: DOS has read 512 bytes from disk with one read operation, so the next three records in the file now reside in memory, not in the slow disk. When your program later tells DOS to get the second record from the file, DOS does not have to read your disk because it already has the information in memory. This is also true for the third and fourth records, as shown in Figure 29-4.

This process reduces the number of slow disk-read operations by a factor of four. Here is what DOS does each time it must read information from disk:

1. Checks to see if the information already resides in memory in a disk buffer

2. Uses that data if it is in a disk buffer

3. If the data does not reside in memory, reads the disk sector containing the data from disk into a disk buffer

The BUFFERS= entry in CONFIG.SYS allows you to specify the number of buffers for which DOS provides space in memory each time your system boots. The format of this entry is

BUFFERS=*number_of_buffers*

where *number_of_buffers* can range from 2 to 255. Most users will achieve maximum performance by using 20 to 25 buffers, as shown here:

BUFFERS=25

If you make the number of buffers too large, you will use memory that DOS may need for other tasks, as well as create a long list of buffers that DOS must examine each time it needs to read information from disk. Therefore, for most applications, the value of 25 disk buffers is recommended.

Specifying Country-Specific Date, Time, And Currency Formats with COUNTRY

The DOS COUNTRY= CONFIG.SYS entry allows you to direct DOS to use the date, time, and currency formats for a country other than the United States. Chapter 31 details this entry discusses the steps that you must take to support international configurations.

Providing Additional Software Support for DOS with DEVICE

Each device on your computer—keyboard, screen, printer, disk drive, or mouse—requires specific software that enables DOS to use it. Such software is called a device driver. For your most common devices, such as your screen, printer, and keyboard, DOS provides all of the software you will require. However, if you purchase a mouse or plotter, you will probably have to install additional software to support it. The process of making such software available to DOS is called *installing a device driver*.

The CONFIG.SYS DEVICE= entry allows you to install a device driver each time DOS boots. The format of the DEVICE= entry is

DEVICE=*FILENAME.EXT*

where *FILENAME.EXT* is the name of the file containing the device-driver software. By default, most device-driver files have the extension SYS. If you list the SYS files in a DOS version 3.3 Program disk, for example, DOS will display

```
A> DIR *.SYS

Volume in drive A is MS330PP01
Directory of  A:\

ANSI             SYS     1647     7-24-87     12:00a
COUNTRY          SYS    11254     7-24-87     12:00a
DISPLAY          SYS    11259     7-24-87     12:00a
DRIVER           SYS     1165     7-24-87     12:00a
                 4 File(s)   5120 bytes free

A>
```

If you examine the Supplemental Programs disk, DOS displays

```
A> DIR *.SYS

Volume in drive A is MS330PP02
Directory of  A:\

KEYBOARD         SYS    19735     7-24-87     12:00a
PRINTER          SYS    13559     7-24-87     12:00a
RAMDRIVE         SYS     6481     7-24-87     12:00a
                 3 File(s)   2048 bytes free

A>
```

As you can see, DOS provides you with several device drivers, which are explained briefly here:

ANSI.SYS	Provides cursor and keyboard control for specific software programs
COUNTRY.SYS	Contains country-specific date, time, currency, and other unique formats to help international DOS users (discussed further in Chapter 31)
DISPLAY.SYS	Provides codepage switching support for the display (discussed in Chapter 31)
DRIVER.SYS	Contains a device driver required for systems using an external floppy disk drive
KEYBOARD.SYS	Contains country-specific keyboard templates
PRINTER.SYS	Provides codepage switching support for the printer (discussed in Chapter 31)
RAMDRIVE.SYS	Contains the device driver required to install a RAM disk drive in your computer's memory

To install the ANSI.SYS device driver, for example, the DEVICE= entry is

```
DEVICE=ANSI.SYS
```

If the ANSI.SYS device driver resides in a DOS directory, your entry might be

```
DEVICE=C:\DOS\ANSI.SYS
```

Many third-party software packages use ANSI.SYS for cursor and keyboard control. The documentation that accompanies such software will instruct you to install the ANSI.SYS driver as shown here:

```
DEVICE=ANSI.SYS
```

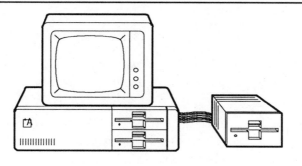

Figure 29-5. *External disk drive*

Advanced DOS users often use the ANSI driver in conjunction with the DOS PROMPT command to redefine keys and change screen colors. That subject, however, is beyond the scope of this book.

All of the computers illustrated in this book have had one or two built-in floppy disk drives. Some systems, however, have external floppy disk drives, as shown in Figure 29-5. Users of this type of system must install the DRIVER.SYS device driver. The format of the command is

```
DEVICE=DRIVER.SYS [ /D:drive_number ] [ /C ]
[ /F:form_factor_index ] [ /H:max_head_number ] [ /N ]
[ /S:sectors_per_track ] [ /T:tracks_per_side ]
```

where the following definitions apply:

- The *drive_number* variable is the physical disk drive number from 0 to 255. Drive A is 0, B is 1, and so on.

- The /C qualifier ensures that DOS will test whether the disk drive door is closed before proceeding.

- The *form _ factor _ index* variable specifies the device type as follows:

Form Factor	Device
0	180K or 360K drive
1	1.2MB drive
2	720K 3.5-inch drive
3	8-inch single density
4	8-inch double density
5	Fixed disk
6	Tape drive
7	1.44MB drive

■ The *max_head_number* variable specifies the maximum number of heads on the disk from 1 to 99. The default is 2.

■ The /N qualifier informs DOS that the device is nonremovable.

■ The *sectors _ per _ track* variable specifies the number of sectors on each track from 1 to 99. The default value is 9.

■ The *tracks _ per _ side* variable specifies the number of tracks per side from 1 to 999. The default value is 80.

To install software support for a third floppy disk capable of storing 720K, you enter

```
DEVICE=DRIVER.SYS /D:2
```

If you purchase an external floppy disk drive, the documentation that accompanies the device should include the correct DRIVER.SYS entry.

Later in this chapter you will examine the RAMDRIVE.SYS device driver, and you will create a RAM disk drive in your computer's memory. As you will see, a RAM drive acts very much like a standard disk drive, allowing you to store programs and files. Unlike mechanical disk drives, which are slow, a RAM drive resides in your computer's memory (known as random access memory, or RAM), which means it is fast. However, because your computer's memory cannot retain its contents when you turn your machine off or restart DOS, RAM drives too will lose their contents. If you have several programs that you use frequently, they may be good candidates for residing in a RAM drive.

Overriding Default Parameters for Disk and Tape Drives with DRIVPARM

DOS supports two types of devices: character mode devices and block mode devices. Character mode devices work with one character of information at a time. Common character mode devices include your screen display and printer. Block mode devices work with blocks or groups of characters. Your disk drive is a block mode device because DOS transfers information to and from a disk in 512-byte sectors.

The DOS DRIVPARM=CONFIG.SYS entry allows you to override the default characteristics for block devices. Its format is

```
DRIVPARM= /D:drive_number[/C]
[ /F:form_factor_index ] [ /H:max_head_number ] [/N]
[ /S:sectors_per_track ] [ /T:tracks_per_side ]
```

where each of the qualifiers are the same as those defined in the DRIVER.SYS entry. Using DRIVPARM to configure a tape drive, for example, your entry might be

```
DRIVPARM=/D:04 /F:6 /H:1 /S:64 /T:10
```

Not all versions of DOS support the DRIVPARM entry (refer to the *MS-DOS User's Guide*). Most of you will never need to use this entry, but you should know that it exists.

Specifying the Number of DOS File Control Blocks with FCBS

Older DOS software packages (those prior to DOS version 2.0) use a facility called a file control block (FCB) to open files. Periodically, under a new version of DOS, you may encounter errors when you invoke these programs. If so, you will need to include the FCBS= entry in CONFIG.SYS. The format of this entry is

FCBS=*max_open,leave_open*

where the following is true:

■ *max_open* specifies the number of file control blocks, from 1 to 255, that DOS can have open at one time. The default for *max_open* is 4.

■ The *leave_open* value specifies the maximum number of files, from 1 to 255, that DOS cannot automatically close if it needs to open additional files. The default value is 0.

The only time you will need to include this entry in CONFIG.SYS is when you are experiencing errors in older software applications. In such cases, try this setting:

FCBS=20,4

DOS versions 2.0 and greater no longer use file control blocks for file input or output.

Specifying the Number of Files DOS Can Open at One Time with FILES

By default, DOS allows eight files to be open at one time. However, DOS predefines the destination of five of these files in order to support DOS I/O redirection. By default, therefore, your applications cannot open more than three files at one time. For most applications, this restriction is unacceptable. You must use the FILES= entry in CONFIG.SYS to change it. The format of this entry is

FILES=*number_of_files*

where *number_ of _ files* specifies the number of files, from 8 to 255, that DOS can have open at one time. Most users select the value 20.

```
FILES=20
```

Even if you do not include any other entries in CONFIG.SYS, you should specify the FILES= entry.

Specifying the Last Valid Disk
Identification Letter with LASTDRIVE

In Chapter 25, you learned that DOS allows you to substitute a logical device name in place of a DOS directory when you use the SUBST command. At that time, if you attempted a command such as

```
A> SUBST  F:  \SUBDIR
```

the command failed and DOS displayed

```
A> SUBST  F:  \SUBDIR
Invalid parameter

A>
```

By default, the last disk drive letter that DOS allows you to specify is E. If you need to specify a disk drive letter greater than E, you must use the LASTDRIVE= entry in CONFIG.SYS. Its format is

```
LASTDRIVE=letter
```

where *letter* is any character of the alphabet from A to Z. For example, this entry allows you to use drives A to I:

```
LASTDRIVE=I
```

Using SHELL to Define Your Command Processor to DOS

In Chapter 6, you learned that COMMAND.COM contains the internal DOS commands, such as CLS, DIR, and TYPE. In addition, COMMAND.COM is responsible for displaying the DOS prompt and processing the commands that you enter. COMMAND.COM, therefore, is your default command processor.

When you become an experienced programmer, you may want to write your own command processors. You need a means of making your command processor, instead of COMMAND.COM, active at system start-up. The DOS SHELL= entry allows you to do so as follows:

SHELL=*FILENAME.EXT*

If your new command processor is called MYPROC.COM, for example, the SHELL= entry would be

SHELL=MYPROC.COM

In Chapter 18, you learned that the root directory of your fixed disk root should only contain the AUTOEXEC.BAT, CONFIG.SYS, and COMMAND.COM files. The SHELL= entry allows you to remove COMMAND.COM from the root directory and place it into a DOS directory. If all your DOS files reside in a directory called DOS, your SHELL= entry is

SHELL=C:\DOS\COMMAND.COM /P

The /P qualifier is mandatory and tells DOS to leave the command processor permanently installed in memory after the start-up procedures are complete. Without /P, DOS would remove the command processor from memory before executing AUTOEXEC.BAT.

When you move COMMAND.COM to a DOS directory, you must place a corresponding SET command in your AUTOEXEC.BAT file. This tells DOS where COMMAND.COM resides.

```
SET COMSPEC=C:\DOS\COMMAND.COM
```

If DOS cannot locate COMMAND.COM when it reboots, it will display the message

```
Bad or missing Command Interpreter
```

If this occurs, use your original DOS Program disk to reboot so that you can fix your error.

By default, DOS sets aside 127 bytes for your environment. Unless you install memory-resident software, such as the DOS GRAPHICS command, DOS allows the environment space to grow to meet your needs. It is usually recommended that you issue all your SET commands before installing memory-resident software. Even when you do this, DOS may eventually display the message

```
Out of environment space
```

If this occurs, the DOS SHELL= CONFIG.SYS entry allows you to allocate space for the DOS environment at system start up. For example, if you use the SHELL= entry

```
SHELL=COMMAND.COM /P /E:4096
```

you have allocated environment space for 4096 bytes or characters of information. DOS allows you to allocate up to 32,767 bytes of environment space with the /E qualifier.

Controlling Hardware Interrupts With STACKS

Many of the hardware devices on your system perform specific tasks and then interrupt DOS when they are done. A good example of such a device is your disk drive. DOS tells your disk drive to write a sector (512 bytes) of information to disk and to let DOS know when it is done. When the disk drive is done, it interrupts the work DOS is currently performing to notify DOS. If many devices interrupt DOS simultaneously, DOS may display the message

```
Fatal: Internal Stack Failure, System Halted
```

If DOS is handling one interrupt and another occurs, it must set the work it is doing aside on a stack. In this context, a stack is simply a location at which DOS can place the work that it is currently performing in order to handle the interrupt. DOS can quickly use up stack space. Although this is not a likely occurrence, if it does happen you must allocate more stacks for DOS to use. The STACKS= entry in CONFIG.SYS shown here can accomplish this:

```
STACKS=number_of_stacks,size_of_stack
```

The *number_of_stacks* value specifies how many stacks are available for DOS to use and can range from 0 to 64. The *size_of_stack* value specifies the size of each stack from 0 to 512. This setting is usually adequate:

```
STACKS=8,512
```

Using a RAM Disk

Earlier in this chapter you were introduced to the fact that the RAMDRIVE.SYS device driver allows you to install a RAM drive in your computer's memory. In general, you can think of a RAM drive as a fast disk that you access with a single-letter disk drive identification. The major difference between a RAM disk and your standard disk drive is that whenever you turn your computer off or reset DOS, the contents of your RAM disk are lost. RAM disks are thus good candidates for storing frequently used programs, but not necessarily their data.

To install a RAM drive, use RAMDRIVE.SYS, as shown here:

```
DEVICE=RAMDRIVE.SYS [disk_space] [sector_size]
[directory_entries] [/E | /A]
```

where the following definitions apply:

- The *disk_space* variable specifies the size of your RAM disk in kilobytes (K). The default size is 64K. The minimum size is 16K.

- The *sector_size* variable specifies the size of each sector in bytes. The default is 128 bytes. Acceptable values are 128, 256, 512, and 1024.

- The *directory_entries* variable specifies the number of files that the disk can store. The default value is 64. The minimum value is 4, and the maximum is 1024.

- The /E qualifier directs DOS to use extended memory for the disk.

- The /A qualifier directs DOS to use extended memory that meets the Lotus/Intel/Microsoft Expanded Memory Specification for the disk.

For example, the following entry creates a 128K RAM drive:

```
DEVICE=RAMDRIVE.SYS 128
```

If you need to store more than 64 files on your RAM drive, you might specify

```
DEVICE=RAMDRIVE.SYS 128 512 128
```

Some versions of DOS call the device driver DOS uses to create a RAM drive VDISK.SYS. If you cannot find RAMDRIVE.SYS on your disk, search for VDISK.SYS. In either case, the command's format is the same.

Hands-On Practice

If you are using a floppy-disk-based system, remove the write-protect tab from your floppy disk and place it in drive A. If you are using a fixed disk, select the root directory as your current default.

Issue the command

```
A> DIR  CONFIG.SYS

Volume in drive A is MS330PP01
Directory of  A:\

File not found

A>
```

If your disk already contains the CONFIG.SYS file, use the DOS TYPE command to display the file's contents.

```
A> TYPE  CONFIG.SYS
```

If CONFIG.SYS does not exist, create a new configuration file, as shown here:

```
A> COPY  CON  CONFIG.SYS
FILES=20
BUFFERS=25
^Z
                    1 File(s) copied

A>
```

Reboot your system. Since DOS will now locate your CONFIG.SYS file, it will use the values that it contains to override the defaults. If for some reason your system does not restart, use your original DOS Program disk to get the system booted so that you can correct your error.

Just so that you can experiment with a RAM drive, create one by using RAMDRIVE.SYS. First, format a bootable system disk.

```
A> FORMAT B:/S
```

Make sure that the COMMAND.COM file resides on the disk. If it does not, use the COPY command to copy it. Next, copy the RAMDRIVE.SYS file to this new disk. Remember, RAMDRIVE.SYS may reside on your Supplemental Programs disk. A directory of that disk now reveals

```
A> DIR  B:

Volume in drive B has no label
Directory of  B:\

COMMAND     COM     25307     5-11-88   2:05p
RAMDRIVE    SYS      6481      7-24-87  12:00a
            2 File(s)  276480 bytes free

A>
```

Create the following CONFIG.SYS file on your new disk:

```
A> COPY  CON  B:CONFIG.SYS
DEVICE=RAMDRIVE.SYS
^Z
                1 File(s) copied

A>
```

Place this disk in drive A and then reboot. When DOS starts, it will display

```
Microsoft RAMDrive version 1.19 virtual disk D:
Disk size: 64k
Sector size: 128 bytes
Allocation unit: 1 sectors
Directory entries: 64
```

which tells you that DOS has created a RAM disk with the disk identification D. To select your RAM drive, type

```
A> D:
D>
```

A directory of this disk reveals

```
A> DIR  D:

Volume in drive D is MS-RAMDRIVE
Directory of  D:\

File not found

A>
```

Place your DOS Program disk back in drive A and copy several files from your DOS Program disk to drive D.

```
A> COPY  FORMAT.COM  D:
            1 File(s) copied

A> COPY  LABEL.COM  D:
            1 File(s) copied

A> COPY  DISKCOPY.COM  D:
            1 File(s) copied

A>
```

Again issue the Directory command.

```
A> DIR  D:

Volume in drive D is MS-RAMDRIVE
Directory of  D:\

FORMAT        COM      11671    7-24-87   12:00a
LABEL         COM       2346    7-24-87   12:00a
```

```
DISKCOPY     COM    6264     7-24-87   12:00a
             3 File(s)  42112 bytes free

A>
```

Note how fast DOS displays the files. The major advantage of a RAM disk is its speed.

Place your new disk back into drive A and reboot. When DOS restarts, issue the Directory command

```
A> DIR  D:

Volume in drive D is MS-RAMDRIVE
Directory of  D:\

File not found

A>
```

As you can see, your RAM drive loses its contents whenever you turn your computer off or restart DOS. Many users will place their most commonly used commands in a RAM drive so that they can minimize the swapping of floppy disks.

If you do not want to use a RAM drive, your CONFIG.SYS should at a minimum contain

```
FILES=20
BUFFERS=25
```

Summary

Each time your system boots, DOS examines your root directory for a file named CONFIG.SYS, which contains entries that you specify in order to customize your system for best performance.

CONFIG.SYS is a standard text file that you can create with EDLIN or by copying the file from your keyboard, as shown here:

A> COPY CON CONFIG.SYS

Each entry in CONFIG.SYS is a single line entry that DOS reads at system start up to override the default system parameters.

The BREAK= CONFIG.SYS entry allows you to enable extended CTRL-C checking each time your system boots. The DOS BUFFERS= entry in CONFIG.SYS allows you to specify the number of disk buffers that DOS supports. Each time DOS reads information from your disk drive, it reads at least one sector of information into a location in memory called a disk buffer. When you request that DOS read information from disk, it will first search its list of disk buffers to see if the data already resides in memory. If it does, DOS does not have to perform the slow disk-read operation. Most users should set the BUFFERS= value to 25.

The DOS COUNTRY= CONFIG.SYS entry allows you to specify the date, time, and currency formats for international DOS users. Chapter 31 examines this entry in detail.

Each device on your computer, be it a keyboard, screen, printer, disk drive, or mouse, requires specific software that enables DOS to use it. Such software is called a device driver. For your most common devices, such as your screen, printer, and keyboard, DOS provides all of the software you will require. The DEVICE= entry in CONFIG.SYS allows you to install a device driver each time your system boots.

The DOS DRIVPARM= CONFIG.SYS entry allows you to override the default values that DOS assigns for your block mode devices, such as a tape or disk drive. Not all versions of DOS support DRIVPARM (refer to the *MS-DOS User's Guide*).

Summary (continued)

Many older software programs (prior to DOS version 2.0) use file control blocks (FCBs) to open and manipulate files. If you experience errors when running these older programs, place the entry

FCBS=20,4

in your CONFIG.SYS file.

The DOS FILES= entry allows you to define the maximum number of files DOS can open at one time. By default, DOS supports eight files. Of these eight, DOS predefines five for I/O redirection, allowing your applications to open only three files at one time. Therefore, all users should place the entry

FILES=20

in their CONFIG.SYS file.

The LASTDRIVE= entry in CONFIG.SYS allows you to specify the letter of the last disk drive DOS can support. By default, E is the last valid disk drive letter. If you want to use the DOS SUBST command to create logical disk drives, you may have to increase the LASTDRIVE= entry, as shown here:

LASTDRIVE=I

If you want to disable logical drives, you may instead enter

LASTDRIVE=C

The DOS SHELL= CONFIG.SYS entry allows you to tell DOS what file to use for your command processor. By default, DOS uses COMMAND.COM. If you want to use a different command processor or move COMMAND.COM to a DOS directory, you must use the SHELL= entry, as shown here:

SHELL=COMMAND.COM /P

Summary (continued)

You can also use SHELL= to increase the size of your DOS environment, as shown here:

SHELL=COMMAND.COM /E:4096 /P

Each time a hardware device interrupts DOS, DOS must suspend the task it is currently performing and place the current tasks aside in an area of memory called the stack. If your system fails, displaying the message

Fatal: Internal Stack Failure, System Halted

place the entry

STACKS=8,512

in CONFIG.SYS and reboot.

Glossary

A *disk buffer* is a location into which DOS places at least one sector of information each time it reads information from your disk drive. Each time you request that DOS read information from disk, it first searches its list of disk buffers to see if the data already resides in memory. If it does, DOS does not have to perform the slow disk-read operation. The DOS BUFFERS= entry in CONFIG.SYS allows you to specify the number of disk buffers that DOS supports.

Each device on your computer requires specific software that enables DOS to use it. Such software is called a *device driver.* For your most common devices, such as your screen, printer, and keyboard, DOS provides all of the software you will require. The DEVICE= entry in CONFIG.SYS allows you to install a device driver each time your system boots.

A *RAM drive* is a very fast disk drive that resides in your computer's random access memory. The major differences between a RAM disk drive and your standard disk drive is that the RAM drive is faster because it is not mechanical. However, whenever you turn your computer off or reset DOS, the contents of your RAM disk is lost. The DOS RAMDRIVE.SYS device driver allows you to install a RAM drive each time your system boots.

30 Using BACKUP And RESTORE

One of the most critical tasks that you must perform on a regular basis is making duplicate copies of your files and disks. If you are using a floppy-disk-based system, you have already seen how the DOS DISKCOPY command allows you to duplicate your disks.

```
A> DISKCOPY  A:  B:
```

If you are using a fixed disk system, however, you need a means of backing up all of the files on your disk to floppy disks. The DOS BACKUP command provides that capability.

In this chapter you will examine the DOS BACKUP command in detail. You will learn how to use BACKUP to copy all your fixed disk files to a floppy disk, how to select specific files based on their creation date and time, and how to back up just those files that have been modified or created since your last BACKUP command. In addition, you will learn how to use the DOS RESTORE command to later copy files from your backup disks back to your fixed disk if one or more files are damaged or inadvertnetly deleted. You will create two batch files that will simplify your daily and monthly backup procedures. Finally, you will also learn how to upgrade DOS to a new version when the SYS command fails.

The BACKUP and RESTORE commands exist for one purpose: to help you prevent or reduce loss of programs and data. DOS cannot prevent the loss of your data unless you perform backups on a regular basis.

Before You Get Started
With BACKUP

Before you examine the DOS BACKUP and RESTORE commands, you must do some preparatory work. First, you need to know how many floppy disks your fixed disk backup will require. To determine this number, first use CHKDSK, as shown here:

```
C> CHKDSK

21309440 bytes total disk space
53248 bytes in 2 hidden files
32768 bytes in 13 directories
6492160 bytes in 419 user files
69632 bytes in bad sectors
14661632 bytes available on disk

655360 bytes total memory
331536 bytes free

C>
```

Next, use the following equation to determine how many bytes are in use:

bytes in use = total disk space - bytes available

Using the figures you received when you invoked CHKDSK, the equation becomes

bytes in use = 21,309,440 - 14,661,632
= 6,647,808 bytes

This figure is then used to determine how many disks your backup will require. Use this equation.

Disk Type	Storage Capacity
Single-sided Double-density	184,320 bytes
Double-sided Double-density	368,640 bytes
Double-sided Double-density 3.5	737,280 bytes
Quad-density	1,228,800 bytes
High-capacity 3.5	1,474,560 bytes

Table 30-1. *Number of Bytes Available on Different Types of Disks*

number of disks = bytes in use / storage capacity

Table 30-1 gives you a quick summary of your disk storage capabilities. Using a 360K floppy disk, for example, your equation becomes

number of disks = 6,647,808 / 368,640
        = 18.03
        = 19 disks

Using a 1.2MB disk produces this equation:

number of disks = 6,647,808 / 1,228,800
        = 5.41
        = 6 disks

You should determine a safe location for storing your floppy disks. The media storage box shown in Figure 30-1 is a good storage location.

You must know exactly where your disks are should you ever need to restore a file from the backup disks. Find a safe location for your

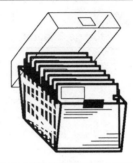

Figure 30-1.   *Media box for disk storage*

media storage box, preferably in a room other than the one containing your computer. Several sources of disk damage, such as smoke, theft, and spills, could also easily result in the damage of your backup disks if they reside in the same room.

It is also important to keep a complete list of all your hardware and software purchases for insurance purposes. A three-ring binder is useful to record your purchases, as shown in Figures 30-2 and 30-3.

Performing backups is a precaution in case you ever lose your files. You should also be prepared with proper records of your computer purchases should your computer ever be stolen or damaged.

Backing Up Floppy Disks

If you are using a floppy-disk-based system, it is imperative that you back up the files that you create on a daily basis. Even though floppy disks cannot store as much information as a fixed disk, they are more susceptible to damage from smoke, fingerprints, and spills; therefore, you must make duplicate copies of the files that you create.

Although you may use several disks throughout your day, you probably create or modify files on only a few disks. Here are two suggestions to help you.

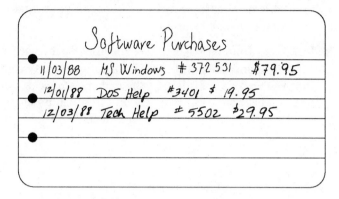

Figure 30-2. *Sample log for software purchases*

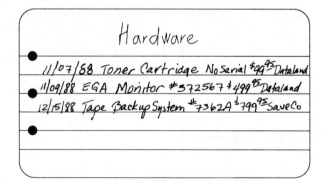

Figure 30-3. *Sample log for hardware*

■ Never use your original disks. Use the DOS DISKCOPY command to make duplicate working copies of your disks placing the originals in a safe location.

■ Purchase a media storage box specifically for your backup disks. Plan to spend the last ten minutes of every day copying the files that you created that day. At the end of each week, go through your backup disks to see if there are any that you no longer need. These can be used again to back up next week's files.

Using the DOS BACKUP Command

Although the DOS BACKUP command allows you to back up the contents of one floppy disk to another, you will not be using BACKUP for that purpose here. You will use BACKUP for fixed disk systems, backing up files from your fixed disk to floppy disks contained in drive A.

In its most basic form, the DOS BACKUP command is

```
C> BACKUP  C:\*.*  A:  /S
```

Here, you are using BACKUP to back up the entire fixed disk in drive C to the floppy disks in drive A. The /S qualifier directs BACKUP to include all of the files contained in DOS directories. Note that this command did not include a file specification on the target drive, A. BACKUP simply requires a disk drive identification letter for the target drive.

How BACKUP Places Files
On the Floppy Disk

BACKUP does not copy files to the target disk in the same manner as COPY or XCOPY. Using a unique file format, BACKUP also keeps track of files and directories. Only BACKUP and RESTORE understand this file format; therefore, once you create a backup disk with the BACKUP command, the only way you can manipulate the files that it contains is by using the RESTORE command. Do not try to copy the files. BACKUP places information at the front of each file that RESTORE later removes. If you simply copy the files, this header information will still reside at the beginning of the file, making the file invalid.

The BACKUP Qualifiers

BACKUP is a powerful command that allows you to back up all the files on your disk and select groups of files based on the file's creation date and time, or just those files that you have created or modified since the last BACKUP command.

The complete format of the BACKUP command is

BACKUP *source _ files target _ drive* [/S] [/M] [/A] [/F]
[/D:*mm:dd:yy*] [/T:*hh:mm:ss*] [/L:*log _ file _ path*]

where the following definitions apply:

- The *source _ files* variable specifies the files that BACKUP is to back up to your target drive.

- The *target _ drive* variable is the disk drive letter of the drive containing the floppy disk to which the files are to be copied.

- The /S qualifier directs BACKUP to also back up files contained in directories.

- The /M qualifier directs BACKUP to back up only those files whose archive flag is set in the file's attribute field.

- The /F qualifier tells BACKUP to format each disk before copying files to it.

- The /D:*mm:dd:yy* qualifier directs BACKUP to copy only files modified or created since the specified date.

■ The /T:*hh:mm:ss* qualifier directs BACKUP to copy only files modified or created since the specified time.

■ The /L:*log _ file _ path* qualifier directs BACKUP (DOS version 3.3) to create a file that logs the disk on which each file is placed.

Backing Up Specific Files

Usually you want BACKUP to examine your entire disk to ensure that all your files are backed up. There may be many times, however, when you want to back up one specific file or a directory of files. For example, this command directs BACKUP to back up all files in the DOS directory.

```
C> BACKUP  C:\DOS\*.*  A:
```

If all of the files in the directory do not fit on the floppy disk in drive A, DOS will prompt

```
Insert backup diskette 02 in drive A:

Warning! Files in the target drive
A:\ root directory will be erased
Strike any key when ready
```

If this occurs, place a formatted disk in drive A and press ENTER to continue.

This BACKUP command backs up just the PAYROLL.DAT file in the BUDGET directory.

```
C> BACKUP  \BUDGET\PAYROLL.DAT  A:
```

Should You Use Formatted or Unformatted Disks?

The BACKUP /F qualifier allows you to use an unformatted disk for your BACKUP operations. If you specify the /F qualifier, as shown here,

```
C> BACKUP  C:\*.*  A:  /S  /F
```

BACKUP will format each disk that it uses during the BACKUP operation. Although this seems very convenient, it slows down your backup process considerably.

Whenever possible, format all the disks that you plan to use with BACKUP. Do not, however, format the disks as bootable system disks. Avoid using up a significant portion of the disk's storage capacity by simply using this command instead.

```
C> FORMAT  A:
```

Backing Up Your Entire Disk

Before you can back up your entire fixed disk to floppy disks, you must determine the number of disks that BACKUP will require, as shown previously in this lesson. Next, assuming that the floppy disks are already formatted, issue the command

```
C> BACKUP  C:\*.*  A:  /S
```

BACKUP will back up all of the files and directories of files on your fixed disk, C, to the floppy disks contained in drive A. Each time a floppy disks fills, BACKUP will display

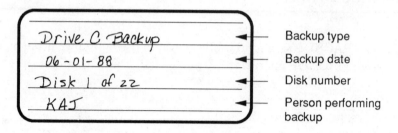

Drive C Backup	◄— Backup type
06 - 01 - 88	◄— Backup date
Disk 1 of 22	◄— Disk number
KAJ	◄— Person performing backup

Figure 30-4.   *Label for disk as BACKUP completes*

Insert backup diskette nn in drive A:

Warning! Files in the target drive
A:\ root directory will be erased
Strike any key when ready

At that time, place a formatted disk in drive A and press ENTER. Make
sure that you label each disk as BACKUP completes its processing,
as shown in Figure 30-4.

Backing Up Newly Created or Recently Modified Files

Although the previous BACKUP command allows you to back up your
entire fixed disk, to do so on a regular basis would be too time consuming. On the first day of each month, therefore, perform a complete
backup of your disk by using the command

```
C> BACKUP  C:\*.*  A:  /S
```

Then, each day for the remainder of the month, using a new set of disks, issue the command

```
C> BACKUP  C:\*.*  A:  /S  /A  /M
```

This command directs BACKUP to back up only those files created that day (or since the last backup, which probably was the day before). You will end up with two sets of disks: the first set is your complete disk backup or monthly backup; the second set includes your daily backup disks.

Because you are backing up your files on a daily basis, it may take you several days or even a week to have enough files to fill up a floppy disk. Using the /A qualifier, you can continue to use the same disk each day for daily backups until it becomes full and DOS displays

```
Insert backup diskette 02 in drive A:

Warning! Files in the target drive
A:\ root directory will be erased
Strike any key when ready
```

At that time, start using a second formatted disk, making sure you label the first disk and place it in a safe location.

Using a Backup Log File

If you are using DOS version 3.3, BACKUP allows you to log which disk your files are stored on with the log file directive /L. The contents of your log file will be

```
C> TYPE  BACKUP.LOG

5-18-1988  14:19:36
001 \COMMAND.COM
```

```
001  \AUTOEXEC.BAT
001  \CONFIG.SYS
001  \DOS\COMMAND.COM
001  \DOS\ANSI.SYS
001  \DOS\COUNTRY.SYS
001  \DOS\DISPLAY.SYS
001  \DOS\DRIVER.SYS
001  \DOS\FASTOPEN.EXE
 .           .
 .           .
 .           .
```

If you are using DOS 3.3, create a directory on your fixed disk called \BACKUP.

```
C> MKDIR  \BACKUP
```

When you invoke your monthly and daily BACKUP commands, include the /L qualifier, as in the command

```
C> BACKUP  C:\*.*  A:  /S  /L:C:\BACKUP\BACKUP.LOG
```

or the command

```
C> BACKUP  C:\*.*  A:  /S  /A  /M  /L:C:\BACKUP\BACKUP.LOG
```

If you later need to restore a file, you can examine the log file to determine on which disk the file resides.

Creating a Backup Policy

The only way your backups will ever be helpful is if you perform them on a regular basis. The easiest way to do that is to create a backup policy and then to implement the policy with DOS batch files.

To begin a good backup policy, you will need sufficient floppy disks to perform three complete fixed disk backups. Format each of these disks with the command

```
C> FORMAT  A:
```

Place these disks safely in a disk media storage box. On the first day of the month, issue the command

```
C> BACKUP  C:\*.*  A:  /S
```

or, if you are using DOS version 3.3, issue the command

```
C> BACKUP  C:\*.*  A:  /S  /L:\BACKUP\BACKUP.LOG
```

Label each disk, as shown in Figure 30-5. When BACKUP completes, place all of the disks in the media storage box.

Each day, using a set of daily backup disks (not your monthly backup disks), issue the command

```
C> BACKUP  C:\*.*  A:  /S  /A  /M
```

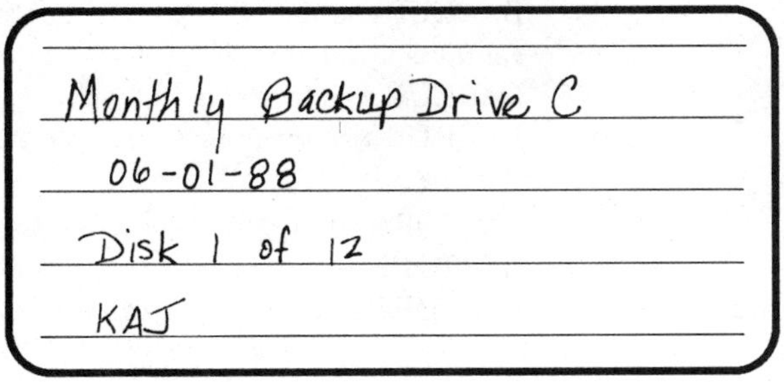

Monthly Backup Drive C
06-01-88
Disk 1 of 12
KAJ

Figure 30-5.   *Label for monthly backup*

or, if you are using DOS version 3.3, issue the command

```
C> BACKUP  C:\*.*  A:  /S  /A  /M  /L:\BACKUP\BACKUP.LOG
```

BACKUP will back up only those files created since your last backup. Continue to use the same disk for your daily backups until it fills and DOS displays the message

```
Insert backup diskette 02 in drive A:

Warning! Files in the target drive
A:\ root directory will be erased
Strike any key when ready
```

At the first of the next month, use your unused floppy disks to perform a complete disk backup. If this backup is successful, you can recycle the previous monthly and daily backup disks.

The batch files presented here are called MONTHLY.BAT and DAILY.BAT, respectively. You can use these files to perform your complete disk backup at the beginning of the month, as well as your daily backups. Place both of these files into your \BACKUP directory.

Each file is based on the fact that BACKUP and RESTORE support the following exit status codes:

Code	Meaning
0	BACKUP successfully completed
1	BACKUP found no files to back up
2	BACKUP could not back up files due to sharing conflicts
3	BACKUP was terminated by a user-entered CTRL-C
4	BACKUP was terminated by an error
0	RESTORE successfully completed
1	RESTORE encountered a command-line error
2	RESTORE could not find specified file

Code (*continued*)	Meaning (*continued*)
3	RESTORE could not find specified path
5	RESTORE could not continue; access denied
8	RESTORE could not continue; insufficient memory
15	RESTORE encountered an invalid disk drive id

The first file presented here implements MONTHLY.BAT, and the second implements DAILY.BAT.

```
ECHO OFF
REM MONTHLY BACKUP PROCEDURES
REM
REM If you are using DOS 3.3, add
REM the /L:C:\BACKUP\BACKUP.LOG qualifier
REM
BACKUP C:\*.* A: /S
REM
IF ERRORLEVEL 4 GOTO FATAL_ERROR
IF ERRORLEVEL 3 GOTO USER_TERMINATED
IF ERRORLEVEL 2 GOTO SHARING_CONFLICT
IF ERRORLEVEL 1 GOTO NO_FILES
:SUCCESSFUL
PAUSE SUCCESSFUL BACKUP -- BACKUP COMPLETE
GOTO DONE
:NO_FILES
PAUSE NO FILES FOUND TO BACKUP
GOTO DONE
:SHARING_CONFLICT
PAUSE FILE SHARING CONFLICTS -- BACKUP INCOMPLETE
GOTO DONE
:USER_TERMINATED
PAUSE USER TERMINATION OF BACKUP -- BACKUP INCOMPLETE
GOTO DONE
:FATAL_ERROR
PAUSE FATAL BACKUP ERROR -- BACKUP INCOMPLETE
:DONE
```

```
ECHO OFF
REM INCREMENTAL BACKUP PROCEDURE
REM
REM If you are using DOS 3.3, add
REM the /L:C:\BACKUP\BACKUP.LOG qualifier
REM
BACKUP C:\*.* A: /S /M /A
REM
IF ERRORLEVEL 4 GOTO FATAL_ERROR
IF ERRORLEVEL 3 GOTO USER_TERMINATED
IF ERRORLEVEL 2 GOTO SHARING_CONFLICT
IF ERRORLEVEL 1 GOTO NO_FILES
:SUCCESSFUL
PAUSE SUCCESSFUL BACKUP -- BACKUP COMPLETE
GOTO DONE
:NO_FILES
PAUSE NO FILES FOUND TO BACKUP
GOTO DONE
:SHARING_CONFLICT
PAUSE FILE SHARING CONFLICTS -- BACKUP INCOMPLETE
GOTO DONE
:USER_TERMINATED
PAUSE USER TERMINATION OF BACKUP -- BACKUP INCOMPLETE
GOTO DONE
:FATAL_ERROR
PAUSE FATAL BACKUP ERROR -- BACKUP INCOMPLETE
:DONE
```

Restoring Files from Your Backup Disk

As stated earlier in this chapter, the only way to access files contained on a backup disk is with the DOS RESTORE command. If you inadvertently delete a file or the file becomes damaged, locate the disk containing your file by using the log file that BACKUP created.

```
A> PRINT  C:\BACKUP\BACKUP.LOG
```

Insert the correct disk into drive A, and invoke a RESTORE command in this format:

```
C> RESTORE A: C:\PATHNAME\FILENAME.EXT
```

For example, this command restores the LABEL.COM file to the DOS directory:

```
C> RESTORE A: C:\DOS\LABEL.COM
```

This command restores all the files in your EXPENSES directory:

```
C> RESTORE A: C:\EXPENSES\*.*
```

If EXPENSES contains additional DOS directories, add the /S qualifier, as shown here:

```
C> RESTORE A: C:\EXPENSES\*.*  /S
```

To restore your entire fixed disk, use the RESTORE command

```
C> RESTORE A: C:\*.* /S
```

RESTORE will not restore the hidden DOS system files. Later in this chapter you will take a look at how to upgrade your system to a new version of DOS.

Here is the complete format of the DOS RESTORE command:

```
RESTORE source_drive: target_drive:file_specification [/S]
[/P] [/A:mm:dd:yy] [/B:mm:dd:yy] [/E:hh:mm:ss]
[/L:hh:mm:ss] [/M] [/N]
```

where the following definitions apply:

■ The *source_drive* variable is the drive letter of the floppy disk drive containing the backup disk.

■ The *target_drive:file_specification* variable specifies the files that RESTORE is to restore from the floppy disk.

■ The /S directive directs RESTORE to restore DOS directories.

■ The /P qualifier directs RESTORE to pause and requests permission to restore files that have been marked Read-only on your fixed disk.

■ The /A:*mm:dd:yy* qualifier directs RESTORE to restore only those files modified or created after the specified date.

■ The /B:*mm:dd:yy* qualifier directs RESTORE to restore only those files modified or created before the specified date.

■ The /E:*hh:mm:ss* qualifier directs RESTORE to restore only those files modified or created before the specifed time.

■ The /L:*hh:mm:ss* qualifier directs RESTORE to restore only those files modified or created after the specifed time.

■ The /M qualifier directs RESTORE to restore only those files modified since the last backup.

■ The /N qualifier directs RESTORE to restore only those files that no longer exist on your fixed disk.

Upgrading to a New Version of DOS

In Chapter 28, you learned that the SYS command

```
A> SYS  C:
```

can fail, displaying the message

```
No room for system on destination disk
```

If DOS displays this message, you must reformat your disk by using the command

```
A> FORMAT  C:/S
```

Before you reformat, boot the new version of the operating system and use this BACKUP command to save your disk's contents.

```
C> BACKUP  C:\*.*  A:  /S
```

Only if this BACKUP command is successful can you boot the new version of DOS (if you have not done so yet) and issue the FORMAT command

```
A> FORMAT  C:  /S
```

When FORMAT completes, restore your disk's contents with the following command:

```
A> RESTORE  A:  C:\*.*  /S
```

When RESTORE completes, copy the COMMAND.COM file from your new DOS disk to the root directory of your fixed disk. Copy all of the DOS external commands and system files to the DOS directory on your fixed disk, as shown here:

```
A> COPY  COMMAND.COM  C:\
A> COPY  *.*  C:\DOS
```

Don't forget about your Supplemental Programs disk.

```
A> COPY  *.*  C:\DOS
```

Your DOS upgrade is now complete.

Hands-On Practice

If you have a floppy-disk-based system, use the DOS DISKCOPY command to make duplicate copies of each of your original disks. Place the originals in a safe location, preferably not in the same room as your computer. Purchase a disk media storage box into which you can place your daily backups. Plan on spending the last ten minutes of each day copying the files that you created that day.

If you have a fixed disk system, purchase enough floppy disks to perform three complete disk backups. Also obtain a disk media storage box to store your backup disks. Using the DOS FORMAT command, format all of your new disks.

```
C> FORMAT A:
```

Create the BACKUP directory on your fixed disk.

```
C> MKDIR \BACKUP
```

Create the following batch files by using EDLIN, and place each into the BACKUP directory:

```
A> TYPE MONTHLY.BAT
ECHO OFF
REM MONTHLY BACKUP PROCEDURES
REM
REM If you are using DOS 3.3, add
REM the /L:C:\BACKUP\BACKUP.LOG qualifier
REM
BACKUP C:\*.* A: /S
REM
IF ERRORLEVEL 4 GOTO FATAL_ERROR
IF ERRORLEVEL 3 GOTO USER_TERMINATED
IF ERRORLEVEL 2 GOTO SHARING_CONFLICT
IF ERRORLEVEL 1 GOTO NO_FILES
:SUCCESSFUL
PAUSE SUCCESSFUL BACKUP -- BACKUP COMPLETE
GOTO DONE
:NO_FILES
```

```
PAUSE NO FILES FOUND TO BACKUP
GOTO DONE
:SHARING_CONFLICT
PAUSE FILE SHARING CONFLICTS -- BACKUP INCOMPLETE
GOTO DONE
:USER_TERMINATED
PAUSE USER TERMINATION OF BACKUP -- BACKUP INCOMPLETE
GOTO DONE
:FATAL_ERROR
PAUSE FATAL BACKUP ERROR -- BACKUP INCOMPLETE
:DONE

A> TYPE  DAILY.BAT
ECHO OFF
REM INCREMENTAL BACKUP PROCEDURE
REM
REM If you are using DOS 3.3, add
REM the /L:C:\BACKUP\BACKUP.LOG qualifier
REM
BACKUP C:\*.* A: /S /M /A
REM
IF ERRORLEVEL 4 GOTO FATAL_ERROR
IF ERRORLEVEL 3 GOTO USER_TERMINATED
IF ERRORLEVEL 2 GOTO SHARING_CONFLICT
IF ERRORLEVEL 1 GOTO NO_FILES
:SUCCESSFUL
PAUSE SUCCESSFUL BACKUP -- BACKUP COMPLETE
GOTO DONE
:NO_FILES
PAUSE NO FILES FOUND TO BACKUP
GOTO DONE
:SHARING_CONFLICT
PAUSE FILE SHARING CONFLICTS -- BACKUP INCOMPLETE
GOTO DONE
:USER_TERMINATED
PAUSE USER TERMINATION OF BACKUP -- BACKUP INCOMPLETE
GOTO DONE
:FATAL_ERROR
PAUSE FATAL BACKUP ERROR -- BACKUP INCOMPLETE
:DONE

A>
```

Now that you understand the DOS BACKUP command, use it to back up all of the files on your fixed disk. With your formatted floppy disks ready, issue either the MONTHLY.BAT batch file or the command

```
C> BACKUP  C:\*.*  A: /S
```

Be prepared to spend up to an hour or so on this backup process, depending on the number of files on your disk. Tomorrow, when you perform your backup operations, BACKUP will only back up those files created or modified since this BACKUP command completed. Your daily backups, therefore, normally take only a few minutes.

Summary

Backing up the contents of your disks is one of the most important functions you must perform on a regular basis. In only a few minutes each day, using the DOS BACKUP command, you can minimize data loss.

If you are using a floppy-disk-based system, immediately make working copies of your original disks and place the originals in a safe location. At the end of each day, spend at least a few minutes copying the files that you modified or created that day to another floppy disk. The first time you inadvertently delete a critical file will make you a true believer in backups.

If you are a fixed disk user, the DOS BACKUP command allows you to back up your entire fixed disk, specific files based on their creation date and time stamp, or files that have been created or modified since the last BACKUP command. Your backup procedure will take two steps: a monthly backup and a daily backup.

On the first day of each month, issue the following BACKUP command:

C> BACKUP C:*.* A: /S

This command directs BACKUP to copy all of the files from your fixed disk to the backup disks in drive A.

With a new set of daily backup disks, perform daily backups by issuing the command

C> BACKUP C:*.* A: /S /A /M

This command directs BACKUP to back up only those files that have been created or modified since the last BACKUP command (usually this is the previous day). These daily backup procedures should only take you a few minutes.

BACKUP does not just copy files to the disks in drive A. Instead, it places each file on the disk in a unique format that only the BACKUP and the RESTORE commands understand. If you

Summary (continued)

attempt to copy a file from the backup disk by using the DOS COPY command, the file will contain backup header information that makes it invalid.

The DOS RESTORE command is BACKUP's counterpart. It allows you to retrieve a file or files from your backup disks should one of the files on your fixed disk become damaged or deleted.

If the DOS SYS command is unable to transfer the hidden DOS operating system files to your fixed disk, you must reformat your fixed disk before you can upgrade to a new version of DOS. Before you issue the FORMAT command, however, use BACKUP to copy all of the files on your fixed disk to floppy disks. When the FORMAT command completes, use RESTORE to place all of your files back onto the disk as desired.

31 *DOS Goes International*

When you first started this book, you were told that you would have to spend about 15 minutes a day for a month on its exercises. If you live in the United States, Chapter 30 concluded your month. However, if you live across the international date line, your month has 31 days.

This chapter discusses the international considerations that are built into DOS. Over the past few years, the international computer marketplace has grown as quickly as it has here in the United States. In fact, many software companies have found that 25% to 30% of their sales are to dealers in Europe and abroad. In order to fully support its international users, DOS provides several commands that offer country-specific character sets and keyboard layouts. DOS thereby simplifies the international user's interface.

In this chapter you will examine the DOS NLSFUNC, CHCP, KEYB, and SELECT commands. You will also take a look at the DISPLAY.SYS, KEYBOARD.SYS, PRINTER.SYS, and COUNTRY.SYS device drivers. Finally, you will use the CONFIG.SYS COUNTRY= entry to select the date, time, and currency formats of a specific country.

If you are not an international DOS user, you will probably never have to issue any of these commands. You can skip ahead to Part Four of this book, the Command Reference section.

What Is a Codepage?

Throughout this chapter the term "codepage" is used extensively. In general, a codepage defines the set of characters used for a specific language. A codepage, therefore, is really nothing more than a character set. Many of you have probably seen typewriters that allow you to change the letter associated with each key simply by changing the typewriter ball. A DOS codepage functions in a similar manner. When you change codepages under DOS, you change the set of letters that DOS will display on your screen or printed output.

Codepages are new to DOS with version 3.3. If you are not using DOS version 3.3, you cannot issue the commands used to manipulate codepages—NLSFUNC, CHCP, and the enhanced MODE commands.

DOS supports the following codepages:

Codepage	Country
437	United States
850	Multilingual
860	Portuguese
863	French-Canadian
865	Nordic

Specifying Country-Specific Formats

Just as most countries have unique languages, they also have unique date, time, and currency symbols. The DOS COUNTRY= entry in CONFIG.SYS (discussed in Chapter 29) allows you to tell DOS to use the country symbols and character set for a specific country. Under DOS version 3.3, the format of this entry is

COUNTRY=*country _ code* [,[*codepage*][,*country _ info _ file*]]

where the following definitions apply:

■ The *country _ code* variable is the three-digit number that identifies your desired country. See Table 31-1.

■ The *codepage* variable is the three-digit codepage number.

■ The *country _ info _ file* variable is the name of the file containing the country-specific formats. In most cases, this file is called COUNTRY.SYS. If COUNTRY.SYS does not reside in the root directory, you must tell DOS which directory the file is in.

For example, to direct DOS to use the French symbol set, your COUNTRY= entry is

COUNTRY=033

Country Code	Country
001	United States
002	French-Canadian
003	Latin America
031	Netherlands
032	Belgium
033	France
034	Spain
039	Italy
041	Switzerland
044	United Kingdom
045	Denmark
046	Sweden
047	Norway
049	Germany
061	English
351	Portugal
358	Finland
785	Arabic countries
972	Israel

Table 31-1.   *Country Codes*

Keyboard Code	Country
US	United States
CF	French-Canadian
LA	Latin America
NL	Netherlands
BE	Belgium
FR	France
SP	Spain
IT	Italy
SF,SG	Switzerland
UK	United Kingdom
DK	Denmark
SV	Sweden
NO	Norway
GR	Germany
PO	Portugal
SU	Finland

Table 31-2.   *Keyboards*

If you are using DOS version 3.3, you can specify a desired code-page, as shown here:

    COUNTRY=033,850

With DOS version 3.3, if the COUNTRY.SYS file does not reside in your root directory, you must tell DOS where the file is located.

    COUNTRY=033,850,C:\DOS\COUNTRY.SYS

The COUNTRY= entry does not define a keyboard layout. To do so, you must issue the DOS KEYB command.

Defining a Keyboard Layout

Different countries use different keyboard layouts or templates. Under DOS version 3.3, the KEYB command allows you to select your desired keyboard from the list of keyboards in Table 31-2.

To choose the French keyboard, for example, your command is

```
C> KEYB FR
```

This command assumes that the KEYBOARD.SYS file (which contains your keyboard templates) resides in the current directory. If this is not the case, you must tell DOS where KEYBOARD.SYS resides, as shown here:

```
C> KEYB FR , , C:\DOS\KEYBOARD.SYS
```

Older versions of DOS (prior to version 3.3) use several different keyboard commands, such as those shown here:

Command	Country
KEYBFR	France
KEYBGR	Germany
KEYBIT	Italy
KEYBSP	Spain
KEYBUK	United Kingdom

For example, to select the French keyboard template with DOS version 3.2, your command is

```
C> KEYBFR
```

Regardless of whether you are using KEYB or a KEYBxx command, DOS allows you to toggle between the international keyboard and the U.S. keyboard by using the following keyboard combinations:

- CTRL-ALT-F1 selects the U.S. keyboard.

- CTRL-ALT-F2 selects the international keyboard.

If you plan to use an international keyboard on a regular basis, you should place the appropriate KEYB or KEYB*xx* command in your AUTOEXEC.BAT file. DOS will then enable the international keyboard each time your system starts.

What You Need to Do
To Get Started

If you are like most international users, the COUNTRY= entry in CONFIG.SYS and the KEYB command are enough to get you started. All you need to do is place the COUNTRY= entry in CONFIG.SYS along with the entries FILES=20 and BUFFERS=25. Also, you should place the appropriate command in the AUTOEXEC.BAT file.

NLSFUNC and CHCP

If you work in multiple languages, you may need to switch quickly from a French character set and keyboard layout to a German configuration. To perform such switching processes, DOS provides the NLSFUNC and CHCP commands, as well as enhancements to the DOS MODE command.

The NLSFUNC (or National Language Support Function) command prepares your system for switching between codepages as your language changes require. If you need to be able to change codepages, the first command you must execute is NLSFUNC.

The basic form of the NLSFUNC command is

```
A> NLSFUNC
```

NLSFUNC uses the COUNTRY.SYS file and assumes that the file is in the current directory. If COUNTRY.SYS does not reside in the current directory, you must tell NLSFUNC where to find it, as shown here:

```
C> NLSFUNC  C:\DOS\COUNTRY.SYS
```

If you anticipate the need for codepage switching, place NLSFUNC in your AUTOEXEC.BAT file.

Once you issue the NLSFUNC command, you can use CHCP to change the current screen and printer codepage to a codepage that has been prepared for use by your system. Later in this chapter you will learn how to prepare codepages. Before you do this, however, you must examine two critical device drivers, DISPLAY.SYS and PRINTER.SYS.

Providing Codepage Switching Support for Your Display

Not all devices support codepage switching. If, however, you are using an EGA, LCD, or VGA monitor, the DISPLAY.SYS device driver provides codepage switching support. Before you can prepare codepages for use by DOS, you must specify DISPLAY.SYS by using the DEVICE= entry in CONFIG.SYS. The format for the DISPLAY.SYS entry is

DEVICE=DISPLAY.SYS CON:=[(*display_type* [,*hardware_codepage*] [,(*additional_codepages, subfonts*)])]

where the following definitions apply:

■ The *display_type* variable specifies your display type. Valid entries are MONO, CGA, EGA, and LCD.

■ The *hardware_codepage* variable specifies the codepage supported by your screen display. Valid entries include 437, 850, 860, 863, and 865.

■ The *additional_codepages* variable specifies the number of code-pages that DOS can prepare for use. MONO and CGA systems do not support codepage switching and must be set to 0. EGA can be set to 2, and LCD to 1.

■ The *subfonts* variable specifies the number of subfonts supported by your display.

For example, a DISPLAY.SYS entry for an EGA monitor is

DEVICE=DISPLAY.SYS CON:=(EGA, 437, (2, 1))

Remember, the only time you need to include this entry in CON-FIG.SYS is when you are going to perform codepage switching.

Providing Codepage Switching Support for Your Printer

Just as some display monitors do not support codepage switching, some printers do support it. If your printer does support codepage switching, the documentation that accompanied your printer should provide you with the correct PRINTER.SYS entry for your printer. In general, the format of PRINTER.SYS is

DEVICE=PRINTER.SYS LPT*n*:=[(*printer_type* [,(*hardware_codepage*) [,*additional_codepages*])]]

where the following definitions apply:

■ LPT*n* specifies the desired printer port number (LPT1, LPT2, and so on).

■ The *printer_type* variable specifies your printer type. Valid entries include 4201 for the IBM ProPrinter and 5202 for the IBM Quietwriter.

■ The *hardware_codepage* variable specifies the codepage that is supported by your printer. Valid entries include 437, 850, 860, 863, and 865.

■ The *additional_codepages* variable specifies the number of code-pages that DOS can prepare for use. This number is printer specific.

For example, to use a ProPrinter connected to LPT1 with the French codepage, use the following PRINTER.SYS entry:

```
DEVICE=PRINTER.SYS LPT1:=(4201, 863, 1)
```

Using CHCP

After you have enabled codepage switching for your display and printer, issue the NLSFUNC command to provide codepage switching support.

```
A> NLSFUNC
```

Next, type **CHCP** and press ENTER. DOS will display the current codepage, as shown here:

```
A> CHCP

Active code page:   437

A>
```

To select the multilingual codepage, 850, enter the command

```
A> CHCP  850
```

If the CHCP command is successful, again type **CHCP** and press ENTER.

```
A> CHCP

Active code page:  850

A>
```

As you can see, DOS has changed your codepage as you desired. The DOS CHCP command changes codepages on a system-wide basis. If you issue the DOS CHCP command, DOS changes the codepage for your screen display and printer. If the CHCP command fails and DOS displays

```
A> CHCP  850

Code page   850 not prepared for system

A>
```

make sure that you have invoked the NLSFUNC command. In addition, to prepare a codepage for use by DOS, you must use new enhancements to the DOS MODE command.

MODE Revisited

The DOS MODE command is a key component in codepage switching, and it has several new forms.

Preparing a Codepage

The first MODE command you will learn about here allows you to prepare a codepage for use by your screen display or printer. To prepare your screen display, the format of this MODE command is

```
MODE CON CODEPAGE PREPARE=(codepage, codepage)
display_type.cpi
```

where *display_type.cpi* is a file containing codepage information (CPI) for your specific display type, such as EGA.CPI. For example, the command

MODE CON CODEPAGE PREPARE=(863,865) EGA.CPI

prepares an EGA monitor to use codepages 863 and 865. The command

MODE CON CODEPAGE PREPARE=(850) EGA.CPI

prepares codepage 850 for use.

Once you have prepared a codepage for use, the CHCP command allows you to select it.

```
A> CHCP  850
```

Note that the previous commands assume that the EGA.CPI file resides in the current directory. If this is not the case, specify a complete DOS path name for the file, as shown here:

MODE CON CODEPAGE PREPARE=(850) C:\DOS\EGA.CPI

Preparing a codepage for use by your printer is a similar process. In this case, use the MODE command

MODE LPT*n* CODEPAGE PREPARE=*(codepage) device.cpi*

where LPT*n* is the printer port desired, and *device.cpi* is the file containing your codepage information for your printer (4201.CPI or 5202.CPI). For example, the command

```
A> MODE  LPT1  CODEPAGE  PREPARE=(865)  4201.CPI
```

prepares codepage 865 for use by your printer.

Selecting a Codepage

The DOS MODE command also allows you to select codepages on a device-by-device basis. Once you have prepared a codepage, you can select it for use, as shown here:

MODE CON CODEPAGE SELECT=*codepage*

or

MODE LPT1 CODEPAGE SELECT=*codepage*

For example, the following command selects codepage 865 for your screen display:

```
A> MODE  CON  CODEPAGE  SELECT=865
```

Refreshing a Codepage

Each time you select a codepage for a device, DOS downloads codepage information to the device. If DOS downloads codepage information to your printer and you later turn your printer off, the codepage information is lost. To have DOS restore the current codepage for the device, you will need to use the DOS MODE command, as shown here:

```
A> MODE  LPT1  CODEPAGE  REFRESH
```

Displaying Your Current Codepage Status

If you forget which codepages are active, issue the MODE command

```
A> MODE  CON  CODEPAGE  /STATUS
```

or the MODE command

```
A> MODE  LPT1  CODEPAGE  /STATUS
```

DOS will display sommething like this for the first command:

```
Active codepage for device CON is 850
hardware codepages:
Codepage 437
prepared codepages:
Codepage 850
Codepage not prepared
MODE Status Codepage function completed
```

Abbreviating MODE Commands

Because many of these MODE commands can become quite long, MODE allows you to abbreviate several of the command's keywords as shown here:

Keyword	Abbreviation
CODEPAGE	CP
PREPARE	PREP
SELECT	SEL
REFRESH	REF
/STATUS	/STA

What Is the SELECT Command?

The DOS SELECT command helps you build a bootable disk for a specific country. In general, SELECT places the correct CONFIG.SYS and AUTOEXEC.BAT entries on a floppy disk for you. The format of the SELECT command is

SELECT *source_drive*: *target_drive*: country_code keyboard

where the following definitions apply:

■ The *source_drive* variable is the disk that contains the required country-specific files.

- The *target_drive* variable is the disk to prepare (SELECT will format the target drive, making it bootable).

- The *country_code* variable is the desired three-digit country code.

- The *keyboard* variable is the two-letter keyboard associated with the KEYB command.

For more information on and examples of SELECT, see the Command Reference section (Part Four) of this book.

Hands-On Practice

Because DOS provides country-specific support, a "Hands-On Practice" section for each specific country is impossible. This section will simply review the steps for getting started with your own country-specific attributes.

If you want to support only one country's character set, place the COUNTRY= entry that corresponds to that country in CONFIG.SYS. Remember that DOS version 3.3 requires you to specify the location of the COUNTRY.SYS file if it is not in the current directory.

If you are not using DOS version 3.3, you can enter

```
COUNTRY=049
```

If you are using DOS version 3.3, your entry could be

```
COUNTRY=049,,C:\DOS\COUNTRY.SYS
```

In your AUTOEXEC.BAT file, invoke the corresponding keyboard command. If you are not using DOS version 3.3, your keyboard command will be similar to

```
KEYBGR
```

If you are using DOS version 3.3, your keyboard command will be
something like

```
KEYB GR,,C:\DOS\KEYBOARD.SYS
```

Your system is now ready for use by DOS.

Summary

The international market is quickly becoming one of the most influential computer marketplaces. In order to fully support its international users, DOS provides country-specific support by means of keyboard layouts and character sets.

A codepage is a character set. Each country has a unique set of characters in the alphabet, just as it has a unique language. A codepage helps DOS display and print characters for a specific country.

The DOS COUNTRY= entry in CONFIG.SYS allows you to select the currency, date, and time formats for a specific country, along with the default character set that DOS will use when it starts.

The DOS KEYB command allows DOS version 3.3 users to select a keyboard template for a specific country. If you are not using DOS version 3.3, you will instead issue a KEYB*xx* command, where *xx* is the two-letter identifier of the desired country. Once you install an international keyboard, you can toggle between that keyboard and the U.S. keyboard by using the following key combinations:

■ CTRL-ALT-F1 selects the U.S. keyboard.

■ CTRL-ALT-F2 selects the international keyboard.

To get started, most users simply place a COUNTRY= entry in CONFIG.SYS and a KEYB command in AUTOEXEC.BAT.

Some of you work in environments that require you to use several languages. DOS version 3.3 allows you to perform codepage switching from one character set to another as your language needs change. To perform codepage switching, you must follow these steps:

1. Install the DISPLAY.SYS device driver in CONFIG.SYS, enabling codepage switching for your display.

Summary (continued)

2. If your printer is supported, install the PRINTER.SYS de-vice driver in CONFIG.SYS, enabling codepage switching for your printer.

3. Place the NLSFUNC command in your AUTOEXEC.BAT file. Remember to tell NLSFUNC where the COUNTRY.SYS file resides.

4. Use the DOS MODE command to prepare your codepages.

5. Use the DOS CHCP command to select system-wide code-pages.

To support codepage switching, DOS version 3.3 enhances the MODE command to include the following commands:

- MODE *device* CODEPAGE PREPARE=(*codepage*) *device.cpi*

- MODE *device* CODEPAGE SELECT=(*codepage*)

- MODE *device* CODEPAGE REFRESH

- MODE *device* CODEPAGE /STATUS

Most of you will probably never require codepage switching, but if you do, DOS fully supports your needs.

Glossary

A *codepage* is a character set. Just as all countries have a uni-que language, so too do they have a unique set of characters in the alphabet. A codepage helps DOS display and print charac-ters for a specific country.

Command Reference Section

Part Four

Having made it through all the exercises in this book, you have been exposed to a tremendous amount of information on each of the DOS commands. Although you may retain a considerable amount of information regarding the function of each DOS command, you would never be expected to remember all of the details. Part Four of this text provides a Command Reference that you can use to quickly look up specifics on each DOS command. In this section you will find command formats, discussion, brief notes, and several examples.

Take some time now to skim through this section. You probably will be happily surprised with how much you remember about each DOS command. By completing the lessons in this book, you have laid a very strong foundation upon which to build your computer knowledge. Don't forget how you mastered DOS, however; it wasn't by luck, but rather by doing hands-on exercises. DOS is just the first of the software programs you will work with that is both complex and fast. You've mastered DOS, which proves you can master any program. You should simply view software packages as new challenges.

Even though most of your early DOS exercises now seem far behind you, take time periodically to skim the "Hands-On Practice" sections of each chapter. In so doing, you will remind yourself of the tricks and shortcuts that can make your life easier. For those of you ready for more information, your next book purchases should include *DOS: The Complete Reference* (Osborne/McGraw-Hill, 1987) and *DOS Power User's Guide* (Osborne/McGraw-Hill, 1987).

Also, *DOS: The Pocket Reference* (Osborne/McGraw-Hill, 1988) provides a complete desktop guide to each DOS command. The book fits easily in a briefcase for work or school.

For those who are ready to learn more time-saving shortcuts to DOS, consider *DOS Secrets, Solutions, Shortcuts* (Osborne- McGraw-Hill, 1988).

A Command Reference Section

The following section takes a detailed look at each DOS command. As you examine the commands, pay particular attention to the examples that accompany each.

APPEND

FUNCTION   Defines the data-file search path that DOS uses each time it fails to locate a file in the current directory or in a specified directory.

FORMAT

[*drive:*][*path*]APPEND [*d:*][*p*][;[*d:*][*p*]...]

or

[*drive:*][*path*]APPEND [/X][/E] (DOS version 3.3)

or

[*drive:*][*path*]APPEND ;

where the following is true:

drive: specifies the disk drive containing the APPEND.COM file. If you do not specify a disk-drive identification, DOS uses the current default disk drive.

path is the DOS path name of the subdirectory that contains the APPEND.COM file. If you do not specify a DOS path name, DOS uses the current default directory.

d specifies a disk drive that DOS is to include in the data-file search path.

p specifies a DOS directory to be included in the data-file search path.

... indicates that the disk drive and directories can be specified several times.

/X aids in SEARCH FIRST, FIND FIRST, and EXEC options. This is a DOS 3.3 version qualifier.

/E places an APPEND entry in the DOS environment similar to the PATH entry. Therefore, the DOS SET command can effect APPEND. This is a DOS version 3.3 qualifier.

NOTES Each time DOS cannot find a data file in the specified directory or in the current directory, it checks to see if the user has defined a data-file search path. The DOS APPEND command allows you to define disk drives and directories to be included in the data-file search path.

By default, not all DOS commands use the APPEND data path. If you are using DOS version 3.3, the /X qualifier increases the number of applications that search the data-file search path.

If you invoke APPEND with simply a semicolon, DOS removes the data-file search path.

EXAMPLES If DOS cannot find the data file in the current directory, the following command tells DOS to search the root directories on drives C, B, and A, in that order:

```
C> APPEND C:\;B:\;A:\
```

The following APPEND command directs DOS to search \DOS, \UTIL, and then \MISC, in that order:

```
C> APPEND \DOS;\UTIL;\MISC
```

If you are using DOS version 3.3, the /E qualifier directs DOS to place an entry containing the data-file search path in your environment, as in this command:

```
C> APPEND C:\DOS;C:\UTIL /E
```

If you are using DOS version 3.3, you can increase the number of applications that support the data-file search path by using the /X qualifier, as shown here:

```
C> APPEND C:\DOS;C:\UTIL
```

If you simply specify a semicolon in the command line, DOS removes the data-file search path, as in this command:

```
C> APPEND  ;
```

ASSIGN

FUNCTION Routes disk-drive references from one disk drive to another.

FORMAT

ASSIGN [*source_drive=target_drive*[...]]

where the following is true:

source_drive is the disk-drive identification of the disk from which I/O references are routed.

target_drive is the disk-drive identification of the disk to which disk I/O operations will be routed.

... indicates that the command can be repeated several times.

NOTES   Many older software packages look on drive A for data or overlay files. If you want to install this kind of software on your fixed disk, you must trick the software into looking on the fixed disk for the files. ASSIGN allows you to do this.

If you invoke ASSIGN without any command line parameters, AS-SIGN restores its original disk-drive assignments.

Do not place a colon after each disk-drive identification in the AS-SIGN command line.

To maintain compatability with future releases of DOS, you should consider using the DOS SUBST command instead of ASSIGN.

Do not use the following commands with an assigned disk:

BACKUP
DISKCOPY
FORMAT
JOIN
LABEL
PRINT
RESTORE
SUBST

EXAMPLES   In the following example, DOS disk I/O operations that reference drive A will be routed to disk C:

```
C> ASSIGN  A=C
```

If you invoke a command such as

```
C> DIR  A:
```

DOS actually lists the files contained on drive C, as shown here:

```
Volume in drive C has no label
Directory of  C:\MISC

HARDWARE    <DIR>    10-05-87  2:20p
```

```
SOFTWARE     <DIR>     10-05-87     2:24p
LEDGER       <DIR>     10-05-87     2:24p
             3 File(s)  1209344 bytes free
```

If you invoke ASSIGN without any command-line parameters, DOS restores its original disk-drive assignments.

This command illustrates that you can perform multiple disk-drive assignments on one command line. In this case, DOS will route the disk drive request for either drive A or B to drive C.

```
C> ASSIGN  A=C  B=C
```

ATTRIB

FUNCTION   Displays or modifies a file's attribute byte.

FORMAT

[*drive:*][*path*]ATTRIB [+A|-A] [+R|-R] *file_specification* [/S]

where the following is true:

drive: specifies the disk drive containing the ATTRIB.EXE file. If you do not specify a disk-drive identification, DOS uses the current default disk drive.

path is the DOS path name of the directory that contains the ATTRIB.EXE file. If you do not specify a DOS path name, DOS uses the current default directory.

+A directs ATTRIB to set a file's archive bit.

-A directs ATTRIB to clear a file's archive bit.

+R directs ATTRIB to set a file's Read-only bit.

-R directs ATTRIB to clear a file's Read-only bit.

file_specification is the complete DOS file specification, including a disk drive and path name of the file(s) to modify. ATTRIB supports DOS wildcard characters.

/S directs DOS to process all files in the directories below the specified directory. This is a DOS version 3.3 qualifier.

NOTES   Each DOS file has a directory entry that contains the following fields:

Field	Offset
File name	0
Extension	8
Attribute byte	11
Reserved for DOS	12
Time	22
Date	22
Starting cluster number	26
File size	28

The DOS ATTRIB command modifies a file's attribute byte.

Several DOS commands use a file's attribute to enable selective file processing, such as BACKUP, RESTORE, and XCOPY. By using these commands in conjunction with ATTRIB, you can gain considerable file processing control.

Get in the habit of using ATTRIB to set your EXE and COM files to Readonly, protecting them from errant DOS commands such as

```
C> DEL *.*
```

EXAMPLES   If you don't specify the A or R qualifier as in this command,

```
C> ATTRIB *.*
```

ATTRIB displays the current attributes of each file, as shown here:

```
A       C:\DOS\ANSI.EXE
A       C:\DOS\ATTRIB.EXE
A       C:\DOS\FDISK.EXE
```

```
A     C:\DOS\GWBASIC.EXE
A     C:\DOS\SUBST.EXE
A     C:\DOS\XCOPY.EXE
```

In this command

```
C> ATTRIB +R CONFIG.SYS
```

ATTRIB will set the file CONFIG.SYS to Read-only. In so doing, DOS cannot modify the file's contents. If you attempt to delete a file marked as Read-only, for example, DOS displays

```
Access Denied
```

The DOS BACKUP /M qualifier directs BACKUP to back up only those files modified since the previous backup. By issuing the command

```
C> ATTRIB +A \*.* /S
```

you can set the archive bit of every file on disk to indicate that a backup is required. The command

```
C> ATTRIB +A \*.* /S
```

marks each file as being backed up.

ATTRIB can be used in conjunction with XCOPY to copy the entire contents of a fixed disk to floppy disks while maintaining the original disk structure. First, mark all the files on disk as requiring a backup, as shown here:

```
C> ATTRIB +A \*.* /S
```

Next, invoke XCOPY, as shown here:

```
C> XCOPY C:\*.* A: /S /M
```

When the floppy disk fills, XCOPY displays a message stating that fact and then terminates. Insert a new floppy disk in the drive and repeat this process. XCOPY will pick up with the first file marked as archived and resume the process at the correct location. Repeat this process until XCOPY finds no files to copy.

The following command sets all of your EXE files to Read-only while also setting each to Archive Required:

```
C> ATTRIB +R +A *.EXE
```

BACKUP

FUNCTION   Backs up one or more files to a new disk.

FORMAT

[*drive:*][*path*]BACKUP *source:*[*file_spec*] *target* : [/A][/D:*mm-dd-yy*]
[/L:*logfile*][/M][/S][T:*hh:mm:ss*][/F]

where the following is true:

drive: specifies the disk drive containing the BACKUP.COM file. If you do not specify a disk-drive identification, DOS will use the current default disk drive.

path is the DOS path name of the directory that contains the BACKUP.COM file. If you do not specify a DOS path name, DOS uses the current default directory.

source : specifies the source disk that contains the file(s) to be backed up.

file_spec is the DOS path name(s) for the file(s) to back up.

target : specifies the target disk.

/A directs BACKUP to append source files to files on the target disk.

/D:*mm-dd-yy* directs BACKUP to back up files modified since the specified date.

/F tells BACKUP that the target disk is unformatted. This is a DOS version 3.3 qualifier.

/L:*logfile* places an entry for all of the files in the log file specified. BACKUP.LOG is the default file name.

/M directs BACKUP to back up files modified since the last backup.

/S directs BACKUP to back up all directory files.

/T:*hh:mm:ss* directs BACKUP to back up files modified since the specified time. This is a DOS version 3.3 qualifier.

NOTES   BACKUP displays the name of each file as the file is successfully backed up.

A 10MB disk requires approximately twenty-five 360K floppy disks or eight 1.2MB disks for a complete backup.

To determine the exact number of disks required to perform a backup, first use the DOS CHKDSK command. Here is an example:

```
C> CHKDSK

Volume DOSDISK created Dec 30, 1988  9:46pm

21309440 bytes total disk space.
        0 bytes in 1 hidden files.
   206848 bytes in 90 directories.
13946880 bytes in 1694 user files.
    20480 bytes in bad sectors.
  7084032 bytes available on disk.

C>
```

The number of disks required is computed by

Disks required = (Total space - Available space)/Floppy disk size

Based on the figures in the example, the equation becomes

Disks required = (21309440 - 7084032)/1213952
$$= 11.718$$
$$= 12 \ (1.2\text{MB}) \text{ floppy disks}$$

Although DOS version 3.3 allows you to use unformatted disks in your backup procedures, this adds a considerable amount of time to your backups. If possible, therefore, always start your backups with sufficient formatted disks.

To support batch processing, BACKUP provides the following exit status codes:

Code	Meaning
0	Successful back up
1	No files found to back up
2	Some files not backed up due to sharing conflicts
3	BACKUP terminated by user CTRL-C
4	BACKUP terminated by error

EXAMPLES The following command backs up all of the files on drive C, including those in DOS directories, to the floppy disk in drive A:

```
C> BACKUP C:\*.* A: /S
```

This command uses the BACKUP /A qualifier to add the C:TEST.DAT file to the files contained on the backup disk in drive B:

```
C> BACKUP C:TEST.DAT B: /A
```

This command directs BACKUP to back up only the files created since December 31, 1988:

```
C> BACKUP C:\*.* A: /S /D:12:31:88
```

The following command directs BACKUP to back up all of the files created or modified since your last BACKUP command:

```
C> BACKUP C:\*.* A: /S /A /M
```

BREAK

FUNCTION   Enables or disables DOS's extended CTRL-BREAK checking.

FORMAT

BREAK [ON | OFF]

where the following is true:

ON enables extended CTRL-BREAK checking.

OFF disables extended CTRL-BREAK checking.

NOTES   By default, DOS checks for a user-entered CTRL-BREAK upon completing keyboard, screen, and printer I/O operations. If you enable extended CTRL-BREAK checking, DOS also checks for a user-entered CTRL-BREAK upon completing each system service, such as disk read or write operations.

If you invoke BREAK without a command-line parameter, BREAK displays the current state of processing, either ON or OFF.

By enabling extended CTRL-BREAK processing, you increase the system overhead because DOS must check for a CTRL-BREAK upon completing each system service. Therefore, you may want to enable this checking during program development. Most users, however, will leave BREAK set at OFF.

By default, DOS boots with BREAK set at OFF. If you want extended CTRL-BREAK processing enabled at system startup, use the BREAK=ON entry in CONFIG.SYS.

EXAMPLE   This command enables DOS extended CTRL-BREAK checking:

```
C> BREAK  ON
```

As stated, if you invoke BREAK without a command-line parameter,

```
C> BREAK
BREAK is on
```

BREAK displays its current state of extended CTRL-BREAK checking, either ON or OFF.

CALL

FUNCTION   Invokes a nested batch procedure from within a DOS batch file.

FORMAT

CALL *batch_file* [*argument* [...]]

where the following is true:

batch_file is the name of the batch file containing the CALL nested procedure.

argument is the command-line parameter for the nested batch procedure.

NOTES   DOS has difficulty invoking one batch file from within a second batch file when the invocation of the procedure appears in the middle of the batch file. If you must invoke a batch procedure in this manner, the CALL command enables you to do so.

This command functions similarly to the DOS command COMMAND /C within a batch file. This is a DOS version 3.3 command.

EXAMPLE   As the following example shows, CALL can be included in a batch file to invoke a nested procedure:

```
CLS
CALL MYPROC
DATE
```

CHCP

FUNCTION Displays or changes the current codepage.

FORMAT

CHCP [*code _ page*]

where the following is true:

code _ page specifies the desired codepage. *Code _ page* must have been previously prepared by the system as either the primary or secondary codepage in CONFIG.SYS.

NOTES Each time DOS displays a character on the screen, it must first map the ASCII value of the character to a specific letter in a character set. DOS uses codepages to map letters to specific characters.

DOS allows you to use a different character set for your DOS session, offering you international support. To select an alternate codepage, you must previously issue the NLSFUNC command.

Valid codepage entries include the following:

437	United States
850	Multilingual
860	Portugal
863	French Canadian
865	Nordic

If you invoke CHCP without a command-line parameter, CHCP displays the current codepage. This is a DOS version 3.3 command.

EXAMPLE The following command directs CHCP to select the Nordic codepage. Remember that this codepage must have previously been prepared by a NLSFUNC command.

```
C> CHCP  865
```

CHDIR

FUNCTION   Changes or displays the default directory.

FORMAT

CHDIR [*drive:*][*path*]

or

CD [*drive:*][*path*]

where the following is true:

drive: specifies the disk drive that contains the directory you want as the default. If you omit the disk drive, CHDIR uses the current default disk drive.

path specifies the DOS path name of the directory that you want to be the current directory. If you omit the path, CHDIR displays the current directory.

NOTES   CHDIR changes or displays the current directory name for the specified disk drive. If you do not specify a drive, CHDIR uses the current default drive. If you do not specify a path name, CHDIR displays the current default directory name.

CHDIR performs the following processing each time you specify a DOS path name. If the path name is preceded with a backslash (\), DOS begins its search for the directory at the root. However, if the path name does not begin with a backslash, the directory must reside below the current default directory.

DOS predefines two directory names.

.. parent directory of the current directory.

. current default directory.

Verify this by performing a directory listing of a DOS directory, as shown here:

```
Volume in drive C is DOSDISK
Directory of C:\SUBDIR

   .          <DIR>      11-01-87  11:34a
   ..         <DIR>      11-01-87  11:34a

           2 File(s)  7182336 bytes free
```

If you simply issue the following directory command

```
C> DIR  .

Volume in drive C is DOSDISK
Directory of C:\SUBDIR

   .          <DIR>      11-01-87  11:34a
   ..         <DIR>      11-01-87  11:34a

           2 File(s)  7182336 bytes free
```

DOS displays a directory listing of the current directory. However, if you use

```
C> DIR  ..
```

DOS displays the files in the parent directory.

EXAMPLES   If you invoke CHDIR without a path name, CHDIR displays the current directory.

```
C> CD
C:\SUBDIR
```

This command is valid with a disk drive specifier, as shown here:

```
C> CHDIR B:
B:\UTIL
```

The following DOS CHDIR command selects the directory DOS\CMDFILES on drive B as the current default directory:

```
C> CHDIR B:\DOS\CMDFILES
```

You could issue this command as two separate commands, first selecting the directory DOS

```
C> CD B:\DOS
```

and then selecting CMDFILES

```
C> CD B:CMDFILES
```

Note the use of the leading backslash in the first command

```
C> CD B:\DOS
```

When the backslash is used, DOS looks for the directory DOS in the root directory of drive B. In the second command, however,

```
C> CD B:CMDFILES
```

CHDIR does not look for the directory in the root, but rather in a directory below the current directory (which is the DOS directory). If you had instead issued the command

```
C> CHDIR B:\CMDFILES
```

CHDIR would not have found the directory because it would have looked in the root instead of the current directory.

CHKDSK

FUNCTION   Checks a disk's current status.

FORMAT

[*drive:*][*path*]CHKDSK [*d:*][*p*][*filename*] [/F] [/V]

where the following is true:

drive: specifies the disk drive containing the CHKDSK.COM file. If you do not specify a disk-drive identification, DOS uses the current default disk drive.

path is the DOS path name of the directory that contains the CHKDSK.COM file. If you do not specify a DOS path name, DOS uses the current default directory.

d: is the disk drive that CHKDSK is to examine.

p specifies a DOS directory containing files that CHKDSK is to examine for disk fragmentation.

filename is the file name and extension of file(s) that CHKDSK is to examine for disk fragmentation.

/F directs CHKDSK to fix errors found in a directory or file allocation table (FAT).

/V directs CHKDSK to display the names of all files on the disk.

NOTES   CHKDSK reports on the status of the following disk conditions:

■ The amount of free, used, and corrupted disk space

■ The number of hidden files

■ The amount of free and used memory

Periodically, because the normal day-to-day disk operations cause wear and tear on the storage media, files become corrupted and lose sectors. The DOS CHKDSK command allows you to view and repair such descrepancies.

During the everyday use of a disk, DOS files can also become fragmented, which means their contents are dispursed throughout the entire disk. Fragmented files increase system overhead on file I/O operations because the disk drive must rotate the disk several additional times in order to read the disk. The DOS CHKDSK command displays information on fragmented files. Once your disk becomes severely fragmented, you should consider a system backup-and-restore operation.

CHKDSK does not work with a JOINed or SUBSTed disk.

If you operate a local area network, do not try to repair your disk. When DOS has files open (as may be the case with a network) it cannot correctly update the file allocation table (FAT).

By default, CHKDSK will only report disk errors; it will not attempt to fix them. To write the actual corrections to disk, you must use the /F qualifier.

EXAMPLES   This command displays the state of the current disk:

```
C> CHKDSK
```

An example output might be

```
Volume DOSDISK created Oct 30, 1988  9:46pm

21309440 bytes total disk space.
        0 bytes in 1 hidden files.
   208896 bytes in 91 directories.
13871104 bytes in 1714 user files.
    20480 bytes in bad sectors.
  7206912 bytes available on disk.

   524288 bytes total storage
   401184 bytes free
```

If you specify a file or use DOS wildcard characters, CHKDSK reports on disk fragmentation.

```
C> CHKDSK *.*
```

If fragmented files exist, CHKDSK displays

```
C:\FILENAME.EXT
contains n non-contiguous blocks.
```

If CHKDSK discovers errors while examining your disk contents, it displays

```
Volume DOSDISK created Oct 30, 1988  9:46pm

Errors found.  F parameter not specified.
Corrections will not be written to disk.

1 lost clusters found in 1 chains.
Convert lost chains to files (Y/N)?
2048 bytes disk space would be freed.
```

To direct CHKDSK to repair the error, use the /F qualifier, as shown here:

```
C> CHKDSK /F
```

You can also use CHKDSK to locate a file quickly. If you invoke CHKDSK with the /V qualifier, CHKDSK displays the name of every file on the disk.

```
C> CHKDSK /V
```

CLS

FUNCTION   Clears the screen display.

FORMAT

CLS

NOTES CLS does not affect video attributes. CLS places the cursor and DOS prompt in the home (upper-left) position.

EXAMPLE In the following example, DOS erases the current screen contents, placing the cursor and the current DOS prompt in the home position:

C> CLS

COMMAND

FUNCTION Loads a secondary command processor.

FORMAT

COMMAND [*drive:*][*path*] [/C *string*][/E:*num_bytes*][/P]

where the following is true:

drive: specifies the disk-drive identification of the disk containing the secondary command processor. If you do not specify a disk drive, DOS uses the current default disk drive.

path is the DOS directory that contains the command processor. If you don't specify a path name, DOS uses the current default directory.

/C *string* directs DOS to execute the command specified by *string*. You can use this parameter for nested batch-file invocations.

/E:*num_bytes* specifies the space DOS must allocate for the secondary command processor environment. *Num_bytes* must be between 160 and 32,767 bytes. The default value is 160.

/P directs DOS to leave the secondary command processor permanently in memory.

NOTES   Each time you load a secondary command processor, it obtains its own copy of the DOS environment space.

Most users use COMMAND to invoke nested batch procedures, as shown here:

```
CLS
COMMAND /C BATFILE
DATE
```

If you use the /P and /C parameters together, COMMAND ignores /P.

To terminate a secondary command processor, use the DOS EXIT command.

EXAMPLES   In the following example, DOS will load the secondary command processor into memory only long enough to execute the CHKDSK command.

```
C> COMMAND /C  CHKDSK
```

When the command terminates, DOS will remove the secondary command processor.

If you invoke COMMAND from the DOS prompt with no parameters, as shown here:

```
C> COMMAND
```

DOS loads a secondary command processor, which displays its system prompt. You can verify that a secondary processor is indeed installed by noting the amount of free memory displayed by CHKDSK.

Note the number of bytes of free memory and issue the DOS EXIT command

```
C> EXIT
```

to terminate the command processor. Then invoke CHKDSK again. Much more free memory is now availabe.

COMP

FUNCTION   Displays the first ten differences between two files.

FORMAT

[*drive:*][*path*]COMP *file_spec1 file_spec2*

where the following is true:

drive: specifies the disk-drive identification of the disk containing the COMP.COM file. If you do not specify a disk, DOS uses the current default disk drive.

path specifies the name of the directory that contains the COMP.COM file. If you do not specify a directory, DOS uses the current default directory.

file_spec1 and *file_spec2* are the complete DOS path names of the files to compare. COMP supports DOS wildcard characters.

NOTES   COMP displays the differences as hexadecimal offsets into the file.

If the files are identical, COMP displays the message

```
Files compare OK
```

Upon completion of the file comparison, COMP will display

> Compare more files (Y/N)?

To compare additional files type **Y**; otherwise type **N**.
If COMP locates more than ten differences, it displays

> 10 Mismatches - ending compare

COMP does not compare files of different sizes.

EXAMPLES In the following example, COMP compares the contents of the A.DAT file to B.DAT.

> C> COMP A.DAT B.DAT

Assuming that each file contains

```
C> TYPE  A.DAT
A
AA

C> TYPE  B.DAT
B
BB
```

the command displays

```
Compare file C:A.DAT and file C:B.DAT

COMPARE error at OFFSET 0
File 1 = 41
File 2 = 42

Compare error at OFFSET 3
File 1 = 41
File 2 = 42

Compare error at OFFSET 4
File 1 = 41
File 2 = 42
```

> Do you want to compare more files (Y/N)?

If you omit the file name from the secondary file, DOS matches the file name on the specified drive with the primary file.

> C> COMP A.DAT B:

If you do not specify a file in the COMP command line, COMP prompts you for them, as shown here:

```
C> COMP
Enter the first filename.
A.DAT

Enter the second filename.
B.DAT
```

COPY

FUNCTION   Copies one or more files to a new destination.

FORMAT

COPY *source_ file target_ file* [/V][/A][/B]

or

COPY *source1+source2* [...] *target_file* [/V][/A][/B]

where the following is true:

source _ file specifies the complete DOS file specification of the file to be copied.

target _ file is the name of the destination file. If a file matching the name of *target _ file* exists, COPY overwrites it.

/V tells COPY to use disk verification to ensure that a successful copy occurred. This qualifier adds processing overhead; however, it prevents a hardware error from rendering the contents of the source and target files inconsistent.

/A informs COPY that the preceding file was an ASCII file.

/B informs COPY that the preceding file was a binary file.

NOTES COPY fully supports DOS wildcard characters.

To combine multiple files into one file, use the plus sign (+) between the source files desired.

COPY will not allow you to copy a file to itself. If you attempt to do so, COPY displays.

```
File cannot be copied onto itself
0 file(s) copied.
```

WARNING: COPY overwrites target files with the same name.

EXAMPLES The following command copies the contents of the CONFIG.SYS file to a file on drive B with the same name:

```
C> COPY A:CONFIG.SYS B:CONFIG.SYS
```

The function of this command is identical to

```
C> COPY A:CONFIG.SYS B:
```

or

```
C> B:
B> COPY A:CONFIG.SYS
```

The following command copies all of the files on drive A to drive B:

```
C> COPY A:*.* B:*.*
```

If you want to copy files contained in directories below the current directory, use the XCOPY command.

This command uses the plus sign to append the B and C files to the A file, thus creating a file called D:

```
C> COPY A+B+C D
```

The following command allows you to append text from the keyboard to an existing file, creating a new file.

```
C> COPY FILENAME+CON: NEWFILE.EXT
```

CTTY

FUNCTION   Selects a new device from which commands are issued.

FORMAT

CTTY *device_name*

where the following is true:

device_name specifies the device from which commands are received (either CON or AUX).

NOTES   Most users will never issue this command.

If you have a terminal attached to your serial port, you can direct DOS to obtain its commands from that port by entering the command

```
A> CTTY AUX
```

To resume normal operations, you must enter the following command from the terminal device:

```
A> CTTY CON
```

DATE

FUNCTION   Sets the DOS system date.

FORMAT

DATE [*mm-dd-yy*]

or

DATE [*dd-mm-yy*]

or

DATE [*yy-mm-dd*]

where the following is true:

mm is the desired month (1-12).

dd is the desired day (1-31).

yy is the desired year (80-99). DATE also allows you to include the century in the form 19*yy* or 20*yy*.

NOTES   The DATE format that you use depends on the COUNTRY= specifier that is in CONFIG.SYS. If you do not specify a date, DATE displays the current date.

In DOS versions prior to 3.3, DATE modifies the AT system clock. Users of these earlier versions must use the SETUP disk provided with the *Guide to Operations* to change the AT system clock. DOS version 3.3 TIME and DATE commands actually set this clock.

The actual date is an optional command-line parameter. If you omit the date, DATE prompts you for it.

EXAMPLES   In the following example, because the date was not present on the DOS command line, DATE prompted the user for it.

```
C> DATE

The current date is: Sun 11-21-1988
Enter the new date: (mm-dd-yy)
```

If you want to display the system date without modifying it, press ENTER at the date prompt. DATE leaves the system date unchanged. In this example, DATE sets the system date to 8 December 1988.

```
C> DATE  12/08/88
```

This command is identical to

```
C> DATE  12/08/1988
```

DATE fully supports a four-digit year. Use this command to set a date from the DATE prompt:

```
C> DATE

The current date is: Sun 11-01-1988
Enter the new date: (mm-dd-yy) 12-08-88
```

DEL

FUNCTION   Deletes a file from disk.

FORMAT

DEL [*drive:*][*path*]*filename* [*.ext*]

where the following is true:

drive: specifies the disk drive containing the file to delete. If you omit the drive qualifier, DEL uses the current default disk drive.

path specifies the name of the DOS directory that contains the file to be deleted. If you omit the path entry, DEL uses the current directory.

filename[.ext] is the name of the file to delete. DEL fully supports DOS wildcard characters.

NOTES DEL will not remove directories. Use RMDIR for this purpose.

Unless overridden with a drive or path specifier, DEL will delete files in the current directory only.

DOS allows you to delete several specific files at one time by placing each file name on the command line.

If you attempt to delete all of the files in a directory, DOS first prompts you with

```
A> DEL *.*
Are you sure (Y/N)?
```

to ensure that you actually want the command performed. If you want to delete the files, type **Y** and press ENTER; otherwise type **N** and press ENTER.

> **WARNING:** Once you have deleted a file, DOS cannot retrieve it.

EXAMPLES In the following example, DEL erases the contents of the CONFIG.OLD file from drive B:

```
C> DEL  B:CONFIG.OLD
```

The following command deletes a file in a DOS subdirectory:

```
C> DEL \DPS\COMMANDS\AUTOEXEC.BAK
```

If you attempt to delete all of the files in the current directory, as shown here:

```
C> DEL *.*
```

DEL responds with

```
Are you sure (Y/N)?
```

If you want to delete the files, type **Y** and press ENTER; otherwise type **N** and press ENTER.

DIR

FUNCTION   Displays a directory listing of files.

FORMAT

DIR [*file_specification*] [/P] [/W]

where the following is true:

file_specification is the complete DOS file specification for the file(s) for which DIR is to display the directory listing. It can contain a disk-drive identification and path name. If you do not place a file specification in the command line, DIR displays a directory listing of all of the files in the current directory. DIR fully supports DOS wild card characters.

/P directs DIR to pause after each screenful of information to display the prompt

```
Press any key when ready.
```

/W directs DIR to display the files in short form (filename) only with five filenames across the screen.

NOTES   For each file, DIR will display its complete name, size in bytes, and the date and time of its creation or last modification. DIR also displays the amount of free disk space in bytes.

To list all of the files on disk, including files in DOS directories, use the TREE command.

DIR does not display hidden system files.

DIR always displays the drive and directory in which the files are stored.

```
Volume in drive A is DOSDISK
Directory of  A:\

SUBDIR          <DIR>    11-01-87  12:53p
                1 File(s)  1213440 bytes free
```

If you invoke DIR with a file name, the extension defaults to *.

```
C> DIR  FILENAME
```

EXAMPLES   In the following example, DIR displays a directory listing of each of the files on drive B:

```
C> DIR  B:
```

This command is functionally equivalent to

```
C> DIR  B:*.*
```

or

```
C> B:
B> DIR
```

If several files exist on drive B, many may scroll off the screen during the directory listing. If this happens, invoke DIR with the /P qualifier, as shown here:

```
C> DIR  B:*.*  /P
```

Each time DIR completes a screenful of files, it will pause and display the prompt

```
Press any key when ready.
```

When this occurs, press any key and DIR will continue.

The file specification of the DIR command can be quite specific, as shown here:

```
C> DIR  \DOS\CONFIG.OLD
```

DIR displays the directory listing of the CONFIG.OLD file that resides in the directory DOS of the current disk.

If you have no interest in file sizes or their date and time stamps, invoke DIR with the /W option.

```
C> DIR  /W                        .
```

DIR displays a directory listing of file names only, five files across the screen, as shown here:

```
Volume in drive C is DOSDISK
Directory of  C:\DOS

               ..     ANSI      EXE   APPEND  COM  ASSIGN   COM
ATTRIB       EXE    BACKUP    COM   CHKDSK  COM  COMP     COM   DISKCOMP COM
DISKCOPY     COM    EDLIN     COM   FDISK   EXE  FIND     COM   FORMAT   COM
FORMATS      TBL    GRAFTABL  COM   GWBASIC EXE  HELP     EXE   JOIN     EXE
PRINT        COM    README          REPLACE EXE  RESTORE  COM   SORT     EXE
       25 File(s)  7106560 bytes free
```

You can also use the DOS redirection operators with DIR. In this example, DOS displays a sorted directory listing.

```
C> DIR | SORT
```

This command prints the files in the current directory.

```
C> DIR > PRN:
```

DISKCOMP

FUNCTION   Compares two floppy disks.

FORMAT

[*drive:*][*path*]DISKCOMP [*primary_drive:*[*secondary_drive*]] [/1] [/8]

where the following is true:

drive: specifies the disk drive that contains the DISKCOMP.COM file. If you omit the drive specifier DOS uses the current default disk drive.

path specifies the DOS directory name that contains the DISKCOMP.COM file. If you do not specify a path name, DOS uses the current default directory.

primary_drive: specifies one of the floppy disk drives to be used in the disk comparison. If you do not specify a primary drive, DISKCOMP uses the current default disk drive.

secondary_drive specifies the second drive to be used in the disk comparison. If you do not specify a secondary drive, DISKCOMP uses the current default disk drive.

/1 directs DISKCOMP to perform a single-sided disk comparison.

/8 directs DISKCOMP to perform an eight-sector- per-track disk comparison.

NOTES   If you have a single-floppy system, DISKCOMP performs a single-drive comparison, prompting you to enter the source and target disks at the correct time.

If the contents of the disks are identical, DISKCOMP displays the message

```
Compare OK
```

Otherwise DISKCOMP displays the side and track (in hexadecimal form) of the differences.

DISKCOMP provides the following exit status values to support your batch processing.

0	Comparison OK
1	Disks were not the same
2	User terminated using CTRL-C
3	Termination due to disk error
4	Insufficient memory of invalid disk drive

If DISKCOMP displays the message

```
Insert disk with COMMAND.COM in drive A
and strike any key when ready
```

insert your DOS disk in drive A and press ENTER.

EXAMPLES   In the following example, DISKCOMP will compare the contents of the disk in drive A to that in drive B:

```
C> DISKCOMP  A:  B:
```

If the disks are identical, DISKCOMP displays

```
Compare OK
```

Otherwise DISKCOMP displays the locations of the differences, as shown here:

```
Compare error on
side n track n
```

If you need to compare single-sided disks, use this DISKCOMP command:

```
C> DISKCOMP A: B: /1
```

DISKCOMP

DISKCOPY

FUNCTION   Copies a source floppy disk to a target disk.

FORMAT

[*drive:*][*path*]DISKCOPY [*source_drive:* [*target_drive*]][/1]

where the following is true:

drive: specifies the disk drive containing the DISKCOPY.COM file. If you do not specify a disk drive, DOS uses the current default disk drive.

path specifies the DOS directory that contains the DISKCOPY.COM file. If you do not specify a path name, DOS uses the current default directory.

source_drive: specifies the disk drive containing the floppy disk to copy. If you do not specify a source drive, DISKCOPY uses the current default disk drive.

target_drive specifies the disk drive containing the disk to be copied to. If you do not specify a target drive, DISKCOPY uses the current default disk drive.

/1 directs DISKCOPY to copy only the first side of the source disk to the target disk.

NOTES   DISKCOPY copies the contents of one floppy disk to another. If you have a single-floppy system, DISKCOPY performs a single-drive copy prompting you to enter the source and target disks at the correct time.

DISKCOPY formats an unformatted disk during the copy.

DISKCOPY does not correct disk fragmentation. Use the DOS XCOPY command for this purpose.

DISKCOPY destroys the previous contents of the target disk.

If the source and target disks are not the same type (for example, a 360K and 1.2MB disk), DISKCOPY displays a message and terminates.

Do not use DISKCOPY with JOINed or SUBSTed disks.

If the target disk has not been formatted yet, DISKCOPY formats the disk during the copy operations, displaying the message

```
Formatting While Copying
```

If DISKCOPY displays the message

```
Insert disk with COMMAND.COM in drive A
and strike any key when ready
```

insert your DOS disk in drive A and press ENTER.

DISKCOPY supports the following exit status code values to support your batch processing:

0	Successful copy
1	Unsuccessful due to nonfatal disk error
2	User terminated by using CTRL-C
3	Unsuccessful due to fatal disk error
4	Insufficient memory or invalid disk drives

EXAMPLES The following command assumes that you have two compatible floppy disk drives on your system:

```
C> DISKCOPY  A:  B:
```

When DISKCOPY begins copying a disk, it reads several tracks of data from the source and then writes them to the target disk. In a single-floppy-drive system, DISKCOPY repeats this process and prompts you for the source and target disks as shown here:

```
[A:\] DISKCOPY
Insert SOURCE Diskette in Drive A:

Press any key when ready

Copying 40 tracks
9 Sectors/Track, 2 Side(s)

Insert TARGET Diskette in Drive A:

Press any key when ready

Insert SOURCE Diskette in Drive A:

Press any key when ready

Insert TARGET Diskette in Drive A:

Press any key when ready

Copy another diskette (Y/N)?
```

ECHO

FUNCTION   Displays or suppresses batch command messages.

FORMAT

ECHO [ON | OFF | *message*]

where the following is true:

ON enables the display of batch commands as they execute.

OFF disables the display of batch commands as they execute.

message is the text message ECHO is to display to the user.

NOTES   By default, each time you execute DOS batch files, DOS displays the names of each command as it executes. For example, the file

```
A
B
C
```

displays the following.

```
C> A

C> B

C> C
```

ECHO allows you to suppress the display of command names within a DOS batch file as the command executes. For example, the file

```
ECHO OFF
A
B
C
```

will display

```
C> ECHO  OFF
```

ECHO also provides a convenient method of displaying messages to the end user.

If you invoke ECHO without a command-line parameter, ECHO displays its current state, ON or OFF.

If you are using DOS version 3.3, you can proceed each command with the @ character to suppress display of the command name.

EXAMPLES   In the following command, DOS continues to display command names within a DOS batch file as it executes:

```
C> ECHO  ON
```

This command disables command name display.

```
C> ECHO  OFF
```

ECHO can be used with batch parameters. For example, this command displays the name of the batch file that is currently executing.

```
ECHO %0
```

This batch procedure displays each of its command-line parameters:

```
ECHO OFF
:LOOP
SHIFT
IF '%0'== " GOTO DONE
ECHO %0
GOTO LOOP
:DONE
```

This ECHO command displays a simple message to the user.

```
ECHO This is a message via ECHO
```

The following batch file fully exploits ECHO, displaying copyright information on the screen:

```
ECHO OFF
ECHO ****************************************
ECHO * Kevin Shafer Software, Inc. 1988  *
ECHO *                                    *
ECHO * Giant's Baseball -- 1988           *
ECHO *                                    *
ECHO ****************************************
```

When invoked, the procedure will display

```
ECHO OFF

****************************************
* Kevin Shafer Software, Inc. 1988   *
*                                    *
* Giant's Baseball -- 1988           *
*                                    *
****************************************
```

Under DOS version 3.3, you can suppress the display of ECHO OFF by changing the line ECHO OFF to

```
@ECHO OFF
```

ERASE

FUNCTION   Erases a file from disk.

FORMAT

ERASE [*drive:*] [*path*] *filename* [*.ext*]

where the following is true:

drive: specifies the disk drive containing the file to be deleted. If you omit the drive qualifier, ERASE uses the current default disk drive.

path specifies the name of the DOS directory that contains the file to be deleted. If you omit the path entry, ERASE uses the current directory.

filename[.ext] is the name of the file to be deleted. ERASE fully supports DOS wildcard characters.

NOTES   ERASE does not remove directories. Use RMDIR for this purpose.

ERASE and DEL are functionally equivalent. Most users use DEL.

Unless overridden with a drive or path specifier, ERASE deletes files in the current directory only.

If you attempt to erase all of the files in a directory, DOS first prompts you with

    Are you sure (Y/N)?

to verify that you want the command performed. If you want to delete the files, type **Y** and press ENTER; otherwise type **N** and press ENTER.

WARNING: Once you have erased a file, DOS cannot retrieve it.

EXAMPLES   In the following example, ERASE erases the contents of the CONFIG.OLD file from drive B:

```
C> ERASE  B:CONFIG.OLD
```

The following command erases a file from within a DOS subdirectory:

```
C> ERASE  \DOS\COMMANDS\STARTUP.BAK
```

If you attempt to delete all of the files in the current directory, as shown here:

```
C> ERASE  *.*
```

ERASE will respond with

```
Are you sure (Y/N)?
```

If you want to delete the files, type **Y** and press ENTER; otherwise type **N** and press ENTER.

EXE2BIN

FUNCTION   Converts an EXE file format to a COM file.

FORMAT

[*drive:*][*path*]EXE2BIN *source _ file target _ file*

where the following is true:

drive: specifies the disk drive containing the EXE2BIN.COM file. If you do not specify a disk drive, DOS uses the current default disk drive.

path specifies the DOS directory that contains the EXE2BIN.COM file. If you do not specify a path name, DOS uses the current default directory.

source _ file is the name of the EXE file that DOS is to convert to a COM file.

target _ file is the name of the converted COM file.

NOTES   If you do not specify a file extension on the source file, EXE2BIN assumes EXE. If you do not specify a file extension on the target file, EXE2BIN assumes BIN.

If a drive or path is not specified for either file, EXE2BIN uses the current defaults.

COM files contain memory images of the program; therefore, they result in a more compact file, which DOS can load quickly into memory. However, there are several requirements that the EXE file must meet before it can be converted. For more information on this, refer to the *MS-DOS Technical Reference Manual.*

If EXE2BIN cannot convert a file, it displays

```
File cannot be converted
```

This is a programmer's tool that you probably will never execute.

EXAMPLE   The following command converts the TEST.EXE file to TEST.COM:

```
C> EXE2BIN TEST.EXE TEST.COM
```

EXIT

FUNCTION   Terminates a secondary command processor.

FORMAT

EXIT

NOTES   EXIT allows you to terminate a secondary command processor.

Many software packages (such as word processors and spreadsheets) allow you to access the DOS prompt by creating a secondary process from your application. Once you are done issuing your DOS commands, invoke EXIT to return to your application.

EXAMPLE   The following command EXIT terminates a secondary command processor:

C> EXIT

FASTOPEN

FUNCTION   Increases the number of directory entries that DOS keeps in memory, thus increasing the speed in which DOS locates files on disk.

FORMAT

[*drive:*][*path*]FASTOPEN *d:* [=*entries*] [...]

where the following is true:

drive: specifies the disk drive containing the FASTOPEN.COM file. If you do not specify a disk drive, DOS uses the current default disk drive.

path specifies the DOS directory that contains the FASTOPEN.COM file. If you do not specify a path name, DOS uses the current default directory.

d: specifies the disk-drive identification for which DOS is setting aside storage to contain directory entries.

entries specifies the number of directory entries that DOS is reserving space for. This value must be in the range 10-999. The default is 10.

... indicates that FASTOPEN can reserve space for several disks in one command.

NOTES   FASTOPEN is a DOS version 3.3 command.

When you specify several disks, remember that the sum of the entries cannot exceed 999.

Each directory entry stored requires 35 bytes.

Each time DOS accesses a directory, it places that directory name into a list of the directory names. Each time you perform a directory manipulation command, DOS first checks its list of directories in memory to see if it can locate the directory on disk instead of reading the disk in search of the directory.

If you use the value of 999 for directory entries, DOS spends a considerable amount of overhead searching its directory list. Most users, therefore, find the value of 34 acceptable.

EXAMPLE   In the following command, DOS remembers 50 directory entries for drive C.

```
C> FASTOPEN C:=50
```

FC

FUNCTION   Compares two files and displays the actual differences between them.

FORMAT

[*drive:*][*path*]FC [/A][/B][/C][/LB *n*][/N][/T][W][/*nnnn*]
file1   file2

where the following is true:

drive: specifies the disk drive of the disk containing the FC.EXE file. If you do not specify a drive identification, DOS uses the default disk drive.

path specifies the directory containing the FC.EXE file. If you do not specify a subdirectory path, DOS uses the current default directory.

/A directs FC not to display all of the lines that differ between two ASCII files, but rather the first and last line in a group of lines that differ.

/B directs FC to perform a binary comparison of the files.

/C directs FC to ignore the difference between upper- and lowercase letters.

/L directs FC to perform an ASCII file comparision.

/LB *n* directs FC to use an internal buffer of *n* lines.

/N directs FC to display the line numbers of lines that differ in two ASCII files.

/T directs FC not to expand tabs into spaces.

/W directs FC to compress white space (spaces or tabs).

/*nnnn* specifies the number of lines that must again match following a difference for FC to assume the two files are synchronized. The default is 2.

NOTES FC displays differences between two files by displaying the first file name followed by the lines that differ between the files. Next, FC displays the second file name followed by the first line that matches in both files and the differences.

   If FC is comparing binary files, it displays differences in the form

   aaaaaaaa bb cc

where *aaaaaaaa* is the offset address of the values that differ, while *bb* and *cc* are the values that differ.

   If FC encounters too many errors, it terminates and displays the message

```
Resynch failed. Files are too different.
```

FC is often a more convenient command to use when comparing two files than is the COMP command.

EXAMPLES The following command compares two binary files, usingthe /B qualifier:

```
C> FC /B TEST.EXE OLDTEST.EXE
```

The output might be

```
00000002: 9A 66
00000004: 06 20
00000006: 01 03
0000000A: 00 CE
0000000E: 20 14
0000000F: 00 04
00000011: 02 08
00000012: 32 97
```

Assuming that the A.DAT file contains

```
1
2
3
4
5
A
A
A
6
7
8
9
10
```

and B.DAT contains

```
1
2
3
4
5
B
B
B
6
7
8
9
10
```

the command

```
C> FC A.DAT B.DAT
```

displays the following:

```
***** A.DAT
5
A
A
```

```
A
6
***** B.DAT
5
B
B
B
6
*****
```

If you include the /N qualifier,

```
C> FC /N A.DAT B.DAT
```

FC displays

```
***** A.DAT
5: 5
6: A
7: A
8: A
9: 6
***** B.DAT
5: 5
6: B
7: B
8: B
9: 6
*****
```

If the DAYS.DAT file contains

```
SUNDAY
MONDAY
TUESDAY
WEDNESDAY
THURSDAY
FRIDAY
SATURDAY
```

and WEEKDAYS.DAT contains

```
MONDAY
TUESDAY
WEDNESDAY
THURSDAY
FRIDAY
```

the command

```
C> FC DAYS.DAT WEEKDAYS.DAT
```

displays

```
***** DAYS.DAT
SUNDAY
MONDAY
TUESDAY
***** WEEKDAYS.DAT
MONDAY
TUESDAY
*****

***** DAYS.DAT
SATURDAY
***** WEEKDAYS.DAT
*****
```

If you want FC to ignore differences between upper- and lowercase letters, add the /C qualifier, as shown here:

```
C> FC /C FILE.1 FILE.2
```

FDISK

FUNCTION   Defines disk partitions on a DOS fixed disk.

FORMAT

FDISK

NOTES DOS allows you to divide your fixed disk into logical collections of cylinders, known as partitions. This allows you to place several different operating systems on one fixed disk.

The DOS FDISK command allows you to add, change, display, and delete disk partitions.

The first sector on every fixed disk contains a master boot record. This record actually contains partition information, which defines the partition the computer uses to boot from. FDISK is your interface to the master boot record.

EXAMPLES FDISK is a menu-driven program. Invoke FDISK with

```
C> FDISK
```

FDISK responds by displaying the first menu, as shown here:

```
Fixed Disk Setup Program Version 3.30
(C)Copyright Microsoft Corp. 1987

FDISK Options

Current Fixed Disk Drive: 1

Choose one of the following:

1. Create DOS partition
2. Change Active partition
3. Delete DOS partition
4. Display Partition Information


Enter choice: [1]

Press ESC to return to DOS
```

If DOS responds with

```
Invalid drive specification
```

when you enter the command

```
A> FORMAT  C:
```

you must create a DOS partition by selecting option 1. FDISK responds with

```
Create DOS Partition

Current Fixed Disk Drive: 1


1. Create Primary DOS partition
2. Create Extended DOS partition
3. Create logical DOS drive(s) in
the Extended DOS partition


Enter choice: [1]

Press ESC to return to FDISK Options
```

If you want to create your first fixed disk partition (drive C), select option 1. Once you define this partition, you can exit back to DOS and then use FORMAT to prepare your fixed disk.

If you have a disk larger than 30MB and want to create multiple partitions, select option 2 after you have defined your primary DOS partition.

To create two DOS partitions, a primary and an extended partition, select option 4. FDISK displays

Display Partition Information

Current Fixed Disk Drive: 1

Partition	Status	Type	Start	End	Size
C: 1	A	PRI DOS	0	523	524
2		EXT DOS	524	964	441

Total disk space is 965 cylinders.

The Extended DOS partition contains
logical DOS drives. Do you want to
display logical drive information? [Y]

Press ESC to return to FDISK Options

You now have drives C and D. Use the ESC key to exit back to DOS.

FIND

FUNCTION Searches a file(s) or piped input for a string.

FORMAT

[*drive:*][*path*]FIND [/C][/N][/V] "*string*" [*file_spec* ...]

where the following is true:

drive: specifies the disk drive containing the FIND.COM file. If you don't specify a disk-drive identification, DOS uses the current default disk drive.

path specifies the name of the DOS directory that contains the FIND.COM file. If you do not specify a directory path, DOS uses the current default directory.

string specifies the string for which FIND is to search. It must be in quotes.

file_spec is the file name that is to be searched for the string. It can be a series of file names separated by spaces. FIND does not support DOS wildcard characters.

... indicates that several file names can reside in the command line.

/C directs FIND to display a count of occurrences of the string.

/N directs FIND to precede each line containing the string with its line number.

/V directs FIND to display each line that does not contain the string.

NOTES   FIND allows you to quickly locate a sequence of characters within a file or redirected output. FIND can also be used as a filter of piped input.

If /C and /N are used together, FIND ignores /N.

The string FIND is searching for must be in quotes. If the string has nested quotes within, you must use two quotes at each nested quote, such as

```
C> FIND """WOW!""" she said" FILENAME.EXT
```

EXAMPLES   In the following example, FIND is a filter used to list each directory in the current directory.

```
C> DIR A: | FIND "<DIR>"
```

If the current directory contains

```
Volume in drive A is DOSDISK
Directory of  A:\
```

```
SUBDIR          <DIR>      11-01-87  12:53p
A               <DIR>            11-01-87   1:44p
B               <DIR>            11-01-87   1:44p
C               <DIR>            11-01-87   1:44p
WSSTRIP         EXE    2816  10-03-84   10:33p
TAB             EXE   12326  5-05-85    6:25p
SUM             EXE    2834  10-24-87   2:20p
PIPE            EXE    2814  10-26-87   6:47p
PIPE2           EXE    7528  10-23-87   12:37p
                9 File(s)  1182208 bytes free
```

the previous command displays

```
SUBDIR          <DIR>          11-01-87   12:53p
A               <DIR>          11-01-87   1:44p
B               <DIR>          11-01-87   1:44p
C               <DIR>          11-01-87   1:44p
```

To list all files that are not directories, use the FIND /V option, as shown here:

```
C> DIR  A:  |  FIND  /V  "<DIR>"
```

The following command displays each occurrence of the string "begin" in the TEST.PAS file:

```
C> FIND  "begin"  TEST.PAS
```

This command displays each occurrence of the string "begin," and each line is preceded by its line number.

```
C> FIND  /N  "begin"  TEST.PAS
```

The following command displays a count of the number of occurrences of "begin" in the file:

```
C> FIND  /C  "begin"  TEST.PAS
```

FOR

FUNCTION   Provides repetitive execution (iterative processing) of DOS commands.

FORMAT

FOR %%*variable* IN (*set*) DO *DOS_command*

where the following is true:

%%*variable* is the FOR loop control variable that DOS manipulates with each iteration. The variable name is restricted to a character, but 0-9 cannot be used because they are reserved for DOS batch parameters.

set is a list of valid DOS file names. *Set* can be a list of DOS file names separated by commas (A, B, C), or it can contain a wildcard character (*.*), or both (A, B, *.DAT).

DOS_command is the command to execute with each iteration.

NOTES   FOR is used most commonly within DOS batch files; however, FOR can be used from the DOS prompt. The %% symbols before the variable name are used in batch files, while the % symbol is used from the DOS prompt.

The set processing that FOR performs is straightforward. Consider this example:

FOR %%V IN (AUTOEXEC.BAT, CONFIG.SYS, S.CMD) DO TYPE %%V

FOR assigns the file name AUTOEXEC.BAT to the variable during the first iteration and displays its contents. On the second iteration, FOR assigns the variable the file name CONFIG.SYS and displays its contents. On the third iteration, FOR assigns the file name S.CMD to the variable and again displays the file's contents. When FOR prepares for the fourth iteration, it fails to find any more file names so its processing is complete.

EXAMPLES   The following command has been issued from the DOS prompt. Note that the variable name is only preceded by one % symbol:

```
C> FOR %I IN (*.FOR) DO TYPE %I
```

In this command, a DOS batch file is using FOR to compile all of the C files on the current directory.

```
FOR %%F IN (*.C) DO CC %%F
```

FORMAT

FUNCTION   Formats a disk for use by DOS.

FORMAT

```
[drive:][path]FORMAT [d:][/S][/V][/4][/T:tracks]
[/n:sectors][/1][/8][/B]
```

where the following is true:

drive: is the disk drive containing the FORMAT.COM file. If you omit the disk-drive specifier, DOS uses the current default disk drive.

path is the name of the DOS directory containing the FORMAT.COM file. If you omit the directory specifier, DOS uses the current default directory.

d: specifies the disk drive containing the disk to format.

/n:sectors defines the numbers of sectors per track. This is a DOS version 3.3 qualifier.

/S directs FORMAT to place the DOS system files on the disk to make the disk bootable.

/T:*tracks* defines the number of tracks per side. This is a DOS version 3.3 qualifier.

/V directs FORMAT to include the volume label.

/4 directs FORMAT to format the disk double- sided in a quad-density disk drive.

/1 directs FORMAT to format the disk as a single-sided disk.

/8 directs FORMAT to format the disk with eight sectors per track. Most disks use 9 or 15.

/B directs FORMAT to reserve space for the system files on the target disk. Unlike the /S option, /B does not actually place the files on disk.

NOTES   The original manufacturer of disks you purchase has no way of knowing what computer the disks will be used on, nor on what operating system. Before you can use a new disk, therefore, you must format it under DOS.

The FORMAT /S command copies the DOS hidden files to the target disk that are required to boot DOS.

Because inadvertantly formatting a fixed disk can be disastrous, FORMAT first prompts you with

```
WARNING, ALL DATA ON NON-REMOVEABLE DISK
DRIVE N: WILL BE LOST!
Proceed with Format (Y/N)?
```

To proceed with the FORMAT, type **Y**; otherwise type **N**.

Upon completion FORMAT displays

```
Total disk space
Corrupted disk space marked as defective
Total disk space consumed by the operating system
Total disk space available for file utilization
```

As you can see, FORMAT reports on defective space that it finds during formatting. In addition, FORMAT places entries for each defective sector into a table called the file allocation table, which prevents DOS from using the corrupted sectors for data storage.

Do not use FORMAT in conjunction with ASSIGN, JOIN, or SUBST.

FORMAT does not allow you to use the /S and /V qualifiers with the /B qualifier.

To support batch processing, FORMAT uses the following exit status values:

0	Successful format
3	User has terminated using CTRL-BREAK
4	Termination due to an error in processing
5	User has terminated using N to fixed-disk prompt

FORMAT will not work with drives currently in a network configuration.

The following are valid FORMAT qualifiers:

160/180K disks	/1 /4 /8 /B /N / T /V /S
320/360K disks	/1 /4 /8 /B /N / T /V /S
720K disks	/N / T /V /S
1.2MB disks	/N / T /V /S
1.44MB disks	/N / T /V /S
Fixed disks	/V /S

If FORMAT displays the message

> Insert disk with COMMAND.COM in drive A
> and strike any key when ready

insert your DOS disk in drive A and press ENTER.

> **WARNING:** FORMAT destroys any of the information contained on the target disk.

EXAMPLES The following command creates a bootable disk on the disk contained in drive B:

> C> FORMAT B:/S

Many users often have to format double-density disks in their 1.2MB drives. The /4 qualifier in the FORMAT command directs FORMAT to create a 360K disk:

```
C> FORMAT A:/4
```

This command displays

```
Insert a new diskette in drive A:
and press Enter when ready.
```

The FORMAT /B and /S qualifiers are very similar. The following command directs FORMAT to reserve space for the operating-system boot files as opposed to actually placing the files on disk:

```
C> FORMAT A: /B
```

When you include the /B qualifier, the DOS SYS command can later update the disk as required.

The following lists the commands used to format various disks commonly used for XT, AT, 386, and PS/2 computers:

Size	Description	Command Used to Format Disk to 360K
5 1/4"	360K	FORMAT A:
5 1/4"	1.2MB	FORMAT A:/4

Size	Description	Command Used to Format Disk to 720K (PS/2 Computers)
3 1/2"	720K	FORMAT A:
3 1/2"	1.44MB	FORMAT A: /N:9 /T:80

GOTO

FUNCTION   Branches to the label specified in a BAT file.

FORMAT

GOTO *label_name*

where the following is true:

label_name specifies the name of a label within a DOS batch
procedure.

NOTES   DOS label names contain any of the characters valid for
DOS file names. If the label does not exist, DOS terminates execution of the batch file.

DOS label names can be virtually any length; however, DOS only
distinguishes the first eight characters. For example, DOS considers
the label names DOS_LABEL1 and DOS_LABEL2 as equivalent.

EXAMPLES   The following batch procedure displays a continuous
directory listing until the user presses CTRL-C or CTRL-BREAK.

```
:LOOP
DIR
GOTO LOOP
```

When this procedure is invoked, it repeatedly displays a directory
listing of the current drive.

When DOS cannot find a label specified in a GOTO command, it
terminates the processing, as shown here:

```
GOTO DOSLABEL
DATE
TIME
:DOSLABL
```

Upon invocation the procedure displays

```
Label not found
```

The following procedure illustrates that DOS only examines the first eight characters of a label name. Although the GOTO command branches to the label DOS_LABEL2, DOS first finds DOS_LABEL.

```
GOTO DOS_LABEL2
:DOS_LABEL
ECHO LABEL1
GOTO DONE
:DOS_LABEL2
ECHO LABEL2
:DONE
```

GRAFTABL

FUNCTION   Enables display of the extended character set when the display is in graphics mode.

FORMAT

[*drive:*][*path*]GRAFTABL [*codepage* | /STATUS]

where the following is true:

drive: specifies the disk drive containing the GRAFTABL.COM file. If you do not specify a disk drive, DOS uses the current default disk drive.

path is the DOS path name of the directory that contains the GRAFTABL.COM file. If you do not specify a DOS path name, DOS uses the current default directory.

codepage specifies one of the following codepages to be used for display:

437	United States
850	Multilingual
860	Portugal
863	French Canadian
865	Nordic

/STATUS directs GRAFTABL to display the codepage that is currently in use.

NOTES   The DOS GRAFTABL command allows users to display extended ASCII characters when the display is in medium resolution graphics mode.

GRAFTABL loads memory-resident code when it is invoked; therefore, it can be invoked only once.

To support your batch processing, GRAFTABL provides the following exit status values.

0	Successful
1	Graphics table already loaded
2	File error occurred during load
3	Invalid parameter specified, load not performed
4	Incorrect DOS version

EXAMPLES   If you specify the /STA qualifier in the GRAFTABL command line, as shown here:

```
C> GRAFTABL /STA
```

GRAFTABL displays the number of the current codepage, as shown here:

```
USA version of Graphic Character Set Table is already loaded.
```

The following command directs GRAFTABL to use the codepage for the United States when it displays extended characters.

```
C> GRAFTABL 437
```

GRAPHICS

FUNCTION   Allows screen contents containing graphics to be printed by means of print screen operations.

FORMAT

[*drive:*][*path*]GRAPHICS [*printer_type*][/B]
[/R][/P:*port_id*][/LCD]

where the following is true:

drive: specifies the disk drive that contains the GRAPHICS.COM file. If you do not specify a disk drive, DOS uses the current default disk drive.

path is the complete DOS path name of the directory that contains the GRAPHICS.COM file. If you don't specify a path name, DOS uses the current default directory.

printer_type specifies one of the following target printer type:

COLOR1	Color printer with black ribbon
COLOR4	Color printer with RGB ribbon
COLOR8	Color printer with cyan, magenta, yellow, and black ribbon
COMPACT	Compact printer
GRAPHICS	Graphics printer
THERMAL	Thermal printer

/B directs GRAPHICS to print the background color. The default is not to print the background color.

/LCD directs GRAPHICS to print the LCD display from the PC Portable.

/P:*port_id* specifies the parallel printer port that GRAPHICS is to use. Valid values include 1, 2, or 3. The default is 1.

/R directs GRAPHICS to reverse the color of the screen image. Black images on the screen will be printed as white and white images as black.

NOTES GRAPHICS is a memory resident program; therefore, you must install it only once.

EXAMPLE The following command loads the memory-resident software required to support print screen operations that contain graphics images:

```
C> GRAPHICS
```

IF

FUNCTION Provides conditional processing within DOS batch files.

FORMAT

IF [NOT] *condition DOS_command*

where the following is true:

NOT performs a boolean NOT on the result of the condition. *condition* must be one of the following:

- ERRORLEVEL *value* (true if program exit status >= *value*)

■ EXIST *file_spec* (true if the file specified exists)

■ *string1==string2* (true if both strings are identical)

DOS_command is the name of the command that DOS is to perform if the condition is true.

NOTES   Although the DOS IF statement is used most commonly from within DOS batch files, DOS fully supports IF from the command line, as shown here:

```
C> IF  EXIST  CONFIG.SYS  TYPE  CONFIG.SYS
```

EXAMPLES   In the following command, if the CONFIG.SYS file exists in the current directory, DOS copies the file to drive B:

```
IF EXIST CONFIG.SYS COPY CONFIG.SYS B:
```

If the program DOSPGM exits with a status greater than or equal to 3, this command directs DOS to display the message T H R E E

```
ECHO OFF
DOSPGM
IF ERRORLEVEL 3 ECHO T H R E E
```

Note how you can add the boolean NOT to this expression to direct the program to terminate if the exit status is less than three, as shown here:

```
ECHO OFF
DOSPGM
IF NOT ERRORLEVEL 3 GOTO DONE
ECHO T H R E E
:DONE
```

In this command, the DOS IF command it used to determine whether or not the value of the batch parameter is NULL:

IF '%1' == '' GOTO NULL

If you use this expression within the following batch file, you can echo each of the batch file parameters to the screen:

```
ECHO OFF
:LOOP
SHIFT
IF '%0'=='' GOTO DONE
ECHO %0
GOTO LOOP
:DONE
```

When you invoke the procedure with

```
C> ECHOTEST 1 2 3 4 5
```

it displays

```
C> ECHOTEST 1 2 3 4 5
C> ECHO OFF
1
2
3
4
5
```

JOIN

FUNCTION   Joins a disk drive to a DOS path.

FORMAT

[*drive:*][*path*]JOIN [*d1:* [*d2:path*]][/D]

where the following is true:

drive: is the disk-drive identification of the disk that contains the JOIN.EXE file. If you do not specify a disk drive, DOS uses the current default disk drive.

path is the name of the DOS directory that contains the JOIN.EXE file. If you do not specify a disk drive, DOS uses the current default directory.

d1: specifies the disk drive to join to the path provided.

d2:path specifies the join directory.

/D directs JOIN to disconnect a previously joined disk.

NOTES   JOIN makes two disks appear as one by joining a disk to a DOS path.

If you issue a JOIN command without any parameters, JOIN displays the current joins.

DOS joins a disk only to an EMPTY DOS directory.

Do not use JOIN in conjunction with the following commands:

CHKDSK
DISKCOPY
FDISK
FORMAT
LABEL
RECOVER
SYS

EXAMPLES   Before you can JOIN a disk to a directory, you must use MKDIR to create an empty directory:

```
C> MKDIR \JOINDIR
```

Use JOIN to connect a disk to the directory, as shown here:

```
C> JOIN B: \JOINDIR
```

References to C:\JOINDIR are identical to references to drive B. If drive B contains DOS directories, refer to them as

```
C> DIR \JOINDIR\SUBDIR
```

If you invoke JOIN without any command-line parameters,

```
C> JOIN
```

JOIN displays the current joins.

To disconnect a join, use the /D qualifier, as shown here:

```
C> JOIN A: /D
```

KEYB

FUNCTION   Loads a foreign keyboard set.

FORMAT

[*drive:*][*path*]KEYB [*keyboard_code* [,*codepage*],[*filespec*]]

where the following is true:

keyboard_code specifies one of the following two-letter codes associated with the desired keyboard:

US	United States	FR	France
GR	Germany	IT	Italy
SP	Spain	UK	United Kingdom
PO	Portugal	SG	Swiss German
DK	Denmark	BE	Belgium

NL	Netherlands	NO	Norway
LA	Latin America	SV	Sweden
SU	Finland		

codepage is the desired codepage (see CHCP for a list of valid values).

filespec is the name of the file containing the keyboard definitions, normally KEYBOARD.SYS.

NOTES   To fully support international configurations, DOS provides support for various keyboard templates.

KEYB loads memory-resident software to replace the standard keyboard layout supported by the ROM-BIOS.

When a new keyboard is installed, you can toggle between it and the default keyboard by pressing CTRL-ALT-F1 for the default, and CTRL-ALT-F2 for the foreign keyboard.

EXAMPLES   In the following command, DOS will use the United Kingdom keyboard template:

```
C> KEYB UK
```

This command selects the French keyboard template and informs DOS that the KEYBOARD.SYS file resides in the subdirectory \DOS.

```
C> KEYB FR , , \DOS\KEYBOARD.SYS
```

LABEL

FUNCTION   Specifies a disk volume label.

FORMAT

[*drive:*] [*path*] LABEL [*target_drive:*] [*volume_label*]

where the following is true:

drive: is the disk-drive identification of the disk containing the LABEL.COM file. If you do not specify a disk drive, DOS uses the current default disk drive.

path is the name of the DOS directory that contains the LABEL.COM file. If you do not specify a disk drive, DOS uses the current default directory.

target_drive: is the disk drive containing the disk to label.

volume_label is the 11-character volume label desired. All of the characters that are valid in DOS file names are valid volume label characters.

NOTES DOS allows you to define a name for each of your disks. Each time you issue the DOS DIR command it displays the volume label of the disk as well as its directory label, as shown here:

```
Volume in drive A is DOSLABEL
Directory of  A:\
```

It is also possible to use software to obtain the disk volume label from within your DOS programs. You can then be sure that the user has the correct disk in each drive.

The DOS VOL command also displays the disk volume label, as shown here:

```
C> VOL  A:

Volume in drive A is DOSLABEL
```

If you do not specify a volume label in the command line, LABEL prompts you for one, as follows:

```
Volume in drive C is DOSDISK
Type a volume label of up to 11 characters
or press Enter for no volume label update.
```

If you do not want to change the disk label, press ENTER; otherwise type in the volume name desired.

Do not use the following characters in DOS volume names:

* ? \ / | . , ; : + = < > ( ) & ^

EXAMPLES   The following command names the floppy disk contained in drive B as DOSDISK:

```
C> LABEL  B:DOSDISK
```

The command line contains the desired label name, so LABEL did not have to prompt the user for any information.

In this command

```
C> LABEL
```

the label name is not specified in the command line; therefore, LABEL will prompt

```
Volume in drive C is DOSDISK
Type a volume label of up to 11 characters
or press Enter for no volume label update.
```

Again, either type in the volume label that you desire or press ENTER to leave the current label name unchanged.

MKDIR

FUNCTION   Creates the DOS subdirectory specified.

FORMAT

MKDIR [*drive:*]*path*

or

MD [*drive:*]*path*

where the following is true:

drive: specifies the drive on which to create the directory. If a drive is not specified, MKDIR uses the current default disk drive.

path specifies the name of the DOS directory that MKDIR is to create.

NOTES If you do not use DOS directories, your disks are restircted to a limited number of files, as shown here:

Disk Space	Maximum Number of Files in the Root Directory
160K	64
180K	
320K	112
360K	
1.2MB	224
Fixed Disk	Based upon partition size

Every DOS directory has a root directory from within which all other directories grow.

The maximum path name that DOS can process is 63 characters.

MKDIR has two choices when creating a DOS directory. First, if the directory name starts with a backslash, such as \SUBDIR, DOS will start with root directory to create the directory. If, however, the name does not start with a backslash, as in SUBDIR, DOS will create the directory within the current directory.

Use the following guidelines when you create your DOS directories:

■ DOS directory names conform to the same format as DOS file names—an eight-character name followed by an optional three-character extension. Examples of valid DOS directory names are FILENAME.EXT, HARDWARE.SAL, and SOFTWARE.INV.

■ If you do not specify a complete DOS path name when you create a directory, DOS assumes that you are creating the directory in the current directory.

■ To manipulate directories contained on other disks, precede the directory name with a disk-drive identification, such as B:\FINANCE\CAR.

■ Do not create directory names that are identical to names of files contained in the same directory.

■ Do not create a directory called \DEV. DOS uses a hidden directory called \DEV to communicate with hardware devices.

■ DOS path names cannot exceed 63 characters.

■ Root directories on each disk are restricted to a specific number of files due to the disk layout. Directories that you create, however, can contain an unlimited number of files.

■ Logically divide your disk into directories.

EXAMPLES In the following example, MKDIR creates a directory called IBM in the root:

```
C> MKDIR \IBM
```

The following command creates a directory called NOTES in the IBM directory.

```
C> MKDIR \IBM\NOTES
```

This command is equivalent to the commands C> CHDIR \IBM and C> MKDIR NOTES. Note that the second command does not have a slash in front of the directory name. If it did, MKDIR would create the directory in the root as opposed to the \IBM directory.

Assuming that the current directory is still the root, the following command also creates a directory off of the root:

```
C> MKDIR  MISC
```

The directory name does not contain a slash, so MKDIR creates the
directory in the current directory, which, in this case, is still the root.
Had the current directory been other than the root, the correct command would be

```
C> MKDIR  \MISC
```

MODE

FUNCTION   Specifies device characteristics.

FORMAT

[*drive:*][*path*]MODE *n*

or

[*drive:*][*path*]MODE [*n*],*m*,[*t*]

or

[*drive:*][*path*]MODE COM # [:] *baud* [,*parity* [,*data* [,*stop* [,P]]]]

or

[*drive:*][*path*]MODE LPT# [:] [*cpl*] [,*vli*][,P]

or

[*drive:*][*path*]MODE LPT# [:] =COM# [:]

or

[*drive:*][*path*]MODE *device* CODEPAGE *operation*

where the following is true:

> *drive:* specifies the disk-drive identification of the disk containing the MODE.COM file. If you do not specify a disk drive, DOS uses the current default disk drive.
>
> *path* specifies the name of the DOS directory that contains the MODE.COM file. If you do not specify a directory name, DOS uses the current default directory.
>
> *n* specifies the screen display attribute. It must be one of the following:
>
> 40 specifies 40-column display.
> 80 specifies 80-column display.
> BW40 specifies a black and white 40-column display.
> BW80 specifies a black and white 80-column display.
> CO40 specifies a color 40-column display.
> CO80 specifies a color 80-column display.
> MONO specifies a monochrome display.
>
> *m* specifies the direction to shift the screen display, one character to either the left or right.
>
> *t* tells MODE to display a test pattern to aid in character alignment.
>
> *baud* specifies the device baud rate: 110, 150, 300, 600, 1200, 2400, 4800, 9600, or 19200. MODE requires you to specify only the first two digits of the baud rate.
>
> *parity* specifies the device parity: E for even parity, N for no parity, O for odd parity. The default is even parity.
>
> *data* specifies the number of data bits, either 7 or 8. The default is 7 data bits.
>
> *stop* specifies the number of stop bits, either 1 or 2. For 110 baud, the default is 2; otherwise it is 1.

cpl is characters per line, either 80 or 132.

vli is vertical lines per inch, either 6 or 8.

P specifies continuous retries on timeout errors.

LPT# specifies the parallel printer number, such as LPT1.

COM# specifies the serial port number, such as COM1.

device specifies the device for which to manipulate a codepage, either CON or LPT*n*.

operation is the codepage operation desired:

PREPARE=[[*codepage*][*filename*]]
SELECT=*codepage*
REFRESH
/STATUS

NOTES   Many hardware devices require unique data communications setups, such as 4800 baud and parity. The DOS MODE command allows you to set the characteristics of a port on the PC.

By default, DOS uses the parallel printer port for printed data. If your printer is connected to a serial device, you can redirect the parallel output to the serial device by using MODE.

If a device requires modification each time it is used, place the mode command in AUTOEXEC.BAT.

If you are using DOS version 3.3, the MODE command allows you to prepare and select codepages for your screen display and printer. The PREPARE operation directs DOS to get a codepage ready for use for the specified device. The SELECT operation chooses a specific codepage to be used by the device.

In some cases you may download a codepage to your printer device, and the printer is turned off. To restore the codepage, you must use the REFRESH operation. The /STATUS operation lists the codepages that are currently in use or are prepared for the device specified.

MODE supports the following abbreviations:

CP   CODEPAGE
/STA   /STATUS
PREP   PREPARE

SEL   SELECT
REF   REFRESH

EXAMPLES   This command sets the screen display to 40 columns
per line.

```
C> MODE 40
```

The following command resets the screen to 80 column mode.

```
C> MODE 80
```

Many users have serial printers connected to their systems. To
route the printer data to the serial printer, you must use MODE, as
shown here:

```
C> MODE LPT1:=COM1:
```

This command routes the parallel data from LPT1 to the serial port
COM1. The following command specifies the data communication
parameters for COM1.

```
C> MODE COM1 96 , N , 8 , 1
```

If you are using DOS version 3.3 and an EGA monitor, this command prepares the display for the Multilingual and Portuguese
codepages.

```
C> MODE CON CODEPAGE PREPARE=(850,860) \DOS\EGA.CPI
```

You must specify the codepage information file (CPI) in the command
line. Once you prepare a codepage for a device, you select the codepage
using the SELECT option, as shown here:

```
C> MODE CON CODEPAGE SELECT=860
```

If your printer supports codepages, the following command prepares the printer for the Multilingual and Portuguese codepages.

```
C> MODE LPT1 CODEPAGE PREPARE=(850,860) \DOS\4201.CPI
```

MORE

FUNCTION   Displays a command's output one screenful at a time.

FORMAT

DOS_command | [*drive:*][*path*]MORE

or

[*drive:*][*path*]MORE < *DOS_command*

where the following is true:

drive: is the disk-drive identification of the disk containing the MORE.COM file. If you omit the disk drive, DOS uses the current default disk drive.

path is the name of the DOS directory that contains the MORE.COM file. If you omit the directory name, DOS uses the current default directory.

NOTES   The DOS MORE command reads data from the standard input device and displays the information to the standard output device one page at a time until the end of the file. Each time a page of data is displayed on the screen, MORE displays the message

```
-- MORE --
```

Press any key to continue the output, or press CTRL-C to terminate the command.

EXAMPLES   In the following command, MORE is used as a filter, obtaining its input from the standard input device (stdin).

```
C> SORT < DATA.DAT | MORE
```

To display the contents of DATA.DAT one screenful at a time, use MORE as shown here:

```
C> MORE < DATA.DAT
```

When you issue the MORE command from the DOS prompt, MORE expects its input from the keyboard.

```
C> MORE
```

Type in a screenful of information and then press CTRL-Z. MORE will process as normal.

NLSFUNC

FUNCTION   Provides device support for international codepages.

FORMAT

[*drive:*][*path*]NLSFUNC [*file_spec*]

where the following is true:

drive: is the disk-drive identification of the disk containing the NLSFUNC.COM file. If you omit the disk drive, DOS uses the current default disk drive.

path is the name of the DOS directory that contains the NLSFUNC.COM file. If you omit the directory name, DOS uses the current default directory.

file_spec is the complete DOS file specification for the file containing the country information. This file is usually COUNTRY.SYS.

NOTES The NLSFUNC command works in conjunction with CHCP. You must invoke NLSFUNC before you invoke CHCP.
This is a DOS version 3.3 command.
The COUNTRY.SYS file contains the country-specific information.

EXAMPLE The following command informs DOS that the country information file (COUNTRY.SYS) resides in the directory \SYS-FILES on drive C:

```
C> NLSFUNC  C:\DOS\COUNTRY.SYS
```

PATH

FUNCTION Defines the command-file search path that DOS uses each time it fails to locate a command as an internal command or within the current directory or the specified directory.

FORMAT

PATH [*drive:*][*path* [;[*drive:*][*path*]...]

or

PATH ;

where the following is true:

drive: specifies a disk drive that DOS is to include in the command-file search path.

path specifies a DOS directory to include in the command-file search path.

... indicates that the disk drive and directories may be specified several times.

NOTES   Each time DOS can't find a command as an internal command or as an EXE, COM, BAT, or CMD file in the current directory, it searches to see if the user has defined a command-file search path.

The DOS PATH command allows you to define disk drives and directories to be included in the command-file search path.

EXAMPLES   In the following command, if DOS cannot find the command, DOS searches the root directories on drives C, B, and A, in that order:

```
C> PATH  C:\;B:\;A:\
```

The following PATH command directs DOS to search \DOS, \UTIL, and then \MISC, in that order.

```
C> PATH  \DOS;\UTIL;\MISC
```

PAUSE

FUNCTION   Pauses batch file execution to display an optional message.

FORMAT

PAUSE [*message*]

where the following is true:

message is an optional message that PAUSE is to display each time it suspends batch processing. The message can contain up to 123 characters.

NOTES Each time DOS encounters PAUSE within a batch file, it displays the following:

```
[ optional message text ]
Strike a key when ready . . .
```

To continue batch processing, press any key; otherwise press CTRL-BREAK. If you press CTRL- BREAK, DOS displays

```
Terminate batch job (Y/N)?
```

To terminate the batch file, type **Y**; otherwise type **N**.

The DOS ECHO OFF command supresses the display of messages from PAUSE.

EXAMPLES In the following command

```
PAUSE Enter a blank disk in drive B
```

when DOS encounters the PAUSE command with the batch procedure, it pauses and displays

```
C>  PAUSE  Enter a blank disk in drive B
Enter a blank disk in drive B
Strike a key when ready . . .
```

This PAUSE command displays

```
C> PAUSE
Strike a key when ready . . .
```

PREDEFINED FUNCTION KEYS

FUNCTION   DOS Function Keys.

NOTES   Whenever you enter one of the following commands, DOS buffers it in a location in memory that you can access to simplify your command entry.

F1	Copies one character from the previous command buffer.
F2	Copies all characters in the buffer that precede the next character typed.
F3	Copies all characters in the command buffer.
F4	Copies all characters including and following the next character typed.
F5	Edits the current command buffer.
F6	Places a CONTROL-Z (^Z) end-of-file marker at the end of a file.
INS	Inserts characters in the current command buffer.
DEL	Deletes the character that precedes the cursor.
ESC	Cancels the current command line without executing it.

PRINT

FUNCTION   Prints a DOS file from the print queue.

FORMAT

[*drive:*][*path*]PRINT [/D:*device_name*][/C][/T]
[/B:*buffersize*][/D:*device*][/M:*maxticks*][/P][/Q:*queuesize*][/S:*timeslice*][/U:*busy ticks*]*file_spec* [...]

where the following is true:

drive: is the disk-drive identification of the disk that contains the PRINT.COM file. If you do not specify a disk drive, DOS uses the current default disk drive.

path is the name of the DOS directory that contains the PRINT.COM file. If you do not specify a disk drive, DOS uses the current default directory.

/D:*device_name* specifies the name of the device DOS is to print, such as LPT1. The default device is LPT1.

/C directs PRINT to cancel the print job of the file whose name precedes the /C and all those that follow.

/T directs PRINT to cancel all print jobs in the printer queue.

/B:*buffersize* specifies the amount of memory (in bytes) that is set aside for PRINT. The default size is 512. Increasing this size in multiples of 512 (1024, 2048, 4096) decreases the number of disk I/O operations required, and thus improves PRINT's performance. Increasing this value does, however, consume memory.

/D:*device* specifies the printer device (such as LPT1, LPT2, or LPT3). This qualifier is only valid the first time you invoke PRINT.

[/P] adds all of the file names that precede the /P in the command line to the print queue. This allows you to add and delete files (via /C) in the same command.

/M:*maxticks* specifies the maximum number of CPU clock ticks that PRINT can consume before it must return control to DOS. This value ranges from 1-255, and the default value is 2. This qualifier is only valid the first time you invoke PRINT. Increasing this value improves PRINT's performance by giving it more control of the CPU. However, if you make this value too large, the rest of your applications become sluggish when PRINT is working.

/Q:queuesize specifies the number of entries that the PRINT queue can store. The value must be in the range of 1-32, and the default value is 10. This qualifier is only valid the first time you invoke PRINT.

/S:timeslice specifies the PRINT time slice. This value must be in the range of 1-255, and the default value is 8. This qualifier is only valid the first time that you invoke PRINT.

/U:busyticks specifies the number of CPU clock ticks that PRINT will wait for the printer to become available for the next series of characters. The value must be in the range of 1-255, and the default value is 1. This qualifier is only valid the first time that you invoke PRINT.

file_spec is the complete DOS path name of the file to be added to or removed from the print queue. PRINT supports DOS wildcard characters.

... indicates that several file names can be placed on the PRINT command line.

NOTES   CPU clock ticks occur 18.2 times per second on an IBM PC computer.

PRINT sends files to the printer in background mode, which allows you to continue your processing in the foreground.

Do not remove a disk that contains a file to be printed until the printing process has finished. If you do so, your printed listing fills with unrecognizable characters, and you must reissue the PRINT command.

EXAMPLES   The following command installs a PRINT queue with storage for 32 files:

```
C> PRINT /Q:32
```

Remember that many qualifiers are valid only when you first issue a PRINT command.

This command sends all of the files in the current directory that have the the DAT extension.

```
C> PRINT *.DAT
```

This command prints the CONFIG.SYS file:

```
C> PRINT  CONFIG.SYS
```

The following command terminates all of the current print jobs:

```
C> PRINT  /T
```

This command removes the AUTOEXEC.BAT file from the print queue.

```
C> PRINT  AUTOEXEC.BAT  /C
```

PROMPT

FUNCTION   Defines the DOS prompt that appears on your screen display.

FORMAT

PROMPT [*prompt_string*]

where the following is true:

prompt_string is the character string that defines the DOS prompt. It can contain characters or the following metastrings:

$b	| Character
$d	Date
$e	ESC
$h	BACKSPACE
$g	> Character
$l	< Character
$n	Current drive
$p	Current directory
$q	= Character
$t	Current time
$v	DOS version
$_	CR LF
$$	$ Character

NOTES   If no string is specified, PROMPT resets the system prompt to the current default drive.

EXAMPLES   The following command sets the users prompt to YES>:

```
C> PROMPT YES$g
YES>
```

The following command sets the system prompt to the current system time:

```
C> PROMPT $t
```

This command displays

```
15:20:18.81
15:20:43.78
15:20:87.12
```

To display only the hours and minutes, you can change the prompt to

```
C> PROMPT $t$h$h$h$h$h
```

Next, many users use the DOS prompt to help keep track of the current directory. The following PROMPT command directs DOS to display the current directory name as the system prompt:

```
C> PROMPT [$p]

[C:\SUBDIR]
```

RECOVER

FUNCTION   Recovers a damaged disk or file.

FORMAT

[*drive:*][*path*]RECOVER [*d:*][*p*]*filename.ext*

where the following is true:

drive: specifies the disk drive containing the RECOVER.COM file. If you do not specify a disk drive, DOS uses the current default disk drive.

path is the DOS path name of the directory that contains the RECOVER.COM file. If you do not specify a DOS path name, DOS uses the current default directory.

d is the disk-drive identification of the file or disk to recover. If you do not specify a disk drive, RECOVER uses the current default disk drive.

p is the DOS path name of the directory containing the file to recover. If you do not specify a DOS path name, DOS uses the current default directory.

filename.ext is the name of the damaged file to recover.

NOTES   If a DOS disk or file becomes damaged and loses sectors, the DOS RECOVER command allows you to retrieve portions of the file up to the point of the corruption.

If the file is a text file, you can later edit the file and restore the missing contents. If, however, the file is an executable file, you should not execute it. Remember, the file is missing sectors. Instead, maintain a good backup of your files so that you do not have to rely on RECOVER.

If you use RECOVER to recover a complete disk, RECOVER creates files in the root directory with names in the form FILE*nnnn*.REC where *nnnn* is a four-digit number beginning with 0001 (FILE0001.REC).

RECOVER does not work with disk drives connected to a network.

EXAMPLES   The following command attempts to recover the contents of the disk in drive A.

```
C> RECOVER A:
```

RECOVER creates several files whose names are in the format FILE*nnnn*.REC.

The command

```
C> RECOVER FILENAME.EXT
```

recovers the contents of the FILENAME.EXT file up to the point of the damaged sector.

REM

FUNCTION Displays comments during batch file execution.

FORMAT

REM [*message*]

where the following is true:

message is a character string of up to 123 characters.

NOTES REM allows you to display messages to the standard output device during the execution of batch (BAT) files. *Message* is an optional command-line parameter that contains the message. The DOS command ECHO OFF inhibits the display of messages by REM.

EXAMPLE The following procedure shows the use of REM in a batch file:

```
:LOOP
REM About to display the directory listing
DIR
REM Directory listing complete
REM
GOTO LOOP
```

RENAME

FUNCTION Renames the file(s) specified.

FORMAT

REN *file_specification filename[.ext]*

or

RENAME *file_specification filename[.ext]*

where the following is true:

file_specification is the complete DOS path name of the file to rename. It can contain a drive and DOS directory path. RENAME supports DOS wildcard characters.

filename[.ext] is the target file name for the rename. It cannot have a drive or DOS directory path. RENAME supports DOS wildcard characters.

NOTES   The target file must reside in the same directory on the same disk drive as the source file because RENAME does not copy file contents, but rather renames the file in its directory entry.

EXAMPLES   The following command gives all of the files on drive B that have the extension BAK the same file name and a new extension of SAV:

```
C> REN B:*.BAK *.SAV
```

This RENAME command changes the extension of all of the files with the extension SYS that are contained in the directory \DOS to XXX.

```
C> RENAME \DOS\*.SYS *.XXX
```

The target file must reside in the same disk and directory as the source. If you specify a disk drive on the target file, for example, REN displays

```
Invalid parameter
```

REPLACE

FUNCTION   Allows selective file replacements and updates when new versions of software become available.

FORMAT

[*drive:*][*path*]REPLACE *source_filespec* [*target_filespec*] [/A][/P][/R][/S][/W]

where the following is true:

drive: specifies the disk drive containing the REPLACE.EXE file. If you do not specify a disk drive, DOS uses the current default disk drive.

path is the DOS path name of the directory that contains the REPLACE.EXE file. If you do not specify a DOS path name, DOS uses the current default directory.

source_file is the complete DOS file specification of the files that REPLACE is to use in the file replacements. REPLACE supports DOS wildcard characters.

target_filespec is the complete DOS file specification of destination of the files being added or released.

/A directs REPLACE to add files to the target directory instead of replacing them. With this qualifier, REPLACE places only those files onto the target that are not currently present.

/P directs REPLACE to prompt you with

```
Do you want to replace drive:filename.ext (Y/N)?
```

before adding or replacing files.

/R directs REPLACE to also replace files on the target location that are currently marked as Read-only. Without this qualifier, REPLACE stops replacement operations with the first file marked Read-only.

/S directs REPLACE to search the directories on the target location for other occurrences of the file to be replaced. This qualifier cannot be used with /A.

/W directs REPLACE to prompt

> Press Enter to begin replacing files.

before starting the file replacement operations.

NOTES   REPLACE is a convenient utility for software developers. It allows you to easily select specific files for replacement.

To support your batch processing, REPLACE provides the following error status values.

0	Successful
1	Invalid command line
2	File not found
3	Path not found
5	Access denied
8	Insufficient memory
15	Invalid drive

EXAMPLES   The following REPLACE command replaces any files in the root directory on drive A that have the extension A:

> C> REPLACE *.A A:\

The following command replaces all of the files in the directory \A on drive A that have the extension A:

> C> REPLACE *.A A:\A

The command

```
C> REPLACE *.* A:\ /S
```

updates all of the files on the entire disk in drive A (even those in directories) that are found on the source disk.

RESTORE

FUNCTION Restores files saved by BACKUP.

FORMAT

[*drive:*][*path*]RESTORE *source_drive target_drive:file_spec*
[/P][/S][/B:*mm-dd-yy*][/A:*mm-dd-yy*][/E:*hh:mm:ss*][/L:*hh:mm:ss*][/M][/N]

where the following is true:

drive: is the disk-drive identification of the disk that contains the RESTORE.COM file. If you omit the disk-drive specifier, DOS uses the current default disk drive.

path is the name of the DOS directory that contains the RESTORE.COM file. If you do not specify a path name, DOS will use the current default directory.

target_drive is the disk-drive identification to which the files will be restored.

source_drive:file_spec specifies the files to restore. The file name must match the name of the file as it was originally backed up. *Source_drive* is the drive that contains the backup files.

/A:*mm-dd-yy* directs RESTORE to restore only files modified on or after the specified date.

/B:*mm-dd-yy* directs RESTORE to restore only files modified on or before the specified date.

/E:*hh:mm:ss* directs RESTORE to restore only files modified on or before the specified time. This is a DOS version 3.3 qualifier.

/L:*hh:mm:ss* directs RESTORE to restore only files modified on or after the specified time. This is a DOS version 3.3 qualifier.

/M directs RESTORE to restore only files modified since the last backup.

/N directs RESTORE to restore only files that no longer exist on the target disk.

/P directs RESTORE to prompt the user before restoring files that have been modified or set to Readonly since the backup.

/S directs RESTORE to restore files contained in directories.

NOTES   The DOS BACKUP command places files onto a disk in a manner only accessible by RESTORE. To copy a file from the backup disk, you must use RESTORE.

RESTORE does not restore the hidden system files or the DOS command processor COMMAND.COM.

To support DOS batch processing, RESTORE provides the following exit status values.

0	Successful restoration
1	No files found to restore
2	Shared files not restored
3	User has terminated using CTRL-C
4	Restoration error

EXAMPLES   This command restores all of the files from the backup disk in drive A, including those in directories.

```
C> RESTORE  A:  C:*.*  /S
```

If the backup used several floppy disks, RESTORE prompts you to place subsequent disks in the specified drive each time it needs a new backup disk.

This command restores all of the files from the backup disk that contain the extension DAT.

```
C> RESTORE  A:  C:*.DAT  /P
```

RESTORE prompts the user with

Warning! File FILENAME.EXT was changed after backed up.
Replace the file (Y/N)?

before it restores files that have been modified since the backup.

RMDIR

FUNCTION   Removes the specified directory.

FORMAT

RMDIR [*drive:*]*path*

or

RD [*drive:*]*path*

where the following is true:

drive: specifies the drive from which to remove the directory. If a drive is not specified, RMDIR uses the current default disk drive.

path specifies the name of the DOS subdirectory to remove.

NOTES   RMDIR removes only empty directories that don't contain files. The largest path name that DOS can process is 63 characters.

EXAMPLES   This command attempts to remove the IBM directory from the root directory of the current drive.

C> RMDIR \IBM

If the directory contains files, RMDIR cannot remove the directory.
This command

```
C> RMDIR  MISC\IBM\SALES
```

removes the directory SALES from the directory \MISC\IBM on the
current drive.

SELECT

FUNCTION   Selects an international format for a new disk.

FORMAT

[*drive:*][*path*]SELECT [[A: | B:] *d*:[*p*]] *country keyboard*

where the following is true:

drive: is the disk-drive identification of the disk containing the
SELECT.COM file. If you omit the disk drive, DOS uses the
current default disk drive.

path is the name of the DOS directory that contains the
SELECT.COM file. If you omit the subdirectory name, DOS
uses the current default directory.

A: | B: specifies the source drive of the keyboard files.

d is the target drive to which international files are copied.

p is the target path for the file copy.

country is one of the following three-digit codes that specifies the country to use:

001	United States	002	French-Canadian
003	Latin America	031	Netherlands
032	Belgium	033	France
034	Spain	039	Italy
041	Switzerland	044	United Kingdom
045	Denmark	046	Sweden
047	Norway	049	Germany
061	English	351	Portugal
358	Finland	785	Arabic countries
972	Israel		

keyboard is the two-character identifier of the keyboard layout to use (see KEYB).

NOTES   SELECT uses the DISKCOPY command (DOS version 3.2 uses XCOPY) to make a copy of the DOS disk. SELECT creates the CONFIG.SYS and AUTOEXEC.BAT files that are required for international support on the target disk.

Upon completion, SELECT places the line

COUNTRY=xxx

in CONFIG.SYS and

KEYB XX

in AUTOEXEC.BAT on the target disk.

SELECT supports one- or two-floppy-drive systems.

EXAMPLE   The following command directs SELECT to create a disk that fully supports GERMAN characteristics.

```
C> SELECT A: 049 GR
```

SET

FUNCTION   Places or displays DOS environment entries.

FORMAT

SET [*name*=[*value*]]

where the following is true:

name is the name of a DOS environment entry to which you are assigning a value.

value is the character string that defines the value assigned.

NOTES   Each time DOS boots, it reserves an area of memory called the environment.

The DOS SET command sets or displays entries in the DOS environment. The DOS environment provides a storage location for system specifics. DOS commands such as PROMPT and PATH place entries in the environment. The SET command with no parameters displays the current environment.

SET converts all entry names to uppercase.

DOS version 3.3 supports named parameters that use environment entries in conjunction with DOS batch files.

EXAMPLES   The following SET command, with no command-line parameters, directs SET to display the current environment entries.

```
C> SET

COMSPEC=C:\COMMAND.COM
PATH=C:\DOS
```

In this command, SET creates a new environment entry called FILE and assign it the value TEST.DAT.

```
C> SET FILE=TEST.DAT
```

You can verify this by again issuing the SET command, as shown here:

```
C> SET
COMSPEC=C:\COMMAND.COM
PATH=C:\DOS
FILE=TEST.DAT
```

If you are using DOS version 3.3, you can create a named parameter called FILE in a DOS batch file, as shown here:

```
CLS
TYPE %FILE%
```

When DOS encounters %FILE%, it searches the environment for a matching entry (in this case TEST.DAT) and, if found, displays the file's contents.

To remove the value for an entry, use SET as shown here:

```
C> SET FILE=
```

Invoking SET now displays

```
C> SET
COMSPEC=C:\COMMAND.COM
PATH=C:\DOS
```

SHARE

FUNCTION   Supports DOS file sharing.

FORMAT

[*drive:*][*path*]SHARE [/F:*file_space*][/L:*locks*]

where the following is true:

> *drive:* is the disk-drive identification of the disk containing the SHARE.COM file. If you omit the disk drive, DOS uses the current default disk drive.
>
> *path* is the name of the DOS directory that contains the SHARE.COM file. If you omit the directory name, DOS uses the current default directory.
>
> /F:*file_space* allocates memory (in bytes) for the area in which DOS stores file-sharing information. Each open file requires 11 bytes, plus the length of the file name (up to 63 characters). The default file space is 2048 bytes.
>
> /L:*locks* allocates memory for the number of file locks desired. The default value is 20.

NOTES   DOS versions 3.0 and greater support file and record locking. Each time a file is opened with file sharing installed, DOS checks to see if the file is locked against the open operation. If so, the file cannot be opened. In addition, DOS checks for locking during each read or write operation.

SHARE is a memory-resident software program that performs the file and record locking; therefore, it can be installed only one time.

Once installed, the only way to remove file sharing is to reboot. SHARE places considerable overhead on all of your file operations; therefore, install SHARE only when file sharing is in effect.

EXAMPLES   The following command invokes file sharing with the default values of 2048 and 20 locks.

```
C> SHARE
```

This command installs file sharing support with 40 locks.

```
C> SHARE  /L:40
```

SHIFT

FUNCTION   Shifts each batch parameter one position to the left.

FORMAT

```
SHIFT
```

NOTES   If more than ten parameters are passed to a DOS batch procedure, you can use the SHIFT command to access each parameter past %9. If no parameter exists to the right of a parameter, SHIFT assigns the parameter a NULL string.

EXAMPLE   The following batch file displays all of the batch parameters specified on the command line.

```
ECHO OFF
:LOOP
SHIFT
IF '%0'== '' GOTO DONE
ECHO %0
GOTO LOOP
:DONE
```

If the previous file was named TEST.BAT, invoking the batch file as

```
C> TEST 1 2 3 4
```

would display

```
C> ECHO OFF
1
2
3
4
```

SORT

FUNCTION   Activates the DOS SORT filter.

FORMAT

DOS_command | [*drive:*][*path*]SORT [/R][/+n]

or

[*drive:*][*path*]SORT [/R][/+n] < *file*

where the following is true:

drive: is the disk-drive identification of the disk containing the SORT.EXE file. If you do not specify a disk drive, DOS uses the current default disk drive.

path is the name of the DOS directory that contains the SORT.EXE file. If you do not specify a directory name, DOS uses the current default directory.

/R directs SORT to sort the data in reverse order.

/+*n* allows you to specify the column to sort the data on.

NOTES   The DOS SORT command reads data from the standard input device, sorting and displaying the information to the standard output device until the end of file.

You can use SORT as a filter with the DOS redirection operators < or |.

EXAMPLES The following command directs SORT to sort the information contained in the DATA.DAT file.

```
C> SORT < DATA.DAT
```

This command directs SORT to sort the same file, this time in reverse order.

```
C> SORT /R < DATA.DAT
```

Assume that your data file contains the following:

```
Bill M
Mary F
Kris M
Kal  M
Andy F
Jim  M
Mike M
Ed   M
```

The following command directs SORT to sort the file based upon the data starting in column 6.

```
C> SORT /+6 < FILENAME.EXT
```

SORT displays

```
Mary F
Andy F
Bill M
Kris M
Kal  M
Jim  M
Mike M
Ed   M
```

If you do not redirect input to SORT,

```
C> SORT
```

SORT expects its input from the keyboard. Type in the following letters and then press CTRL-Z.

```
C> SORT
A
F
D
E
B
C
^Z
```

SORT sorts the data and displays

```
C> SORT
A
F
D
E
B
C
^Z

A
B
C
D
E
F

C>
```

SUBST

FUNCTION   Substitutes a drive name for a DOS path name.

FORMAT

[*drive:*][*path*]SUBST [*d:*] [*pathname*][/D]

where the following is true:

drive: is the disk-drive identification of the disk containing the SUBST.EXE file. If you do not specify a disk drive, DOS uses the current default disk drive.

path is the name of the DOS directory that contains the SUBST.EXE file. If you do not specify a directory name, DOS uses the current default directory.

d is the disk drive identification that will be used to reference the path.

pathname is the DOS path name to abbreviate.

/D directs SUBST to remove a previous disk substitution.

NOTES   Because DOS path names can become quite large, DOS allows you to substitute a drive identifier for a path name.

If you invoke SUBST without any parameters, current substitutions are displayed.

If you plan to perform multiple disk-drive substitutions, you must use the LASTDRIVE= entry in CONFIG.SYS.

EXAMPLES   In the following command, DOS will now allow you to abbreviate the subdirectory \DOS\HELPFILE\COMMANDS with the drive letter E:

```
C> SUBST  E: \DOS\HELPFILE\COMMANDS
```

The following command displays the contents of the directory \DOS\HELPFILE\COMMANDS.

```
C> DIR  E:
```

If that directory contains other directories, you can still use the drive letter.

```
C> DIR  E:SUBDIR
```

If you invoke SUBST without any command-line parameters, SUBST displays the current substitutions, as shown here:

```
C> SUBST
E: => C:\DOS\HELPFILE\COMMANDS
```

SYS

FUNCTION   Transfers to the target disk the hidden operating system files that perform the initial system start-up processing.

FORMAT

   [*drive:*][*path*]SYS *target_drive:*

where the following is true:

drive: specifies the disk drive containing the SYS.COM file. If you do not specify a disk-drive identificationn, DOS uses the current default disk drive.

path is the DOS path name of the directory that contains the SYS.COM file. If you do not specify a DOS path name, DOS uses the current default directory.

target_drive specifies the target disk drive for the hidden operating system files.

NOTES   SYS does not copy the COMMAND.COM file to the target disk. You must do this with the DOS COPY command.

SYS does not work with a JOINed or SUBSTed disk.

DOS transfers files only to an empty target disk or to a disk previously formatted with the /S or /B qualifiers.

EXAMPLE   The following SYS command transfers the hidden operating system files to the disk in drive A.

```
C> SYS  A:
```

Verify the procedure by issuing the CHKDSK command, as shown here:

```
C> CHKDSK  A:

362496 bytes total disk space
 53248 bytes in 2 hidden files
 25600 bytes in 1 user files
283648 bytes available on disk

655360 bytes total memory
586912 bytes free
```

If the target disk cannot store the required system files, SYS displays

```
No room for system on destination disk
```

TIME

FUNCTION   Sets the DOS system time.

FORMAT

TIME [*HH:MM*[:*SS* [.*hh*]]]

where the following is true:

HH is the desired hours (0-23).

MM is the desired minutes (1-59).

SS is the desired seconds (0-59).

hh is the desired hundredths of seconds (0-99).

NOTES   If you do not specify a time, the TIME command displays the current time.

In the past, most DOS users had to set their system clock using the SETUP disk provided in the *Guide to Operations* manual. The DOS version 3.3 TIME command modifies the AT system clock, thus removing this requirement.

EXAMPLES   The following command does not specify a time on the command line.

```
C> TIME
```

TIME prompts you for one, as shown here:

```
Current time is 16:08:41.15
Enter new time:
```

To leave the time unchanged, press ENTER. Otherwise type in the desired time.

This command sets the clock to 12 noon.

```
C> TIME  12:00
```

This command sets the clock to midnight.

```
C> TIME  00:00:00.000
```

If the time that you specify is invalid,

```
C> TIME  15:65:00
```

TIME displays an error message and reprompts you for the time.

```
Invalid time
Enter new time:
```

TREE

FUNCTION   Displays a directory structure.

FORMAT

[*drive:*][*path*]TREE [*d:*][/F]

where the following is true:

> *drive:* specifies the disk-drive identification of the disk containing the TREE.COM file. If you do not specify a disk drive, DOS uses the current default disk drive.
>
> *path* specifies the name of the DOS directory that contains the TREE.COM file. If you do not specify a directory, DOS uses the current default directory.
>
> *d:* is the disk-drive identification of the disk, the directory of which TREE is to display.
>
> /F directs TREE to also display the name of each file in a directory.

NOTES   By default, TREE displays the name of each directory on a disk. To also display each file name, use the /F qualifer.

EXAMPLES   The following command displays the directory structure of the disk:

```
C> TREE
```

The output is similar to

```
Directory path listing

Path: \IBM

Subdirectories:  SALES


Path: \IBM\SALES

Subdirectories:  None


Path: \MS

Subdirectories:  None
```

Use the following command to also display the files in each directory:

```
C> TREE  B:/F
```

When you invoke the command, your display is similar to this:

```
Directory path listing

Files:        None


Path: \IBM

Subdirectories: SALES

Files:        NOTES  .TXT


Path: \IBM\SALES

Subdirectories: None

Files:        JULY   .DAT


Path: \MS

Subdirectories: None

Files:        C   .TXT
              PRES   .TXT
```

TYPE

FUNCTION   Displays a text file's contents.

FORMAT

TYPE *file_specification*

where the following is true:

file_specification is the complete DOS file specification for the file to be displayed. It can contain a disk-drive identification and a DOS path name.

NOTES   TYPE is restricted to ASCII files. Do not use TYPE on COM or EXE files because these files contain unprintable characters that cause your screen to beep and display uncommon characters.

EXAMPLES   The following command directs TYPE to display the contents of the CONFIG.SYS file:

```
C> TYPE  CONFIG.SYS
```

The command

```
C> TYPE  B:\DOS\AUTOEXEC.SAV
```

directs TYPE to display the contents of the AUTOEXEC.SAV file in the directory DOS on drive B.

If the file specified in the TYPE command line does not exist, TYPE displays

```
Invalid filename or file not found
```

VER

FUNCTION   Displays the DOS version number.

FORMAT

VER

NOTES DOS version numbers are comprised of one major and one minor version number. For example, DOS version 3.2 has a major version number of 3 and a minor version number of 2.

EXAMPLE The following command directs VER to display the current version number:

```
C> VER
```

For DOS version 3.3, the output is

```
MS-DOS Version 3.30
```

VERIFY

FUNCTION Enables or disables disk verification.

FORMAT

VERIFY [ON | OFF]

where the following is true:

ON enables DOS disk verification.
OFF disables DOS disk verification.

NOTES Periodically a disk drive may not correctly record the information on disk as DOS intended. Although rare, such occurrences can leave incorrect data on disk.

If you enable disk I/O verification, DOS will double-check the data it writes to disk by rereading each sector and comparing it to the original data. If a descrepancy exists, DOS can detect it.

If you invoke VERIFY without a command-line parameter, VERIFY displays its current state, ON or OFF.

Because VER requires DOS to reread each sector that it writes to disk, disk verification has significant system overhead.

EXAMPLES   The following command enables disk I/O verification:

```
C> VERIFY ON
```

If you invoke VERIFY without command-line parameters, VERIFY displays its current state, ON or OFF, as shown here:

```
C> VERIFY
VERIFY is on.

C>
```

VOL

FUNCTION   Displays a disk volume label.

FORMAT

VOL [*drive:*]

where the following is true:

drive: specifies the disk-drive identification of the disk of whose volume VOL is to display. If you do not specify a disk identification, VOL will use the current default disk drive.

NOTES   DOS volume labels are 11-character names assigned to a disk.

Volume names use the same characters as DOS file names.

If you do not specify a target drive, VOL uses the current default.

To assign a volume label, use the DOS LABEL command.

EXAMPLE   In the following command, VOL displays the disk volume label of the disk contained in the current drive:

```
C> VOL
Volume in drive C is DOSDISK
```

XCOPY

FUNCTION   Copies source files and directories to a target destination.

FORMAT

[*drive:*][*path*]XCOPY *source_filespec* [*target_filespec*]
[/A][/D:*mm-dd-yy*][/E][/M][/P][/V]
[/S][/W]

where the following is true:

drive: specifies the disk drive containing the XCOPY.EXE file. If you do not specify a disk drive, DOS uses the current default disk drive.

path is the DOS path name of the directory that contains the XCOPY.EXE file. If you do not specify an OS/2 path name, DOS uses the current default directory.

source_filespec is the complete DOS file specification for the source files that XCOPY is to copy.

target_filespec is the destination name for the files copied by XCOPY.

/A directs XCOPY to copy only files that have their archive bit set.

/D:*mm-dd-yy* directs XCOPY to copy only files created since the specified date.

/E directs XCOPY to place directories on the target disk if the directory is currently empty.

/M functions like the /A qualifier; however, /M directs XCOPY to clear each file's archive bit as it copies them.

/P directs XCOPY to prompt

```
FILENAME.EXT (Y/N)?
```

before copying each file.

/V directs XCOPY to compare the contents of the target file and the source file to ensure that the file copy was successful.

/S directs XCOPY to copy the contents of lower- level directories to the target location.

/W directs XCOPY to prompt

```
Press any key to begin copying file(s)
```

before beginning.

NOTES   XCOPY is more functional then COPY and DISKCOPY because it selectively copies files contained in DOS directories. In fact, many users use XCOPY to repair disk fragmentation or as a system back-up mechanism.

EXAMPLES   If you have a blank disk in drive B, the following command creates a disk structure on the disk in drive B identical to that of the disk in drive A.

```
C> XCOPY A:\*.* B:\ /S
```

The following command copies all of the files contained in or below the directory \A on drive A to the disk in drive B:

```
C> XCOPY A:\A\*.* B:\ /S
```

To copy the entire contents of a fixed disk to floppy disks, first set the attribute of each file on the fixed disk to indicate that each requires a backup, as shown here:

```
C> ATTRIB +A \*.* /S
```

Next, issue the command

```
C> XCOPY \*.* A:\ /M /E /S
```

XCOPY begins transferring files to the floppy disk while maintaining the existing disk structure. When the target disk becomes full, insert a new floppy disk in drive A and invoke this command.

```
C> XCOPY \*.* A:\ /M /E /S
```

XCOPY continues where it left off because it has been clearing the archive bit on each file it successfully copies to the target disk.

TRADEMARKS

Apple®	Apple Computer
AT™	International Business Machines
Commodore®	Commodore Business Machines, Inc.
IBM®	International Business Machines
Intel®	Intel Corporation
Lotus®	Lotus Development Corporation
Microsoft®	Microsoft Corporation
OS/2™	International Business Machines
PS/2™	International Business Machines
Sprint™	Borland International
WordPerfect®	WordPerfect Corporation
WordStar®	MicroPro International

Index

?, as wildcard character, 68
*, as wildcard character, 70
^ character, 82
@ character, 373, 376

A

Abort, Retry, Fail, 134-35, 142, 146
Access denied, 491, 508, 520, 526
Additional hardware, 14-15
Album, record, 102
All files canceled by operator, 218
ALT key, 32, 35
ANSI.SYS, 564
APPEND command, 485, 489, 498,
    503, 627-29
    /E qualifier, 490, 498, 628
    /X qualifier, 490, 498, 503, 628
Append redirection operator, 398,
    400, 415
Apple, 101
Application software, 21, 23
Archive attribute flag, 536, 538, 543
    setting, 509
Archive bit, 631
Archive required, 506, 519, 538,
    539, 543

Archiving, 528
Are you sure, 341, 655, 667
ASCII file, 449, 515, 527, 740
ASSIGN command, 547, 552, 555,
    629-31, 685
Asterisk (*), 67, 74, 75
    EDLIN prompt, 227, 228, 231,
        233, 242, 247
    in the three-character file
        extension, 69
    wildcard character, 127, 143
ATTRIB command, 505, 506, 519,
    526, 539, 631-34
    +A qualifier, 509
    +R qualifier, 508, 509
    -A qualifier, 509
    -R qualifier, 508, 509
    /S qualifier, 509
    wildcard characters, 632
Attribute byte, 631, 632
Attribute field, 506, 538
Attributes, 505
AUTOEXEC.BAT, 354, 355, 357,
    379, 392, 387-88, 451, 454, 488,
    523, 570, 612, 619, 620, 703, 725
AUX, 281, 291, 549, 555, 652